M

p.176

JUN 0 4 2004

BEYOND
THE MIRACLE

*It is not given to every generation that it should be present
during and participate in the act of creation.*
— THABO MBEKI, APRIL 1997

To Sue Sparks
who shared so much of this dream with me

BEYOND THE MIRACLE

INSIDE THE NEW SOUTH AFRICA

Allister Sparks

The University of Chicago Press
Chicago

The University of Chicago Press, Chicago 60637
Profile Books, London, United Kingdom, EC1N 8LX
Jonathan Ball Publishers, Johannesburg and Cape Town, South Africa

12 11 10 09 08 07 06 05 04 03   1 2 3 4 5

ISBN: 0-226-76858-9 (cloth)

Library of Congress Cataloging-in-Publication Data
Sparks, Allister Haddon.
   Beyond the miracle: the making of the new South Africa / Allister Sparks
   p. cm.
Includes bibliographical references (p.) and index.
ISBN 0-226-76858-9 (alk. paper)
   1. South Africa—Politics and government—1994– I. Title.
   DT1974 .S737 2003
   968.06'5—dc21   2003012649

CONTENTS

FOREWORD

This book completes a trilogy on the thunderous history of my country, South Africa, as I have observed it as a journalist over the past 52 years. The first of the books, *The Mind of South Africa,* attempted to present a sweeping historical study of a complex country whose different races had been in conflict for three-and-a-half centuries, and of how those conflicts had culminated in first the rise and then the crisis of apartheid. The second book, *Tomorrow is Another Country,* recounted the events that led to that crisis being resolved through a remarkable series of secret negotiations that culminated in the abandonment of apartheid and an attempt, instead, to build a nonracial democracy in which all these different peoples who have been in conflict for so long resolved to attempt what many thought the impossible – to bury their historical enmities and forge themselves into a single, united nation, a nonracial democracy. Some called that astonishing negotiated revolution, carried out by South Africans themselves without outside mediators, a miracle, so improbable had it seemed.

Now comes the third book, an assessment of what has taken place since the miracle of that transformation; an assessment in other words of the status of Nelson Mandela's dream of building a single nation of many races and colours, languages and religions.

The three emerge as separate phases in an ongoing saga of racial oppression, confrontation and transformation, each written in the midst of the events themselves. So they are not retrospective histories in the classical sense, written with the wisdom of hindsight. They are works of journalism, written from the front line, as it were, as the events were unfolding. Yet hopefully they hold together as a continuous story of contemporaneous history. It is, I believe, an important story of conflict resolution in a shrinking world riven by racial, ethnic and cultural differences which some fear may be headed for a war between civilizations. A story not only of the ending of the most systematic programme of racial segregation and oppression that the modern world has seen, but also of the peaceful resolution of a conflict over national sovereignty. At a time when the world is witnessing such bitter conflict between Israelis and Palestinians over their rival claims to the same patch of earth in the Middle East, and when Catholics and Protestants are doing the same in Northern Ireland, white Afrikaners and black Africans have resolved their similar conflict through peaceful negotiation and a merging of national identities here at the southern tip of the world's most impoverished and derided continent.

It is also, of course, an unfinished story. To that extent I am a little uneasy about the use of the word "miracle" to describe the South African transformation, for a miracle implies a single amazing event due to some supernatural agency. It also implies an event that is complete. The change that has taken place in South Africa is neither. It was brought about not by some Damascus Road revelation but by ordinary, fallible human beings who ultimately recognized that they had been cast together by forces of history that could not be undone and that in the final analysis they were dependent on one another to a degree where they could either live together or perish together, and who then followed the painful and difficult logic of that recognition. And the change is certainly not complete. There is still a long road to travel, much reconstruction to be undertaken to bring about economic as well as political justice and much soul-searching in the quest for cross-cultural bonding and a coherent national identity.

Nonetheless, I have used the "miracle" word in this title because it captures the essense of what a marvellous event that transformation was, what an unexpected triumph of the spirit on the part of a people who had become the pariahs of the world. In that sense a greater event, surely, than any economic miracle. In doing so I am indebted to Professor Ben Turok, an ANC Member of Parliament, who first suggested the title to me and used it himself for a valuable reader on the economy which he published in 1999.

I am indebted to many other people, too, for their help in preparing this work. To Steven Lagerfeld, editor of the Wilson Quarterly, who published an initial article on the subject in the Spring 1999 issue of that fine magazine which later evolved into the concept for this book. And to the magazine's parent organization, the Woodrow Wilson International Center for Scholars in Washington DC, which gave me an invaluable research scholarship that enabled me to study the complex new globalization revolution within which the South African revolution is taking place.

I am doubly indebted to the Public Policy Institute at Duke

University and the School of Journalism and Mass Communication at the University of North Carolina for visiting professorships that enabled me to do much of the writing of this book at those fine institutions, and at the same time engage with their rich intellectual resources as the United States and the world as a whole struggled to come to terms with the transforming shock of the 11 September 2001 terrorist attacks on New York and Washington. It was an experience that drove home the realization that the South African transformation was indeed taking place within a dramatically changing global context.

There are many others to be thanked at a more personal level: Cabinet Ministers and senior government officials, including President Thabo Mbeki, who gave generously of their time during busy schedules to speak openly and on the record of their roles in this remarkable story and to share their perspectives with me. There were others with specialist knowledge who read specific chapters for accuracy, including Phillip van Niekerk, Govin Reddy, Tamela Hultman and that marvellous media lawyer, Gilbert Marcus, who read the important chapters on the media and made valuable suggestions; Iraj Abedian, who played a key co-ordinating role in drafting the ANC's turnaround economic policy known as GEAR and who is now Group Chief Economist at the Standard Bank of South Africa; to my old friend and journalistic colleague, Richard Steyn, who read the whole text and offered constructive advice; to my son Michael Sparks, a fine copy-editor, who edited each chapter as it came off my computer and enabled me in the end to submit a clean manuscript to the publishers; and to Barry Streek, another old colleague who now works for Jonathan Ball, my South African publisher, whose sharp eye and long experience also picked up a number of errors. To Jonathan Ball himself for his enthusiasm and energetic support, to my agent, Isobel Dixon, for her unflagging commitment to her native country and its writers; and last but most important to my wife, Jenny Gandar, for her endurance and that essential encouragement every author needs when the going gets hard and the spirits are low.

Rivonia
17 March 2003

THE WORLD IN MICROCOSM

Then the Lord said to Cain,
"Where is your brother Abel?"
"I do not know," he replied.
"Am I my brother's keeper?"
— GENESIS 4:9

THE OLD APARTHEID REGIME used to display a tourism poster abroad which proclaimed South Africa to be "A World in One Country". The intention, of course, was to advertise the apartheid vision of a "multinational" land with independent tribal nations linked together with a big white-dominated one in a kind of ethnic confederation. It was political fantasy, venal fantasy in its dishonest attempt to Max-factorize the face of an evil system, and mercifully both the fantasy and its rationalizations have gone the way of all nightmares come the dawn. Yet paradoxically that sobriquet now finds a new validity in the national reincarnation that has taken place. The new South Africa is indeed the world in microcosm, in its population mix, its wealth gap, and above all in the impact which the powerful new forces of globalization are having on it both internally and in its relationship with the rest of the African continent.

Here is where the First and Third Worlds meet, or in the new lexicon of post-Cold War geopolitics, the developed and developing worlds, the dark-skinned and light-skinned worlds, the rich and the poor, in the same proportions as the rest of the global village of roughly one to five. It is where the white-skinned First Worlders tried to keep the dark-skinned Third Worlders out of their islands of affluence in the cities with pass laws and influx control regulations, just as the developed nations try to stop them crossing the global poverty barriers of the Rio Grande, the Mediterranean and the Pacific Rim, and with as little suc-cess. It is where the forces of globalization are tending to widen the gap between the stinking rich and the dirt poor, just as they are in the world as a whole. And it is where South Africa, as the regional superpower in the world's most marginalized continent, finds itself in much the same situation as the United States does internationally – growing richer and more resented in its relationship to the rest, both envied and feared, with the power and the obligation to help the less developed in its neighbourhood but constrained in what it can do for fear of being considered imperialist and domineering. Of being the *gringos* of Africa.

But there is one big difference. The Third Worlders rule the new South Africa, and so are in a position, and have the motivation, to redress the imbalances and close the gaps as they are nowhere else. That makes South Africa the test case for a new global dispensation. I will argue that the success of the new South Africa is vital for the salvation of Africa, and that the salvation of Africa is vital to the world as a whole.

At a workshop of Africa specialists that I attended in Washington, the question was posed: "Why does Africa matter?" The implicit suggestion was that the continent was drifting off the world's radar screens because of a failure to project a compelling answer to that question to the movers and shakers of international affairs who were increasingly preoccupied with interacting with one another and with playing the new casino game of globalized free trade among themselves. Africa, with its pathetic two percent of global production and no purchasing power – more than half its 800 million people have to survive on less than $1 a day – simply didn't belong in that league and so was being ignored. Its economic insignificance aside, the developed world was turning away in exasperation from Africa's endless conflicts and self-destructive misrule. The international news media, too, had grown weary and were giving less coverage to its endless woes and impenetrable complexities. *The Economist* had dismissed it as "the hopeless continent". All of which gave rise to the question: Does Africa matter? And if so, why?

So I offered my contribution. "Africa matters," I suggested, "because in the global village you *are* your neighbour's keeper. Because if you are not, if you ignore your neighbour's plight as you grow wealthier and he sinks ever deeper into poverty and despair, he may pollute your property, his family may contract diseases that infect yours, he may burgle your home, he may try to invade and occupy it, and in his resentment at your indifference he may even throw a bomb at it."

A year later suicide pilots flew three hijacked airliners into the twin towers of the World Trade Centre and the Pentagon. As the United States reeled with shock and anger, and as President George W Bush declared "war on terrorism", naming the Islamic militant, Osama bin Laden, as his prime target, an American academic tried to warn that an attempt to hunt down a guilty party might aggravate rather that alleviate "a residual enmity against America" that was at large in the world. "The root cause is not terrorist activity," wrote Professor William Beeman, a specialist in Middle East culture at Brown University. "It is the relationship between the United States and the Islamic world. Until this central cancerous problem is treated, Americans will never be free from fear."[1]

Indeed. Except that I would say the root cause of this residual enmity goes beyond the Islamic world. And beyond the United States, too. It is the relationship between the First and Third Worlds that is the primary cancer threatening to metastacize as this century progresses. The suicide attacks on New York and Washington were a first experience of a major terrorist blow against the American homeland which its citizens had come to regard as a safe haven amid the storms of global events, but the fact is that such acts have long been a symptom and a warning of a growing resentment that is spawning cells of aggressive fanaticism. In the 33 years since 1968 there have been 500 hijackings around the world and more than 4 000 recorded terrorist bombings[2].

The poor two-thirds of the globe are angry. They are angry at global inequity and what they see as the First World's, the white world's, arrogance and indifference to their concerns. Ever since the self-centred Reagan-Thatcher years and the collapse of communism, the developed nations have been too wrapped up in what John Kenneth Galbraith has called "the culture of contentment" to be overly concerned about the deepening plight of the world's poorer countries. And as Thomas Friedman's "electronic herd" thunders across the globe whipping up ever bigger profits for the already wealthy and sometimes trampling on the poor,[3] there are some ritual murmurings of concern among the global nabobs who gather annually in Davos, but no one does anything about it. The inequalities remain unattended, and the anger grows.

Yet even as the United States began preparing a strategy to respond to the terrible attacks on its home soil, one truth suddenly became clear – the strategy would have to be global and would have to include allies in the developing world if it was to stand any chance of success. A sudden awareness that the Third World *does* matter, that you can't ignore your neighbour in the global village. That is a start. What is needed now is for the First Worlders to enter into an exhaustive political engagement with their deeply aggrieved neighbours and to show some sensitivity to the economic, cultural and religious concerns that are turning them into such bitter foes. That is what South Africa learned just in time to avoid its own Armageddon.

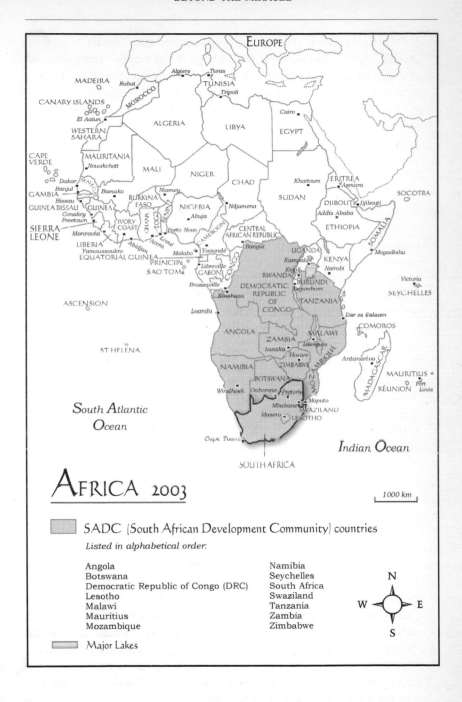

AFRICA 2003

1000 km

SADC (South African Development Community) countries

Listed in alphabetical order.

Angola
Botswana
Democratic Republic of Congo (DRC)
Lesotho
Malawi
Mauritius
Mozambique

Namibia
Seychelles
South Africa
Swaziland
Tanzania
Zambia
Zimbabwe

Major Lakes

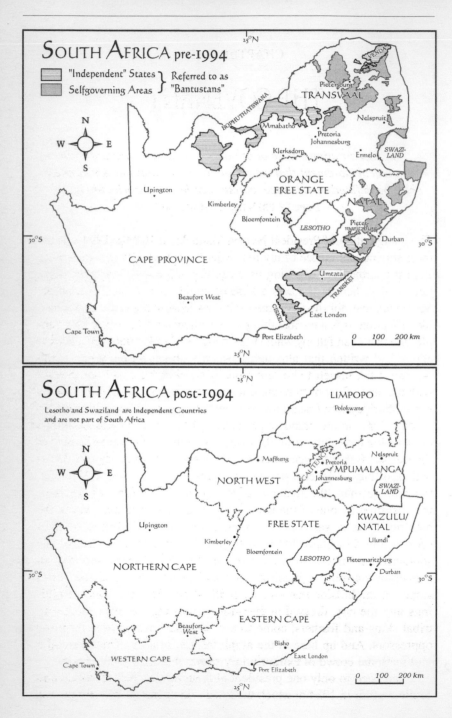

SOUTH AFRICA pre-1994

"Independent" States
Selfgoverning Areas
} Referred to as "Bantustans"

25°N

N
W   E
S

BOPHUTHATSWANA

VENDA

Pietersburg

TRANSVAAL

Mmabatho

Nelspruit

Pretoria
Johannesburg

Klerksdorp

Ermelo

SWAZI-
LAND

ORANGE
FREE STATE

NATAL

Upington

Kimberley

Bloemfontein

LESOTHO

Pieter-
maritzburg

30°S   30°S

Durban

CAPE PROVINCE

Umtata

Beaufort West

TRANSKEI

CISKEI

East London

Cape Town

Port Elizabeth

0   100   200 km

25°N

SOUTH AFRICA post-1994

Lesotho and Swaziland are Independent Countries
and are not part of South Africa

LIMPOPO

Polokwane

N
W   E
S

Mafikeng

Nelspruit

Pretoria

GAUTENG

MPUMALANGA

NORTH WEST

Johannesburg

SWAZI-
LAND

KWAZULU/
NATAL

Upington

FREE STATE

Kimberley

Ulundi

Bloemfontein

LESOTHO

Pietermaritzburg

30°S   30°S

Durban

NORTHERN CAPE

EASTERN CAPE

Beaufort
West

Bisho

Cape Town

WESTERN CAPE

East London

Port Elizabeth

0   100   200 km

25°N

xiv

CHAPTER ONE

THE COVENANT

*"The Constitution whose adoption we celebrate constitutes an
unequivocal statement that we refuse to accept that our Africanness
shall be defined by our race, colour, gender or historical origins."*
— DEPUTY PRESIDENT THABO MBEKI

The inauguration of President Nelson Mandela on 10 May 1994 was the
most stirring experience of my life. After more than 40 years of writing
against apartheid, of exposing its inequities and cruelties and the sheer
lunacy of it, here at last was a kind of vindication, a kind of triumph.
More than that, for the first time I felt the stirrings of a sense of national
identification. It is a terrible thing to feel alienated from one's own people, and that I had felt my whole life. In my first book, published a decade
ago, I had written that although I was a fifth-generation white South
African, I felt myself to be "emotionally stateless": I could not identify
with the land of my birth because it stood for things I abhorred; I felt no
sense of pride when I heard my national anthem or saw my national flag.

Now here, in the grand amphitheatre of Pretoria's Union Buildings
overlooking the capital from the slopes of a hill which inspired architect
Sir Herbert Baker 80 years before with visions of the Acropolis dominating the city of Athens, stood the tall, frail figure of Nelson Mandela,
the miracle man, the living martyr who had withstood 27 years of
incarceration by one of the world's most heartless regimes, taking the
oath of office. It was a clear, cloudless day, the bright-brittle sunlight
crisp in the thin highveld air, with just the first chill touches of the
southern hemisphere autumn. But from the crowd there throbbed an
exuberant warmth. A hundred thousand people thronged the lower
slopes of the hillside that sweeps gently down from the Union Buildings into the city, dressed in everything from rags to work clothes to
tribal skins and feathers, come to see their hero take power from the
oppressors. And up here in the amphitheatre, in all its finery, stood a
multinational crowd of extraordinary sartorial and political variety.

I had been to only one presidential inauguration before, a thin and
soulless affair in 1984 at which the tough old militarist P W Botha was

installed in the presence of just one foreign leader – the Angolan rebel, Jonas Savimbi. Now the whole world was here: Hillary Clinton and Al Gore and Fidel Castro, John Major and Yasir Arafat, the kings of Belgium and Greece, Swaziland and Lesotho, the Duke of Edinburgh and the lord chamberlain to King Hussein of Jordan, Israelis and Arabs, Iranians and Turks and Greeks and Russians, Europeans and Asians and Latin Americans, and, of course, the whole of Africa. The pariah state had emerged like a butterfly from its chrysalis into the sunlight of international acceptance.

The Old Man stepped forward and the great crowd hushed. Tall and thin and still, with that immobile face, so like his own wax image in Madame Tussaud's, with not a muscle moving, not a flicker of emotion, until after the oath – and then the smile that everyone has come to know, broad, beaming, radiant. Then back into its immobile mode once more for the speech. A speech that seemed aimed at all the alienated souls of Alan Paton's beloved country. The closing words, slow and measured, booming out across the great crowd: "We enter into a covenant that we shall build a society in which all South Africans, both black and white, will be able to walk tall, without any fear in their hearts, assured of their inalienable right to human dignity – a rainbow nation at peace with itself and the world." And then the pledge, from a man who had once told the judge who was about to sentence him to life imprisonment that he was prepared to die for the cause of nonracialism. "Never, never, never again shall it be that this beautiful land will again experience the oppression of one by another, and suffer the indignity of being the skunk of the world."

A military band began playing the lilting harmony of the new national anthem, *Nkosi sikelel' iAfrika* (God bless Africa), and I felt the hairs stand up on the nape of my neck. My first experience in all my three score years of a sentiment that was, what, patriotism? Six jet fighters, which only a few short years before had been strafing Mandela's men in the bush of Angola, flew low overhead trailing long smoke streamers in the six colours of the new national flag, followed by six helicopter gunships flying the flag itself. Down below, a rock band struck up. The great crowd burst into song, swaying and rocking to the music and forming snakelike trains that wove through the crowds holding the new flag high in the air. The occasion turned, as is wont to happen in Africa, from formal ceremonialism into an impromptu Woodstock.

A rainbow nation. What a wonderful promise in a world riven by ethnic conflicts. What a stunning turnaround for a country bedevilled by half a century of institutionalized racism. Gripped by the symbolism of it, Archbishop Desmond Tutu, the Nobel laureate, was moved to predict that South Africa, with its own intersection of First and Third World populations, would transform itself from global pariah into global role model. "Once we have got it right," Tutu said, "South Africa will be the paradigm for the rest of the world."

But promises are one thing, fulfilling them another. Can South Africa, with its long history of racial intolerance, really buck the global trend and become a truly nonracial, multiparty democracy? Is non-racialism itself in any event not a pipe dream that ignores the hard realities of human nature? Is democracy not something that can exist in only a handful of developed countries with a high degree of homogencity and what the political scientists call social balance?

* * *

Looking back after nine years, almost a decade, one can credit the new South Africa with many excellent achievements. We have entrenched a new democratic Constitution, perhaps the most progressive in the world, and bedded it down through four national, provincial and local elections which have been manifestly peaceful and fair. We have a Constitutional Court presided over by world-class jurists to interpret and defend it, and we have established a number of other institutions to give effect to the Constitution, including an Independent Electoral Commission, a Human Rights Commission and a Commission for Gender Equality. Not least we have managed a smooth transition from the Founding Father of our new nation to his young successor in a continent where this is rare.

We have scrapped all the old race laws, guaranteed freedom of speech and the press, abolished the death penalty, legalized abortion on demand, protected the rights of gay people, and advanced women in many spheres of life.

We have brought clean water to more than 9 million people who did not have it before, electricity to more than 2 million, and telephones – that vital connection to the new Information Age – to 1,5 million. We have integrated, at least nominally, more than 30 000 public schools that used to be racially segregated, as well as all the country's universities and other institutions of higher learning, raised the literacy rate of 15-to-24-year-olds to 95%, and brought free health care to millions of children.[1] We have ended diplomatic isolation and rejoined the community of nations to play an influential role on the international stage.

We have resuscitated an economy that was on its deathbed, restoring fiscal discipline, cutting the budget deficit, reducing the national debt, bringing inflation down from double figures to within a target range of 3% to 6%, slashing interest rates from a high of 24% under apartheid to 14% prime; lifting trade barriers, removing a maze of tariffs and import duties, and generally winning universal praise for establishing a sound macroeconomic base from which hopefully to build future prosperity.

It is indeed another country.

But the greatest achievement by far has been to avoid the bloodbath that was so widely predicted for so long by so many as the inevitable destiny of apartheid South Africa. Within the first two years of his presidency, Nelson Mandela had defused the threat of a counter-revolution by the white right and put an end to the internecine violence between his ANC and Chief Mangosuthu Buthelezi's Inkatha Freedom Party (IFP) which claimed some 25 000 lives between 1983 and 1996 – the so-called "black-on-black" violence that much of the media portrayed as a grim indicator of what lay in store for the new South Africa. Mandela did so through a series of extraordinary gestures of reconciliation, which included drawing the IFP into his government and Buthelezi into a senior Cabinet post, having tea with Betsie Verwoerd, widow of the chief architect of apartheid, Hendrik Verwoerd, and even visiting Percy Yutar, the Uriah Heep figure who was the prosecutor in the trial that sent Mandela and his colleagues narrowly past the gallows to their long, harsh incarceration.

The prospect of a counter-revolution was the most real, and feared, danger at the time of the 1994 election, when right-wing Afrikaner extremists formed themselves into militia movements that threatened to link up with the Defence and Police Forces and take over the government by force of arms. But the threat was defused when an attempted putsch in one of the tribal bantustans, or "homelands", BophuthaTswana, collapsed ignominiously. Mandela then met with the putative leader of the putsch, former Chief of the Defence Force General Constand Viljoen, and persuaded him to campaign for his separatist cause by constitutional means instead. Viljoen did so, forming the far-rightists into an Afrikaner separatist party called the Freedom Front and winning seven seats in the new Parliament.

Today the separatist movement is dead. The Freedom Front won less than 1% of the vote in the 1999 election, and Viljoen retired – while Eugene Terre'Blanche, the bearded demagogue who thundered his

4

threats of a Third Boer War and led the charge into BophuthaTswana, has served a prison sentence, faces another, and says he has given up the gun for God.

More than that, Afrikaner nationalism, that powerful force spawned by the twin agonies of the Boer War and the Great Depression and which shaped and drove South African politics as a malign force for nearly the whole of the twentieth century, is itself dead, its rump subsumed first into the old party of white liberals led by an English-speaking Jew, and then later into an alliance with the ANC where it will surely shed the last vestiges of its traditional support.

All this the world has hailed as a miracle and venerated its prophet.

Yet you will not travel far into this society without encountering many, on both left and right, who are writing the old President's covenant off as a failure. With unemployment rising and the wealth gap between whites and the vast majority of blacks still painfully wide, it is easy to find disenchanted blacks who will tell you that the new regime has done too much to appease the whites and that for them "nothing has changed". They see whites still dominating the economy and still living in big houses in salubrious suburbs while the black ghettos and pullulating squatter camps on the fringes of every town and city remain. Many are irked, too, by what they see as an unrepentant attitude among whites and a resentful reluctance to have any of the social and economic privileges they acquired under apartheid diminished. As returned author and playwright Mandla Langa puts it, the new South Africa is a country "immured in amnesia, where the past never happened".[2]

For their part many whites, especially the Afrikaner majority among them who ruled the country for nigh on half a century and came to regard it as their God-given right to do so, feel disempowered and confused about whether they have a role and even about their own identity. "Many of us feel alienated because so little thought was given to our place and our role once the war against racism was won," writes Chris Louw, an Afrikaans broadcaster whose first ancestor arrived in South Africa three-and-a-half centuries ago and who has written with angry confusion about his sense of cultural and national alienation. "We still do not know where we fit in if we are unfortunate enough to have been born African, but not black."[3]

Afrikaner nationalism is dead, so what does it mean now to be an Afrikaner? Some even worry about the survival of their language. Five of South Africa's 21 universities were established specifically to nurture the

Afrikaans language and the "Christian National" culture that were considered the quintessential elements of national existence. Today those five universities have had to integrate and adapt to the needs of a large number of students who do not speak the language or identify with the culture. That has meant dual-medium instruction, with lectures in English as well as Afrikaans. The Rand Afrikaans University, established in 1967 as the newest and most triumphalist assertion of this *volkskultuur* with the architectural profile of a protective laager in the heart of metropolitan Johannesburg, now has an enrolment of 13 000 students only 5 000 of whom are Afrikaans-speaking. Many feel it is no longer an Afrikaans university and that without such conservatories the language itself will die. The questions abound. Can a *volk*, a nation, exist, can a *volksgeist*, Herder's national spirit, be sustained without a nation-state to call its own? What, ultimately, is to be the identifying culture of the new rainbow nation which faces the paradoxical challenge of trying to build national unity while preserving cultural differences and 11 official languages?

There are practical concerns, too, within the white community and it is not only the Afrikaners who are affected. The English-speaking South Africans, who number 40% of the white population and have remained politically powerless for more than a century in the country they dominate economically, don't suffer from the same sense of disempowerment and don't feel the same threat to their cultural identity, but they too are profoundly conservative, they are less deeply rooted in South Africa, they don't have the same sense of *blud en boden*, they feel themselves to be members of a global community of English-speakers, and they are more mobile than the Afrikaners.

Two things in particular trouble these English-speakers: the country's high crime rate and the new government's policy of affirmative action which places blacks first and women next in the job queue. Young white men, "pale males" as they call themselves in tones tinged with bitterness, feel themselves disadvantaged. They fear their career prospects and those of their children will be stunted, that they will lose out in the competition for advancement and success in life because of their skin colour rather than their ability. It's a reversal of roles which some may see as poetic justice, but the result is a brain drain which is damaging the economy and restricting the growth needed to provide jobs for the swelling ranks of unemployed young black people.

But deeper down beneath these real concerns about role and identity and fears lies a subliminal unease among many whites, rooted in generations of assumed cultural superiority, that black people can't really run

6

things efficiently, that over time the new South Africa for all its promise is bound to go "the way of the rest of Africa", of *The Economist's* "hopeless continent". So they sit on the sidelines watching for every sign of mismanagement or corruption that will reinforce these dark forebodings. And expecting the worst, they see it. The result is a persistent negativism that rankles with the new government and raises its hackles, which in turn prompts accusations of hyper-sensitivity, so setting up a polarizing vicious cycle.

Nor is it only white South Africans who display this negativism. It is evident throughout the white Western world where Afro-pessimism is widespread. There are good reasons, of course, for the developed world to look with scepticism and even disgust at Africa's many failures which too often have been caused by its own kleptocratic rulers who have raped and plundered its resources with a greed that surely matches its maligned colonizers. But the generalization, the reluctance on the part of many to see that South Africa with its industrialization and its maturity is manifestly different, the too-easy assumption that some kind of inherent deficiency is at work, bespeaks the same kind of subliminal racism which exists in South Africa. It is abetted of course by negative media reporting abroad and the word-of-mouth of those South Africans who have fled the imagined terrors of nonracial democracy to settle in Australasia, Canada, Europe and the Sunbelt of America. Too often for comfort I find when I travel abroad that people address me with words like: "You poor fellow, after all you have done it must be terrible to see what is happening in your country." Or as our Nobel laureate for literature, Nadine Gordimer, notes: "Again and again, when I am interviewed by European or US journalists or find myself in encounters with other people from their countries, the burning question is: 'What is happening to whites?'"

There are two obvious assumptions, Gordimer says, to be made of this approach to South Africa by Europeans and North Americans. "The majority of them being white, they identify only with whites whether consciously or unconsciously. Because I am white they assume I do the same. It's the Old Boys/Old Girls Club producing its dog-eared membership card. The projection is of the priorities of *their* lives, along with the old colonial conditioning that these belong with whiteness and are incontrovertibly, forever, threatened by Otherness – blacks."[4]

But it is not only whites who harbour deep-rooted race prejudice. Black South Africans are profoundly xenophobic. They are fiercely hostile, often violently so, towards economic refugees from other

African countries who flock to what they perceive to be a cornucopia of opportunity. While such economic self-protectiveness may be understandable and is pretty well universal in similar circumstances of large-scale unemployment, in South Africa's case there is more than just a whiff of ethnic superiority in the attitudes displayed towards the black immigrants. The foreigners themselves describe the black South Africans as arrogant, and they resent it particularly because South Africa's liberation movements were hosted and supported and even funded by their own countries for decades, often at great cost to those countries. To no small degree the economic distress that now drives these refugees southwards was a price paid for helping to liberate the very people who now resent them.

Nor is black racism confined to attitudes towards these black immigrants. While it is not of the same order as white racism, in that it stems more from a sense of grievance and outrage rather than a deeply ingrained sense of inherent superiority, racist attitudes towards whites are nonetheless a factor that is revealing itself more and more as the inhibitions of oppression fade, and which poses its own threat to the realization of the rainbow dream. It reveals itself in power plays in the scramble for advancement. Black South Africans have a lien on the collective guilt of their white fellow-countrymen, which equips them with a devastating weapon with which to demolish any white competitor for a job, or white critic of government policy. All they have to do is label the competitor, or the critic, a racist. It is a charge that cannot be credibly denied, for no racist in history has ever admitted the fact. And silence means consent. So the target of this charge has no way of countering it. There is no defence. And the more successful it proves to be, the more frequently it is used. As Mondli Makhanya, then Political Editor of the mass circulation *Sunday Times*, once observed: "Today we are seeing the re-emergence of a raw, uncouth black consciousness (as distinct from Steve Biko's more sophisticated concept of the philosophy) among members of the new elite, who wield blackness like a weapon as they climb the ladder of privilege."[5]

In its most striking instance, this weapon was used to destroy the career of the widow of the liberation struggle's most celebrated white hero, Joe Slovo, leader of the South African Communist Party and Chief of Staff of the ANC's guerrilla army, *Umkhonto we Sizwe* (Spear of the Nation). Helena Dolny, who married Slovo after his first wife, Ruth First, was killed by a parcel bomb sent her by an agent of the apartheid state, is an agricultural economist whom Mandela appointed to head the Land Bank and transform it into an institution that would help re-establish a black agricultural class after nearly a century of disinheritance.[6] Dolny was tackling her job with a passionate commitment when out of the blue in May 1999 the chairman-designate of the Bank, one Bonile Jack, wrote a letter to President-in-waiting Thabo Mbeki, with a copy deliberately slipped to *The Star* newspaper, accusing her of "racism, nepotism and mismanagement". A judge later found the allegations to be "defamatory and baseless", but after six gruelling months of public traducement during which it became clear that this was part of an orchestrated campaign to squeeze her out of her job, Dolny resigned in despair – and with a parting jibe about "ethnic cleansing" in the Land Affairs Department which had shed seven whites with "land struggle activist backgrounds" from senior positions in five months.[7]

Three years later *The Star* published a front-page apology to Dolny in which it acknowledged that the statements it had published about her were not true. But the damage was done – to herself and the country.[8]

It is a trend that has alienated many members of the white left who identified with the liberation movement and in many instances paid a heavy price for doing so. The effect has been unfortunate because, as Saki Macozoma, a prominent black business executive, has noted, this group, though small, is influential especially in the media and academia and has served as an important bridge between South Africa's black elite and the white community. "Their alienation has had a great impact on how the discourse between the black political elite and the white community is conducted," Macozoma writes. "The casualty of this tension has largely been the project of creating a nonracial society." Deploring this, Macozoma calls on the country's leaders "to rise above the chaff and the noise" and find ways to build bridges between the races. "The ideal of creating a nonracial society is unique to South Africa," he adds. "There is no society in the world today that has achieved this ideal, and thus there are not many precedents to follow. Those of us who believe that this is the only type of society that will deliver harmony and prosperity to our people have to be steadfast, patient, creative and committed. We will zig and we will zag in our attempts to create a nonracial society, but we must continue to go forward."[9]

* * *

Nine years on the honeymoon is certainly over. Gone is the euphoria of that first election day with its spirit of camaraderie in the long snaking queues of people waiting for hours to cast their votes, and of black people dancing in the streets of Johannesburg the night our rugby team, the pride of white Afrikaners, won the 1995 World Cup and a beaming Mandela donned the number six jersey of captain François Pienaar. Now South Africa is facing its harder realities. There is also a new brittleness in the air and, some think, a recrudescence of racism.

The cut and thrust of adversarial politics is partly responsible for this, as is the outspokenness of a press flexing its wings of critical freedom for the first time since the first newspaper was founded at the Cape in 1824 and promptly fell into conflict with the British Governor. There is a complication of paradoxes here: South Africa needs healing and for this it needs a lowering of voices and a climate of restraint and constructive engagement to enable the different groups to find one another and build mutual trust; yet South Africa also needs to build a vigorous political opposition, for that is the essence of parliamentary democracy. South Africa also needs a free and vigorous press that can play the role of public watchdog and a brake on the abuse of power, for that, too, is an organic necessity in a democratic society. The criticism is vital, yet it also divides and when the political divisions run along ethnic or racial lines that inevitably causes polarization along those lines.

To an unfortunate degree this has happened in South Africa. Two landmark events have brought it about. The first was former President F W de Klerk's decision to withdraw prematurely from the Government of National Unity. For two years six Ministers of his National Party and 18 ANC Ministers had worked together in the GNU Cabinet, and although the relationship was difficult given that it was an unnatural coalition of ex-enemies with different agendas and no agreed common policy framework, it worked surprisingly well. Mandela played an elder statesman role, delegating De Klerk and Thabo Mbeki as the two Deputy Presidents to chair Cabinet meetings on a rotational basis, and gradually the Ministers settled into a practical working relationship which produced a considerable degree of mutual understanding and even camaraderie. But ultimately De Klerk could not adjust to his lesser role or to the ANC's adamant refusal to accept his concept of permanent "power-sharing" in the new Constitution. Moreover he resented the fact that Mandela never really trusted him and on one occasion had attacked him angrily in a Cabinet meeting. Mandela felt De Klerk had betrayed him by conniving in the "Third Force" of police and intelligence agents who sponsored the massive political violence between supporters of the ANC and Chief Buthelezi's Inkatha Freedom Party.

So in June 1996 De Klerk pulled the NP out of the Government of National Unity, to the dismay of some of his colleagues. "At the best of times," he wrote later, "it is hardly possible for a former chief executive to serve in the same board as his successor. No matter how sensitively he conducts himself, the former CEO will always wish to provide the board with the benefit of his experience. No matter how sound that advice might be, his successor will nearly always resent it."[10]

The result was an end to a collaborative experience across the racial and political divide at the executive level. At the same time the Constitutional Assembly completed its work, bringing to an end another constructive negotiating experience between white and black MPs of different parties. It also saw the departure from active politics of Cyril Ramaphosa and later Roelf Meyer, the two key negotiators for the ANC and the NP who had been the pivot around which the whole negotiating process had turned from its earliest days in the Negotiating Council. Thereafter Parliament became a much more combative arena.

The second watershed event was the 1999 general election. It brought together into the adversarial contest two men both of high intelligence but otherwise as different in personality, culture and style as it is possible to find – Thabo Mbeki, the new ANC leader, and Tony Leon, leader of the Democratic Party. The DP, an amalgam of opposition groups from old regime days headed by the liberal Progressive Party and therefore still the residual home of white liberalism, had won only seven seats in the first democratic election with a paltry 1,7% of the vote. But soon after pulling out of the Government of National Unity De Klerk had resigned as leader of the NP, so dealing his party a fatal double blow. With Meyer out of the picture, having clashed with De Klerk over the future role of the party, the leadership fell to a 37-year-old former youth organizer, Marthinus van Schalkwyk. Though bright and well-meaning, Van Schalkwyk's chubby, boyish face and general lack of gravitas earned him the crippling Afrikaans nickname of *Kortbroek* (Short Pants) which he was unable to shake. Thus weakened at the top and uncertain how to shed the albatross of its apartheid past without also shedding its white conservative support base, the New National Party (NNP), as it now called itself, entered the lists looking vulnerable – and Tony Leon went for the jugular.

Determined to oust the NNP as the main opposition party, Leon launched a campaign aimed blatantly at winning over the white conservative vote. He had been fishing in these waters for some time, coming out strongly against the ANC's policy of affirmative action. In

February 1998 the DP brought out a stinging pamphlet called *The Death of the Rainbow Nation,* in which it accused the Mandela government of reintroducing racial politics with a law that required employers to draft a plan showing how they intended to advance blacks in their work force and then submit annual progress reports to the government. In a crude bit of overstatement the DP claimed this effectively reintroduced a system of race classification and criminalized "colour-blindness", and warned that "racial legislation is a very slippery slope: apartheid, American segregation and Nazi Germany all had small beginnings".

Now Leon chose to run his election campaign on an emotive slogan that said simply, "Fight Back". To black South Africans that meant only one thing – fight back against black majority rule! Although the DP claimed belatedly that the slogan meant fighting back against crime, corruption and misrule, it was stretching credulity not to recognize that it was a not-very-subtle call to conservative whites to come out of the woodwork and fight back against the ANC and all it represented. The polarizing impact was massive, but from Leon's short-term strategic perspective it was successful. The DP gained spectacularly, winning 38 seats, gaining more Afrikaner votes than the NNP and so ousting it as the official Opposition in Parliament. Even far-rightist supporters of the Freedom Front flocked to Leon's banner. As a bewildered General Viljoen confessed to a fellow Afrikaner: "One of them told me, 'That Jew fights harder against the kaffirs than you do.'"[11]

What followed compounded the political felony. Soon after the election the DP merged with the New National Party to form a consolidated and overwhelmingly white opposition, called the Democratic Alliance (DA), with Leon as leader and Van Schalkwyk as deputy leader. It made for a stronger opposition, but it polarized Parliament racially with an overwhelmingly black governing party facing an overwhelmingly white opposition. While Mandela was President this would have mattered less, for with his enormous prestige he was, in Macazoma's phrase, able to "raise himself above the chaff and the noise". But with his departure the chaff and the noise became more evident. The change from Mandela to Mbeki also brought with it a change of emphasis, from the phase of reconciliation to that of delivery and an increasing emphasis on the poverty gap with Mbeki speaking, like Disraeli, of "two nations", one white and rich and the other poor and black, together with a sharpened criticism of continued white racism and a reluctance to help narrow that gap.

Perhaps fortunately the Democratic Alliance did not last. Leon and

Van Schalkwyk fell out after little more than two years, and Van Schalkwyk then took the NNP into an informal relationship with the ANC in a manoeuvre that smacked more of opportunism than political principle. It resulted in the new ANC/NNP alliance grabbing control of the Western Cape Provincial Administration which the DA had controlled before, and Van Schalkwyk later ending up as provincial Premier. This did at least have the merit of breaking up the black-white political alignment, but the brittle relationship between Mbeki and Leon remains, with the latter still leading the opposition in the national Parliament and likely to move further to the right as he seeks to capture the rest of Van Schalkwyk's traditional and by now thoroughly confused Afrikaner support base.

Mbeki and Leon are diametric opposites. Mbeki is quiet and undemonstrative, a reflective thinker and a subtle strategist with a fine analytical mind; but above all he is essentially African in seeing himself as part of a political community with a common purpose rather than as an individualist in the Western liberal sense. This makes him a collectivist who gives and requires total loyalty, whose style is to strive for inclusiveness and consensus, and who has a visceral dislike of open confrontation. He is a negotiator and a manipulator, not a fighter.

Leon by contrast is essentially Eurocentric with not an ounce of empathetic sensitivity to traditional African ways of debate and conflict resolution. As Frederik van Zyl Slabbert, a former leader of the Progressive Party and of the opposition in the old South African Parliament, has said, his style is pure Westminster and he would doubtless have done well there, probably as a Tory. In the words of retired editor/columnist Ken Owen, his style is that of "a cocky little bantam" whose weapons of choice are cleverness and historical contempt. He gets up black people's noses in an extraordinary way and the chemistry between him and Mbeki is the worst South Africa could possibly have at this juncture.

Yet for all that, at the social level South Africans of all races are mixing together as never before. They are living together, working together, playing together, going to school together, even making love and marrying together, which only a few years ago was a criminal offence under an equivalent of Hitler's Nuremberg laws. With remarkable speed the old cellular society, in which each group was born, lived out their lives and even died and were buried in separate social compartments, is breaking down. It is a process that has started and which has no end and which fills those of us who have spent our lives here with hope. Nadine Gordimer writes of her feelings as she drives past a school in her neighbourhood which used to be for whites only. "I see the kids coming out, the small boys scuffling with one another, the little girls tangling hands and giggling together. They are all shades of colour – SA black, SA Indian, SA Coloured, SA white. They are growing up with a common initiating experience, into life. They will never be subject to the horrors that the Truth Commission has exposed to us, and that has been so vital for us to face what we did or what we allowed to happen. These children are not being kept apart to learn to hate, to fear the unknown, the untouched in each other."[12]

That is where the new South Africa is being incubated.

CHAPTER TWO

A THREE-IN-ONE REVOLUTION

Every revolution is the consequence of one revolution
and the beginning of another.
— FRANCOIS CHATEAUBRIAND, *REVOLUTIONS ANCIENNES*

By any reasonable standard of judgement, the balance between success and failure over these nine years does not warrant the gloomy assessments of the state of the nation that one hears at home and particularly abroad. Rather the contrary. Yet barely had the sounds of Mandela's great inaugural party died away than the pessimistic prognostications began, and they have continued ever since. As *The Economist* noted a mere three years after the transition: "If scare stories were an export-earner, South Africa would be a rich place these days."[1] Of course the country has never lacked for doomsday prophets. Apartheid was always expected to end in an apocalyptic catastrophe, and even when the time of transition came many international journalists arrived with their video cameras primed for a bloodbath, and when it didn't happen they packed up and flew to Rwanda where conveniently there was one. In part this is because of the pervasive expectation of disaster associated with the continent of Africa, of Joseph Conrad's *Heart of Darkness*, which the white Western world has always seen as primitive and frightening and whose post-colonial history too often has been a tale of new presidents stepping off the inaugural podium onto a slippery slope of economic collapse, tribal warfare, lawlessness and corruption.

But what is even more responsible for the gloomy assessments is a gross underestimation of the task that has confronted the new majority government. It has been infinitely more complex and difficult than anyone, particularly those involved in the government itself, imagined it would be. As Gill Marcus, who was involved with the ANC in exile for more than 20 years and is now Deputy Governor of the Reserve Bank, puts it: "There was a feeling that if you dealt with apartheid a lot of other things would automatically fall into place, but that has not been the case. It is much harder than we expected; a lot of problems are much more deep-seated." Moreover there are simply too many problems clamouring for immediate attention. "So much is expected of us simultaneously," says Marcus, "that there is no room for sequencing. There is too much to do and we are trying to do it all."

To begin with, the new regime inherited an economic mess. In their exile dreams the ANC imagined South Africa to be an economic cornucopia that would provide them with ample resources to do their socioeconomic restructuring, such was the myth of monetary and military might and of administrative efficiency that the old regime had propagated, and which most whites and many foreigners believed. But the ANC leaders were in for a shock. When they moved into the seats of power they found the coffers near empty, with gross foreign exchange reserves down to less than three weeks of imports, and a budget deficit that had reached a record 8,6% of gross domestic product. "There was simply no money to do what we had planned," says Mac Maharaj, a veteran of the liberation struggle who became Minister of Transport in the first government. "We had to dump our blueprints and start from the beginning." The first task was to stabilize this shaky economy to prevent capital flight, then try to find at least some money to provide better social services to 80% of the population who had not had them before. No easy task. "The ANC inherited an economy that was in severe distress," says Pamela Cox, former head of the South Africa Division at the World Bank, "and what they have done to put the economy on a right footing is, I think, almost miraculous."[2]

But an even bigger challenge lies in the fact that, again unexpectedly, circumstances have forced South Africa to undertake not only a sociopolitical revolution, working to democratize the modern world's most deeply entrenched system of institutionalized racism and political authoritarianism, daunting though that is in itself. It is attempting three simultaneous revolutions rolled into one.

The first of these, the transformation from apartheid to a nonracial society, has itself been much more profound than is generally recognized. To outsiders particularly, apartheid appeared to be simply an extreme form of segregation, and therefore its ending was seen as roughly analogous to the desegregation of the American South, with Nelson Mandela in the role of Martin Luther King Jr. But in fact, while apartheid was indeed the most deeply entrenched and institutionalized system of segregation in the modern world, at its core the South African struggle was about much more than that. It was a struggle between two ethno-nationalisms claiming sovereignty over the same piece of territory – the black Africans, who claimed South Africa by indigenous right, and the white Afrikaners, who claimed it on grounds of the 350-year occupation – as long as whites have been in the United States – and by a God-given right extrapolated from their interpretation of Calvinist theology and given divine sanction by their Dutch Reformed Church. The essence of the struggle was: Whose county is it? Which is an infinitely bigger issue than segregated busses and lunch counters and schools, and makes the South African struggle more appropriately analogous to the conflicts between Israelis and Palestinians over the same blood-soaked patch of Middle Eastern earth, and between Protestants and Catholics in Northern Ireland.

Apartheid, with its ten tribal bantustans all supposedly evolving towards sovereign independence, was the means by which Afrikaners sought to achieve a multi-state settlement that would enable them to retain sovereignty over the main body of South Africa, in much the same way as the Oslo Agreement sought to achieve a two-state settlement in the Middle East.

The essence of the first revolution, therefore, is that the Afrikaners have abandoned their claim to sovereignty over South Africa as their historic, God-given homeland, and accepted a settlement that creates a single unitary state in which, thanks to a remarkable spirit of forgiveness and reconciliation on the part of the black South Africans, they are now a disempowered minority in a country ruled by others. An equivalent settlement in the Middle East would see Israel, the West Bank and the Gaza Strip consolidated into a single secular state which before long would be ruled over by a Palestinian majority government and in which Jews could live in peace and security as a minority group.

That is the measure of South Africa's achievement, the scale of its political revolution.

But it is, as I say, only the first of the three simultaneous revolutions. The issue of relinquishing sovereignty and political power aside, the task of ending segregation and beginning to integrate a society divided by 350 years of segregation and 45 of apartheid – that part which is equivalent to the integration of the American South – has itself been massive. It has involved much more than simply erasing apartheid legislation from the statute books and integrating schools and living areas and workplaces and every public and private institution in the land, or even of negotiating and writing and enacting a new national Constitution, designing a new national flag and coat-of-arms, and acquiring a new, integrated national anthem. It has involved more than just the explosive element of white-black racism and defusing the threat of a right-wing counter-revolution, for this is a society riven by cleavages of tribe and class and religion as well as race, of traditionalists who want to cling to the powers of the chiefs over their subjects, and modern democrats who see that as inimical to the building of a modern society, of largely illiterate rural masses who are dirt poor and an upwardly mobile urban class that is opening a gap between itself and the masses as wide as that between white and black.

This first revolution has also involved redrawing the geo-political map of South Africa – in itself a transformation of quite remarkable scale. A country that previously consisted of four provinces and ten nominally autonomous tribal "homelands", four of them independent, has been redrawn into one of nine completely new provinces with their own premiers, executives and legislatures, and with the so-called "homelands" eliminated as separate entities and subsumed into the provinces. At the city, town and country level, a hodge-podge of local government institutions with their roots in the incredibly complex apartheid system, where the races were kept physically and politically apart, has been restructured into a compact system of six metro, or mega-cities, 231 local councils and 47 district councils. In December 2000, 30 477 candidates from 79 political parties and 690 independents contested local government elections to fill these new governing bodies.

But more challenging than that is the second revolution, which has been to transform South Africa from an isolationist siege economy into a player in the new global marketplace. South Africa has had to transform itself from a highly protected, inward-looking economy into an internationally competitive one. This has meant opening itself to international competition, reducing barriers, abolishing exchange-control regulations on non-residents, and allowing the rand currency to float to a market-related level. These have been courageous and necessary steps, but they have exposed the country to the blasts of international financial instability.

When South Africa went to the polls so hopefully in April of 1994, no one realized that it was also about to plunge into a second, global revolution as powerful in its socio-economic impact as the industrial revolution of the nineteenth century. The fall of the Berlin Wall and the collapse of the Soviet Empire were phenomena that had stripped the ANC of its material support base and so helped to make our own negotiated revolution possible. But no one noticed immediately that they had also changed the world in a profound way. No longer was it divided into two separate and mutually exclusive economic systems, with each of the two superpowers defending the most distant and least important outpost of its empire with the threat of its nuclear capability so that the bipolar world seemed to be frozen in that form for all time. Suddenly the division was gone, and overnight the whole world became one big capitalist marketplace; and with the fortuitous coinciding of the information revolution with its miracle of instant electronic communication, suddenly traders could trade across the whole of this new worldwide marketplace at the click of a mouse. Suddenly companies could locate themselves in whatever parts of the planet made economic sense, with a headquarters in New York, a production plant in Bangkok and their accounting services in India or Bangladesh. It is a revolution that is changing the world in ways yet to be experienced – and with our own domestic revolution subsumed into it.

At the same time, South Africa is having to move rapidly from a primary producing economy based on agriculture and mining to one based on exports of manufactured goods. This is the third revolution. The country's gold resources, once the richest in the world, are dwindling and the price of gold is falling. In 1980 gold sales accounted for 15% of South Africa's gross domestic product; in 2000 they accounted for less than 3%. South Africa's industries, meanwhile, were mostly geared towards the mining industry or towards import substitution, a pattern intensified by international sanctions during the 1980s. Only a few, such as Rothmans, a major tobacco transnational, South African Breweries, which was then the world's fourth-largest beer manufacturer, and the country's highly rated wine and fruit-canning enterprises, were significant exporters[3]. This has had to be turned around rapidly, from inward-looking to export orientation, to make up for the loss of foreign exchange earnings from gold. In the decade since Mandela's release South Africa's manufactured exports have increased from 6,7% of gross domestic product in 1990 to 39,7% in 2000.

Down on the farm, meanwhile, another part of this turnaround revolution has seen the new government withdraw fat agricultural subsidies that the apartheid regime paid to its white farming constituents to keep them on the land. Much of the farming in what is largely a semi-arid country was profitable only at enormous cost to the state through these subsidies, which at their peak in 1970 consumed the largest slice of the national budget at R108 million (the equivalent of R2,8 billion in 2001 rands, or $346 million).[4]

19

Land had long been part of the mythology of Afrikaner Nationalism, woven around the heroic folklore of the pioneer Voortrekkers struggling their way northward in the Great Trek of the early nineteenth century to escape British colonization and stake out their own vast estates in their own independent republics and then defend these to the death in a titanic struggle against the armies of the British Empire at the height of its power. The land may not have been much good except for some fertile strips around the Indian Ocean coastline, but to the Afrikaner Nationalist regime it had a value in political nostalgia that was priceless. And so the subsidies were paid. They took the form of special rates for financial and technical assistance to groups of farmers who formed cooperative societies. After the Great Depression the government introduced price support schemes that cushioned the farmers against fluctuating prices in the open market. There were 21 marketing control boards, covering every kind of agricultural product from meat to maize and from eggs to dried beans, through which farmers sold their produce at fixed prices. Since their profits were assured and directly related to the quantity produced, the farmers produced as much as they could. This resulted in massive surpluses in some sectors, particularly maize, which the state then exported at a loss.

All this the new government has abolished. At a stroke it deregulated the industry in 1996, abolishing all the marketing boards and leaving the farmers to cope with competition and the complex business of relating production to market needs. Many have gone under. Small operations have been taken over by larger ones. In the 20 years between 1980 and 2000 the number of farmers declined from 70 000 to 50 000, and the number of farm workers from 1 235 000 to 914 000. At the same time agriculture's contribution to the gross domestic product shrank from 6% to 3,4%.[5]

* * *

Compounding the difficulty is a crippling conflict between the requirements of these three simultaneous revolutions. On the one hand, the ANC faces the political imperative of having to deliver more jobs and better pay to its expectant and long-deprived constituencies. On the other hand, the harsh reality of competitive participation in the global market is that it leads to increased unemployment and pressure on wages, at least in the short term. In seeking to transform South Africa from a producer of primary goods into a manufacturing exporter, the government has to deal with the fact that the old economy required an abundance of cheap, unskilled labour, while the new one requires a smaller but highly skilled work force – and the apartheid regime, as a matter of policy, prevented the black population from acquiring skills. The purpose of the policy was not only to protect white jobs but to attempt the Sisyphean task of reversing the relentless influx of rural black people to the cities. They were supposed to stay in their own little tribal "homelands", which were one day supposed to become independent, leaving the greater part of the country as the white man's land.

The result was that black people were deliberately given a separate and inferior education (most, in fact, got no education at all). They were barred from the major universities. They were prohibited by law from doing skilled work. A black man could carry a white craftsman's toolbox for him and hand him the tools, but he could not do the skilled job himself. He could mix the paint and clean the paint brushes and set up the ladder, but he could not paint the wall himself. Such work was reserved for whites under the Job Reservation Act.

Until 1979 black people were not allowed to join trade unions, so they could not acquire skills by becoming apprentices. They were not allowed to form partnerships or companies. They could not establish businesses, except simple shops selling perishable produce – and even then their trading licences had to be renewed annually. It must be the only instance in history in which a government deliberately crippled the skills base of its country's working class. Cyril Ramaphosa, the trade union leader who became the ANC's chief constitutional negotiator and is now a tycoon, has described this planned neglect as the worst of all apartheid's crimes against humanity. Its legacy is now the new democratic regime's greatest liability.

But even that is only the half of it. More taxing still is having to cope with the uncharted winds of destabilization that keep blowing through this newly globalized world. No sooner do we have our macro-economic house in order and the analysts start predicting a good growth year ahead, than a new blast gusts from some distant part of the globe over which we have no control, and it blows us off course.

* * *

The first of these storms blew up on 8 December 1997 in Thailand, a country 10 000 km from South Africa and with which we had no significant economic interaction. On that day the Thai government announced that 56 of the country's top 58 financial institutions had gone bankrupt and were to be closed.[6] The institutions had been

21

stoking a spectacular boom that made Thailand one of the leading "Asian Tigers" and transformed its capital, Bangkok, from a quaint oriental Ruritania for Anna and her king into a skyscraper metropolis with elevated motorways and skytrains and the world's worst traffic jams. They had done so by borrowing large quantities of US dollars and lending these to Thai businesses to build the towering apartment and office blocks that were the monuments to the new prosperity. They thought they were safe doing this because the government was committed to keeping the local currency, the baht, pegged to the US dollar, but they had reckoned without a new phenomenon of the globalization era. Currency speculators, monitoring the state of economies around the globe, decided the Thai economy was weaker than it looked and launched a massive speculative attack on the baht. The speculators do this by selling the currency short – in other words selling large amounts of baht that they don't have, thereby driving its value down so that when eventually they have to deliver the currency to the buyers anything between one to six months later it is substantially cheaper than what they were paid for it. The speculators can make a killing this way, which is what happened to the baht in 1997. The currency plunged 30%, which meant the businesses that had borrowed the dollars couldn't pay back their loans, which meant the finance houses in turn couldn't repay their foreign lenders. They went bust and were shut down.

But the Thai crash was simply the first domino to fall. Alarmed investors began looking more critically at other countries in Southeast Asia that had excited something of a feeding frenzy until then. Click, click, click went the computer mice and their investments were whipped away to safer havens in the developed world. The currencies of South Korea, Malaysia and Indonesia all plummeted as the baht had done. And as the Southeast Asian recession set in, the prices of raw materials that the boom had been consuming also slumped – gold, copper, aluminium and oil. This in turn hit other economies. Russia, still struggling to find its feet after the collapse of the communist system, was particularly dependent on its oil exports and was having to raise foreign loans at ever higher interest rates to balance its operating budget. As the oil revenues dwindled, Russia found it could not pay the interest and principal on these loans. Suddenly it devalued and defaulted at the same time, leaving banks, speculators and investors around the world with massive losses.

It was the signal for a panic flight of investors from emerging economies everywhere, which threw 38% of the world's economies into recession. South Africa was one of those hit hard. A billion dollars left the country in the third quarter of 1998, the rand currency plummeted 26% in two months, and by the time the Johannesburg Stock Exchange bottomed out in September the all-share index was 40% down from its April high. Interest rates shot up from 18,25% in June to a record high of 25% in August, and growth was stopped in its tracks. Instead of a projected 2,3% growth rate for 1998, the country ended with a miserable 0,5%.

Slowly Southeast Asia recovered, although investor confidence never returned fully to the emerging economies. The rand steadied at just over six to the US dollar and just under ten to the British pound, the Johannesburg Stock Exchange climbed back 30%, interest rates returned to 18%, and consumer inflation, which had reached a scorching 25,5% under the apartheid regime, fell below 5% for the first time in 20 years.

But steadiness is not the norm in the new globalization era. Other storms blew up in Turkey and Argentina, but the next big one came from the opposite end of the earth and of the economic spectrum. As the Clinton Administration gave way with a little help from the Supreme Court to that of George W Bush, the dot-com bubble burst in the world's only Superpower. The Nasdaq crashed and America's unprecedented run of prosperity came to an abrupt end. At the same time the Japanese economy entered its fourth recession in a decade, and in Europe the German economy, too, slipped into recession. For the first time the world's three leading economies were in recession at the same time. It was in that dismal climate that the Al Qaeda suicide pilots launched their devastating attack on the World Trade Centre and the Pentagon – America's "vital organs", as Osama bin Laden put it – and sent the mighty US economy reeling.

Once again the impact on South Africa was severe, stripping 15% off the Johannesburg Stock Exchange and knocking the hapless rand down to a desperate 11,26 to the dollar by the end of the year. In all the currency lost 30% of its value against the dollar in the course of the year, despite a general agreement that South Africa had among the best economic fundamentals of any of the emerging economies. All as a result of events far beyond its borders over which it had no control.

* * *

On a crisp winter's day in 1999 the citizens of Pretoria beheld an extraordinary sight. Bobby Godsell, chief executive officer of Anglogold, the world's biggest gold mining company, and chairman of the South

African Chamber of Mines, walked arm-in-arm with the General Secretary of the National Union of Mineworkers, Gwede Mantashe, through the streets of the capital at the head of a crowd of 5 000 miners and mine managers in a protest march to the Swiss Embassy and the British High Commission, where they presented a petition objecting to a decision by the central banks of those countries to sell off portions of their gold reserves. "The Chamber Digs Gold", read the slogan on Godsell's yellow tee-shirt, while his young daughter, who rode on his shoulders, carried a poster declaring "Not One Ounce More". Beside them strode Mantashe in a socialist red shirt and cap.

It presented an improbable show of comradeship between white and black and between bosses and workers in an industry historically associated with race discrimination and exploitation. But the two had a binding common interest, for if these central banks went ahead with their decision it would clearly mean the beginning of the demonetizing of gold and thus of the element that had given it a special value since antiquity. It would become just another mineral, useful in the manufacture of jewellery but not much more. That would obviously cost the mining companies heavily in profits and the union in jobs. So the old antagonists marched together.

It was a brave show but a largely futile one. Godsell and Mantashe also undertook a joint mission to the United States, where they managed to persuade the International Monetary Fund to abandon a plan to sell off its own gold reserves to enable it to help some of the world's most heavily indebted countries, arguing that this would do more harm than good since many of these poor countries were also gold producers. But other than that the central banks of a number of developed countries went ahead with their sales. It was a watershed event. For generations there had been a relationship between the number of bank notes a central bank issued and the amount of gold it held. Now the central banks realized that with the growing sophistication of economic mechanisms they could hold their reserves in other forms that were as good as gold – such as US Treasury Bonds – and that would earn interest, which gold did not. It meant that gold had effectively lost its age-old value as money. It had also lost its value as a hedge against inflation as that dragon was seen to have been slain. And so gold's special glitter was gone – and with that its role as the central pillar of the South African economy.

As the price declined, more and more South African mines became marginal. Nature had bestowed a great gift upon South Africa with the world's most bountiful gold resources, but it was a problematic gift. The gold is deep under the earth, three to four kilometers down, in narrow veins averaging only a metre wide, and in exceptionally hard rock. That makes the mining of it difficult, dangerous and expensive. Indeed had gold been discovered at these depths at the end of the nineteenth century in Australia or the US it would probably have stayed under the ground. What made the mining of it possible in South Africa was the abundance of dirt-cheap labour. Cheap because it was black. In 1910 black miners on the Witwatersrand were paid two shillings a day, compared with a white miner's 20 shillings, and when after a decade they asked for a three-shilling raise the Chamber of Mines replied that to grant that would close down the whole industry.[7] That is how marginal it was. Throughout most of the twentieth century black miners in South Africa continued to be paid miserable wages, but the granting at last of trade union rights to black workers in 1979 saw that start to change. Tough union negotiations with the Chamber of Mines resulted in wages beginning to rise quite sharply, pushing up the costs of mining South African gold to the highest in the world and forcing the mining companies to modernize their old apartheid practices to improve productivity – which meant culling jobs. "Under apartheid you had two people doing just about every job," Godsell explains. "One to do the work and another to sign the paper." Anglogold found that while it was employing 200 workers in its metallurgy plants, Australian gold mines were using 30. "As we were able to employ whole people doing a whole cycle of work, rather than for that work to be broken down into different categories (to protect white jobs), we saw efficiency gains that enabled us to take more than $100 an ounce off our costs."[8]

Another paradox ensued. The peaking of the price above $800 in 1980 set off a rush of new exploration that saw world gold production grow by eight percent a year over the next two decades. This increased production just as demand from the central banks was declining sent the price down further. More significant still, among the new finds were a number of shallow and alluvial deposits, particularly in Australia and the United States. According to Godsell, this new gold costs exactly half as much to mine as South African gold.[9] The profit margins on South African gold shrank dramatically. Whereas a kilogramme of gold earned R120 000 in 1980 at a cost of R35 000, giving a profit margin of R85 000, in 2000 it earned R60 000 at a cost of R55 000, giving a profit margin of only R5 000.[10] The threat of war in the Middle

East caused the price of gold to spike above $350 an ounce in early 2003, but the boost seemed likely to prove temporary.

To stay profitable, South African gold companies have had to mine only higher-grade veins, closing down lower-grade shafts and even whole mines. So production has slumped, from 680 tonnes in 1980 to 428 tonnes in 2000. From providing 50% of all South Africa's merchandize exports in 1980, gold has shrunk to a mere 16%.

Worse still, the closing of shafts and the modernizing of mining practices has seen a staggering fall in the number of miners employed, from a peak of 553 000 in 1987 to 214 000 in 2000. More than half the total workforce in South Africa's premier industry have lost their jobs in 13 years.[11]

Of course gold is not all that is mined in South Africa. The country has an amazing array of important minerals, from the world's largest deposits of platinum, chromium, manganese and vanadium to diamonds, coal, iron ore, copper, uranium, zinc, nickel, fluorspan, zirconium and vermiculite. Some of these have boomed in recent years, the production of platinum group metals, chrome and coal doubling since 1980. With its price rocketing thanks to its use in catalytic converters for automobiles, platinum in fact exceeded gold as an export earner in 2000, bringing in R28 billion to gold's R26 billion. The beneficiation of many of these minerals, adding value by producing ferro alloys, steel, chemicals from coal and so on, has also been an important growth sector. So mining is far from being a sunset industry.

But even so, the total contribution of all minerals to South Africa's gross national product has declined from 22% in 1980 to 6% in 2000, and with the modernization of production methods more than 300 000 jobs have been lost in the total mining industry in that time. Add to that the 350 000 agricultural workers who have lost their jobs since 1970, and one has a picture of the magnitude of the government's task in trying to transform the economy so that the growth of the manufacturing industry can absorb this huge pool of unemployment as well as the 600 000 new workers who come onto the labour market every year.

* * *

Needing an economic miracle to follow its political miracle, South Africa has suffered repeated setbacks instead.

The harsh reality of globalization, of competitive participation in the new worldwide marketplace, is that it leads to increased unemployment and pressure on wages. The theory is that if you can get your macroeconomic structures right the benefits will come later, but that can take time and in the meantime the rich grow richer and the poor poorer, between countries as well as within them. "A rising tide raises all boats," said John F Kennedy. True maybe of tides but not necessarily of economies, where some are manifestly more equal than others.

The brute fact is that in the nine years since it came to power with the declared intention of delivering a better life for all, and especially for the black majority who had suffered all those years of degradation and exploitation, the ANC government has seen more than half a million jobs lost. Haroon Bhorat, senior researcher at the University of Cape Town's School of Economics, explains how the shifts have taken place, both between economic sectors and within them, with the poorly educated and unskilled losing out heavily in both.[12] As the economy has changed, the demand for labour has shifted away from the primary sectors – mining and agriculture – to the manufacturing and particularly the service sectors, where the demand is for people with skills; while within those sectors the computer revolution has meant a demand for workers with higher and higher skills levels "matched by an alarming decline in the demand for unskilled employees".[13] Africans, the ANC's core constituency, have suffered most. African men particularly, for more than a century the heart of the unskilled manual labour force in the primary sectors, have taken the hardest knock of all, with serious psychological consequences for family and community relationships as well as social distress. The knock-on effects extend to an increase in the crime rate, while for the ANC itself it is a major political headache.

Unemployment stands at somewhere between 25% and 35% depending on how unemployment is defined and whether or not one includes the informal sector of the economy. The official figure was 29,4% in February 2002[14], which is almost as high as the United States experienced during the Great Depression. Franklin D Roosevelt introduced the New Deal with its big public works projects to deal with that great social trauma. But in the new world of neo-liberalism, or what is called the "Washington consensus", such state interventionism is considered a heresy and it is difficult to swim against the current of approved economic behaviour if you wish to attract the foreign direct investment that all developing countries need.

And so the new South Africa finds itself trapped in a Catch 22. The ANC was elected to free its people from generations of oppression and exploitation, yet finds itself having to undertake a radical reconstruction of the economy that is inflicting even greater hardship on many of its people. It is doing so in the hope that there will be a long-term payoff for the painful reforms it is making. But there can be no certainty about this. Investors in this hard new world go where they think they can make the greatest profits. There is no sentiment involved, no favour offered. Their investments are heat-seeking, scanning the globe for the hottest growth prospects, and if your economy remains cool, no matter how impeccably orthodox it may be or how many academic accolades it may receive, they will stay away.

The problem for a country like South Africa is that it needs foreign direct investment to kick-start growth, but the foreign investors are looking for growth before they will invest. A chicken-and-egg conundrum. Meanwhile the tough macroeconomic reforms go on swelling the ranks of the unemployed, and the government waits for the theory to turn into reality. There was a flash of hope in the last quarter of 2000 when employment in the private sector rose for the first time in a decade. But then came the US recession.

CHAPTER THREE

OUT OF THE BUSH

We were taken from the bush, or from underground
inside the country, or from prisons, to come and take charge.
We were suddenly thrown into this immense responsibility
of running a highly developed country.
— NELSON MANDELA

If the task facing the new regime was not daunting enough, the 27 Cabinet Ministers that Chief Justice Michael Corbett swore in on the morning of 11 May 1994 looked an unlikely lot to be able to meet the challenge. Some, as Mandela says, had literally come out of the bush, from guerrilla camps in Angola and Tanzania; others, like himself, had spent long years in jail acquiring such esoteric skills as learning to crush stones and dig in lime quarries; yet others had returned from precarious lives scattered about the world as exiles; and then there were the street activists who had confronted the security forces at home and rendered parts of the country ungovernable. They were tough, smart and dedicated, but none had the skills required to run a complex country with a sophisticated economy. Thanks to the restrictions imposed by apartheid on people of colour, and the limited opportunities in exile, none had in fact run anything at all except of the most rudimentary kind. Now they were confronted with this enormous challenge, having to learn on the job while an expectant nation and a whole world beyond kept a critical watch on their every move.

There were among them, of course, half a dozen who did have experience of governance, members of De Klerk's old regime party, the National Party, who qualified for seats in the Government of National Unity under the proportional representation system that had been agreed at the constitutional negotiations. There were also three members of Chief Mangosuthu Buthelezi's Inkatha Freedom Party who had acquired some administrative experience through that party's participation in apartheid's bantustan system. But they were essentially yesterday's people, and everyone knew it was the 16 ANC Ministers who would have to be the agents of change. And they were all rookies.

To make matters worse they were going to have to work through an

29

alien, perhaps hostile, bureaucracy. The ANC had no army of civil servants of its own waiting in the wings to take over. In any event the ANC had agreed to so-called "sunset clauses" in the settlement agreement that guaranteed job security for five years to all existing civil servants. It was a gesture of political magnanimity that helped open the way to the agreement, but it was also one of necessity for they would not have been able to govern without these experienced administrators. But it did mean there would inevitably be conflicts, for the bureaucracy had taken on the habits of mind and outlook of the successive apartheid administrations it had served for half a century. They were the same people with the same backgrounds, speaking the same language and sharing the same philosophies and prejudices as the masters they had served all their working lives. And in the course of those lives they had been infused with the belief that the ANC were their mortal enemies, communist terrorists intent on destroying the Afrikaner *volk* and everything it stood for. There could be no easy working relationship, and both sides had awaited this day with trepidation.

That the relationship worked at all is remarkable. That it has worked as well as it has is as much a miracle as any other aspect of the South African transition. Jay Naidoo, the fiery former trade union radical, recalls how startled police officers guarding the Union Buildings were when he greeted them cheerfully as he arrived for his first day as Minister Without Portfolio charged with implementing the new government's Reconstruction and Development Programme. The men in blue were accustomed to the austere aloofness of the dark-suited Nationalist Ministers so filled with a sense of their own importance as princelings of the *volk*. Now here were working-class Ministers accustomed to mixing with the hoi-polloi.

Mandela himself found his first day chilling. He had waited his whole life for this moment, endured more that 27 years in prison, talked and pondered endlessly about how to emancipate his people and build the new society of his covenant. Now here at last he was approaching the seat of power and the opportunity to realise those dreams. It was a moment to savour. But as he entered the President's office in the Union Buildings he found it empty. There was no staff around. There was no-one to serve him coffee, there were no memos or briefing papers on his desk. Everyone had scuttled away in anxiety. As his biographer, Anthony Sampson, recounts, Mandela eventually summoned a senior civil servant in the late afternoon and asked him to assemble the staff next morning. Mandela then shook hands with them, reminded them that a new government had taken over, and assured them no-one would be dismissed. He soon established warm relations with them all. They became totally loyal to the genial old man who remembered their names and their families.[1]

* * *

Mac Maharaj is a lean, wiry man who fits all of Mandela's descriptions of where his Cabinet came from: he was out of the bush as a guerrilla fighter, out of prison, out of exile, and he had been an underground agent who had moved in and out of the country in a multitude of disguises organising internal resistance and sending coded messages back to ANC exile headquarters on a laptop computer.

As a man of action Maharaj wasted no time assuming his new role as Minister of Transport. The moment the swearing-in ceremony was over he hurried to the President's office to find out where the Transport Ministry offices were in Pretoria, then jumped in his car and drove there, sprinted up four flights of stairs and strode in to his new domain.

The staff were startled to see him. A flustered Director-General, Dr C F Scheepers, rushed up to apologise. "We didn't expect you today," he spluttered. "We thought you would take a few days and then make an appointment to come over." But Maharaj was eager to get to work and he didn't see why a Minister should make an appointment to see his own staff. "Everyone seemed very nervous," he told me. "From the DG down they all came up to me very deferentially, saying Minister I am so-and-so. I am here at your service if you need me. Scheepers, too, told me he had six months to go in his term as DG and that he, too, would stay if I wanted him, but if I didn't he could return to the body of the department. They were all jittery."

I asked Maharaj how he felt as he moved into his seat of power, the first of the new Cabinet to do so, after all those years of struggle. Did he feel a sense of the occasion, a sense of history in the making? "Ah," he responded with a long pause. "Actually all my feelings were overwhelmed by the enormity of the task that lay ahead of us and a feeling that, look, you had better get down to work immediately. We had all come from backgrounds that had given us no experience of how government works and I felt the need to learn what transport was about very quickly. I had studied in prison for a BA Admin degree which included a one-year course in transportation. But that was all."

Maharaj's impatience was to be frustrated by a factor that was to bug all members of the new regime in the years ahead, a dislocation between them and the civil servants with whom they had to work. De Klerk had told the incoming Ministers they would all be given briefing papers on where their departments stood on key issues, but Maharaj found there was nothing based on the ANC's transport policy perspectives. It was as though the civil servants had no idea what the new majority party's policies were. This annoyed him. "This is standard practice in the major democracies," he told me. "Once an election is declared all heads of department liaise with the competing parties to find out their policy positions and prepare implementation proposals based on that. I thought something like that would be done with regard to the ANC, particularly since it was obvious we were going to win the election or at least be a major force in the Government of National Unity. But it wasn't."

Maharaj's other concern was his private secretary. A young man who turned out to be super-efficient. Too efficient for the Minister's liking. Perhaps because of his own espionage background, Maharaj became suspicious. "He knew absolutely everything about how government functioned," Maharaj said. "You raised any query and he knew which button to press to get the answer. If I phoned airline reservations and they told me a flight was fully booked, he would take over and in five minutes the ticket would be on its way. Nothing was too difficult for him. I began to get the impression he was trying to control my life, to be the gatekeeper as to who saw me."

So Maharaj began to interrogate his secretary, and learned that he had spent 10 years as personal assistant to Magnus Malan, the apartheid regime's Minister of Defence and arch-enemy of the ANC. He had even followed Malan to the Ministry of Water Affairs when De Klerk shunted his controversial security hawk there as the constitutional negotiations began, and had only moved to the Ministry of Transport two weeks before Maharaj's arrival. "I decided he had been sent to spy on me and had him moved," Maharaj told me.

* * *

When it comes to being thrown in at the deep end none had to learn to swim with such desperate urgency as Trevor Manuel at Finance. Starting from scratch with no academic training or practical experience in the dark world of economics, he found himself plunged into it at the politically tender age of 40, since when he has been the one primarily responsible for charting South Africa's course through the wild currents of the Three-in-One Revolution.

32

Mercifully Manuel did not have to face the worst of it right away. He began in the less onerous position of Minister of Trade and Industry, while Derek Keys, a shrewd and experienced businessman whom De Klerk had head-hunted two years before from the big mining house of Gencor where he was CEO, retained the position of Minister of Finance for the first four months of the Government of National Unity (GNU); and when Keys retired Mandela turned to another business-man whom he had come to know and trust, Chris Liebenberg, then CEO of Nedcor, a major banking group. But when Liebenberg, too, retired in March 1996 the President called on Manuel, who had already impressed his colleagues as a fast learner at Trade and Industry. Manuel faced a double disadvantage in terms of public perceptions: he was both "coloured" and inexperienced, and painfully aware that the reason Mandela had kept two white men in the Finance portfolio dur-ing the birthing of the new democracy was to preserve the confidence of the international investment community. The worldly-wise old President knew the extent of white racial prejudice, in South Africa and internationally.

In fact Manuel's first plunge into the world of finance had come five years earlier, in July 1991, when he was elected to the National Executive Committee of the ANC and told to take charge of its Department of Economic Planning. Nothing in his background had prepared him for this kind of work. After leaving high school he had worked for a construction company, eventually qualifying as a civil engineering technician. Then he quit that job to devote himself to com-munity affairs in Cape Town's coloured townships. "My skills were the skills of an activist," he says reflectively now. "I worked in community organisations, in what were called civics, and in the United Democratic Front (the internal front of the ANC while it was still outlawed in the 1980s). I ran a little resource agency for a while. I could do a number of things. I could write pamphlets. I could type. I could do letraset headings for the pamphlets. I worked intensively on a community newspaper called *Grassroots*. But I had no background in economics, no academic training at all. And I never had any dream of ever occu-pying an office like this. There was never a set of steps that I took to have this as a kind of career plan. It was just never there. I was just working from day to day. The 1980s was a time of very harsh repres-sion, jail and so on. I mean, you just didn't think beyond that stuff."

So when the call came from the ANC's secretary-general, Cyril Ramaphosa, to tell him he had been elected not only to the National

Executive Committee but to its inner National Working Committee, and that each member of the NWC was expected to take charge of a portfolio, Manuel was taken aback. He recalls the conversation in the racy township speech of the day: "Cyril calls me and says, 'Hey bro', we thought you should get Economic Planning.' I say, What Cyril, me? I can't do this thing, man. He says, 'No, we think you must. In fact the decision has been taken.'"

And so Manuel found himself committed, and much against his will relocated from Cape Town to ANC headquarters in downtown Johannesburg. The place was a madhouse: it was just over a year since the ANC had been unbanned, exiles were streaming back and the organisation was struggling to re-establish its structures in South Africa and prepare for the forthcoming negotiations. "I was dropped in by parachute and I had to find my feet in this environment," he recalls. Manuel also found he had to be a jack-of-all-trades at the headquarters office. Among other things Mandela commissioned him to write the speech he was to deliver at the opening session of the first negotiating council, called Codesa, in December 1991. He was given an old laptop for the job. "I knew how to type but I hadn't worked this computer thing. I took it home and worked on the speech until about 2 am – and then I lost it all because I hadn't saved it. I didn't know how to save. So I had to do it all again, working until daybreak and then I telephoned someone who could tell me what I had to do to save it."

But there were people around who helped him focus on the subject he was supposed to specialise in, suggesting books he should read. An intensive series of conferences, workshops and policy planning sessions followed. And so the steepest of all learning curves began.

Then came the election and Manuel's appointment as Minister of Trade and Industry, with Gill Marcus, now Deputy Governor of the Reserve Bank, as his deputy. Keys was at Finance, with a smart young trade unionist, Alec Erwin, who had been a lecturer in economics at the University of Natal as well as a member of the Communist Party and the radical National Union of Metalworkers of South Africa (Numsa), as Deputy Minister. The foursome formed an economics brains trust, with the experienced Keys as mentor. All acknowledge the importance of Keys's influence as a man with wide practical experience.

When Liebenberg took over from Keys, the banker made it clear to Mandela he would remain in the job only for a relatively brief period. Six months before Liebenberg's departure in March 1996, the President summoned Manuel to tell him he would be taking over this most daunting of jobs. He had six months to work closely but confidentially with the departing Minister to ensure a smooth handover. In fact even after Manuel had taken over, Liebenberg took the new Finance Minister on an overseas trip in his own time to introduce him to the heads of important financial institutions he had come to know during his career as a banker. "It was a wonderfully magnanimous gesture," Manuel acknowledged to me some years later.

Although Manuel already had two-and-a-half years experience as a Cabinet Minister, he found the move to Finance a much more daunting experience than his first day in political power. Partly because the department was bigger and partly, as he puts it, because "the levels of decrepitude were much greater." The place, he says, "was an archaic mess." He also sensed a resentment among some of the civil servants. There was an early clash with the Director-General, Estian Calitz. Incongruously, it was over pictures. When Manuel entered his new offices on the 26th floor of the Finance Department building in Pretoria, he noticed a row of portraits, in thick black frames, of all the country's Ministers of Finance up to the end of the apartheid era hanging in the foyer. Derek Keys and Chris Liebenberg were not there. Manuel was incensed and he confronted Calitz.

"I said to him, 'Estian, it's nice to have a sense of history but can we please take those pictures out of the foyer?' He didn't want to. He said, 'No, I'm still the DG and I'd like to keep them there.' So I said, 'Estian, we're going to clash on this if you don't take them down today. You can have them, you can hang them in your study at home, you can do whatever you like with them, but they are coming off the wall.' I said if it had been a complete history I might have been willing to bend, but Derek was not there, Chris was not there, so out they go. He was very, very upset, but it was indicative of a wish to hang on to something of the past. It was still very much there."

According to Manuel, he also found that all the black staff who had been recruited after the 1994 election had been accommodated together on a separate floor. "A little bantustan where they could go and play together," as Manuel put it. He soon changed that, and boasts today that his Ministry has the largest number of black economists in the country.

Calitz left. He had told Liebenberg he would ask for a transfer when he heard that Manuel was going to take over, and he duly did so. He was replaced by Maria Ramos, a brilliant young economist of Greek immigrant parentage who had undergone graduate studies in Britain and lectured at the London School of Economics. She and Manuel are widely regarded today as forming the most competent team of financial managers in the developing world.

* * *

But not all the new brooms have swept as clean as that. There have been failures. As Winston Churchill and Ulysses Grant revealed, the qualities needed to lead a people in war or a struggle for a great cause are not always the same as those that make good governors. Thus Joe Modise, who had been commander-in-chief of the ANC's military wing, *Umkhonto weSizwe* (Spear of the Nation), was a less than successful Minister of Defence who led the country, while it was struggling to recover from the economic mess inherited from the old regime, into a staggering R32-billion arms procurement deal which swelled to R53-billion as the rand devalued and which dragged the government into a morass of scandals over the awarding of contracts. Professor Sibusiso Benghu likewise. He was a reasonably competent Vice-Chancellor and Principal of Fort Hare University, the *alma mater* of a whole generation of liberation movement leaders, managing to redeem it in the final years of apartheid from some of the damage its absorption into the iniquitous system had inflicted on it. But he failed as Minister of Education in the Mandela Administration to make an effective start in restructuring the dysfunctional education system that the country's skills needs require. In at least one respect Benghu actually made things worse. Anxious to bring about greater equality of education between the richer and poorer provinces and between urban and rural schools, he ham-handedly tried to pressurise teachers into moving by making them either accept relocation or take retrenchment packages. For the country's most experienced, long-service teachers who stood to pick up the fattest retrenchment packages it was a carrot to encourage them to leave and start a second career rather than a stick to get them to move into the boondocks. At a stroke the country lost hundreds of its best, most experienced teachers, at significant financial cost to the department.

Then there was dear Raymond Mhlaba – "Uncle Ray" as he was affectionately known – a sweet man with a long and honourable record of service to the liberation cause but who in his declining years was sadly not up to the job of Premier of the Eastern Cape Province which Mandela gave him out of loyalty to an old comrade who had been a "lifer" with him on Robben Island. Under Mhlaba's shaky hand the province sank to the level of the most poverty-stricken and poorly governed in the country.

The worst problem, though, lies in the civil service and its often difficult relationship with the new political leadership. The "sunset clauses" served a vital purpose, for without them there could have been no negotiated transition to majority rule, or if there had been the new regime would have been unable to govern, but the downside is that in combination with the need for affirmative action appointments they have resulted in a bloated bureaucracy that was both costly and inefficient. It comprises an ossified old guard and inexperienced newcomers, an uncomfortable mix that leads to mutual resentment and insecurity. The five years are up now and the sun has set on the clauses, but it is difficult to downsize the civil service in the face of the country's high level of unemployment. Moreover the new labour legislation, introduced to protect black workers from the servitude conditions they suffered under apartheid, makes retrenchment difficult and expensive, while the public service unions are fiercely protective of all their members, white as well as black. Indeed the government's efforts to downsize the civil service have resulted in some of the most acrimonious conflicts between it and the big trade union federation, Cosatu, which is its most important alliance partner in the administration.

The result is a problem of delivery. Bureaucratic thrombosis means the ANC government has acquired a disconcerting record of formulating excellent policies which it then has difficulty implementing. Budget allocations in crucial sectors like health and education often remain underspent, especially at the provincial level where inefficiencies are worst. Seven years after the transition, government services output fell 0,8% in 2001.[2]

There is also a problem of corporate governance, particularly in the big public sector companies which form a large part of the South African economy. Unlike private sector companies, where directors represent the shareholders and often have their own personal investments in the company, or, in the case of executive directors, have their remuneration linked to the company's performance, those who run public companies have no such vested interest in the success of their enterprises. The government is the sole shareholder, represented by the Minister under whose portfolio the company falls, and it is the Minister who appoints the board of directors. Neither the Minister nor the directors stand to lose anything if the company underperforms, nor is there any effective form of accountability.

This weakness is compounded in the new South Africa by the fact that many of the newcomers to the public sector companies do not have

37

a clear understanding of the different roles the parties involved are supposed to play. Lacking personal incentives and effective accountability in these roles, the field becomes prone to turf wars and power struggles between ambitious people trying to scale the ladder of opportunity after generations of servitude. Some use old lines of political influence to further their own ends; problems between board members and the Minister get exacerbated by public service interference; direct political interference sometimes renders boards ineffective; and civil servants have been known to do behind-the-scenes deals with trade unions to confront their board with a *fait accompli*. And, as Helena Dolny, who had a stormy term as head of the Land Bank, has noted, the Minister-as-shareholder sometimes appoints a board to represent the state's interests, then usurps the board's authority by bringing in consultants or civil servants as advisers "some of whom are enamoured of their licence to play god with public assets worth hundreds of millions of rands."[3] All this has turned a number of South Africa's para-statals into battle zones and efficiency has suffered.

But for all that, the new regime is immeasurably more competent than the old. In the economic field especially, as Pamela Cox says, it has achieved a miracle of transformation, while elsewhere the problems are the birth pains of a new nation struggling to emerge from the ashes of its scorched past. They stem from the legacy of a wretched education system and a lack of administrative experience which together give rise to a sense of insecurity and its usual over-compensating responses of excessive assertiveness, stubborn defensiveness and a hunger for the reassurance of status. These are problems that will fade as increasing competence and experience bring about a greater self-confidence that over time will erase those negative responses.

CHAPTER FOUR

PORTRAITS OF CHANGE

Hark, hark! The dogs do bark,
The beggars are coming to town;
Some in rags and some in jags,
And some in silken gown.
— NURSERY RHYME

I arrived in Johannesburg in February 1959 and immediately found myself both repelled and fascinated by the curious mix of vitality and tension that seemed to permeate the atmosphere of this extraordinary city. For Johannesburg was then, and still is, the cutting edge of the country's racial and cultural interactions, the place where its First and Third World elements are drawn together by the irresistible magnet of a dynamic economy. I had grown up on a farm in the backwaters of the eastern Cape Province, alongside the country's largest black reserve, where I had come to know rural tribal people in all their slow and amiable ways. Now I was in the big city, where the black folk were sharp and streetwise and the whites brash and on the make. Though I had spent time in London, working for the big Reuters news agency on Fleet Street, this was different, with none of Europe's assured maturity and depth of culture and courtesy. I found it frightening but also fascinating, for I realized from the start that it was a place of primal issues and moral challenges, a place to engage the passions like no other on earth. If I wished to understand my country, this was where to do it.

Quickly I came to realize that the essential character of Johannesburg stemmed from the fact that it was still really an overgrown mining camp. It had that instant and transient air about it, as though everyone had come there for a quick buck and nothing was meant to last. The city had sprung into life only 68 years before, scarcely six months after a penniless gold prospector stumbled upon a rocky outcrop that proved to be the signpost to the world's richest gold deposits. Because the gold was deep underground and expensive to mine, an elaborate financial structure soon followed. It took less than a year to establish the city's first stock exchange. Brothels and bars arrived almost simultaneously. The boom was so headlong that no one bothered to record which official, speculator or digger had been honoured in the city's name. It thus became the city of the unknown Johannes. Long before the first decade had run out, the first generation of mining millionaires had staked out the high ground above the bustle of the mining compounds and started competing with one another in the erection of grandiose mansions. Thus was established the first class distinction, based on money, that was to overlay the basic racial stratification of the society that continues to the present day. Thus was established, too, a spirit of vigour, of entrepreneurship, of acquisitiveness, and of greed.

The city still had a honky-tonk atmosphere when I arrived, an impression accentuated by the yellow mine dumps and ungainly mine headgears that dotted its periphery. Somehow the city seemed a lot bigger than it really was, partly because of its pace and partly because its black population, numbering two-thirds of the total, lived beyond its fringes in dormitory townships and thronged its streets by day. It was regarded as a skyscraper city, even though its tallest building, Eskom House, was only 12 floors high. But the paradox was that unlike every other metropolis in the world, this one died at night. At 5 pm, when businesses closed, the inhabitants fled to their segmented ghettos, the blacks to their dormitory townships and the whites to their suburban homes. The central city streets fell silent, dark, and sinister.

I had come there to work as a copy-editor on the country's biggest morning newspaper, the *Rand Daily Mail,* which under a new editor was showing signs of becoming the first mainstream paper to crusade for racial justice in South Africa's history. It was a challenging time for such a venture. African colonies were reaching for their independence, and as British Prime Minister Harold Macmillan warned during a visit to South Africa in 1960, a "wind of change" was beginning to blow through the continent. In the black population a new assertiveness was stirring. But in South Africa a new Prime Minister, Hendrik Verwoerd, had taken power and was beginning to elaborate the apartheid ideology and implement it with intensified thoroughness. Every day brought news of more forced removals as the bulldozers flattened black residential areas deemed too close to the "white" city, leaving their residents to be dumped on a stretch of open *veld* a sanitary distance away in a new conglomerate to be called South Western Townships – Soweto.

So the great multiracial metropolis was being segmented into a series of self-contained, inward-looking ethnic enclaves. But the African independence movement was pumping adrenaline into the young black intelligentsia, who were churning out books, poetry, and powerful pieces of protest theatre. Many were journalists working for a black publishing company established by Jim Bailey, the maverick son of a pioneer mining magnate. Jim had launched two publications, *Drum* magazine and a weekly newspaper called *Golden City Post,* which were themselves great pioneering ventures that provided the first real media platforms for black expression.

The publishing house was just two blocks from our offices, and some of us would meet up with the black journalists at a drinking establishment known simply as Whitey's Place. It was illegal for blacks to enter bars or to buy or consume "white" liquor, even beer, but speakeasies like Whitey's, called *shebeens,* flourished everywhere and became the network for a whole subculture of black social life and interracial bonding. The *shebeen* queen who ran the joint paid the local police protection money, inflating the prices, but the clientele paid up cheerfully.

They were raucous, racy places, sometimes violent, and it was here that I came to know a whole generation of black journalists, writers and artists, many of whom were doomed to die early, rot in jail, or wither away in exile. They were a colourful lot, the journalists writing in a Damon Runyon style of ribald township slang and sometimes affecting a pseudo-American accent gleaned from the movies. The fashion in dress was sharp suits and fedora hats worn at a slant for the men, tight-fitting floral dresses for the women. There were few cars in the townships in those days, but those that there were, battling their way along rutted dirt roads, were mostly huge beat-up American gas-guzzlers. Only some years later did a spirit of anti-Americanism creep into the black community, as the Soviets began training and aiding the exiled ANC's guerrilla fighters.

I became political correspondent of the *Rand Daily Mail* in 1961, and for the next few years sat in the press gallery of the all-white Parliament in Cape Town listening to Verwoerd expound on the philosophy of apartheid in two-hour marathons. It was an eerie experience. He had been a professor of applied psychology, trained in Germany during the 1930s, and he brought a chilling intellectualism to the crude racism that had propelled the Afrikaner National Party to power in 1948. Ethnicity, he explained with paternalistic patience, was the way of human nature, and any attempt to create a multiracial nation was not only fallacious but deadly dangerous. Apartheid, by contrast, was the way of liberation: each ethnic "nation" had a God-given right to its own identity and its own country, and so the white South Africans were prepared to give each black nation its own homeland even as they claimed their own for themselves. It sounded so plausible in that isolated, all-white chamber, cut off like an ocean liner from the pulsating polyglot reality of the society outside. The packed ranks of Verwoerd's party supporters, hugely dominant in that Parliament and becoming more so with every election, sat in fascinated silence as they listened to him give this veneer of respectability to their bucolic prejudices. Outside the bulldozers crunched on, the tensions rose, and the ANC was outlawed.

There followed the bleakest of times. Verwoerd was assassinated in 1966, stabbed to death spectacularly in his seat of power by a deranged white parliamentary messenger. His Minister of Justice and Police, Balthazar Johannes Vorster, took over. No intellectualism here, simply ruthless repression and increasing authoritarianism. Black voices were silenced as the ANC, its leaders imprisoned or exiled, tried to muster the resources to mount a guerrilla war against Africa's most powerful military establishment. The price of gold climbed in international markets and South Africa prospered, by political disaster and economic windfall, it was said. The country entered a triumphalist phase, soon reflected in the architecture of its cities. In Johannesburg real skyscrapers arose, 20, 30, 50 floors high, palaces of chrome and glass and conspicuous affluence. A Dallas on the African *veld*. The centrepiece was a towering glass creation designed in the shape of a diamond by a New York architect. Yet, as always, the reality of the city's heterogeneous character refused to disappear. The new extravaganza was located on a racial boundary called Diagonal Street, and across the road stood a row of decrepit two-storey buildings officially licensed as "black shops" selling used clothes, cheap cuts of meat, and the herbal medicines that African healers prescribe. To their horror, the owners of the sparkling diamond palace found this tacky strip obscenely mirrored in their magnificent glass. Since the business community at that time was trying to present itself to overseas critics as an agent of reform, it could hardly send for the removal squads. The best it could do was present the baffled shop owners with gifts of free paint, but to little avail. The heterogeneous reality of South Africa had triumphed against the odds, as it has continued to do.

* * *

42

It is these images that I hold in my mind as I listen to the protestations that "nothing has changed". For today the city has changed again, more radically than ever before. Today Johannesburg has abandoned its pretensions to being a Dallas or a Minneapolis. It has become an African city, a huge Nairobi, with blacks thronging its streets, taking over its shops, moving into its apartments, setting up hawkers' stalls on its sidewalks that sell all manner of merchandise, and giving the whole a less glitzy, more Third World aspect. Black consumers now account for more than ninety percent of central city trade. Hillbrow, a high-rise apartment quarter that was once the residential heartland of young white Johannesburg and the centre of the city's nightlife, is now overwhelmingly black. From this core, blacks have spread outward into suburbia, to Yeoville and Brixton, to Mayfair and Vrededorp, and even into the most affluent suburbs, Houghton and Sandton. The demographic tide has swept in, and with poetic justice Soweto has taken over the city from which it was once expelled.

As the tide flows, many whites are withdrawing deeper into suburbia, their security walls rising ever higher, office blocks and all-purpose shopping malls following them to make it increasingly unnecessary ever to venture into the city centre. To that extent, a residual apartheid persists. There has also been a considerable amount of white emigration, a flight spurred by a post-apartheid rise in the crime rate and a perceived loss of career opportunities because of the government's affirmative action policies. A survey by the University of South Africa of this brain drain estimates that 39 000 South Africans left the country in 1999 to join 1,6 million already living abroad. In July 2001 the South African Medical Association estimated that a third of all doctors who graduated from the country's world-class medical schools between 1990 and 1997 had left the country. That represents a considerable loss of valuable skills in professional sectors such as law, accounting and the engineering sciences, as well as medicine. But then again labour mobility, at least for those qualified enough and unencumbered enough to move easily, is part of the new globalization phenomenon.

Inward and upward. As black South Africans have moved in from the townships, they have moved up, enjoying a new social and economic mobility undreamed of before, into the boardrooms of big companies such as the mining giant Anglo American Corporation; into companies of their own, such as the highly successful Kagiso Media Limited; and, not surprisingly, into commanding positions in government departments and parastatal corporations such as Eskom, the national electricity supplier, and Transnet, the umbrella body controlling the national transportation network. Blacks are occupying middle management and junior management positions, doing supervision and strategic planning and a host of other jobs that were closed to them before. They are driving Mercedes-Benzes and BMWs and moving into big homes and in every way emulating the *nouveau riche* lifestyles of the white moneyed elite that preceded them. Their children now go to the same suburban schools, play in the same sports teams, and go to the same cafes and cinemas and rock concerts as the white kids. To that extent, an incipient rainbow nation is taking shape.

What is happening, of course, is that a new class restratification is taking place, overlaying the old distinctions based purely on race. A multiracial middle class is emerging, growing socially more distant from the predominantly black working class and the huge underclass. In less than a decade the number of black households earning as much as or more than the average white household income of R20 708 has risen from fewer than 1 000 to 1 200 000. Their share of all income increased from 30% in 1991 to 36% in 2000[1]. A survey conducted for the advertizing industry in early 2000 showed that 43 percent of people in the upper-income bracket were black, and predicted that in five years blacks would be a majority. A year later the Bureau of Market Research at the University of South Africa reported that between 1995 and 2000 the personal disposable income of the 1 500 000 Indian population had increased by 2,8% each year, of Africans by 2,7%, of the 2 600 000 mixed-race Coloured population by 2,1%, and the 5 000 000 whites by 1,1%.[2]

Relatively speaking, therefore, white affluence is shrinking, particularly at the lower end of the income scale. Some working-class whites are joining the big black trade unions, and a sprinkling of white beggars are appearing on the streets. For the first time since the Great Depression, poor-whiteism, the searing experience that hit the poorly educated white Afrikaner community particularly hard and began the process of legally enforced job discrimination, has shown its face again. These are developments which to a degree make nonsense of President Mbeki's contention that South Africa consists of two nations, one white and rich, the other black and poor.[3] That there are two nations is indisputable, but the rich one is no longer entirely white. It is increasingly multiracial.

It is in this new class formation that the seeds of discontent lie. It is not that nothing has changed, but that things have not changed for enough people. The gap between the new multiracial middle class and the huge underclass is as wide as the old one between white and black,

44

second only to Brazil among the widest in the world, and it is growing steadily wider. The trouble with this is the jealousy it arouses. Why should some blacks prosper so conspicuously while others continue to languish in poverty? What happened to African socialism and the fellowship of the oppressed?

The gap has become physical as well as economic, for it is the new middle-class blacks – sometimes referred to sarcastically as yummies, or young upwardly mobile Marxists – who have quit Soweto and moved to the old whites-only suburbs. While the apartheid laws were still in force some doctors, lawyers and others who had managed to accumulate a degree of wealth built fancy homes in an elite suburb of Soweto called Diepkloof East. But today they have left for the greater convenience and social status of Johannesburg's northern suburbs, and Diepkloof East is an abandoned white elephant, if that is the appropriate phrase, its fine homes unsaleable since no one who could afford them would choose to stay in Soweto.

This rankles among those who remain. "Our best and brightest are all running away from Soweto," says one long-time resident who runs a bar in the township. "The very people who are leaving are the people with the money and the know-how that Soweto needs. They are cowards, driving their BMWs home to the suburbs while the people suffer."[4] Others express resentment that comrades who marched alongside them in the days of the struggle now seldom set foot in Soweto and are too snooty to greet them when they meet in the streets of the city.

But even Soweto, in the wide spectrum of South Africa's society of extremes, represents a relative elite, a settled urban community with a higher level of employment than the rest of black South Africa. Foreign visitors, remembering news reports and television coverage of the violent police repression that took place there, are often surprised to find that it is not the desperate slum they imagined. The fact is Soweto was always the home of the black intellectual and economic elite, which of course is why it was the centre of political activism and became such a household name among all who followed the South African struggle. But South Africa's real Third World, the poorest of its poor, are to be found elsewhere, in a massive migration from rural poverty to the fringes of the cities. For them, too, the new South Africa is radically transforming their way of life and in their totality they present the new government with the greatest challenge to its pledge to deliver "a better life for all".

* * *

45

But before dealing with that I want to touch on what, for me as a reporter who spent most of his career chronicling the evolution and implementation of apartheid and experiencing its frightening evocation of ethno-nationalist fervour, is the most remarkable change of all. This is the sudden and total collapse of the whole system and the visual manifestation of that in the legislative arena where it all happened. Sitting today in the press gallery of the National Assembly where I once spent all those hours listening to Verwoerd deliver his long lectures on the Fichtean fundamentalism of national identity and the global importance of South Africa's quest to divide the country into a patchwork of "separate freedoms" for each ethnic entity in its population, with his party members listening in silent awe as though to Moses bringing the divine word down from Mount Sinai, I sometimes get the feeling that what is before me now cannot possibly be real. The change is too great. The building and furnishings, even the procedural rituals, are the same, and the same old ghosts still stalk the corridors and haunt my head. But where before there were serried ranks of white males, all alike in their dark suits and closed faces and immovable ideas – except for the solitary woman, the brave and combative liberal, Helen Suzman – today the whole of South Africa's multi-hued population is represented.

A system of proportional representation with no minimum cutoff line has meant that eight political parties are represented. In a National Assembly of 400 members the ANC alliance holds 268 seats, having won 67% of the national vote in the second democratic election on 2 June 1999. Next is the liberal Democratic Party, which replaced the party of the old regime, the New National Party, as the official Opposition in the 1999 election. It won 39 seats. The Inkatha Freedom Party came third with 33, the NNP fourth with 28 (down from 82 in the 1994 election), the black militant Pan-Africanist Congress and the Afrikaner separatist Freedom Front won three each, and the Black Consciousness Azanian People's Organization and the African Christian Democratic Party have one each.

The National Assembly chamber presents a kaleidoscopic picture of ethnic and sartorial variety: colourful saris, flowing African gowns, long white Muslim robes, gaudy head scarves, and of course the dark suits. One-third of the members are women, including the sari-clad Speaker and her deputy. The mood is much less inhibited: the honorable members sometimes cheer, clap, or sing. There has even been a fistfight on the floor of the Assembly – not, as it happens, involving the new African lawmakers, but between two white Afrikaners, one representing the new regime and the other the old (with neat irony, the old guard MP subsequently joined the ANC and now sits on the same benches as his boxing opponent). At moments of special enthusiasm, some of the women are liable to break into ululation. When Mandela was first installed in his seat of power, an *imbongi,* or praise singer, was in attendance, clad in skins and beads to prance and chant the new President's history and virtues. Here, certainly, is a rainbow legislature.

The change of content is even more striking than the visual picture. In the old House of Assembly the white men, every one a self-appointed amateur ethnologist, would talk endlessly about the black South Africans who were not present – what they were like, how they thought, what their real aspirations were, how they were different in their wants and ways. Now the black people are there to speak for themselves with a riveting authenticity. The old sense of unreality that used at times to overwhelm me has gone. With that has come a new openness, for what has happened is much more than just the abandoning of apartheid and the enfranchizing of the black majority. It has also been a change from authoritarianism to democracy to a degree unique in Africa and equaled in only a handful of developed countries. The new Parliament gives expression to one of the most liberal constitutions in the world, with an entrenched Bill of Rights guaranteeing all the fundamental human rights, including the right to life, liberty, and freedom of expression. The result has been some of the most progressive decision-making in the world, including the prohibition of the death penalty and the legalization of abortion.

The meetings of Parliament and its committees are open to the public and the news media. Official information is much more easily obtainable. There is an Open Democracy Act giving members of the public the legal right of access to information. In my 23 years at the *Rand Daily Mail,* as a political correspondent, columnist, assistant editor and editor, I could count on the fingers of one hand the number of one-on-one meetings I had with Cabinet Ministers. And with Presidents none at all. Today's Ministers are much more accessible, and during the Mandela years particularly the President exhibited a degree of informality and casual spontaneity unique in the modern world that exasperated his security staff and enchanted everyone else. Compared with the dour and reclusive personalities of the old regime, Daniel Malan the unsmiling preacher, Hans Strijdom the firebrand "Lion of the North", Verwoerd the interminable lecturer, John Vorster the grim-faced police chief, the finger-wagging P W Botha and even the little cock-sparrow figure of F W de Klerk, it is a contrast as stark as the philosophies they espoused.

* * *

All these changes are taking place in the First World and therefore the more visible sector of South African society. In the Third World sector a very different story is unfolding. The massive migration from countryside to cities is, of course, a global phenomenon and it is not new. It began with the Industrial Revolution and produced the social and economic conditions of Charles Dickens's novels, but it has accelerated enormously now with globalization. All over the world a tide of humanity is moving from rural communities to the cities, invading public and private lands as they set up informal shantytowns that are doubling and trebling the size of urban populations.

Brazil has its *favelas*, Peru its *pueblos juvenes*, Venezuela its *ranchos*, Mexico its *barrios marginales*, the Philippines its *barong-barongs*, Haiti its *bidonvilles*, Turkey its *gecekondus*, and South Africa its squatter camps. In Cairo thousands of people live in the city's main Muslim cemetery, a place of family tombs where the newly urbanized underclass have moved in with the deceased to establish what locals, with a macabre humour, call "the city of the dead".

Robert D Kaplan, writing in *The Atlantic Monthly* about a journey through West Africa, depicts a population flow from the interior draining like rivers into dense slums along the coast where they are forming "one burgeoning megalopolis" that spans the boundaries of five countries.[5]

It is everywhere in the Third World, driven by the imperatives of modern economics which are impoverishing Third World agriculture and sending its desperate people like moths to the city lights. But in South Africa it is driven by something else besides. Back in 1913, the newly independent whites-only government, faced with pressures from both white farmers and the mining industry for more cheap labour, passed a law prohibiting black people from owning land outside the small tribal reserves – which later became apartheid's bantustans – that together constituted 13% of the total land area of the country for 75% of the population. Since land inside the reserves was communally owned and vested in the chiefs, it meant no black person could own land individually anywhere. The Land Act brought an abrupt end to black commercial farming, which at the time was beginning to take

48

root and give a small but growing sector of the black population a degree of economic independence for the first time since the defeat of their tribes by the colonial armies in the nineteenth century frontier wars.

At a stroke the entire black population was rendered landless, and although a small amount of subsistence agriculture was possible in the reserves during the early years, this soon became impossible on any meaningful scale as the reserves became hopelessly overcrowded.

Thus the black peasantry was destroyed nearly a hundred years ago. From that moment the entire black population, wherever they lived, became economically dependent on the cities. It was not an easy dependency, for a complex web of influx control regulations and pass laws controlled the flow of workers to the mines and industrial cities to match the needs of employers. In effect the reserves, or bantustans, became labour reservoirs, to be tapped as needed by the urban economy. The system kept wages low and, since blacks were prohibited from forming or joining trade unions, kept them totally dependent on their employers. To lose one's job meant to lose one's legal right to remain in the urban area and to be forcibly returned to the jobless reservoir that was supposedly one's homeland of Verwoerd's "separate freedoms".

The economic dependence on the cities was total, for those who managed to acquire permanent rights to work in urban areas, for the migrant workers who came and went on a contract basis, for the women and children in the reserves who waited, hopefully, for remittances from their menfolk working in the cities, and even for the elderly and the disabled who survived on meagre state pensions. The bantustans themselves supported hardly anyone, aside from the swelling armies of civil servants and their hangers-on who were themselves paid from the coffers of the central government. The only black people who remained economically anchored in rural South Africa were the farm workers, and they were both miserably paid and subject to large-scale retrenchments as agriculture began to mechanize after World War II.

The result was that when apartheid ended, indeed even from when it began to crumble in the mid-1980s, black South Africans began moving to where they logically belonged. To the source of their economic support. The cities.

It was like the bursting of the reservoir walls. Thousands flooded out. Many came from intermediate settlement areas, where they had settled after being moved off the farms, or from bits of the fragmented bantustans which were in long-distance commuting range of the cities.

It was an urban rush on a scale that Kaplan never saw in West Africa. To fly over South Africa today is to see not one megalopolis but many, only here it is not a drainage of humanity towards the coast but to the interior, for South Africa's economic hub is in the centre of the country around Johannesburg. Drive south from Johannesburg along the N1 and after you pass the outskirts of Soweto you will see them, huge conglomerates of crude and scabrous shacks, not so much shantytowns as shanty-cities, with disconcertingly charming names like Orange Farm, Finetown, Beverly Hills and Palm Springs. Drive up the coast from Cape Town along the N2 and you will see them again, packed close and pressing up against the highway, a sea of slums swamping the Cape Flats that stretch between the majestic grandeur of Table Mountain and the crenulated peaks of the Hottentots-Holland range. Fly north from Durban and there they are like a mushroom field beneath you. They are around every city and sizeable town in the country, and they are all growing exponentially.

Life in these communities is tough. The crime rate is high, and predatory slumlords preside over the allocation of living space and exact tribute from the inhabitants. Turf wars break out between rival gangs. The fabric of traditional African social systems, with its extended family and age-group networks of mutual support and reciprocal responsibilities, was badly shredded years ago by the migrant labour system and the disruption of tribal life; now it is under further assault with this massive urbanization and the alienation that goes with it. Yet despite all this, a remarkable spirit of communal life survives in these bleak settlements. People stand by one another, help one another, share what little they have.

In part this social cohesion is provided by the rapid growth of new religious sects which have arisen to fill the vacuum left by the collapse of traditional society. There are more than 5 000 of these sects countrywide, most of them a syncretization of pentecostal Christianity and animism in which people of the same tribe, or from the same village, can bond together and find solace through the intercession of their ancestors buried back home. One can see them on Sundays on their way to religious services clad in crisply-pressed blue and white robes, or hear their sonorous choral singing at baptismal ceremonies beside muddy streams, and sometimes the wailing and shrill hysteria of congregants as they are gripped by the spirit.

This is the underside of the new South Africa. It is not pretty. Millions of people live in these squatter camps, and because they are

50

unskilled and poorly educated and therefore unemployed in the new changing economy, they represent an enormous problem for the government of liberation.

Yet even in the face of this, the new government has done a remarkable job in building new houses and roads, and bringing sanitation, water, electricity and telephone connections to many of these settlements. Even more remarkable is the survivability of the people themselves. I am constantly amazed at how people with absolutely nothing, no job, no assets, no prospects, manage to survive, even to improve the material conditions in which they live. Enter these rudimentary shacks, of sticks of wood and strips of cardboard and black plastic sheeting with stones holding down a roof of corrugated iron, and you will usually find them neat and spotless inside, the floors meticulously swept and the walls sometimes decorated with pictures clipped from newspapers and magazines. And if you return a year or so later you will find they have been upgraded into something more substantial.

* * *

For Sylvia Malala, aged 55 when I met her, life in one of these settlements had been an endless drudge. She spent a large part of her waking hours exhausting herself in a daily quest for the two most basic commodities of her family's subsistence – firewood and water. To get them involved pushing a wheelbarrow half a dozen kilometres across hot sandy *veld*, then scrambling through a fence into a thicket of scrubbush on land belonging to an irascible Afrikaner farmer whom the local black folk nicknamed *Skiet-hom-dood,* for he would occasionally threaten to shoot them with his 12-bore shotgun, where she would hack at the stubborn stems and branches of the *mopanie* bushes until she had enough to fill her barrow which she would then heave heavily back over the sand to her wood-and-iron shack in the indelicately named settlement of Stinkwater, north of Pretoria.

That done, Mrs Malala would set out again in a different direction, this time with a 25-litre bucket balanced on her head, on an hour-long hike to a water reservoir outside the settlement. There would be a crowd there and she would have to wait in line, sometimes for an hour or more, as others scooped water into their buckets. Then she would fill hers, hoist it onto her head, and walk home again bearing her load. Every day the same routine. In the heat of summer and the bitter cold of the highveld winter. And every year the thicket would recede a little more and the stripped bushes would have less wood to yield and the queue at the reservoir would be a little longer and Mrs Malala would be a year older and a little more bent and a little more exhausted from the endless drudgery.

Wood and water. Those were the defining elements in the lives of millions of black women all over South Africa. In 1984 a comprehensive study of poverty in South Africa produced the appalling statistic that the average rural black South African woman had to walk 12 km every day of her life to fetch firewood and water to cook, heat, wash, iron and scrub for her family. Where the countryside was stripped bare they collected cow dung for fuel, and often the water was from pools muddied and fouled by livestock. That in a country with reticulated water systems for every white household, and which generates more electricity than the whole of the rest of the African continent – sufficient to electrify every home south of the equator, but which somehow couldn't manage to get it to Mrs Malala and millions like her.

It struck me at the time that a single photograph which would have captured the essence of this inequality would have been of a black woman with a huge load of firewood on her head, an ubiquitous sight in those days, walking beneath the giant Eskom powerlines that span the South African countryside but which did not lead to her home.

But when I visited Mrs Malala five years after the transition, I found her relaxing on a settee watching television. She rose to switch on an electric kettle and offer me tea. The water came from a communal tap at the street corner, 100 metres from her home. She still had no job and she was still living in a rural slum which still had the awful name Stinkwater. The dirt road was still rutted, there was still a pit lavatory in the garden and the family still had to bath in a battered tin tub. In purely economic terms the ending of apartheid had brought Mrs Malala nothing. But the provision of water and electricity had transformed her life. The daily drudgery was over. For the first time in her life she had leisure. And entertainment. Her son, who has a good job in the city, had given her the TV set, as well as the kettle, an electric stove, an electric iron and a refrigerator. Even shopping for groceries had become less onerous. Whereas it, too, had been a daily chore of having to "buy-cook-and-eat" since there was no way to store food, the refrigerator meant she could now space out her shopping and cooking chores more conveniently.

"I am nothing, I have nothing, I'm just an African mother," Mrs Malala, who never went to school and whose husband abandoned her 13 years ago, murmured as she served me the tea. "But now I have got time to rest, and I've got more time for my church work on Sundays and Thursdays." Leisure, fellowship, entertainment. They may seem modest enough gains, but given the drudgery of the past they amount to a dramatic improvement in her quality of life.

It is an improvement that now, nine years after Mandela's inauguration, has touched the lives of millions of South Africans, in rural areas and squatter communities around the big cities, as more and more water pipes and electric cables reach out to them. By mid-2001 half the population of the country had access to clean water.

Water and electricity and telephones. Another appalling statistic of inequality is that there are more telephones in New York City than in the entire continent of Africa with its 800-million people. In this information age, when the Internet is the gateway to participation in the new globalized economy, how can you become a player when you have no phones? And when the new ideology requires that you must privatize state enterprises if you hope to attract foreign direct investment to create the jobs you need for your people, how can you rely on private enterprise to extend services to communities that don't have the means to make those services profitable?

Grappling with this dilemma, the new South African Government is attempting what might be called "privatization with strings". Its initial sale of 20 percent of the state-owned Telkom granted the partially privatized company a five-year monopoly on condition that it provided a specified range of services to such communities. The goal is that by 2004 every village in the country, every school, community centre and police station, will be connected. Meanwhile the cellular telephone, a yuppie toy that has become a vital instrument in South Africa's black communities, is providing another part of the answer.

* * *

Boksburg is a name redolent of the worst manifestations of apartheid racism. It is an old mining town which arose on the gold reef of the Witwatersrand east of Johannesburg, but the gold was exhausted some thirty years ago and the mines have shut down, forcing the town to turn to other forms of industry and leaving it with a has-been air and a population living lower on the economic scale. Here is where working-class whites and blacks, Indians and Coloureds have been thrown together in economic competition and physical proximity to a greater extent than almost anywhere else in South Africa. Racial animosities flourished as a result. Through the 1980s, the decade of the great black uprising, Boksburg and its neighbouring mining town of Brakpan were constantly in the news as white extremists of the *Afrikaner Weerstands-beweging* (Afrikaner Resistance Movement) fought pitched battles with local blacks who began using the public parks.

The town's notoriety reached a peak in July 1991 when the white residents of one of its newer suburbs, Dalpark Extension Six, built a "Berlin Wall" to seal themselves off from a nearby black squatter camp called Tamboville. One of the white residents, James Lammont, whose house was closest to the squatter camp, was appalled as he watched the makeshift shacks of plastic, wood and cardboard creep ever closer to his garden fence. He wrote a letter of protest to then President F W de Klerk, and when he received no reply he raised a petition among the other white residents of Dalpark Six which he presented to their local town councillor, Steve Erasmus.

Erasmus was a solitary independent on a council dominated by the far rightist Conservative Party, and as he confessed to me at the time he had won his seat only because he had not run on the ticket of the National Party of which he was a member. In the reactionary atmosphere of white Boksburg, the National Party was considered leftist. When Erasmus put the residents' case to the council, sympathy for their situation was instant. The council voted a sizable sum to build the wall, a two-metre high structure of prefabricated concrete that ran for two kilometres along the outer edge of Dalpark Six, cutting it off from Tamboville and an older-established black township called Wattville beyond, where a swelling population of more than 50 000 lived.

Then a strange thing happened on the way to the inauguration. James Lammont began to have second thoughts. "When I raised the petition it was with a feeling of anger," Lammont recalled at the time. "One associates squatters with squalor and I was angry that they were being allowed to encroach on our suburb. But then I began to realise they were here to stay. I guess it was a matter of acceptance. And I decided that if they were going to live next to me I had better get to know about them." So he went to see Steve Erasmus again and with the councillor's help made contact with Abe Nyalunga, chairman of the Wattville Concerned Residents Association. Abe, a savvy 34-year-old, invited the whites to meet his community. And so it came to pass that five conservative and rather anxious white men drove to Wattville one night. They were led to a small church hall where a singing, cheering crowd of about 400 people awaited them.

What followed was a strange mixture of awkward paternalism and warm response that seemingly changed the lives of the five white men.

More meetings followed, at which the two communities agreed on a good-neighbourliness pact which in turn culminated in one of the most extraordinary rituals of racial reconciliation that white and black South Africans have ever engaged in. On a sunny spring day a mere three months after the wall went up, a hundred white residents of Dalpark Six spent the morning together with 800 black residents of Tamboville and Wattville clearing litter from the 50-metre stretch of land between them and around the shores of a little lake called Leeupan, or Lion Pan, that they shared as a recreation spot. They planted a tree to symbolize their new relationship, taking turns to dig in the hard-baked earth while the crowd formed a circle, held hands and sang a Zulu song with the words, "Come together people of Africa". Finally everyone sat down together beside the wall for a *braaivleis* (barbecue) party.

The whites made patronizing remarks about "the wonderful way you people sing", and the blacks responded with uninhibited delight. There was some disarmingly straight talk. "I nursed many of you when you were children," elderly Catharina Hlatswayo told them. "I loved you then and I still love you now, even though you have built this wall which is a pain in my heart."

Ah, the wall. As they sat there singing and grilling their steaks and sausage in the noonday sun, symbolizing the new South Africa with their togetherness, the wall loomed behind them, symbolizing the old. The whites, their faces glowing with their conversion like born-again liberals, were saying things like, "Together we can show the world that the people of Dalpark Six, Tamboville and Wattville can live side by side." But they were still not prepared to demolish the wall. "The majority of people in Dalpark Six still want it," said Erasmus, "and as their councillor I must respect their democratic wish."

"I don't regret it," said Lammont. "The wall serves a purpose. You could say it provides a comfort zone. It makes people feel less threatened and that is why they have been able to come together like this." The blacks disagreed. To them the wall was a crude symbol of racism, but on Abe Nyalunga's advice they decided not to make it an issue. "We're just going to build relations and the wall will come down on its own," Abe remarked.

So the party of reconciliation went on beside the wall of apartheid, jointly symbolizing the ambiguity of a society in transition where hopes and fears and attitudes and symbols were all in a state of flux and nobody was quite sure what was what any more.

* * *

I returned to Dalpark Six a month after Nelson Mandela's inauguration and the wall was gone. It came down with no fuss; hardly anyone noticed. But by then Dalpark Six itself had changed. Three-quarters of its white residents had left. The hard-liners were the first to go, and as they put their homes on the market property prices dipped. Middle-class blacks, Coloureds and Indians snapped up the bargains and moved in, prompting more whites to leave and so repeating the cycle. Living in close proximity to the blacks of Wattville and Tamboville was one thing, but living in a mixed suburb with its increasingly mixed schools and other facilities was quite another for even some of the star-ry-eyed folk who had been at the *braaivleis* party. For the more com-mitted few who stayed, however, life had settled into comfortable rela-tionships and so over the three years Dalpark Six had become South Africa's most integrated residential suburb. "We purged ourselves of our racists," remarked Andrew Loader, 32, who with his wife Annetjie stayed on at 12 Tafelboom Street. "A few are left but they keep to them-selves. They are in a minority."

According to the Loaders the integration took place without a sin-gle racist incident. In their view, it had been a change for the better. "There's a much better atmosphere here now than three years ago," said Andrew, a social extrovert who seemed to know everyone on Tafelboom Street and cheerfully lent his lawnmower to his black and Coloured neighbours. "Then it was dead. Now everyone knows every-one else. It's much more friendly."

Living in an integrated suburb was not the only change that had taken place in Andrew Loader's life. He worked at the Baker's biscuit factory in nearby Kempton Park where his boss was now a black man, Joe Mnisi. This, too, would have been unthinkable three years before, but Loader said he didn't mind. "Joe's a competent man. I respect him," he said. More than that, the two families had become friends and had even gone on holiday together.

Mnisi had started work at the factory as a floor sweeper 23 years before. Now he was Production Manager with five whites among those working under him. He, too, was now living in Dalpark Six, having moved there from the teeming black township of Tembisa some 20 km away. "My white neighbours came round to welcome us when we moved in," he told me. "I was surprised, but I have found that if you communicate with people nicely they end up liking you." In return Mnisi had been careful – perhaps too careful – not to subject his neigh-bours to any culture shock. He told me he had admonished his wife for conversing loudly across the fence with a black friend two doors away, a feature of township life that makes them noisy, rumbustious places. "Whites find it disturbing and one must respect other people's feelings," Mnisi explained.

George and Lillian Johnson had moved to Dalpark Six from a Coloured township called Ennerdale – and didn't sleep a wink the first night for fear of being attacked by right-wing whites. "But nothing happened and after a while we settled down," said George, a computer programmer working for a bank in Johannesburg. Lillian, a university graduate, was working for an insurance company. They had two small children, two dogs and a new Toyota Corolla car, a quintessentially middle-class family.

"What I like most about living here is that our kids won't have to go through all the stages of learning to relate to other cultures the way we had to," said Lillian. "I went back to Ennerdale the other day," George chipped in, "and felt totally alienated. I couldn't believe I had grown up there. Those people are just surviving, they're not living. Here we feel free and independent."

One sensed, though, that there was still some tension between the Dalpark Six residents and the squatter community. The shacks had crept to within 20 metres of the nearest Dalpark Six houses, a number of which had security fences and "for sale" notices. There were still occasional meetings with Abe Nyalunga and his committee, but there hadn't been another big get-together. The peace tree had disappeared and few people in the transient squatter community seemed aware that there had ever been one. "I think someone cut it down to build a shack," one resident told me.

* * *

Fast-forward seven years and I was back in Dalpark Six once more. The political transition and the onset of economic recession had wrought yet more changes. All traces of the "Berlin Wall" had disappeared from most memories, as well as the last of the wall's detritus, but there were some gated streets in the suburb now testifying to the increased crime rate that has come with liberation. Some of the houses closest to Tamboville's ever-encroaching shacks were abandoned shells that had been stripped and vandalized. The shopping mall had shut down following repeated burglaries that had turned away the traders.

More whites had left, because of the increased crime, the locals said, and so had a number of black householders who had lost their jobs as many East Rand factories and businesses had cut back on staff, leaving the new homeowners unable to keep up their rates and mortgage payments. More Indians, many of them traders who seemed better able to withstand the impact of the recession, had moved in to snap up the bargains as property prices slipped further. Indians now numbered nearly half the suburb's population, while the black population had shrunk to 20% and the whites and Coloureds to 15% each.

James Lammont, the man who had prompted the building of the wall and then its demolition, was among those who had gone, on transfer, neighbours said, to the pleasant Western Cape town of George 1 000 km away. Steve Erasmus, the man who helped him, was no longer on the town council, which in fact no longer existed. It had been subsumed into a much larger metropolitan council called Ekehurleni that included Boksburg and five other East Rand towns, was controlled by the African National Congress and had a black mayor, Bavumile Vilakazi. Erasmús, who had returned to his medical practice, was living in a capacious brick mansion in the centre of Boksburg where he told me he was no longer active in politics. Nor were any of the old Conservative Party councillors who once ran the town with him. "They are all still around," Erasmus told me, "and they have all come to terms with the changes that have taken place. I think the whole transition in South Africa is unique and has surprised a lot of people."

The Baker's biscuit factory was one of the enterprises that had cut back heavily on staff. Both Andrew Loader and his boss Joe Mnisi had taken retrenchment packages. Mnisi had started up his own business, a freight agency, which was doing well after forming a partnership with a German company. The company had offices in Johannesburg and Mnisi drove there every day, but had opted to continue living in Dalpark Six. "I like it here," he said. "It's very quiet and friendly." Meanwhile Loader moved first to another biscuit factory, then when the recession forced its closure he took a job with an engineering company where he was now the workshop manager. But this company, too, was feeling the squeeze so that Loader was working long hours, often seven days a week and late into the night, to ensure that the company survived and that he retained his job.

The Loaders still lived at 12 Tafelboom Street, but told me there were now only three other white families on the street. The kids were growing up: Allan, now 15, was singing in the mixed-race East Rand Youth Choir and was about to embark on a four-week European tour, while Andre, 13, was head boy at the Dalview Primary School and a budding long-distance athlete. "He runs nearly every week in all the black townships," his father told me. "You've got to run there if you want to be noticed because that's where the best athletes are." The Loaders and Mnisis were still friends, they still visited one another though not as often as before, and they had not been on holiday together again. In part this was obviously because they no longer worked together and so their lives had drifted apart, but I sensed, too, that the initial gush of multiracial enthusiasm had spent itself and in the tougher economic climate life had shed some of its post-transitional euphoria.

But for all these changes of mix and mood that I had watched over the years in Dalpark Six, this time it was the adjoining black settlements that caught my eye. Tamboville, once a jumble of flimsy shelters nailed together from strips of wood and cardboard, corrugated iron and black plastic sheeting, the roofs held down with stones and the whole place looking as though a wind storm could carry it all away in a flurry of debris, had now taken on an altogether more substantial and permanent aspect. It was still a Casbah of twisting alleyways, but many of the homes were now built of brick, some with neat little gardens and vegetable patches, and the alleyways themselves were tarred. There were street lights and water taps and telephone lines, and every here and there a TV satellite dish. One of the finer brick homes was built by Abe Nyalunga, but Abe, I learned, was dead. Killed in one of the terrible political clashes that ravaged the East Rand in the early stages of the national transition. But he is not forgotten. The street running past his home is named after him.

As Andrew Loader drove me through Tamboville, where scores of people waved to him in recognition, the narrow thoroughfares were alive with activity, children playing, chickens and dogs scurrying about and people plying various forms of commerce: an array of *shebeens* and liquor stores, spaza shops and alfresco grocers selling everything from cigarettes and canned foods to live chickens and herbal remedies. A modern school had been built in the centre. Here, too, is a cemetery with a large grey marble tombstone marking the burial place of Oliver Tambo, the ANC hero who led the organization through all its years in exile only to suffer an incapacitating stroke on the eve of liberation and to die shortly after it, and after whom this humble settlement with its squatter camp origins is named. It has turned the place into a national shrine.

Behind Tamboville is Wattville and the two had now converged into a single town, with Wattville as the more pretentious quarter. It had some double-storey homes, a proper shopping centre and many more satellite dishes. Beyond Wattville, yet again, a new squatter camp was arising, an array of flimsy shacks mushrooming up daily just as Tamboville had done a decade before. It had no name yet but it was growing apace, its shacks spilling down towards the water's edge on the far bank of the little lake opposite Dalpark Six.

The Government, I was told, had moved some of these newcomers to a low-cost housing development further out on the East Rand, but as fast as they were moved others arrived. And so it will continue, for this is an unstoppable phenomenon as the new South Africa takes shape out of the distorted socio-economic dispensation of the old.

Circling further around the little lake one comes upon two more settlements, Leachville Two and Three. These are new Government projects aimed at redressing the huge housing backlog inherited from the apartheid regime. The townships are properly planned and neatly laid out, with wide streets, open spaces and small but neat homes. A notice outside an estate office informs that the house prices range upwards from R52 000 (about $5 200) with deposits from R2 000 (about $200). Cheap by international standards but beyond the reach of all but the new black middle class.

As I gazed down upon the Lion Pan with the settlements strung around its perimeter, it struck me that there was a tableau of the new South African society in transition. At one end of the little lake, the Mediterranean of this microcosmic world, was the old white suburb now growing increasingly multiracial as more and more black people managed to reach and enter its middle-class status, while at the other end there was the relentless arrival of our own Third World population striving ceaselessly to reach South Africa's affluent urban complexes. And in between, like the rungs of a social ladder, the various sectors of the black underclass struggling to lift themselves up, first into a Tamboville, then a Wattville, then a Leachville, always with the hope that eventually they would be able to buy a home in Dalpark Six. Some will make it the whole way, many won't. And the number who make it will depend on the ability of the economy to grow and absorb members of this huge proletariat. When the economy falters, and the Baker's biscuit factory has to retrench workers, some will fail to meet their mortgage payments and slip back down the social ladder around the little lake. But if the economy were to take off, many more would succeed and the rainbow nation would become a reality.

CHAPTER FIVE

THE ESSENTIAL FREEDOM

*South Africa should put the freedom of its press and media
at the top of its priorities as a democracy. None of our
irritations with the perceived inadequacies of the media
should ever allow us to suggest even faintly that the
independence of the press could be compromised or
coerced. A bad free press is preferable to a
technically good, subservient one.*
— NELSON MANDELA

As a journalist who spent nearly the whole of his professional life
working through the dark days of apartheid censorship and harassment,
nothing has excited me so much or filled me with so much hope as the
new South Africa's commitment to freedom of expression and of the
media. I say this not so much for personal reasons, although there is a
wonderful sense of liberation in that too, but because freedom of the
press is not a luxury; it is an organic necessity for the proper functioning of a democratic system. Once human society developed beyond the
small tribal unit and the Greek city-state, when the citizenry could be
gathered together for discussion and decision-making, it became
impossible for the individual to obtain for himself the information he
needed to function as an informed member of the body politic. The
news of events in today's complex societies must be brought to him by
newspapers, radio, television and the internet, which also provide the
channels for public discussion and analysis. That way the wheels of
democratic decision-making are kept in motion.

More than that. As James Madison put it in his 1798 Virginia Resol-
utions, when a fear of Jacobin terror in France caused the newly established American democracy to clamp down on criticism, freedom of
expression is also "the only effectual guardian of every other right".
Without freedom of expression tyranny can advance in silence, the way is
open for public brainwashing, and then all other democratic rights can be
removed without protest. It is the well-trodden road to authoritarianism.

Judiciaries can be stacked, elections rigged and people detained with impunity. Nowhere in the world is there now, or has there ever been, a democracy without freedom of expression. It is the essential freedom.

It is beyond argument that if the media are to perform this vital role adequately and fearlessly they must be unfettered. And protected, too, as far as possible, from the pressures of government and other powerful interests. All of which means that, next to the enfranchising of the black population and the drafting of the Constitution itself, the lifting of restrictions on freedom of speech and the media and their entrenchment in the Constitution has been the most important democratizing feature of the new South Africa.

This is not to say that all is well on the media scene. There are worrying tensions between the media and the new Mbeki administration, government's tolerance threshold is low, there are serious deficiencies within the media itself, it is racially and ethnically divided and shot through with mutual suspicions, journalism is at a low ebb, proprietorship is unstable, and the industry as a whole is in a fluid condition as it struggles through its own uncertain transformation. Nevertheless it is unquestionably true that the media today is both freer and more representative of all sectors of the population than at any other time.

The history of the South African press has been one of struggle against repressive forces from earliest times. When two of the early British settlers, Thomas Pringle and John Fairbairn, started the country's first newspaper, the *South African Commercial Advertiser*, they were soon forced to close it down in 1824 when the authoritarian governor of the Cape Colony, Lord Charles Somerset, censored the paper for publishing critical material. It took Pringle and Fairbairn four years of persistent argument and representations to the colonial government in London before they won the right to republish. The Colonial Office, overruling Somerset, issued a decree granting "a presumption in favour of the right of individuals to obtain a licence to publish, subject only to the law of libel; their right to engage in political discussion; and their right to report events relating to the government of the colony without pre-publication censorship." It was a safeguard against what media lawyers today call "prior restraint", but there was still no protection against punishment after publication of material deemed to have crossed the boundary of "political discussion" and to be harmful to or disrespectful of the colonial regime or its officials. Out of that struggle was born a robust, British-type press tradition, even though the decree fell short of what would today be regarded as adequate press freedom. It was not constitutionally entrenched, and when the Union of South Africa was established in 1910 the new Constitution was silent on the subject.

That early tradition came under constant pressure in the years that followed as it found itself caught in the conflicts of a deeply polarized society, divided first between English and Afrikaner and then between white Afrikaner nationalism and black African nationalism. In effect the media became caught up in two overlapping revolutions.

Great tensions arose during the Boer War of 1899-1902, between Paul Kruger's South African Republic and the English newspapers of Johannesburg which Kruger understandably saw as mouthpieces of the enemy. There was tension once more during the Great Depression of the 1920s – the furnace in which Afrikaner Nationalism was forged – when striking white miners saw the English-language press as the voice of the mining companies and burned down *The Star* building in Johannesburg.

Tension arose yet again during World War II when Afrikaans news-papers, newly arisen to support the growing National Party, opposed South Africa's involvement in the war and sympathized with Hitler. One of the Afrikaans editors then was Hendrik Verwoerd, later to be Prime Minister and chief architect of apartheid. Jan Smuts, who was South Africa's wartime Prime Minister, decided not to introduce for-mal press censorship but instead set up a series of informal arrange-ments and committees to obtain the co-operation of newspapers in what he regarded as critical war-effort matters. Although the Afrikaans newspapers were hostile to the war effort, they knuckled down to the informal arrangements because they felt these were preferable to full-scale censorship. That established a pattern of internalized control and self-censorship that was later replicated by the National Party regime.

When Afrikaner Nationalism came to power in 1948 committed to implementing apartheid and entrenching Afrikaner-dominated white supremacy in a post-war world that was moving away from racialism and colonialism, the tensions between press and government rose to new heights. The attitude of the new government was rooted not in the Pringle-Fairbairn tradition but rather in the filial relationship between the Afrikaans press and the Afrikaner Nationalist movement. The Afrikaans newspapers had arisen as part of this folk movement, as instruments in the ethnic mobilization of the Afrikaners, and although they were allowed a measure of freedom to criticize the political lead-ership and test reaction to new ideas, it was expected that this criticism would be temperately phrased and essentially constructive in its approach. The essence of the relationship was that the newspapers would at all times be loyal to the movement, would never harm it with embarrassing reports, would serve as instruments of communication between the movement's leadership and its followers, and at election time especially would sound the trumpet call to rally the *volk* to the party's support. In short, it was a "patriotic" press in the narrow context of the ethnic political movement it served, and when the National Party government came to power it sought to impose that same patriotic requirement on the press as a whole. It was inclined anyway to regard the English-language press as the voice of the political enemy. While the government could accept this in the context of white political rivalry between the National Party and the predominantly English United Party, when it came to what it saw as the larger "national interest" – and increasingly this included reports on the implementation of apartheid and the international reaction to it – the press was expected to be loyal and "patriotic". To the extent that the English press continued to exercise its traditional freedom and publish these embarrassing reports, it was seen as disloyal and prepared to damage the national interest for the sake of partisan political gain. Political pressure to control this perceived disloyalty mounted steadily.

Black journalism, meanwhile, struggled to establish itself in this hostile environment. The first black newspaper, *Imvo Zabantsundu* (African Opinion), was founded in 1884 by John Tengo Jabavu, a pioneer figure in black South African politics. In 1903 another, called *Ilanga Lase Natal* (The Natal Sun), was started by John Dube, who later became first president of the South African Native National Congress, forerunner of the African National Congress. Others followed, including *Abantu-Batho* (the word for "people" in both Zulu and Tswana), founded jointly by Dube and Solomon Tshekisho Plaatje, a remarkable man who though having only a primary school education mastered six African languages as well as English, Dutch and German and whose 1916 book, *Native Life in South Africa*, became a classic. But none survived. There was never sufficient operating capital or advertising revenue to sustain them. It was not until the 1950s when Jim Bailey with his Randlord father's inheritance launched *Drum* magazine and *Golden City Post* that black journalism came into its own with a more vigorous voice and an array of wonderful writers and photographers. They established a tradition of savvy, streetwise reporting and the use of a racy Africanized English that captured the flavour of township life and led to a golden age of black South African writing. But then Bailey, too, ran short of funds and withdrew, his publications taken over by big white publishing houses. They and others like them continued to target black readers but their lean revenues and white ownership kept their voices restrained.

Initially the English press focussed entirely on the English-Afrikaner political struggle. The editors of the major English-language newspapers were conservative white men with a suburban mindset. They had grown up in an era when blacks were simply part of the South African landscape, like the animals and the thorn trees, and had no political significance except in so far as they could provide cheap labour and be of service to the white person's needs. As people with hopes and aspirations and as citizens with rights, they simply did not exist. This pervasive blindness was vividly expressed in an editorial which the *Rand Daily Mail* of Johannesburg published in 1923 on the occasion of its 25th birthday.

> "The *Mail* desires to see established in and around Johannesburg, and in the Transvaal generally, a happy and prosperous white community. With this object in view . . . it will do what it can to direct this forward movement into channels leading to the largest possible employment of white men at a fair wage and under decent conditions."[1]

But from the late fifties this began to change – partly in response to the growth of black resistance at home and the wave of decolonization in the rest of Africa, and partly through a generational change of editors and senior staffers on some of the newspapers that brought in people more in tune with the new era. From then on the main thrust of the government's moves against the press was to restrict its reporting of the black resistance.

It did not do this by placing censors in the newsrooms. The control system was more insidious than that. There were 120 pieces of legislation that one way or another restricted what could be published on pain of prosecution.[2] The effect was self-censorship imposed by the journalists themselves.

A key early measure aimed at restricting coverage of the black resistance was the Suppression of Communism Act, later subsumed into a hold-all law called the Internal Security Act. This prohibited newspapers from quoting any utterances, past or contemporaneous, of thousands of political activists placed under a special restriction called a "banning order". Similarly, newspapers could not publish anything deemed to "further the aims" of a banned organization. A few years later the major black nationalist parties, the African National Congress and the Pan-Africanist Congress, were banned together with their leaders, bringing them under the silencing law as well. This was followed by the banning of 19 Black Consciousness organizations in 1977, and then the United Democratic Front and 17 other black political organizations in 1987. The cumulative effect was to silence the whole of the authentic black political opposition within South Africa for nearly forty years.

Other laws effectively prevented the publication of information about conditions in prisons, or activities of the military or the police force, without prior approval by these institutions themselves which was granted only when it cast them in a favourable light. This made it risky for newspapers to publish news of the large-scale torturing of political detainees, the assassination of political opponents and the maltreatment of prisoners. In one spectacular instance it prevented the South African media from reporting the fact that the country's troops had invaded Angola in 1975 to within 100 km of the capital, Luanda. The whole world was aware of this massive military invasion which lasted for months and involved heavy engagements with the Angolan army and Cuban troops supporting them. Body bags came home and young conscripts were hospitalised, yet throughout it all the government maintained the official fiction that South African troops were not in Angola except in small numbers to protect a large dam a few kilometres across the border from Namibia, then called South West Africa. I even attended a background briefing of editors presided over by then Defence Minister (later President) P W Botha at which the Chief of the Defence Force, General Constand Viljoen, pointed out the precise positions of South African troops deep inside Angola – only to conclude by issuing an official statement for publication repeating the falsehood that there were only a handful of South African troops in Angola guarding the Calueque Dam.[3] It must be one of the few instances in history where a country has gone to war and tried to conceal the fact from its own public.

There were laws making it an offence to stir up racial hostility, raising the question of whether one could be prosecuted for exposing and condemning acts of injustice against blacks; to incite anyone to break a law by way of protest at a time when it was illegal for blacks to strike or form "riotous assemblies"; to photograph or publish a picture of any prisoner or place where prisoners were held, which is why Nelson

Mandela's features remained unknown to the world for 27 years. There was a total ban on publishing anything about the development of nuclear energy in South Africa; on where the country obtained its oil imports; on advocating sanctions against it; and, in a bizarre Catch 22, on reporting anything about "key points" whose number, nature and whereabouts remained undisclosed. Under a range of blanket security laws the Security Police also had the power to raid any newspaper office, detain journalists – or anyone else – without trial, and empowered the Minister of Justice to close any newspaper in the name of "national security".

These censorship laws were supplemented by even more stringent restrictions during various states of emergency that were declared during times of black political uprisings. Most restricted journalists' access to trouble spots. The most draconian, imposed during the great township demonstrations of the 1980s, empowered any police officer to instantly declare the area in his vicinity an "unrest area", at which all reporters and photographers had to leave or be arrested. It was aimed particularly at stifling television coverage of the unrest.

Some newspapers tried hard to negotiate this minefield and present a more balanced picture of the total society, exposing injustices, challenging apartheid's basic premises, and giving political dissenters, including such leading black figures who were not imprisoned, exiled or otherwise judicially silenced, a platform to articulate their opposition. These papers distinguished themselves with brave reporting and thunderous editorials. Foremost among them was *The World*, a black daily led by a courageous editor, Percy Qoboza, who was imprisoned for a time before the paper itself was closed, only to re-appear as *The Sowetan*; a black weekly, *New Nation*, edited by Zwelakhe Sisulu, scion of a leading ANC family who was abducted from his home and detained without trial for more than a year and a half; the *Evening Post*, a small daily in Port Elizabeth founded and edited by a former war correspondent, John Sutherland, who was the first white editor to break the conformist mould of the English-language press and begin reporting vigorously on black issues; the *Daily Dispatch* of East London, whose crusading editor Donald Woods was banned and who then escaped into exile to become a highly effective anti-apartheid lobbyist; the *Cape Times* under the editorship of Anthony Heard who had the courage to violate the most stringent of the security laws by publishing a question-and-answer interview with the exiled leader of the ANC, Oliver Tambo; and most influential of all, the *Rand Daily Mail*, the largest morning daily in the country, which under the editorship of an incisive political analyst, Laurence Gandar, gave intellectual leadership to the liberal movement and inspired a whole generation of young South African journalists. The "*Mail*" won international acclaim for its courage, but Gandar was fired by the paper's proprietors who wanted a blander product that would attract less critical attention from the government and from advertisers. So, too, was his equally courageous successor, Raymond Louw. During my own four-year editorship of the paper during the 1970s I was in court six times. Then I, too, was fired. Eventually in 1985 this great newspaper was closed – just five years before President de Klerk unbanned the ANC, released Nelson Mandela and began the transformation process that the paper had been urging for four decades.

The death of the *Rand Daily Mail* was a terrible blow to journalism and to the country, for it resulted in the dispersal of the most talented staff that has ever been assembled in a South African newsroom, a number of whom left the country or left journalism to prosper elsewhere, and it sank a flagship which left journalists and editors elsewhere among the mainstream media feeling vulnerable and less inclined to follow its crusading example. Yet it had sown some fertile seeds. With astonishing chutzpah a small group of young journalists who were retrenched when the *Mail* and a sister paper, the *Sunday Express*, were closed, pooled their retrenchment packages, raised funds elsewhere and launched a small weekly to carry the tradition forward and indeed take it to new heights. Several other small publications followed in the wake of the *Weekly Mail* to form what became known as the alternative press. Among them was another weekly, *Vrye Weekblad* (Free Weekly), run by a tiny staff of courageous anti-apartheid Afrikaans journalists under the leadership of editor Max du Preez. Together the *Weekly Mail* and *Vrye Weekblad* created a whole passage of history of their own by being among the first to expose the apartheid regime's hit-squads and third-force violence which later became the main theme of the Truth and Reconciliation Commission's hearings. Seldom in the history of journalism anywhere can two such small newspapers have played such a large role in the destiny of their country's affairs.

Journalism under apartheid was stimulating in that it gave one a strong sense of mission to expose the truth about such an oppressive regime, but it was tough and sometimes dangerous. Black journalists, who worked for both the black newspapers and the predominantly white English press, were singled out for special harassment. In five years up to 1981, before the major unrest of that decade began, 50 black journalists were detained and 10 were banned, while one white journalist was detained and one editor was banned[4]. Black journalists were also frequently assaulted and tortured in their encounters with the security forces. Few escaped this brutality, and several suffered permanent injury.

Despite these handicaps and the smallness of their numbers – in 1981 there were 250 full-time black and more than 3 500 white journalists[5] – black journalists played an important role in expanding the range of news coverage. They brought new perspectives to newsrooms, and when the explosions of racial violence of 1976 and the mid-1980s made it hazardous for white journalists to operate in the black townships, it was often only black journalists who were able to reach the scene of the action and let the rest of the world know what was happening.

Pressures were intense on the foreign press as well. Although for technical reasons it would have been difficult to prosecute a foreign correspondent under the censorship laws for material published abroad, government nonetheless held the threat of expulsion over their heads. During the two years of uprising in the mid-eighties, the regime expelled 12 western correspondents, including representatives of such high-profile media as *The New York Times*, CBS, BBC-TV and ITN. The intention was to intimidate and to make the foreign correspondents hesitate to report aggressively or run the risk of displeasing Pretoria. Nevertheless enough graphic material was published and broadcast to arouse massive moral concern abroad and lead eventually to the imposition of sanctions against South Africa.

What was particularly galling in those years was that, while some newspapers did their best in difficult circumstances to expose the injustices of apartheid, the national public broadcaster, The South African Broadcasting Corporation (SABC), became the most blatant propagandist of the regime and its odious ideology. It was initially modeled on Britain's BBC, but soon after the National Party came to power it subverted the SABC's independence. The government packed the board of directors with political appointees, who in turn filled all key editorial positions with ideologically reliable apparatchiks. No journalist who was not a true believer could hope to work there. No critical item ever made it on air. Moreover, no other broadcaster was permitted to operate, giving the SABC a monopoly of the air as it broadcast over three television channels and 22 radio stations.

It is difficult to exaggerate the impact of this systematic brainwashing over three decades following the 1960 banning of the ANC and other black political organizations. A 1982 opinion survey showed that 80% of whites believed the government line that communism, not black discontent, was the greatest threat to South Africa's future; 81% of whites supported military attacks on ANC bases in neighbouring countries; and a staggering 71% believed that South African blacks were basically content and had no reason to try to overthrow the apartheid regime. The prevailing white view, instilled by years of managed news reporting by the powerful state-controlled broadcast media, was that South Africa was not facing a domestic threat but an external one, a "total onslaught" directed from the Soviet Union.

At the same time I believe the role played by the small band of courageous newspapers was crucial in enabling the negotiated transformation to nonracial democracy to take place. Despite all the efforts at news management and thought control, the silencing of the black opposition and the pumping out of propaganda over the airwaves, those newspapers managed to bear witness to the truth of what was happening. They kept the country and the world informed, they prodded white consciences, they sustained the morale of the black majority, and they aroused world opinion.

They did more than that too. It was one of the curious features of the apartheid system that while it was authoritarian, even brutal, it was never completely totalitarian. With a strange ambiguity of mind the government wanted to maintain an illusion of democratic institutions and processes. While it created a police state it also maintained an independent judiciary, and while most of the judges were shamefully complicit in their harsh application of wicked laws and their blindness to the routine torturing of prisoners and witnesses who appeared before them, there were some with greater moral integrity who delivered bolder judgments and stretched the common law to mitigate oppression. While the regime refused to grant the franchise to people of colour it maintained a white Parliament with regular elections and a small but articulate anti-apartheid opposition that punched above its weight; and while it tried to limit and control what the press reported it did not snuff it out altogether. The result was that there were interstices in the control system, platforms and arenas that a wide range of dissenting groups were able to use – civil rights lawyers, liberal politicians, student bodies, women's organizations, trade unions and the like. The English press, and particularly the *Rand Daily Mail* as the biggest and most articulate among them, became the sustaining voice of these dissenting groups and individuals. It was the thread that kept them all together in a loose constellation, a group of newspapers which, by being a common denominator to all these groups, gave them a sense of common purpose and mutual support and which in this way managed to sustain each and so keep the spirit of dissent alive in the country.

That is what saved South Africa. Instead of conformity pressures causing white opinion to congeal into a siege mentality, as the country sank deeper into crisis the spirit of dissent grew, ultimately reaching into the ranks of the ruling elite until it became possible for them to consider the impossible – relinquishing power.

Now the media is free. The main censorship laws have been swept away or become dead letters. In their place is a near equivalent of the American First Amendment, a constitutional clause guaranteeing freedom of speech and the press. Section 16 of the Bill of Rights reads:

(1) Everyone has the right to freedom of expression, which includes -
    a. freedom of the press and other media;
    b. freedom to receive or impart information or ideas;
    c. freedom of artistic creativity;
    d. academic freedom and freedom of scientific research.
(2) The right in subsection (1) does not extend to -
    a. propaganda for war;
    b. incitement of imminent violence; or
    c. advocacy of hatred that is based on race, ethnicity, gender or religion, and that constitutes incitement to cause harm.

More recently that has been supplemented by a brace of laws aimed at making South Africa a more open society. The Promotion of Access to Information Act, which became law in February 2000, aims at giving effect to a constitutional clause stating that everyone has the right to any information held by the state; while the Protected Disclosures Act, passed six months later, sets out procedures and protections for employees who blow the whistle on malpractices in the organizations for which they work in both the public and private sectors. Both pieces of legislation are enormously complex: the Promotion of Access to Information Act, for example, has 93 sections of microscopic detail setting out what kinds of information can be disclosed and what cannot, while the whistle-blowers act tried to safeguard against its being abused by employees who want to embarrass a rival or someone against whom they have a grudge.

A new openness and a changed pattern of media ownership. Whereas in the past all of the newspapers were white owned, today all but two of the seven major publishing companies have changed hands or been restructured. At the time of this writing, two of the publishing houses are black controlled, 13 of the 22 editors of mainstream news-papers are black, 34,7% of journalists in those papers are black – compared with 6,7% twelve years before and 11,8% in the United States in 2000 – and 34,5% are women.

The broadcasting scene has changed too. The SABC today has a multiracial board of directors with a black chairman. It has had three black chief executives, several black editors of its radio and television news services, and the editorial staffs of these services are predominantly black. To prevent another hijacking of the airwaves, the SABC's monopoly of broadcasting has been ended with the appointment of an independent licensing body called the Independent Communications Authority of South Africa (ICASA).[6] South Africa now has 22 public, 16 private commercial and more than 100 community radio stations. In addition to the SABC with its three TV channels, there is now a private free-to-air commercial television channel called e-TV together with two encrypted pay channels devoted to movies and sport put out by a consortium called M-Net, and a huge satellite bouquet, also encrypted, of 54 TV and nine radio channels, including the BBC, CNN, Fox and a range of other foreign broadcasters, aired by M-Net's associate company, Multichoice. A far cry indeed from the old state monopoly.

* * *

Freedom of speech is of course a relative concept. It cannot be absolute. One cannot be free to commit blackmail or perjury or fraud or to cause panic by falsely shouting fire in a crowded theatre. Nor can a government be prohibited from making laws to punish such acts. Yet the right to engage freely in public debate is fundamental to democracy and must be protected. How to strike the right balance, then, becomes a matter for legal interpretation. Constitutions typically state broad principles rather than specific detail. It is then up to the courts to give substance to those principles on a case-by-case basis, handing down interpretations which over time build up a body of precedents that form the case law on the subject. Future legal advice and argument is then based on the constitutional clauses as interpreted in those precedents.

Courts generally do not give decisions in the abstract about what a constitutional clause means, but only when particular cases come before them. This has the advantage of not binding the future with precise details. Ideally constitutions should be flexible enough to adjust to changing circumstances over time and not be fixed to the limited vision of any particular age. Anthony Lewis, in his detailed account of the evolution of the American First Amendment, writes of the paradox that this has produced in his country's constitutional system. "We live under a written Constitution, and we rely on its unchanging character to give stability to our turbulent society," he notes. "But the Constitution continues to have meaning and life only because judges apply it in fresh ways to challenges unforeseen by its creators."[7]

So far South Africa's freedom of expression clause has been tested in only a few cases, but already these have laid the foundations for a more liberal body of precedents than prevailed during the apartheid era. This is the start of what will be a long, evolutionary process.

The evolution over time of the US Supreme Court's notions of freedom of speech and of the media is an instructive illustration of such a process. When the first Congress of the United States enacted the First Amendment in 1791, four years after the Philadelphia Convention had written the US Constitution, the legislators almost certainly did not have in mind the wide libertarian meaning the First Amendment has now acquired. "Congress shall make no law . . . abridging the freedom of speech, or of the press," the amendment declares. On the face of it, that restriction applied only to the federal legislature and not to the states, or to the executive branch, and certainly not to media proprietors or advertisers or anyone else in the private sector. It was very far indeed from being a blanket protection of free speech.

Indeed during the republic's first hundred years the US Congress first passed a Sedition Act in 1798 that made criticism of the federal government a crime, then during World War I it passed an Espionage Act making it a crime to oppose America's involvement in the war or to criticize either the government or the armed forces. Hundreds of people were imprisoned under both laws. An opposition member of the House of Representatives, Matthew Lyon, was imprisoned under the Sedition Act for writing a letter to a newspaper accusing President John Adams of power hunger, pomposity and avarice, while Eugene Debs, the leader of the Socialist Party and its candidate for President five times, was among those jailed for criticizing the Espionage Act. A monthly journal, *The Masses*, was closed for running a series of articles and cartoons opposing the war and the draft.

It was only after World War I that the US Supreme Court began incrementally widening the interpretation of the First Amendment. It began with a series of judgments by two icons of the American judicial system, Oliver Wendell Holmes and Louis Brandeis. In an early case under the Espionage Act, in which the defendants had equated conscription with slavery, Holmes noted that while things could be said in peacetime that would not be tolerated when one's country was at war, the test should be whether the words used were of such a nature as to create "a clear and present danger" to the safety of the state.[8] It was a phrase that was to evolve into a litmus test in American case law on freedom of speech. Holmes elaborated on the phrase in a later judgment. "I think that we should be eternally vigilant against attempts to check the expression of opinions that we loathe and believe to be fraught with death, unless they so imminently threaten immediate interference with the lawful and pressing purposes of the law that an immediate check is required to save the country," he said.[9]

Other expanding judgments followed, including one in 1925 which prevented any state of the union, not only the federal Congress, from infringing free speech. It did so on the grounds that the Fourteenth Amendment forbids the states to deprive anyone of "liberty without due process of law" – and that freedom of speech and of the press constitute personal liberties.[10] One opened the way for much freer debate of court cases and the criticism of judges than is permitted in Britain and other Commonwealth countries. "An enforced silence," wrote Justice Hugo Black, "however limited, solely in the name of preserving the dignity of the bench, would probably engender resentment, suspicion and contempt much more than it would enhance respect."[11] In 1972 the famous Pentagon Papers case, in which *The New York Times* and *The Washington Post* defeated a US government attempt to stop them publishing extracts from secret official documents on the origins of the Vietnam War, provided another landmark. "Only a free and unrestrained press can effectively expose deception in government," wrote Justice Black.[12]

Then came the most striking of all, when a city commissioner named L B Sullivan, who was in charge of the police in Montgomery, Alabama, sued *The New York Times* for libel in 1961 and was awarded half a million dollars by a local jury because the newspaper had published an advertisement critical of the city's brutal response to civil rights protests. When the case reached the US Supreme Court, its judgment laid down a powerful new set of rules to prevent critics of official conduct from being silenced by libel actions. It declared that sovereignty was vested in the people, not the government, and set such store on their right to debate public issues freely as to make it virtually impossible for anyone to libel a public official. A critical statement need not even be true; certainly would-be critics should not be deterred by doubts about whether they could prove the truth of their statements in court. "Erroneous statement is inevitable if the freedoms of expression are to have the 'breathing space' that they need," declared Justice William Brennan. The only exception was if an official could prove that a false statement had been made with "actual malice", meaning the critic knew it was false, or had a "reckless disregard" for the truth. Nor could injury to an official's reputation be grounds for damages.[13]

In sum, the judgment wove all previous expressions on the subject together into a comprehensive statement of America's concept of free speech as the most crucial feature of a democratic society. Of the ten amendments to the Constitution that together constitute the Bill of Rights, the first is considered paramount.

* * *

As South Africa embarks on its own long process of evolving a body of case law around its Constitution, it has already shown an inclination to follow a similar libertarian course – although it has stopped short of the American model in some instances, particularly in declining to accord Section 16 a primary position. Instead the courts are taking the view that there is no hierarchy of rights in the Bill of Rights, so that while the importance of free expression is acknowledged it does not take precedence over other entrenched rights.

The first of these judgments, handed down by the Supreme Court of Appeal in October 1998, comes close to *Sullivan* in limiting the grounds on which journalists can be sued for defamation. It is an unusual case in that it was not based on Section 16 and so did not reach the Constitutional Court which is where all constitutional issues have to be decided; and, secondly, in the radical change of judicial thinking it reveals since South Africa's transition to democracy. It is also a particularly important case, since a long line of conservative judgments during the apartheid era had steadily tightened the common law on defamation until it rivalled the 120 censorship laws in its restrictive effect on the media. One of these imposed a doctrine known as "strict liability" which removed the need to show that a defendant was "culpable" – in other words intentional or negligent – in publishing defamatory material. In practice this meant that newspapers which could not prove they had been accurate in all material details of a report exposing apartheid brutality, for example, would be held liable for damages.

Another extended the right to sue for defamation to public companies and even political parties which were deemed to have a right to privacy that entitled them to conceal information from the public.

The see-saw history of this particular libel case reveals with startling clarity the change that has taken place in the judicial climate. In 1992, two years before South Africa's transition to democracy, the little Afrikaans weekly, *Vrye Weekblad*, published reports alleging that Lieutenant-General Lothar Neethling, South Africa's second most senior police officer and head of its forensic division, had been involved in death-squad activities, making sophisticated poisons that were used against ANC members and other activists in the democratic movement. One of the victims, Rev. Frank Chikane, now Director-General in the President's office, became gravely ill during a visit to the United States from a poison sprinkled in his luggage after he had checked it in at Johannesburg airport. Neethling was also said to be searching for a chemical to make black people sterile.

Neethling sued *Vrye Weekblad* for libel, claiming R1 500 000 damages. The *Mail & Guardian*, as the *Weekly Mail* had become by then, which had also published the reports, was a co-respondent. But Neethling lost the case when Judge Johann Kriegler, one of a handful of liberal judges who managed to swim against the tide of judicial complicity during the apartheid era, found that the general had been involved in illegal police activities and that he had perjured himself. In a courageous judgment Kriegler went on to recognize a new category of defence in defamation cases brought by public officials in an attempt to silence newspapers publishing information in the national interest. He held that in certain exceptional circumstances of "burning public interest" an editor might have a duty to publish allegations which he could not prove but which appeared to be correct and capable of proof.

But Kriegler's judgment was overturned by the Supreme Court of Appeal, where Judge Gustav Hoexter wrote a deeply retrogressive judgment which asserted that "the common law does not recognize a duty-interest relationship between a newspaper and its readers sufficient to support qualified privilege".[14] Not only did Hoexter brush aside the notion that newspapers had a democratic duty to be a watchdog against corruption and a critic of public policy, he went on to quote approvingly a sneering comment by an English judge that the media are "peculiarly vulnerable to the error of confusing the public interest with their own interest". Among the Appeal Court judges who concurred with this appalling judgment was the Chief Justice of that time, Michael Corbett. The damages subsequently awarded to Neethling killed the heroic little Afrikaans newspaper.

Fast-forward five years into the new South Africa, and suddenly there is a breathtaking about-face. In September 1998 another libel action involving a newspaper came before the Supreme Court of Appeal.[15] This time the newspaper, *City Press*, a weekly with a high circulation in the black community, had published a report containing allegations not against a public official but against a Pretoria lawyer, Nthedi Bogoshi, whom it accused of defrauding clients and the Motor Vehicle Accident Fund as well as of touting for business. Bogoshi brought nine libel claims for R1 800 000 against *City Press*. The newspaper initially based its defence on the established common-law requirement of "truth and public interest", but later applied to the Johannesburg High Court for an amendment to its defence basis. The High Court refused, and the matter went to the Supreme Court of Appeal.

There it came before a five-judge bench which again included Hoexter, but now in the changed atmosphere of the new democracy. Although the case did not raise the defence of the Constitution's freedom of expression clause, which would have required it to go to the Constitutional Court, the hitherto conservative Appeal Court judges clearly decided they had better get into line with the new Constitution and the spirit of the times.

This time Judge Joos Hefer wrote the judgment, with Hoexter and the other three judges concurring, and they reversed themselves completely, going against the *Neethling* judgment in all key respects. The new judgment held that journalists did indeed have a specific duty to publish information in the public interest and would no longer have to prove the truth of allegedly libellous reports to escape liability for defamation. It would be enough for them to show that they had taken reasonable care. As Hefer put it:

> "The publication in the press of false defamatory allegations of fact will not be regarded as unlawful if, upon consideration of all the circumstances of the case, it is found to have been reasonable to publish the particular facts in the particular way and at the particular time."

In addition, Hefer said, journalists could escape liability by showing that they were not negligent in publishing information even if it turned out to be wrong. This test reversed the doctrine of "strict liability" for any information they published which was defamatory and wrong. "If we recognize, as we must, the democratic imperative that the common good is best served by the free flow of information and the task of the media in the process, it must be clear that strict liability cannot be defended," Hefer said.

The *Bogoshi* test of "reasonable and not negligent" comes close to the *Sullivan* test of "reckless disregard" for the truth to establish malice. In one important respect it falls short: whereas the onus is on a US plaintiff to prove "reckless disregard" for the truth, the onus is on a South African journalist to prove he was "reasonable and not negligent". But in another respect *Bogoshi* goes further than *Sullivan*: it is not limited to the libelling of public officials. It applies to all.

The judgment also marked the first time the Appeal Court has acknowledged that the media have a duty to provide information to the public – the point Hoexter had scorned if not actually refuted in the *Neethling* case. Citing English, Dutch, German, Australian, New Zealand and United States precedents as well as the European Court of Human Rights, Hefer was explicit: "We must not forget that it is the right, and indeed a vital function, of the press to make available to the community information and criticism about every aspect of public, political, social and economic activity and thus to contribute to the formation of public opinion."

Finally, in a ringing statement, the judgment delivered the most emphatic declaration of the importance of freedom of speech and the media yet to be entrenched in our case law.

"Freedom of expression constitutes one of the most essential foundations of a democratic society and is one of the basic conditions for its progress and the development of man."

But important though *Bogoshi* is in laying a new foundation for the case law on libel in South Africa, it did not contribute to an elucidation of the freedom of expression clause in the Bill of Rights. That is the exclusive task of the Constitutional Court, and so far only three cases have had a bearing on this.

The first and most important of these arose from a complicated dispute in which the spokesman for the Department of Correctional Services, Russell Mamabolo, was convicted for contempt of court after issuing a statement criticizing a High Court judge. Eugene Terre'Blanche, the demagogic leader of the right-wing *Afrikaner Weerstandsbeweging*, had been sentenced to two terms of imprisonment after the political transition which he tried so hard to derail – one year for assault with intent to do grievous bodily harm, and a second six-year term for attempted murder. When he was nearing the end of his first term and expecting parole, he applied for leave to appeal against the second term, not against the sentence itself but to have the charge reduced to grievous assault. Leave was granted, and the trial judge, Johan Els, went on to grant Terre'Blanche bail of R5 000 pending the appeal hearing. Startled and confused by this, Mamabolo issued a press statement saying the judge had erred and that Terre'Blanche would not be released since he was still serving his sentence. An outraged Judge Els summoned Mamabolo to appear before him and convicted and sentenced him for contempt of court.

Mamabolo appealed to the Constitutional Court on two grounds – that his constitutional rights to a fair trial and to freedom of expression had been violated. He was joined in his application by three media organizations, a television broadcasting company called Midi-TV, *Business Day* newspaper and the Freedom of Expression Institute, as *amici curiae*, or friends of the court. The court briskly overturned the contempt conviction on the grounds that Judge Els's summary procedure, long standard practice in contempt cases in South Africa and elsewhere, violated the fair trial requirements set out in Section 35 (3) of the Bill of Rights. The judgment, written by Justice Kriegler (now promoted to the highest court in the land) then plunged into a detailed exposition of the freedom of expression clause and its conflict with the Constitution's injunction to uphold the dignity of the courts.

After outlining the long historical roots of contempt of court as a punishable offence in both English and Roman Dutch law, Kriegler then posed the modern-day question increasingly on the ordinary citizen's mind and which has prompted the American courts to exclude criticism of judges as grounds for contempt.

"Why should judges be sacrosanct? Is this not a relic of a bygone era when judges were a power unto themselves? Are judges not hanging on to this legal weapon because it gives them a status and untouchability that is not given to anyone else? Is it not rather a constitutional imperative that public office-bearers, such as judges, who wield great power, as judges undoubtedly do, should be accountable to the public who appoint them and pay them? Indeed, if one takes into account that the judiciary, unlike the

other two pillars of the state, are not elected and are not subject to dismissal
if the voters are unhappy with them, should not judges pre-eminently be subjected to continuous and searching public scrutiny and criticism?"

The case seems incontrovertible, particularly in light of the craven
compliance of many South African judges in administering wicked
laws and turning a blind eye to injustices during the apartheid era, their
steady stifling of the press with the judiciary's increasingly restrictive
additions to the case law on defamation, and the glaring wrongness of
the Appeal Court's decision in the *Neethling* case.

Yet Kriegler turned the argument on its head. Precisely because of
South Africa's undemocratic history, he reasoned, it was particularly
important to protect the reputation of the judicial process and to build
public confidence in it. "No one familiar with our history can be
unaware of the very special need to preserve the integrity of the rule of
law against governmental erosion," he wrote. "The emphatic protection
afforded the judiciary under the Constitution therefore has a particular
resonance."

Kriegler strongly emphasized the importance of free expression and
public criticism, which he said should include criticism of judicial
affairs. Courts were open, he noted, "so that the people can discuss,
endorse, criticize, applaud or castigate the conduct of the courts." Such
"robust and informed" debate was actually good for the public image
of the judicial system and helped promote impartiality, accessibility
and effectiveness. But there had to be limits. "(It) does not mean that
attacks, however scurrilous, can with impunity be made on the judiciary or on individual judicial officers." That could be "downright harmful to the public interest by undermining the legitimacy of the judicial
process as such."

Where to draw the line? Gilbert Marcus, a leading media lawyer
who appeared for the media companies, urged the court to accept
Oliver Wendell Holmes's formula of "a clear and present danger", but
Kriegler said he was "very much unpersuaded by this". One had to be
careful, he said with what sounded like a touch of scorn, not to have "a
wholesale importation of a foreign product".

Kriegler agreed that freedom of expression was of the utmost
importance. "Having regard to our recent past of thought control, censorship and enforced conformity to government theories, freedom of
expression . . . is no less important than it is in the United States of
America. It could actually be contended with much force that the

public interest in the open market-place of ideas is all the more important to us in this country because our democracy is not yet firmly
established and must feel its way." But again Kriegler shied away from
the logic of these compelling arguments, saying the South African
Constitution was inherently different from the US Constitution in that
it was much more detailed and explicit, it entrenched the importance of
protecting the dignity of the courts more emphatically, and the two
countries had different common law origins. "The balance which our
common law strikes between protection of an individual's reputation
and the right of freedom of expression differs fundamentally from the
balance struck in the United States."

Then came the really important declaration. "With us (the right to
freedom of expression) is not a pre-eminent freedom ranking above all
others," Kriegler asserted. "It is not even an unqualified right." Noting
that in its opening statement the Constitution proclaims the three
values of human dignity, freedom and equality as "foundational" to the
Republic, Kriegler said this meant "the right to freedom of expression
cannot be said automatically to trump the right to human dignity . . .
Freedom of expression does not enjoy superior status in our laws." It is
a statement which on the face of it appears to place a limit on the liberalizing door which *Bogoshi* had opened three years before in our case
law on defamation.

And then Kriegler came close to declaring that there is indeed a
hierarchy of rights in the Bill of Rights, with the dignity of the courts
enjoying superior status and trumping freedom of expression.

> "On balance," he said, "while recognizing the fundamental importance of
> freedom of expression in the open and democratic society envisaged by the
> Constitution, there is a superior countervailing public interest in retaining
> the tightly circumscribed offence of scandalizing the court."

Certainly Kriegler's judgment does circumscribe the crime of contempt
of court very tightly. The test, it says, must be "whether the offending
conduct, viewed contextually, really was likely to damage the administration of justice". The difference between *"really likely to damage"*
and Holmes's test of *"a clear and present danger"*, which Marcus
wanted Kriegler to accept, must be regarded as marginal.

Interestingly, one of the Constitutional Court justices, Albie Sachs,
a long-time anti-apartheid activist who was grievously injured in a car-
bomb attack by the South African security forces, submitted a separate

judgment proposing a more specific test almost identical to Holmes's. The test, he said, should be *"a real and direct threat"* to the administration of justice – a difference which Kriegler himself remarked was "more semantic than substantive" from his own *really likely to damage* formula. Quite so. Yet having said that, Kriegler went on to contend that Sachs's formula set the benchmark too high and might put an end to all prosecutions for this form of contempt of court. My strong suspicion is that in shying away from Sachs's formula, Kriegler's real concern was that it was too close to Holmes's and he did not want to adopt an American formula that might open the way for the future evolution of our case law along American lines and ultimately give constitutional primacy to freedom of speech.

The second Constitutional Court case to test Section 16 was one in which the South African National Defence Force Union challenged a clause in the Defence Act prohibiting members of the armed forces from joining trade unions or participating in public protests.[16] The union claimed the clause violated their constitutional right to free expression and the right under Section 23 of all workers to form and join trade unions, to participate in union activities and to strike.

The notion of soldiers striking is, of course, rather outlandish and Justice Kate O'Regan, who wrote the judgment, swiftly ruled it out on the grounds that members of the armed services were required to operate with "strict discipline". But she held that this did not negate the right of members of both the armed services and police from joining trade unions – something that is permitted in the Netherlands, Germany and Sweden, but not in Britain and the US. "It may well be that in permitting members to join trade unions and in establishing proper channels for grievances and complaints, discipline may be enhanced rather than diminished," O'Regan declared.

She held, too, that the prohibition violated the rights of the armed services to free expression. Not only did Section 16 give individuals the right to express opinions, but also the right to form associations and groups of like-minded people to propagate those opinions. O'Regan then went on to declare that "freedom of expression lies at the heart of democracy". But in another case three years later, O'Regan came back to Kriegler's theme that freedom of expression was not the paramount right in the Bill of Rights but that dignity, freedom and equality were "foundational". She was giving judgment in a case in which the leader of a political party, Bantu Holomisa, of the United Democratic Movement, had sued the *Sunday World* for damages after it had published a report alleging he had been involved with a gang of robbers and was under police investigation. It was a serious allegation, to be sure, and one must sympathize with Holomisa for feeling the newspaper should be able to prove what it said. But the newspaper argued that the report was in the public interest, given Holomisa's position as a public figure, and that the onus was on him to show the report was false. In her judgment O'Regan applied the *Bogoshi* test – thus giving it Constitutional Court endorsement – that the newspaper had to show that publication was "reasonable and not negligent", which she said it had failed to do.[17]

Taken together, these four cases amount to a massive, indeed spectacular, rehabilitation of the law on free expression and the role of the media in our new democracy. My only regret is that Justice Kriegler, who demonstrated such boldness in trying to widen the boundaries of freedom during the dark days of apartheid, did not seize the opportunity provided by *Bogoshi* to proclaim the paramountcy of Section 16. Instead both he and O'Regan have emphasized its limitations and placed the rights of dignity, freedom and equality above it. The concept of dignity, especially when applied to public figures and politicians, trumping freedom of speech in our rank order of rights troubles me. I would rather see freedom of expression in the number one spot because, like Madison, I believe that without it no other liberty is secure. At least one eminent South African media lawyer agrees. Wim Trengove, delivering a keynote address at a journalism award function in Johannesburg, made the case for freedom of expression being accorded "special protection" in our courts not only because of the vital democratic role the media performs, but because Section 16 (1) vests that right in *everyone*. Nor does it only protect every individual's right to speak freely, but it also includes the freedom to receive information and ideas from others and to convey information and ideas to them. That in turn, said Trengove, meant everyone also had the constitutional right to demand that the media be free. "Their freedom is protected, not because they are a superior class, but because it is in the interests of all of us that they be free."[18]

Nelson Mandela appears to agree as well. In his keynote address at the tenth anniversary of the founding of the Institute for the Advancement of Journalism in Johannesburg in June 2002, he was quite explicit. "South Africa should put the freedom of its press and media at the top of its priorities as a democracy," Mandela said, adding that a bad press which was free was preferable to a technically good but subservient press.

* * *

It is sadly apparent, though, that our progressive Constitution is well ahead of the new administration and some sectors of the population. As the courts have been expanding the common law on freedom of expression, official hostility to the press has been increasing. The new regime, particularly since Thabo Mbeki became President, has been acutely sensitive to criticism which it sees as being negative and unfair, or, worse still, derisory of black capabilities and intent on portraying a country going to the dogs under black rule.

Mistrust of the press is at several levels. Not surprisingly, in the minds of most black people the upholding of human dignity, rather than freedom of expression, holds prime position among all the rights entrenched in the new Constitution. This is not to say they do not value free expression, but for people who have had their human dignity trampled on for so long, their intelligence, their capabilities, their whole self-esteem impugned in law and in practice, the rehabilitation of their humanity is obviously of paramount importance. It is easy to see, too, why such people are likely to be hypersensitive to criticism of the performance of the liberation movement they have put in power to reinstate their dignity; criticism they are likely to see as yet another manifestation of derogatory attitudes towards them. And the sharper that criticism, the more it is cast in the biting language that is the weaponry of the English media and political tradition, the more it is resented.

There are suspicions that the white community, and the predominantly white media with it, are not genuinely committed to the vision of a new non-racial South Africa – and there are enough tales of racially derogatory remarks at suburban dinner tables to give substance to these suspicions. With that goes a feeling that the so-called white media are not doing as much as they could to counter racism in the white community. It is a continuum of mistrust: some black journalists are inclined to suspect that the white-owned or white-run newspapers give less prominence to reports of overt racism, of a white farmer dragging a black worker to death behind his truck, for example, than they do to black corruption or maladministration. This may not be objectively correct in the journalistic context of the relative importance of different news events on particular days, of how news stories break in relation to deadlines, of the detail and quality of reports received, and a multitude of other factors. But the suspicion is father to the thought.

At a broader level, government's chief accusation is that the media portray only the negative, not the positive, placing undue emphasis on stories about crime, especially rape, corruption, maladministration, HIV/AIDS, the falling value of the rand currency, rising unemployment, President Mbeki's "quiet diplomacy" towards President Robert Mugabe's outrageous land seizures in neighbouring Zimbabwe, allegedly inflexible labour policies and the like – all to the detriment of a country which is struggling to attract badly needed foreign investment. At its worst, a racist motive is seen behind this, of white-controlled publications giving expression to deep-seated beliefs in their community that black people are inherently incompetent and crooked and that black majority rule is bound to fail.

For their part, the media respond that theirs is primarily a watchdog role, and that in any event calamities and failures inevitably make stronger news than the smooth implementation of policies: the airliner that crashes makes news, the thousands that land safely every day do not. There is also a strong feeling among journalists that their role is not to be the government's cheerleaders, that it is big and strong enough to blow its own trumpet, and that their job is to probe the official claims of success to make sure they are not smokescreens to cover failure.

Through all of this, President Mbeki has been meticulous in asserting his government's commitment to media freedom, leaving most of the criticism to his aides and ministers, but he has criticized the media for not doing more to combat racism. He has also accused some newspapers, though not by name, of going beyond watchdogism and regarding themselves as being in opposition to government. It was one thing for the media to have opposed the apartheid government because it represented an unjust system, he once told a delegation from the World Association of Newspapers, but it was wrong that some newspapers had carried that attitude over into the new democratic era. "You are correct to be opposed to any government that is based on injustice," he said, "but I don't believe that, as a general principle, the media is an 'opposition party' by definition. I don't think that is correct."

A moot point, to which the editor of the *Mail & Guardian*, the paper which Mbeki probably had in mind when he spoke those words, had a response in a separate context. "In the old days we had no truck with those in power," the editor, Phillip van Niekerk, said. "We saw ourselves as adversaries of the government. We were broadly anti-apartheid and would not be content until there was a democratic order in this country. Today we support and are proud of the Constitution of this country. We agree with the basic principles upon which our society

85

is based and to which the ruling party has proclaimed its loyalty. And, yes, today we demand a higher standard of behaviour from our public officials, black and white. Why? Because they are our public representatives – they represent everybody. If they steal from the public purse, it is a betrayal of the entire nation's trust."

That powerful mission statement was delivered during a hearing of the South African Human Rights Commission, a body of 11 members appointed by the President, which brought the conflict between the media and their critics to a climax in mid-2000. The hearing stemmed from a complaint lodged in November 1998 by two professional organizations, representing black lawyers and accountants, accusing the *Mail & Guardian* and the country's largest-circulation newspaper, the *Sunday Times*, of racism in their reporting. The complaint was ironic in that the *Mail & Guardian*, under its former title of the *Weekly Mail*, had been in the forefront of exposing apartheid atrocities, while the *Sunday Times* has a black editor and the company which owns it is headed by South Africa's leading black businessman, Cyril Ramaphosa, who left politics after losing to Thabo Mbeki in the contest to become Nelson Mandela's successor. But the consequences of the complaint were explosive as the commission decided to widen the issue into a full-blown investigation into racism in all the media, which the media in turn saw as the most aggressive threat to its freedom since the inception of majority rule.

Some sort of examination of the media's role in the new South Africa and the extent to which it may still be projecting old-style racial stereotypes would no doubt be valuable, even necessary, given the country's history, but the manner in which this investigation was instituted could hardly have been more calculated to cause suspicion and provoke confrontation. First of all, the complaints did not question the accuracy of the reports but simply contended, among other things, that because the *Mail & Guardian* had published 14 reports on black corruption and only four of white corruption over a given period of time it had shown racial bias and given the impression that black people are essentially corrupt and incompetent. This despite the fact that the ratio of white to black in South Africa is about one to seven. Among the accusations against the *Sunday Times* was that it trivialized the deaths of black people by publishing only the statistics of those killed in a massacre while giving more detailed coverage to the death of a white couple allegedly murdered by their son.

The commission then engaged two researchers to determine the extent and nature of racism in the South African media – a near-impossible task in the best of circumstances, but explosively controversial in the short time available and the charged atmosphere of what was beginning to look like a Kafkaesque hearing with ill-defined charges and a pre-trial assumption of guilt. This impression was aggravated by the fact that the commission's chairman, Barney Pityana, had recently co-authored a newspaper article accusing the media of being "an obstacle to change" and asserting that "the press is engaged in negating African excellence in order to gain advantage for the dying and endangered conservative liberal agenda".[19]

The research findings, when they were disclosed, added to the outrage. A young researcher, Claudia Braude, who had been assisted in her research by some of the commissioners, including Pityana, who were then presumably going to sit in judgment of the media, had come to the conclusion that the white controlled media in general were guilty of what she called "subliminal racism." In other words what they wrote, published and broadcast revealed an unconscious hostility towards black people.

That may well be the case: the subconscious mind is a tricky thing. But whether a young researcher with no clinical training and equipped only with the uncertain tools of textual analysis is able to diagnose it is at least questionable. What is certain is that her findings elicited a torrent of ridicule, particularly one relating to a picture of two birds, a pied crow and a marabou stork, sitting on the edge of a refuse bin in the Ugandan city of Kampala which was published in *The Star* of 25 June 1999. The caption made a light reference to the city refuse container as a "pavement cafe whose scraps keep birds like themselves on the wing". It was what journalists would call a "filler" picture, vaguely interesting but unimportant, used at the last minute to get an early page away on deadline. But Braude, with no journalistic experience, saw something much more sinister in it. Linking the picture arbitrarily to a headline in the previous day's paper about the decaying infrastructure and poor refuse disposal system of Johannesburg, she contended that use of the picture of the birds in Kampala was intended to portray an image of South Africa in a state of decline, and to remind readers of the havoc black leaders had created elsewhere in Africa.

"The caption suggests that the bird is enjoying the benefits of Johannesburg's decaying infrastructure under budgetary constraints," she wrote. "'City refuse container' becomes visual shorthand for an Africanized (central business district); and the marabou stork a shorthand for Africa within Johannesburg, for the perceived change from a first-world to a third-world city in which hawkers line the pavements referred to in the caption, their persons and refuse adding to the city's detritus."[20] In another finding, Braude found racial bias in reports about a warrant of arrest issued to the newly elected Premier of Gauteng province, Mbhazima Shilowa, in his capacity as a trustee of a community organization, which she said overshadowed the more important news of his election to lead the provincial administration. But such news is episodic. Had her research covered the period of *The Star's* collaboration in the destruction of Helena Dolny's career at the Land Bank, a sharply different picture might have appeared. Braude also criticized a headline in *The Star* stating that "Those who can least afford bags will go without", over a report on plans to ban the use of non-biodegradable plastic shopping bags in grocery stores. She said the headline implied that blacks, who would be less able to afford the bags, were less clean and hygienic than whites.[21]

In yet another finding, Braude detected subliminal racism in a report about the breakdown of management at hospitals and clinics in Gauteng province, particularly at the giant Chris Hani Baragwanath hospital outside Soweto. She contended that its publication implied that black leadership was incapable of running the nation. She did not contest the accuracy of the report. Nor did she say whether, if true, such information about the state of medical services in a country riven by the AIDS pandemic should be suppressed. Is that what is required to escape the charge of racism?

The second research task was undertaken by the Media Monitoring Project, an organization initially established to monitor media coverage of the first democratic election campaign in 1994 and a body with rather more experience and credibility than Claudia Braude. It adopted a different method of research aimed at trying to measure the extent to which racial stereotypes occur in the South African media. The researchers drew up a list of stereotypes that they believed reflected racism, then tested reports and articles to see whether they supported, challenged or were neutral to those stereotypes. Again it was a system of questionable accuracy for a number of reasons: it failed to distinguish between racist reporting and reporting on race, it failed to establish whether readers actually considered particular texts to be racist, and the study itself was too small and carried out over too short a time. In all 1 430 media items covering six weeks were analysed. While stressing that they were not trying to label the media or any part of it racist but merely to challenge journalists to be more sensitive, the researchers said they had found racial stereotyping was still common in the media and that the legacy of apartheid had "functioned to produce some harmful portrayals of black and white people". An elaborate ascertaining of the obvious, perhaps, but at least it was less infuriatingly subjective than the Braude report.

Then came the bombshell. The Human Rights Commission, anxious in the light of the press furore that journalists would not participate in the hearings that were to follow the research findings, issued subpoenas to force them to testify on pain of imprisonment. Convinced now that they were being summoned to appear before a Star Chamber to be tried on a legally vacuous charge of subliminal racism against which there could be no defence and in which the prosecutors would also be the judges, they dug in their heels – and then split. White editors announced that they would refuse to appear and would challenge the subpoenas in the High Court, even face imprisonment if necessary, while black editors for the most part said they would participate because they agreed the issue of racism in the media warranted a hearing. Racial polarization threatened to split the media community to a degree not experienced since the worst moments of the apartheid era. Significantly, the Media Monitoring Project also refused to participate in the hearings unless the subpoenas were withdrawn. Its chairman, William Bird, protested that the commission had violated the terms of his contract with them by using the project's research to implicate the media it had cited.

Then the commission relented. After a mixed delegation of white and black editors, then of proprietors, met with Pityana a compromise was struck: he would withdraw the subpoenas and the editors would agree to testify voluntarily. At the same time Pityana gave an assurance that no newspaper was on trial and that the hearings would not follow an adversarial line. The editors, only partially mollified, duly appeared. "Two weeks ago," said Phillip van Niekerk when he took the stand, "I faced a situation where I believed I was being dragged before a statutory inquisition, under pain of imprisonment, to answer unsubstantiated allegations about the content of my publication." He said he had agreed to appear because of the assurance that it would not be a trial, then added: "I am here today in a spirit of trust, and in the knowledge that we all carry the mental baggage of race around with us, whether we be editors or Human Rights commissioners."

Van Niekerk went on to challenge what he called "the unarticulated assumption" that all black South Africans were victims. Many, he noted, were now in positions of power and affluence. Beneath the cacophony of racial antagonism there were now new fault-lines in South African society – "between the rich and the poor, the powerful and the powerless, the landlords and the tenants. To be disadvantaged does not derive only from the accident of birth that gave some of us a little more or less of melanin." The question now, Van Niekerk said, was: "How do we prevent the powerful (of whatever colour) from stifling the voice of the powerless?" The answer, he insisted, was for the media to continue to play its watchdog role.

In the end the great inquisition turned out to be a pat-a-cake affair, with the commission producing a relatively mild report which contained no proven cases of racism in the media but broadly supported Braude's thesis of "subliminal racism". The report stated that the heart of the inquiry related to "the manner in which representations of crime, corruption and incompetence by black people in positions of authority are made", but it failed to demonstrate that these "representations" were caused by racial malice. Its worst effect was to sharpen racial divisions within South African journalism, but with time these have largely healed and in the final analysis the commission probably did more damage to its own credibility than to the media.

In an article on the commission's website after the hearings, Pityana proclaimed them a triumph. "They marked a victory for open and accountable democracy," he wrote. "The people of South Africa could see for themselves that powerful and usually faceless editors were brought into the open arena to explain and account." He then went on to reflect on why there had been such a furore. "Having been through the apartheid era controls and interference in the media," he said, "there is clearly fear (in some media circles) that in the democratic South Africa the government of the day may harbour some desire to control the media, and the commission process merely opens the door to that."

Quite so. Once bitten twice shy. If the hearings were an exercise in sensitivity training for the journalists, perhaps they were for the commissioners too. The fact is that media people have to be eternally vigilant to protect their institution, which is vital for democracy but exceedingly vulnerable. Its practitioners are neither powerful nor faceless, as Pityana suggests; they are reporters and commentators whose task is to be the eyes and ears of the public, whose only influence is their own credibility and who must keep watch on those who truly are powerful, the keepers of the national purse and the wielders of the national sword who can demolish them with one blow. The institution of a free press is something that survives in only a handful of countries around the world, and in the African continent hardly at all. It is as fragile as an eggshell and, like Humpty Dumpty, once broken is extremely difficult to put together again.

* * *

Of course nobody of any considerable experience of newsrooms can be under the illusion that governments pose the only threat to media freedom. More newspapers around the world have been closed by their own proprietors than by their governments. For media organizations are in the unique position of being both vital organs of the democratic system and commercial operations which must make a sufficient profit to keep their shareholders satisfied – functions that are not always congruent. Nor is the disposition of proprietors the only factor. Advertising agencies want clear target markets to sell to their clients, which makes them look askance at publications that cut across the racial spectrum or the boundaries of class and income.

On top of all this there are strong conformity pressures in any society, built particularly around its powerful establishment interests, that can make it difficult, even perilous, for a newspaper or broadcasting service to go contrary to what the American media critic Noam Chomsky has called "an elite consensus". The watchdog only barks, says Chomsky, when elite interests are threatened.[22] Not that proprietors and managers give orders to their editorial teams, as many people imagine. It is simply that the conformity pressures are part of the working milieu. Speaking of the US media, Chomsky says they "permit – indeed encourage – spirited debate, criticism, and dissent, as long as these remain faithfully within the system of presuppositions and principles that constitute an elite consensus, a system so powerful as to be internalized largely without awareness."[23]

Journalism's self-image is encapsulated in William Randolph Hearst's famous aphorism that the role of the media is "to comfort the afflicted and afflict the comfortable". But in fact it is a role performed all too seldom, for afflicting the comfortable can be a hazardous business. The *Rand Daily Mail* was closed at the height of its international fame and journalistic success, not by the authoritarian government but by its own proprietors, because what it reported and what it said about the apartheid society was at odds with Chomsky's elite consensus. It afflicted the comfortable. Advertisers disliked it because it appealed more to poor blacks than rich whites; its own board and management disliked it because it rocked the boat and made life difficult for them; and the business elite disliked it because its revelations of apartheid atrocities harmed the country's image and were therefore bad for business, it criticized their discriminatory practices, and it gave too much publicity to the newly legalized black trade union movement. Long after the *Mail's* closure the country's leading businessman, Harry Oppenheimer, whose giant Anglo American Corporation held a controlling interest in the company that owned the paper, stated publicly that the *Mail* had "failed" because it had fallen out with the business community.

All of this indicates that while there is good cause for concern and even indignation at the accusations being levelled at the media, there is also a strong case for introspective analysis within the media itself. There is much wrong with our industry, not least a hypersensitivity of its own that resents criticism to a degree that rivals that of the government. There is even a degree of the same paranoia in that some who are sympathetic to the industry are expected to withhold their criticism because it might encourage those who are hostile to it.

The plain fact is that, just as the South African media is freer now than at any other time in our history, so is our journalism now at its lowest ebb ever. There are many reasons for this, among them the deleterious effects of generations of inferior Bantu education. There is too, perhaps, as Chief Justice Arthur Chaskalson has suggested, "a temptation to see (in the sudden transition from authoritarian rule to an open society) an entitlement to do whatever we like, to place no limits on our behaviour."[24]

But the main problem stems from structural defects in the media industry inherited from the apartheid era. It is still a segmented industry for what was a segmented society, with Afrikaans newspapers for the Afrikaans community, English newspapers for the English community, and black newspapers for the black community. Readership patterns overlap these boundaries, especially in the case of the English newspapers, but a deeply conservative advertising industry still thinks in terms of racial target markets. The result is that, in a country with a low literacy rate compared with the developed world, there are too many low-circulation newspapers feeding off a relatively small advertising cake. The consequent shortage of revenue means newsrooms are understaffed and journalists are underpaid, which in turn means that on average they are young and inexperienced.

It is a problem being compounded in the immediate post-apartheid era by a huge demand for able, well-educated black people to fill key positions in the government service and across the board in the private sector. These jobs pay many times more than even the highest journalism salaries, with the result that newsrooms across the country have been depleted of their experienced black journalists, who were always too few in number anyway, while the need for affirmative action has seen a number of experienced white journalists take retrenchment and early retirement packages. These vacancies have been filled by a crop of young black journalists fresh out of school, many of them talented and eager but with very little experience of journalism or of the world around them. Many middle and top editing jobs, too, are going to journalists of limited experience – and those who shine are quickly snapped up by the higher-paying public and private sectors.

A juniorized news staff is prone to factual errors, bad news judgments, poor writing and a shaky hold on history. The small staffs are also rushed, reduced to press release transcription and assembly line editing. On the daily papers especially these young reporters have to produce four to five news reports a day, which means none can be thoroughly researched or backgrounded. They have to be hacked out as quickly as possible so that the reporter can get on to the next one. Too many are single-source reports based on a quick telephone interview. This is microwave journalism. Like fast food, it is easy to produce but lacks flavour and nourishment.

The competitive pressure for circulation in the segmented marketplace also results in stories being hyped to catch public attention. Once early in my career, when I was unexpectedly given the editorship of the small *Sunday Express* in Johannesburg, I asked Joel Mervis, then editor of the mass-circulation *Sunday Times* and the doyen of that particular craft, what his formula for success was. "You have to go over Niagara in a barrel every Sunday," he told me with a wry grin. Well, tabloid journalism is one thing; reporting and analysing the world on a daily basis, I would hope, requires a little more than repeatedly astonishing the public with some new sensation. Yet with a few honourable exceptions the South African media, dailies as well as weeklies, are locked into just that.

At a time when the new Constitution has given them the freedom to report anything they wish, and the Promotion of Access to Information Act invites them to probe, they are heavily into a mono-diet of crime and scandal. Now there is nothing wrong with that in principle. It is important that the public should know about the country's high crime rate, and exposing corruption is a basic media function. But what is lacking is a searching examination of what lies behind the crime rate. How did the big international crime syndicates manage to move into the country after the 1994 transition, who are they and how do they operate? Why has the tough and crudely efficient police force of the apartheid era suddenly lost its efficacy? What are they teaching in the police colleges to remedy the situation? The truth is reporters are not getting beyond their newsrooms, not moving beyond the official sources in their search for stories. News to most is just what comes to them in handouts, official statements and generic news agency reports.

As for the reporting on corruption, as Steven Friedman, a former journalist who now heads the Centre for Policy Studies in Johannesburg, points out, this is "often based on untested information and riddled with unresearched hyperbole." And, he adds, "while parading as the outcome of exhaustive investigation, it is often the result of the ability to write down the claims of members of the bureaucracy dissatisfied with other members."[25] This is not new, of course: it is the continuation of a malaise that began during the apartheid era, as the dirty-tricksters of that era have recently reminded us. Two members of the Strategic Communications arm of the old State Security Council, Craig Williamson and Paul Erasmus, spoke openly before the Truth and Reconciliation Commission about how they had planted stories in *The Star*, the *Weekly Mail* and *The Citizen* smearing opponents of the apartheid regime.

Williamson recounted how Stratcom, as the dirty-tricks unit was called, planted a story in *The Star* claiming that Joe Slovo, leader of the South African Communist Party at the time, had assassinated his wife, Ruth First, because of ideological differences between them. That by the very organization which had itself killed First with a letter-bomb sent to her in Maputo. A nod, a wink and a hint from a single source who should by definition have been suspect, and this appalling libel was in the paper. What a bitter irony, too, that Slovo's second wife, Helena Dolny, should have become the victim of another venomous leak to the same newspaper in the post-apartheid era.

Erasmus in turn boasted of how he embarrassed the Democratic Party in 1990 by getting *The Star* to publish a story revealing that David Dalling, then one of its MPs, had sent a cheque to the ANC paying his wife Zelda's membership fee. What happened is that Stratcom, which routinely intercepted letters to the recently unbanned ANC's

94

headquarters in Johannesburg, got hold of one containing the cheque and a note from Dalling to Jesse Duarte, who then worked in the ANC president's office. Dalling wrote his name clearly at the end of the note, but the cheque bore an illegible signature. So Erasmus made a photocopy of the cheque, with Dalling's legible name from the note superimposed on it. He also wrote a letter on a bank's letterhead purporting to come from "a concerned and despairing South African working in the bank who feels this should be exposed".

That is about as simple and crude a forgery as it is possible to imagine, but it was enough to entrap an unquestioning reporter and slip past all the paper's editing checkpoints. The reporter never called Dalling, who would have been able to point out that it was not his signature on the cheque. He never called the bank, which would have been able to point out that it had not processed the cheque and that no one there had ever written such a letter. He did not call Jesse Duarte, who would have transferred him to the ANC treasurer, Sheila Weinberg, who would have told him that the cheque had not yet been presented to the bank and was still in the cash box on her desk. Nor did the reporter, or for that matter the copy editor who handled the story and placed it on page one of the newspaper, notice that the cheque had not been stamped by the bank. The paper simply published the single-source, unchecked story – together with the photocopy of the forged, unstamped cheque.

Had any of those checks been made, the reporter would quickly have become aware of the deception and been able to start an inquiry that would have led him to a much better story about what his informant was really up to. It says something about our journalism that the Stratcom dirty-tricks team apparently had no fear of such an inquiry being made and perhaps leading to their exposure.

Erasmus talked, too, of the "mirror effect" achieved by planting stories in British newspapers – particularly right-wing papers such as the *Daily Express* and Rupert Murdoch's *The Times* and *Sunday Times*, which were only too eager to accept anti-ANC material – and having these played back in the South African media. This tells us something, of course, about how standards have declined in the British press as well, under the pressures of intensified profiteering. But it also reflects a tendency by the South African press to lift material from overseas newspapers and republish it here without checking its accuracy.

Nor is it only stories from abroad that are republished in this unquestioning way. Items from local papers are also given a quickie lift and instant follow-up treatment. A reporter is handed a cutting from a rival newspaper; he phones someone to get a reaction to the reported events, and uses this to slap a new lead on a story that is essentially a rehash of the rival paper's. There is no attempt to check the accuracy of the original. Microwave journalism again.

I had a bizarre experience of this soon after my appointment as editor of SABC Television News in June 1997. *The Star* published a report of the appointment that included a paragraph stating that since I was a print journalist who knew nothing about television I had been sent to Australia to be given a crash course in the subject at the Australian Broadcasting Corporation. I sat bemused in my Johannesburg office reading that I was apparently in Sydney at that moment. The reporter had not troubled to telephone my office, or my home, or speak to any other informed source, including my son Michael who was right there in the same newsroom, to check on my true whereabouts. Reaction stories then began appearing in some other newspapers, again without any contact with me to check whether the original was true. Some were simply "lifts", reporting that *The Star* had reported that I had been sent to Australia. I found it a disconcerting experience to appear in the news like this, stay there for some days, then disappear again without a single reporter ever getting in touch with me. I can only presume that a rumour circulated through the corridors of the SABC, which is notoriously prone to such mongering, and that the reporter picked it up and published it on the strength of a single source, after which it was repeated by others as assumed fact.

The structural weaknesses that have given rise to this kind of single-source reporting do more than expose the media to exploitation by dirty-tricks hackers and vengeance-seekers. They go to the heart of why there is so much public and official discontent with the media at the moment. Certainly all governments want the media to highlight the good things they do, and grow resentful when they face critical scrutiny. Ours is no exception. But there is something deeper to their dissatisfaction that is not being articulated, possibly because the people concerned cannot quite put their fingers on what it is that they find unsatisfactory. I suggest it is an absence of context. We are living in one of the most fundamentally transforming societies in modern times, a hugely exciting process of transition, yet our newspapers fail to capture the essence of what is happening. They fix instead on the transient events of the day, superficial snapshots of accidents, crimes, and the public statements and squabbles of public figures as they occur in a passing blur that tells the public nothing of the deeper undercurrents that are reshaping our society.

Bob Haiman, former director of the Poynter Institute for Media Studies in Florida, who paid several visits to South Africa, called this "stenographic reporting". Don Fry, the best journalism trainer to visit our shores, talks of "episodic reporting". Joseph Lelyveld, then executive editor of *The New York Times* who had spent two terms here as a foreign correspondent and held our journalism in high esteem over many years, chided us on a return visit to South Africa in 1995 for failing to mirror what was happening in our exciting society. "You are sitting on one of the truly great stories of our time," he said in a keynote address to a press freedom conference, but asked what we were doing with it. After only a few days in the country Lelyveld listed a whole diary of great potential stories, inquiring as he did so whether our newspapers were working on any of them. "Or is news just what comes to you, what happens in all the old obvious places?" he asked knowingly.

Episodic reporting. Stenographic reporting. Microwave journalism. Whatever you call it, that is our malaise. If we are going to change it, then we must look not only to the training of individual journalists but to fundamental changes in the structure and culture of our newsrooms, to the inculcation of a new value system that is prepared to make long-term investments in quality journalism instead of the preoccupation with cost-cutting and short-term profit margins, which is the culture of the moment. But even as I write this the global recession and the decline of South Africa's currency, which affects the foreign investors in our media particularly, are resulting in more cost-cutting, staff retrenchments and the scrapping of training schemes. Like so much else in South Africa the successful transformation and improvement of our media is ultimately going to depend on the successful growth of the economy as a whole.

CHAPTER SIX

A PRAGUE SPRING

As an African I don't see my village in the global village.
Our mission at the SABC is to put our village in
the global village.
— ZWELAKHE SISULU, FIRST BLACK CEO OF THE SABC

Transforming the SABC has been one of the most challenging, and frustrating, tasks in the new South Africa. For 45 years this giant broadcasting monopoly dominated the airwaves as an explicit and unashamed propaganda machine, controlled and directed by the head of the Broederbond secret society, Piet Meyer, who presided for most of that time as chairman of the corporation's Board of Directors. Meyer, together with Hendrik Verwoerd, Nico Diederichs and other founding fathers of the apartheid ideology, had undergone his graduate studies in Germany during the Third Reich, from which he returned as one of the new Afrikaner movement's more didactic philosophers. Just how deeply this German experience influenced Meyer is evinced by the fact that he named his son Izan, which is Nazi spelled backwards. He in turn left an equally deep imprint on the broadcasting corporation which named its headquarters office tower in Johannesburg's Auckland Park after him. The building was in itself a soaring architectural extension of his personality, dominating the city's western skyline and on a clear day commanding a view from its 30th-floor Panorama Room of the Voortrekker Monument 50 km away on a hilltop outside Pretoria. It was known to cynics on the staff at the time as the *breintoring*, or brain-tower, where the ideological guidelines were laid down that all had to follow with absolute obedience.

At the other extreme the building also mirrored the bunker mentality of Afrikaner Nationalism. All six floors of its radio broadcasting facilities – studios, editing rooms, tape libraries, cafeterias – were built completely underground as a protection against possible revolutionary attack. Even the stairways leading into this broadcasting catacomb are narrow, and wind down in a clockwise spiral to make it more difficult for an assault force (unless they happen to be left-handed) to charge in with automatic weapons in a firing position. There are also recesses in the underground passageways where defenders can take shelter.

Meyer was the quintessential Afrikaner Nationalist ideologue, authoritarian, intellectually arrogant, pontifical and puritanical. "To Afrikanerdom," he wrote not long after his return from Germany, "belong only those who, by virtue of blood, soil, culture, tradition, belief, calling, form an organic unitary society. This nation is by nature an organic wearer of authority with the patriarchal leader as chief bearer of authority of the nation, and with the members of the nation as active and cooperative workers. The national Afrikaner state of the future is therefore the political embodiment and ordering of the whole of Afrikanerdom as an organic articulation of authority."[1]

Meyer's personality permeated the organization he commanded. There was no pretence of objective journalism. Having arrived at the truth for the ordering of human society, not just for South Africa but for the world, Meyer and his co-directors countenanced no such thing as balanced reporting or presenting the other side of the story. The "cooperative workers" of the SABC had to articulate the authority of that national truth. Dissenting voices, my own among them, were on an extensive blacklist of people banned from the air. Pat-a-cake interviews with cabinet ministers were de rigueur. Whenever the print media published a major expose of an apartheid atrocity or other government scandal, the SABC's role was to lead off with an official denunciation of the newspaper concerned and a denial of its disclosures. No attempt at an independent verification of the allegations was made. The facts of Black Consciousness leader Steve Biko's murder in detention in 1977 and of South Africa's military invasion of Angola were never broadcast. Instead there was constant, heavy-handed propaganda spearheaded by what the SABC called its "editorial of the air" – a Spenglerian radio lecture on the decadence of liberalism and the decline of the West, delivered by a Lord Haw Haw figure with a whining voice, named Alexander Steward.

There was an almost Taliban-like fear of the cultural as well as political influences of the West infecting the youth of South Africa. Films, books and magazines were strictly censored, and foreign publications such as *Playboy* and *Penthouse* were banned with a pathological vigour. When John Lennon wisecracked that the Beatles were more popular than Jesus Christ, the SABC ordered that their music should never be broadcast again. Not only were their songs banned but, as I found out later when I joined the corporation, the records themselves were gouged to ensure that no one could play them clandestinely or by mistake.

Most striking of all, this fear of outside influences and of a swamping of Afrikaans culture with an influx of English programming from abroad resulted in the SABC preventing the introduction of television in South Africa until 1976. We were the last industrialized country in the world to get TV. The minister in charge of broadcasting for the first two decades of National Party rule was the most right-wing member of the Cabinet, Albert Hertzog, son of the founder of the National Party, Barry Hertzog, and a man who took his father's relatively pragmatic ethno-nationalist ideas to extremes. Albert Hertzog, a small, wiry, goatee-bearded man with a shrill voice who later broke with the NP to form the extreme right-wing Herstigte Nasionale Party[2], simply said No. No TV. It's decadent. It's corrosive. It's wicked. It's uninteresting. It's just a small bioscope. No. And that was that until well after his departure.

Not until Meyer and his fellow directors of the SABC were satisfied that they could control the feared medium – indeed more than that, until they knew they could turn it to their powerful political advantage – did they introduce it. So that when television came at last to South Africa it did so with the most advanced technology of the time and an impact that was all the greater because of the long delay. It became the apartheid system's most powerful propaganda weapon.

Not surprisingly, as the Negotiating Council got under way at the World Trade Centre near Johannesburg Airport in May 1992, the ANC and other anti-apartheid parties were unwilling to contemplate a democratic election campaign with this powerful propaganda tool still in the hands of the National Party. In a country where three-quarters of the population had never participated in a democratic election before and half of them were functionally illiterate, SABC radio in particular, with its 15 million listeners a day, was going to be crucially important. The corporation would have to be changed – radically and fast.

That in turn led to a power struggle which became a subject for negotiation at the council and in many ways mirrored the struggle for control of the country itself that was taking place there. As Tamela Hultman, a highly respected American journalist and publisher with many years experience covering Africa, was to write in an academic thesis: "The battle for control of the SABC was waged with as much drama and brinkmanship as the struggle to steer South Africa towards elections. In many ways the SABC symbolized what the National Party had built and what it stood to lose."[3]

Meantime, having spent the years since my dismissal as editor of the *Rand Daily Mail* reporting on South Africa for *The Washington Post*, *The Observer* in Britain and Holland's *NRC Handelsblad*, I decided, as I watched the ANC and other exiles return home, that it was time for this "internal exile", as I dubbed myself, to return as well. I felt a need to become more directly involved in the transformation of my country which I had analysed and written about and advocated and longed to see take place for so many years. So realizing that journalism itself would face a crisis of transition, I raised funding and in June 1992 founded the Institute for the Advancement of Journalism (IAJ) in association with the University of the Witwatersrand in Johannesburg – an organization devoted to trying to uplift journalistic standards by giving short, intensive mid-career courses and, anticipating affirmative action, trying to prepare black journalists in particular to move into more senior editorial positions.

The huge challenge of how to transform the SABC became an early concern of those of us working at the IAJ. The SABC was not only the state broadcaster, it was also the broadcast licensing authority, and except for a few small radio stations operating in apartheid's tribal bantustans had preserved its own monopoly position. The result was that there were almost no journalists or media administrators in the country with broadcasting experience other than those who had been trained by the seriously tainted SABC.

With funding from the Australian labour organization, Apheda, we invited a group of two dozen interested people whom we thought might be potential members of a new SABC Board of Directors to participate in a week-long workshop together with some top overseas broadcasters – Peter Manning, head of Current Affairs at the Australian Broadcasting Corporation; Sam Younger, Controller of BBC Radio's World Service; and South African-born David Fanning, producer of the American public television series "Frontline". It was a fascinating and instructive week, but the most important outcome was a commitment by the ABC to send a team of journalism trainers to the IAJ over the next several years to run courses for both SABC staffers and print journalists who would seek jobs at the public broadcaster. At the same time the Canadian Broadcasting Corporation, the BBC and the Thompson Foundation in Cardiff also set up training courses at the SABC. It amounted to a major commitment by foreign broadcasters to help with the crucial task of transforming South Africa's delinquent public broadcaster.

Choosing a new Board of Directors became an elaborate operation. After weeks of tough negotiating between the government and the ANC, Ismael Mohamed and Piet Schabort, two Supreme Court judges known to support the ANC and NP respectively and who were already joint chairmen of the Negotiating Council itself, were asked to be joint chairmen of an eight-person selection panel as well. The group consisted of five blacks and three whites, seven men and a woman. Public bodies were invited to nominate candidates, and more than 500 people from all walks of life were nominated, of whom 45 were short-listed.

The panel began interviewing the short-listed candidates in May 1993. It was a great public circus. The interviews were televised live as the candidates appeared one by one in a cavernous hall at the World Trade Centre to be seated alone in a hard-backed chair in the middle of the room, looking for all the world like prisoners at the bar as they faced the legal eagles lined up on a stage before them. They had to make presentations and face cross-examination by the lawyers. There was a packed audience behind them in the hall and millions more watching on their TV screens at home: the audience ratings for the show, which lasted two weeks, were among the highest the SABC had ever recorded. As Hultman noted, this extraordinary public interest stemmed from the fact that the SABC had acquired an almost iconographic significance in this time of rapid social change, becoming a repository for both the fears and hopes of an uncertain era. "It has long been an institution that anti-government South Africans loved to hate," she wrote, "and because it penetrates into homes and cars and offices it has been despised with an intensity born of intimacy. As the first major organization to undertake top-to-bottom transformation, it has been scrutinized with a voyeuristic fascination."[4]

This voyeurism reached its apex with the public cross-examination of old regime candidates. It was the first time any of the perpetrators of apartheid were called upon to publicly acknowledge their complicity in the policy. Mohamed, an Indian who had been on the wrong side of apartheid, had the time of his life. He had been a brilliant civil rights lawyer, defending countless anti-apartheid activists charged under the security laws, and now in the last-gasp days of the old regime he had been appointed the country's first black judge. When the new government came to power it made him Chief Justice, but sadly he died of cancer soon afterwards. But now, in this hall, he was at his peak, interrogating those who had been associated with the SABC during the apartheid years with the relish of an avenger. The crowds at home loved it. Years of anger at the corporation's blatant bias and lofty arrogance found a cathartic release as Mohamed grilled the old guard candidates on their views about balance and fairness and why they had allowed the perversion to continue for so long – all of it going out on the SABC's own airwaves even as the National Party government was still in power. For the masses outside, it was a sweet foretaste of changes to come.

The SABC's chief executive, Wynand Harmse, at first denied that the corporation had ever suppressed news, but had to backtrack when Mohamed recalled him for further questioning. In the interim the panel had been given a policy document that Harmse had issued in 1989 instructing staff that extra-parliamentary political activity should be silenced. But the most delicious moments came during the testimony of the retiring chairman of the board, Christo Viljoen. When Viljoen insisted that SABC coverage had always been "balanced, objective and fair", excluding only extra-parliamentary, revolutionary views, Mohamed challenged him.

MOHAMED: Extra-parliamentary politics included politics that were perfectly legal, did they not?

VILJOEN: Well, some were at that stage excluded.

MOHAMED: Well, what other politics could black people indulge in other than extra-parliamentary politics?

VILJOEN: I'm not a political expert, sir.

MOHAMED: What other politics could a black person indulge in if he hasn't got the right to vote in Parliament, but to do it outside Parliament? (silence) You have no answer?

VILJOEN: No, I have no answer.

MOHAMED: Well, then, isn't it entirely arbitrary to say that the politics of the majority will not be given any time or airing on the SABC? Is that not an entirely white perception?

VILJOEN: That could be said, yes.

MAHOMED: Don't you think that was an error in news policy?

VILJOEN: In retrospect, yes.

MOHAMED: And don't you think, therefore, that the perceptions that yours was a biased policy are perfectly justified and legitimate in retrospect?

VILJOEN: During the 1980s, yes sir.[5]

Eventually the panel named a 25-member Board, consisting of 12 Africans, ten whites, two Coloureds and one Indian. Eight members were women. The chairman was a highly respected black author and university professor, Njabulo Ndebele, with Ivy Matsepe-Casaburri, a champion of rural women's causes with a PhD from Rutgers University in New Jersey, as his deputy. Seldom can the governing board of any media organization anywhere in the world have been chosen so publicly and so democratically.

Yet President de Klerk refused to accept it. To the dismay of everyone who had been associated with the process, De Klerk rejected Ndebele as chairman on the ground that he could not speak Afrikaans. Given that De Klerk himself does not speak any of the country's African languages, it was a spurious complaint indeed.[6] De Klerk also vetoed seven other members of the selection panel's choice, myself among them, claiming the group as a whole was loaded in favour of the ANC. He replaced them with seven others who had been bypassed by the panel, and appointed the former Leader of the Opposition in Parliament, Professor Frederik van Zyl Slabbert, as chairman. It was a blatant violation of the process agreed to by the Negotiating Council, but De Klerk was still the President and he had the constitutional, if not the moral, authority to do this. The ANC exploded with indignation but could do nothing about it.

I felt outraged. Such a violation of trust by the President, after such a remarkably open and democratic process, seemed an appalling way to begin the transition to a new South Africa. I felt the board named by De Klerk should refuse to take office and demand that the agreed selection process be honoured. But they decided not to. Time was running out and they felt the task of restructuring the SABC should not be delayed.

That was not the end of the matter, however. Two of De Klerk's appointees, including Franklin Sonn who later became South African Ambassador to the United States, refused to accept their appointments but were persuaded by other members to serve provisionally. Slabbert issued a statement declining the chair, but in a four-hour crisis meeting on 3 June was persuaded to accept for two months. As Mandela and De Klerk hurled angry exchanges at each other and protesters demonstrated outside the SABC building, Slabbert called an emergency board meeting on 24 July at which Fatima Meer, a feisty sociologist and long-time political activist, attacked him, saying it was unacceptable at this time of change for control of the pivotally important SABC to move from one white Afrikaner male to another. It was an unfair attack, since Slabbert had an impeccable anti-apartheid record and had played an important role initiating dialogue between influential Afrikaners and ANC exiles during the 1980s, and he was deeply offended. Slabbert promptly resigned from the board, leaving Matsepe-Casaburri to take over the chairmanship.

Slabbert later accused Fatima Meer, Raymond Louw and myself of holding secret meetings at which we plotted to get rid of him.[7] This is completely untrue. No such meetings or discussions of any kind on the subject between any of us ever took place. While I believed at the time, and still do, that it was an error of judgment on Slabbert's part not to have refused to accept the irregular appointment outright, I did not meet with anyone or plot anything about it and I know that Raymond Louw did not either.

As the new board settled in to its task there began an intense clash of cultures, for the old management and staff were still in place. There had been some hasty changes in the last few years as the corporation tried to change its face, to try as the De Klerk government itself was trying to reform the system in an effort to salvage as much of its essential character as possible. "I must emphasize," said Johan Pretorius, head of television news at the time and Broederbond custodian of the corporation's newsroom values, "that nothing will be turned upside down and changed drastically." A few new black appointments were made, but it remained an Afrikaner citadel: all 27 senior managers were men, all but one were white and 22 were Afrikaners. Now a black woman was in charge, and soon a dynamic black man with long struggle credentials moved in as chief executive officer. Zwelakhe Sisulu was 45 when he took over. He was the youngest son of Walter and Albertina Sisulu, two of the most revered figures in the ANC after Nelson Mandela with whom Walter had shared 25 years in prison. Zwelakhe Sisulu had been trained on the *Rand Daily Mail* and gone on to be founding editor of the weekly *New Nation*, to be awarded a Nieman Fellowship at Harvard University, to win its Louis Lyons Award for courageous journalism, and to found the Media Workers Association, a trade union for black journalists and other workers in the media. Most striking of all, he had been harassed and banned by the apartheid regime; the security police had dragged him from his home in the middle of the night and held him in solitary confinement and without trial for more than two years. Now his appointment thrust him into a position of awesome responsibility. As a relatively young man with no management experience beyond editing the small weekly *New Nation*, he had to oversee the operations of three multilingual TV channels, 25 radio stations broadcasting in 11 languages, a signal distribution company, a private subscription service and a staff of 5 000 people. It was like the skipper of a tugboat taking over an aircraft carrier.

More than 15 million people listened to the radio stations each day, and 8 million watched the TV channels. All that Sisulu had not only to manage but to transform, the first major national institution to undertake radical change, and to do so with the entire nation watching his every move. Given his close ANC connections, his appointment ignited black expectations: with one of their own taking over the mighty SABC surely dramatic changes would come, and come quickly. It also ignited Afrikaner fears. As Hultman noted, from then on those who backed the old order were prone to see ideological bias behind every change that was made, while those who had struggled and sacrificed for political change were impatient for discernible differences in programming, staffing and operational procedures.[8]

Other key changes were made too. Govin Reddy, another man with good struggle credentials who had been banned and had gone into exile, where he became deputy editor-in-chief of the Zimbabwe Broadcasting Corporation and then a senior executive of a Third World news agency, Inter-Press Services, was appointed Head of Radio at an early stage. Later Jill Chisholm, a former *Rand Daily Mail* political correspondent and the first woman in South Africa's parliamentary press gallery, became Head of Television. She, too, had left the country and acquired two decades of experience in television abroad, much of it as a senior executive with Britain's ITN and later with a division of Digital, the world's second-largest computer company.

The territory on which the struggle was waged was cultural as much as political. As Hultman notes, what was at stake was not just a political platform for the election but a cultural identity. The SABC, with its extensive reach across the length and breadth of the country, especially into the remote farming areas which constituted the Afrikaner heartland where there were no newspapers and few other sources of entertainment or social interaction, was a link that bonded the *volk* together and sustained their culture. "Through music and poetry and plays and comedies as well as through news and information, SABC radio and television reinforced Afrikaans as a medium of communication and Afrikaners as a community."[9] Now here was the new hierarchy at the SABC planning to bring Sisulu's African village more strongly into the picture, increasing the range and content of African programming and reducing the Afrikaans language from its position of dominance to a status alongside the nine African languages. Although all 11 official languages were supposed to have equal status, in practice English, as the language of business and politics and the urban lingua franca, replaced Afrikaans as the dominant language both on air and in the administration of the SABC. Afrikaners were pained and angered by this. Pieter Aucamp, secretary of the right-wing *Volksfront*, echoed the sentiments of many when he declared that "the storm over Afrikaans, especially by the SABC, shows clearly the concern among Afrikaners over the future not only of their language but also their whole culture."[10]

Just how strongly these feelings ran was illustrated by one Afrikaner who became so angry as he sat watching television in his home one night that he pulled out a pistol and fired a shot through the screen of his TV set, then packed it up and mailed it to Sisulu. The startled CEO took due note of the man's reaction and carefully placed the shattered set in a display cabinet in his office where it remained as a piece of art deco sculpture throughout his tenure. "I decided to keep it," he told me, "as a reminder of the explosive emotions we are dealing with in this country."

Nor was it only Afrikaners who were upset by the changes. As more black voices went on air to give more local colour and authenticity to the English-language radio broadcasts, there were cries of anger at the thick African accents and sometimes mangled grammar. What had become of the purity of Received English? What was happening to standards? With a primness and pedantic arrogance born of their frustration at being the largest, richest community of English-speakers in the world who have never held political power and have always had to knuckle under to those they considered less able than themselves, some members of the English South African community went into a paroxysm of rage at the SABC over the presumed abuse of their language that gave a glimpse into their own thinly veiled racism. What they overlooked was that if English were to be allocated air time proportionate to the size of the English-speaking population, it would come only seventh on the list. Its prime position derives from the fact that it is everybody's *second* language, and its usage reflects this fact.

These multi-fronted battles raged inside and outside the SABC. There were protest demonstrations by Afrikaner groups demanding a better deal for their language, and by black groups demanding more African programming. There were letters, scores of them, to the newspapers from the outraged English listeners. Pressure groups bombarded the board and the management with demands and petitions, some defending Afrikaans, some wanting more local content, yet others wanting deregulation and downsizing of the SABC so that private enterprise could play a bigger role in broadcasting. Old-guard staffers watched affirmative action appointments and worried about losing their jobs; ambitious newcomers complained that the promotion of blacks was too slow and that too many of the old guard were still in gatekeeper positions. Rumours ran rife, and hardly a day passed without the SABC featuring on the front pages of the newspapers.

It was a stormy time but gradually things settled down. With history and credibility on their side the newcomers won out and the hard core of old-guard managers left. Those who remained fell into line, just as they were doing in the civil service generally. The new board settled into the task of mapping out a new role for the corporation as a public broadcaster. Ivy Matsepe-Casaburri, who came to the job knowing nothing about broadcasting or the media in general, threw herself into a learning curve that soon had her coming to grips with the complexities of the vast and hitherto opaque corporation; and the editorial teams began preparing for the awesome task of covering the country's first democratic election. With all the world watching they did a remarkably good job. The coverage was comprehensive and fair, and as the only institution in the country with the facilities to do so the corporation managed to cope with the 3 000 foreign journalists who descended on South Africa for the election. More than 1 500 members of the new polyglot SABC staff played a direct role in the election coverage. For most it was something of a bonding experience, and for the corporation itself the beginning of a Prague spring.

In due time, as Mandela took over and some members of the SABC board were assigned to ambassadorships and other key roles in the public and private sectors, the new President filled the vacancies from De Klerk's veto list. And so I joined the board in 1995, and for the next four years had an insider's view of the challenging, exciting, tumultuous, ego-ridden, power-laden, ambition-driven, racially-stressed, politically-charged transformation of this huge state-owned media corporation – a microcosm, if you will, of the transformation of the country as a whole. It was a fascinating experience, and in the end a little saddening.

* * *

Part-way through that four-year period Sisulu decided the television newsroom wasn't dynamic enough. He had nostalgic recollections of the energy and drive of the *Rand Daily Mail* newsroom while he was undergoing his training there, and was also intrigued by some of the training methods we were using at the Institute for the Advancement of Journalism. He asked me if I would consider leaving the board to take charge of the TV newsroom for a time and try to introduce some of those features there. After much discussion and hesitation, with both of us aware that the appointment of an ageing white male to such a high-profile position would be controversial – particularly since it would involve replacing a highly respected black journalist, Joe Thloloe, who happened also to be a friend of ours – it was agreed that I should be seconded from the IAJ to do the job for one year, and in that time help develop a new team of young black newsroom executives to take over when I left. It was a tough assignment, made tougher by the fact that Sisulu dithered over the announcement so that news of it leaked out in the newspapers, to Thloloe's embarrassment and justifiable outrage. It was made even more difficult by the fact that I took over just as a board decision to retrench 1 400 of the corporation's 4 500 employees was being implemented – the third wave of staff cuts in six years that added mightily to the general atmosphere of uncertainty, insecurity and cynicism.

These problems notwithstanding, that year as a change agent was, I think, successful. The newsroom was an unwieldy conglomerate of reporters serving different bulletin desks which had to cope with a requirement that SABC-TV broadcast the news in all 11 of the country's official languages over three channels: eight of them nationally from the headquarters station in Johannesburg, and three from regional studios in the provinces. I know of no other television broadcaster in the world that attempts anything remotely like this. The multilingual reporting and translation requirements made it a nightmare. Practical difficulties aside, there was also the risk that different language groups, meaning racial and ethnic groups, would get different slants on the news – an unacceptable carry-over from the apartheid era.

I tried to simplify the process by insisting that there should be a single news bulletin delivered in the various languages. The main changes I made were aimed at introducing what I called a "culture of coaching" in the newsroom, which involved experienced people helping to train the journalists in an ongoing way as part of the daily work process. I appointed one of the corporation's brightest young journalists, Gary Alfonso, who had been seconded to the training division, to head a new central news desk that would implement the coaching process. I vacated the palatial editor's office on an upstairs floor and moved into a glass booth in the newsroom where I could be constantly among the staff and join in the coaching process myself. I found the newsroom slow, lethargic and unimaginative. As Jacques Pauw, a fine investigative reporter who had worked for the feisty Afrikaans weekly *Vrye Weekblad* and was one of the first of the new recruits, warned me soon after my arrival, the SABC had never had a culture of journalism. "It's a place where news stories are followed, never broken," he said. To my astonishment I found that the news diary for the evening bulletin was drawn up in mid-afternoon the day before, mainly on the basis of the South African Press Association's laundry list of upcoming events. It was a surefire formula for routine episodic reporting with no room for initiative or getting at the deeper trend of events in a rapidly changing society. So I concentrated on trying to energize the staff, emphasizing the importance of getting to the scene of the action quickly and getting the news on air fast even if this meant using voice-only reports over cellphones from remote regions. There was simply not enough modern transmission equipment. The news conferences became brain-storming sessions on story ideas with the whole staff encouraged to participate. Results were analysed and critiqued, we talked about the critical issues affecting politics, the economy and the society and how to find stories that would illuminate these issues for the public. We introduced a weekly programme called "Special Assignment", featuring the old *Vrye Weekblad* investigative team of Max du Preez and Jacques Pauw; and we introduced a flagship News Hour once a week with the anchors conducting tough, live interviews in the studio. It worked. Morale and energy levels rose and the bulletins improved.

It must be said that, contrary to a widely held belief outside the corporation particularly among critical whites, throughout my four years at the SABC, as a board member and as editor in charge of television news, I was never once subjected to any attempt by any member of the government to interfere with the editorial independence of the corporation. There were complaints certainly – most in fact from the New National Party which was clearly feeling the pain of losing its loyal propagandist – but that is true of all media organizations everywhere and it is the democratic right of everyone, governments included, to complain and to criticize. Freedom of expression is not a one-way street. But of interference, there was none. Whether there were attempts to pressurize the corporation that were blocked by Sisulu, I do not know. He did not tell me of any, and I did not ask.

On one occasion when the government formally requested a regular television time slot to explain its policies to the public, Sisulu firmly rejected the request on the grounds that this was not the public broadcaster's role.

Only once did I have a moment of anxiety. Not long after I moved in to the newsroom, Sisulu told me that Deputy President Thabo Mbeki's two closest aides, his media liaison officer, Thami Ntenteni, and a Deputy Minister in his office, Essop Pahad, wanted to speak to us about the television news coverage. We flew to Cape Town for what was an abrasive meeting. The two aides launched into an harangue of generalized complaints with no specific cases to which one could respond. The gist of it was that they believed the news was negative and unfairly critical of the government, but cited no examples to substantiate their case. Their complaint was groundless and I told them so in no uncertain terms, adding that if they had specific complaints I would deal with them but that I could not respond to broad generalizations. There were no threats and no demands, but I found the summons and the encounter disturbing. As we left Tuynhuys I told Sisulu so. "What do we do now?" I asked him. He grinned. "We go back and carry on doing what we have been doing," he replied.

I cannot vouch for what has happened since my departure, when at times the news bulletins are almost as fawning in their coverage of senior ANC leaders as the old SABC was of the apartheid ministers, but my strong suspicion is that as rival factions jockey for power within the corporation they are trying to ingratiate themselves with the ruling elite. They are delivering what they think the government wants rather than what they are being told to do.

The SABC's main problems in fact stemmed not from outside but internally, and not from conflicts between old and new guard, but increasingly from a growing, deadly rivalry between leading newcomers. While I relished the challenge of the job and delighted in the enthusiastic response of the staff, as the months passed I became aware of burning ambitions among some of the senior black journalists around me who knew my appointment was temporary and that soon one of them would succeed me. Cliques began forming and surreptitious lobbying of the corporate hierarchy began.

In drafting his transformation plans Sisulu had made use of the media consultants, McKinsey and Company. With digital technology looming they had recommended a merging of radio and television news staffs, then being undertaken by both the BBC and the Australian Broadcasting Corporation, as a major cost-saving strategy. Sisulu asked me if I would take over as editor-in-chief of the joint operation, with separate television and radio editors operating under me. I had many reservations: I had doubts about the wisdom of the merger given the SABC's onerous commitment to broadcast in 11 languages; about the job itself which would make me more of an administrator than a newsroom energizer which is what I felt I did best and enjoyed most; and, above all, my wife was suffering from terminal cancer and I did not want to embark on a major new commitment. We had many discussions around this but again, as with my initial appointment, Sisulu stalled and remained indecisive, never in fact coming to a decision. Later I realised he was under immense pressure from the ambitious cliques waiting for my departure.

Then things began to fall apart.

* * *

Looking back, it is clear that the root cause of the trouble lay in the hybrid nature of the SABC. It is a public broadcaster with a strong mandate to serve the public interest – as distinct from the government interest – across a wide range of commitments, yet to raise the revenue to perform that service it has to compete in the commercial marketplace. The two are incompatible. Public service broadcasting is expensive and generates no revenue, while commercial broadcasting requires "dumbing down" to pander to popular tastes and win mass audiences for advertisers. They require diametrically different programming and operating cultures, and the SABC's attempts to do both has resulted in ongoing tensions and confusion. It would do so in any situation, and indeed public broadcasters in other parts of the world have experienced the same problems, but superimposed on the tensions of racial and political transformation in South Africa the stresses became extreme.

The old SABC had operated in a much easier environment, with no competition and a limited public broadcasting mandate. With licence fees contributing only 28% of its revenue, the way the financing worked was that a string of profitable commercial radio stations effectively cross-subsidized the public service arm of the corporation. Even so, when the transition came in 1993 the old regime handed over a fiscally troubled organization that had started running into the red nearly a decade before.

The new regime faced a daunting task from the beginning. Not only did it have to get ready to cover the fast-approaching first democratic election, which included preparing and broadcasting many hours of voter training programmes for the large black population that had never voted before, but for the first time in its history the SABC had to apply for a broadcasting licence to the newly-established Independent Broadcasting Authority (IBA).[11] And it had to do so in the face of strong pressures from other aspirant broadcasters who were petitioning the IBA to trim the public broadcaster's activities to make more room for competition. Some wanted the SABC deregulated altogether, others wanted it cut back to a modest operation that would operate on licence fees alone with no advertising revenue, yet others wanted it trimmed back at least from three to two television channels. Already burdened with the task of having to broadcast in 11 languages and under increasing pressure from the new government to reflect the values of a new multicultural and democratic society, the board made a pledge to widen its public service mandate to justify retaining the three TV channels and its radio stations. After hundreds of hours of internal consultation and debate, it presented its submission.

"It is the SABC's view that the nation needs to have a strong national public broadcaster to assist in enhancing public understanding of a number of major political, economic and social dilemmas at this critical point in its history. The corporation's established broadcasting infrastructure and services represent a unique resource for the community. Its viability needs to be protected, at least in the short to medium term, allowing the corporation to restructure and reorient its activities to reflect the new South Africa."[12]

When Sisulu was appointed chief executive, he pledged in his first address to the staff that he would make the SABC programme driven and not ruled by the bottom line. Now he presented his own commitment to the IBA – a 57% increase in news programming in the first year, a 92% increase in current affairs programming, an increase in local television programming from 40% to 60%, a doubling of local drama for young audiences, a 20% increase in adult drama in the five major African languages, a 50% increase in local music broadcast, massive increases in educational and provincial broadcasting, and a doubling of the training budget.[13]

The costs of this greatly expanded public broadcasting mandate, aimed at making the SABC predominantly South African in its content, would run to R639 million a year when capital costs to extend the provincial television windows and upgrade the African radio stations were added. To cover it the SABC hoped for increased subsidies from the government, but that was not to be. Even as it demanded more public services from the SABC, the government, facing pressing demands elsewhere on its own limited revenues, insisted that all para-statals, including the SABC, had to pay their own way. In mid-1997 it gave the SABC R177 million to defray these costs, but said there would be no more.

Worse still, while the IBA agreed to the SABC retaining its three TV channels, it required the corporation to sell six of its highly profitable commercial radio stations – the revenue generators the old SABC had used to cross-subsidize the loss-making arms of the corporation. The stations were sold for a total of R550 million, which the SABC hoped to invest at a rate that would almost cover the losses in advertising revenue. But the government insisted that, as the sole shareholder in the corporation, it was entitled to the money from the sale. So the SABC lost out doubly. Nor was that the only blow. The SABC was also required to float off its national transmission facility, Sentech, into a separate state corporation. Sentech's earnings had brought the SABC R24 million a year: now the corporation would have to pay Sentech for carrying its signals.

Reduced revenue and increased expenditure, as Mr Micawber found, spells trouble. Facing this Sisulu sought help. He discussed his problems with John Birt, then Director-General of the BBC, who recommended that he call in the glitzy consulting firm, McKinsey and Company. Under pressure from Prime Minister Margaret Thatcher, Birt had used McKinsey to radically restructure the BBC and place it on more of a business footing. It was high-powered advice, difficult for a rookie like Sisulu to reject, and so the consultants moved in. It was, in my opinion, a mismatch. McKinsey have built their international reputation in the commercial world, where one of their stars, Jeffrey K Skilling, built the Texas energy company, Enron, into the high-flying Icarus that soared to the stratosphere where he bailed out just before its meltdown in December 2001. As many at the BBC complained, there was a clash of cultures when McKinsey moved into the public broadcaster, and indeed many of their innovations have been dismantled since Birt's departure in 1999.

At the SABC McKinsey identified nearly everything Sisulu and the board had planned to fulfil the public broadcasting mandate as opportunities for cost-cutting: local content, provincial broadcasting, African language TV programmes, and even the English and Afrikaans radio services. They showed little concern for the political and cultural needs of a country undergoing a profound transition, or for the sensitivity of such issues as the use of the languages. That was not their territory; that was for the board and management to consider. Their eye was on the bottom line, and their aim was to save R450 million while generating an extra R350 million in advertising revenue.

The result was a change in the whole nature and purpose of the SABC. It ceased to be the programme-driven broadcaster that Sisulu had originally envisioned and the board and IBA endorsed, and became bottom-line driven instead. Staff was cut, local programmes fell away and imported spam flooded in. The figures improved, but the whole vision of a public broadcaster was lost. What was the point of having a public broadcaster at all if it could not deliver a public broadcasting service? There was confusion and dissatisfaction all around, from the government, from the board, from the IBA, from the staff, from the public – and Sisulu was in the middle of it all. He received some press praise for turning the SABC's finances around, but the pressures on him mounted as the ambiguities of the corporation's role became more evident.

Earlier, while I was still on the board, I became aware of a growing tension between Sisulu and Matsepe-Casaburri. Sisulu clearly resented the chairperson's increasing assertiveness as she gained in confidence and knowledge of the corporation. It became a low-level territorial war. Sisulu felt that Matsepe-Casaburri, instead of confining herself to broad policy guidelines, was intruding on his territory and becoming too involved in detailed planning and even implementation; that she was beginning to act like an executive chairperson. Though nothing ever emerged in public, it was obvious that Sisulu used his powerful ANC connections to bring about a change. When the board's term expired and a new one was appointed in 1996, Matsepe-Casaburri's name disappeared from the list – to re-emerge as Premier of the Free State province.[14] In ANC terminology, this is called "redeployment". The new chairman, Paulus Zulu, was a Natal University academic with no media experience, who visited the SABC only twice a month to attend board and sub-committee meetings and showed little interest in the inner workings of the corporation. At the same time my own departure for the TV newsroom and that of an advertising executive, Lyndall Campher, left the new board without anyone with media experience.

The weakened board put Sisulu in an all-powerful position, but before long with the pressures mounting he began to show signs of strain and was hospitalized for a time. He had been a fine journalist and was a visionary who could talk inspiringly about building the SABC into a world-class public broadcaster. He had an eye for talent and brought many fine people into the corporation. But he was not a good administrator. His indecisiveness and procrastination, especially as the pressures on him multiplied, caused frustrations to mount and problems to fester, and instead of stamping his authority on the organization and putting an end to the manipulations at middle-management level, he fell in with some of them. At my urging he appointed Reddy as Deputy Chief Executive to relieve him of the day-to-day business of running the corporation and for a time this worked well, but then inexplicably he seemed to lose faith in Reddy.

He lost faith in the experienced Jill Chisholm, too, and she left the corporation in mid-1997, a loss it could ill afford. She was replaced by Molefe Mokgatle, who had been business manager of the *Sowetan* newspaper before joining the new SABC and becoming head of one of the three television channels.

The crunch came when Sisulu himself decided to leave the SABC and take up a more lucrative appointment with the leading black empowerment company, New African Investments Limited (NAIL), which included a significant media arm. In the months before he left, Sisulu put in place a team of loyalists. One was a television reporter, Snuki Zikalala, whom he appointed Deputy Editor-in-Chief of Radio News with a mandate to integrate the radio and television news teams in line with a McKinsey recommendation. It was an incongruous appointment which was to have damaging consequences. In the first place Sisulu did not consult the Editor-in-Chief of Radio, Barney Mtomboti, arguably the best black journalist in South Africa, before making the appointment. Not surprisingly Mtomboti was offended, and later left the corporation. Worse still, the appointment put Zikalala, a tough, assertive man who had been a guerrilla commander during the struggle and later gained a PhD in journalism in Bulgaria, in an exceptionally powerful position. Although only second in command at radio news, Zikalala's mandate enabled him to designate which reporters would cover key assignments for both radio and television as the two news teams were integrated. This diminished the authority of the editors of both and set the scene for fierce turf wars.

Worst of all was the appointment of Sisulu's successor. Reddy seemed the logical choice: as Deputy CEO he was the man in line for the job, he had the experience, he had stood in frequently for Sisulu and done a good job, he had a strong commitment to the public broad-casting ideal, and he had the right anti-apartheid credentials. He also had the initial backing of Sisulu. But Reddy was an Indian, not an African, and this seemed to be a strike against him. The chairman, Paulus Zulu, emerged strongly in favour of an old-regime employee, Rev. Hawu Mbatha, who had succeeded Reddy as Head of Radio when the latter became Deputy CEO. Curiously, Mbatha did not appear to have regarded himself as an appropriate candidate and had not applied for the job until Zulu made a personal appeal to him to submit a late application. Mbatha had run Radio Zulu for the old SABC during the apartheid years, and Zulu, who had listened to the radio regularly dur-ing those years, believed he had done a good job in building a large audience and a healthy operating profit. He felt the SABC needed this ability and pushed hard for his man, eventually causing the rest of the board, Sisulu included, to fall in with his wishes.

It was a terrible mistake. Mbatha was a sweet, amiable man but he lacked the toughness and the leadership qualities to command such a large, disparate and fractious organization with all the pressures bearing in on it. As time would show, he was simply not up to the job. Nor did this come as a surprise to the staff, most of whom were astonished at his appointment. But the reason for this error of judgment was clear enough. The board which had to make the selection had not a soul on it, other than the departing Sisulu, with any media experience. Its decision was therefore based on hunch and a half-hour interview. That is not a sufficient basis for making a critical decision on an appointment that requires fine judgment of professional abilities by a group of peers who know the qualities and track records of the candidates they are choos-ing from. For a group of people with no knowledge of the media to make the country's most important media appointment makes about as much sense as if a Judicial Services Commission without a single lawyer on it were to appoint the country's judges. There was also a bit-ter irony about the appointment: while Sisulu had been incarcerated in jail and Reddy forced into exile, Mbatha had been serving the apartheid regime. In the brouhaha which followed the controversial appointment, Reddy departed – another serious loss of scarce expertise.

Over the next two years the SABC slid to the lowest point in its post-apartheid phase. With a disengaged board and a weak CEO there was a vacuum at the top which resulted in fierce power-plays breaking out at middle-management level. As ambitions burgeoned turf wars broke out everywhere and lines of authority became blurred. When conflicts arose and senior staff members sought clarity from the chief executive, he would smilingly refer them back to the middle managers they were in conflict with. He became known cynically as "the smiling reverend", benign but ineffective. With rumours rampant and the turf-war combatants leaking tendentious barbs to the newspapers every day, the place became a snake pit.

As my own one-year contract as editor of TV news ran out, Mbatha asked me to stay for another three months to head an SABC project to launch a 24-hour Africa news channel in conjunction with Multi-choice, the digital satellite distributor, that would be transmitted throughout the African continent and into part of the Middle East and southern Europe. It was a fascinating project I had begun working on during the Sisulu era and was to be the coda to my role in trying to help orchestrate the transformation of the public broadcaster.

The idea originated with Koos Bekker, the new chief executive of Nasionale Pers, the Afrikaans newspaper company that had taken the lead in launching first M-Net and then Multichoice as the country's first pay-TV broadcasters. Bekker had headed the company's TV operations and acquired a reputation as an innovative executive and a tough nego-tiator. He had been in frequent clashes with the SABC management, both old and new, and relations between the two broadcasters were strained. Now he was on his way to take over M-Net/Multichoice's par-ent company. As he made his way between jobs he contacted me through a mutual friend, saying he had this idea for a collaborative project and because of the tensions between the two broadcasters wanted to plant it with me because of my relatively independent status on secondment to the SABC.

The idea, simple but imaginative, was to draw on the SABC's exten-sive news reporting network, news agency services and tape library resources to prepare bulletins of news about Africa that could be updated through the 24-hour cycle and broadcast to the African continent as part of Multichoice's pay-to-view bouquet of satellite channels. Multichoice would pay for the channel and the SABC would have editorial control over its content. Advertising revenue would be shared. It was a great idea and I immediately agreed to put it to the SABC management. Sisulu liked it and commissioned the corporation's chief operational officer and financial manager, Neil Harvey, and myself to enter into negotiations with Multichoice.

The negotiations were tough, for this was a hard-headed commer-cial company, but they soon opened up wider opportunities for both broadcasters. The SABC had earlier decided to embark on a commercial satellite venture of its own for which it had entered into ten-year leasing agreements for seven transponders, the transmitter arms on communication satellites, at a cost of R1 million a month for each transponder. Three of the transponders were to put the SABC's existing channels on satellite and the remaining four to add sports and entertainment channels to the proposed commercial bouquet. But the project had bogged down because of a shortage of capital, concerns that the corporation had erred in deciding to use analogue instead of the new digital technology, and growing doubts about the project's viability. The result was that the SABC was haemorrhaging R7 million a month in payments for the transponders while earning no revenue from the satellite bouquet. Now in the course of the negotiations about the 24-hour Africa news channel we learned that Multichoice badly needed more transponder space for its expanding digital bouquet. By including a takeover by Multichoice of the SABC's seven transponders, and putting the SABC's three channels on their satellite bouquet together with the 24 hour Africa news channel, the deal became worth R1,1 billion over ten years to the SABC.[15] Harvey, who had worked as a turnaround specialist in the US, described it at the time as the best deal he had ever been party to negotiating.

Yet it ran into trouble. To our astonishment the Director-General of the Department of Posts, Telecommunications and Broadcasting, Andile Ncaba, opposed the deal on the ground that it would strengthen Multichoice to the competitive disadvantage of the government-owned signal distributor, Sentech. He argued that the SABC should retain the six transponders and press ahead with its own satellite project, even though, as Harvey pointed out, that would require capital expenditure of a billion rands which the SABC did not have, and it was doubtful whether there was room for two operators in this field of business. How a civil servant could intervene in a business deal in this way was a puzzle, but Ncaba, a returned exile who had held high rank in the ANC's guerrilla army, had powerful contacts in the ANC hierarchy and his opposition became a major obstacle. The SABC appealed to the Minister of Posts, Telecommunications and Broadcasting, Jay Naidoo, and a long, complex power struggle ensued behind the scenes about which those of us in the front seats could see and hear nothing. As time rolled by my new three-month contract for the project grew short. Eventually government approval came through, leaving me with just six weeks to launch the new channel.

It was a desperate rush. No staff had been engaged and no proper equipment ordered while the uncertainty continued. I sought help from CNN, who sent a brilliant specialist, Ken Tiven, who devised some marvellous improvisation and the channel went on air in what must have been the shortest time in the history of television. Mbatha urged me to stay on to consolidate the new operation, but with my wife's health deteriorating I declined. I offered instead to be available on a part-time consultancy basis, and Mbatha responded positively – but then I became increasingly aware of the grasping ambitions that had been awaiting my departure.

Phil Molefe had succeeded me as editor-in-chief of TV news and current affairs, and now he moved to absorb the new channel into his empire as well. SABC-Africa, as the new channel was called, was a small operation with fewer than 50 staffers and before leaving I had advised Mbatha to ensure that it had its own editorial independence and to use it to groom a future generation of newsroom executives. It would make sense, I pointed out, for a large organization like the SABC to prepare a line of succession, especially in light of the rapid turnover of staff in all the para-statals in this time of transition. I recommended a successor to take over from me, a talented young black journalist I believed had the potential to become a future editor-in-chief of television news. Mbatha agreed enthusiastically with all of this. But none of it happened.

Instead Molefe took nominal charge of SABC-Africa. No formal successor was appointed after my departure, and the channel lost its editorial independence. The person I had recommended to succeed me was sidelined. Nothing ever came of my offer to be a part-time consultant. The new channel limped on, and four years later has developed hardly at all. Part of the rationale behind the Multichoice deal had been to provide a platform for the SABC to expand its broadcasting reach into Europe, North America and elsewhere, and an African-American group had expressed interest in putting the 24-hour Africa news channel on cable in 13 American states. But such was the preoccupation with power-seeking and empire-building that no one ever followed up on any of these exciting prospects.

Worse was to follow. The turf war between Molefe and Zikalala intensified. In an attempt to end it, the board appointed a new editor-in-chief of broadcast news over both of them, naming Enoch Sithole, a Sisulu loyalist who had worked as a reporter on *New Nation* and then headed the licensing division of the SABC. But instead of stopping the conflict this simply turned it into a three-way power struggle. As news-room morale declined, many of the talented young staffers left. The most public and damaging was the summary dismissal of Max du Preez, the courageous Afrikaner who had exposed the death squad activities in *Vrye Weekblad*, had anchored the SABC's award-winning weekly broadcasts on the Truth and Reconciliation Commission's hear-ings, and was now executive producer of the highly successful "Special Assignment" investigative team. He was the most widely respected journalist on television. While his sacking had racial and political over-tones, it also revealed the fragile insecurity of the command structure within the SABC.

The incident blew up over a "Special Assignment" programme on witchcraft called "The Living Fear" that had been produced by two black members of the investigative team. Du Preez was not in the office on the night the programme was scheduled to go on air, but Molefe's number two, Themba Mthembu, viewed it and objected to a scene of a goat being slaughtered which he regarded as offensive. Claiming the programme demeaned African culture by presenting tra-ditional healers as witches, Mthembu stopped the broadcast and ordered a rerun of the previous week's "Special Assignment" programme.

Du Preez, a volatile and outspoken man, was outraged. He con-fronted Mthembu and swore at him. He also wrote a memo calling the banning of the documentary "a grave error of judgment" and an embarrassment to the SABC. The two black producers of the pro-gramme took a copy to a black-run Sunday newspaper, whose editor wrote that he could find nothing offensive about it. He described the programme as "gripping television" and said its canning was "an auto-cratic abuse of power, a reversal of the gains we, as a society, have made with regard to freedom of the press."

Du Preez took the matter to Mbatha, who smilingly assured him not to worry, that his job was safe. But as Du Preez walked back into the newsroom moments later, Molefe called him into his office and told him his contract would not be renewed when it expired a fortnight later. Mbatha made no move to intervene. With telling irony, on the weekend Du Preez left "Special Assignment" won six awards at a television prizegiving. At first the SABC gave no reason for Du Preez's dismissal, but following a public outcry the nightly TV news bulletin announced that he had been fired for "gross insubordination of management".

Meanwhile, as the corporation's financial position continued to decline rumours began to circulate of improper commissioning of expensive television programming. The government at last decided to act. As the SABC board's term expired new public hearings were held and all but two of Paulus Zulu's board, including the chairman himself, were swept from office and a new 15-member team was appointed. A top black businessman, Vincent Maphai, who is Corporate Affairs Manager for South Africa of the giant beer manufacturer, South African Breweries, now the world's second largest, was named chairman. Maphai promptly called in an international consultancy, Gemini, to analyse the corporation's ills. Its report, delivered in March 2000, was damning of the entire top management and its recruiting practices, which Gemini described as based on nepotism and patronage. Most startling of all, the consultants found more than R350 million in television stock, programmes commissioned or bought by the SABC since 1997 but never used, would have to be written off. An auditing firm had meanwhile named two of the corporation's most powerful executives, Molefe Mokgatle, Head of Television, and Theninga Shope, Head of Channel 2, as having violated commissioning procedures. Both left the corporation. Next came newspaper disclosures that Enoch Sithole, the recently appointed editor-in-chief of broadcast news, had falsified a university degree and possibly his South African citizenship as well. He, too, left under a cloud.

Finally Mbatha himself was axed. A head-hunting firm was engaged to find a new chief executive, and Peter Matlare, who had headed the radio division of a commercial broadcasting company, Primedia, took office in January 2001. With him came an entirely new management team. The talented Barney Mthomboti returned to the corporation to replace Sithole as editor-in-chief of broadcasting, with Mantatha Tsedu of *The Star* newspaper joining him as his deputy. Phil Molefe was shunted aside and Snuki Zikalala departed. It looked like a clean-out of the Augean stables, and eight years after that hopeful beginning it seemed to place the SABC in a position to start again. But a year later both Mthombothi and Tsedu left and the place was in confusion once more. Meanwhile, the attempt to merge television and radio is being abandoned and there is a new plan to "corporatize" the SABC and split it into two entities, one to carry out the public broadcasting mandate and the other to be a commercial broadcaster. But it is difficult to see how this will make any significant difference. The only reason the SABC has so many TV channels and radio stations is to enable it to cope with the costly obligation of broadcasting in all 11 official languages – and this will not change with the new arrangement. The SABC cannot afford not to carry advertising on the public broadcasting units, because that would reduce its revenues to below their present unacceptable level, so the units will remain semi-commercial. Indeed the whole exercise merely formalizes what has long been the de facto situation, with the profitable stations cross-subsidizing the unprofitable ones. The only change is that the two arms will now have separate, and therefore more costly, management structures.

I do not believe there is any structural adjustment quick-fix for the SABC's ills. What is required is either a radical reduction of the language requirements on television so that only one channel is needed, or an alternative financing system for public broadcasting through special taxation or an electricity surcharge. But beyond that what the corporation needs most is a culture change, away from the power- and status-seeking impulses that characterized the old regime and sadly carried over to the new, to a culture of broadcasting and journalistic professionalism. That new culture must be implanted and nurtured over time. It will not be easy, but then the hard lesson of the past nine years is that there is nothing easy about transformation. As Hultman concludes in her thesis: "The SABC has learned, as South Africa as a nation must as well, that the process of transformation is slow, messy, fraught with continual setbacks, and much more complicated than anyone setting out to pursue it wanted to believe."[16]

CHAPTER SEVEN

STROKING THE TIGER

"Beware of the tiger in the Afrikaner."
— EX-PRESIDENT PW BOTHA

When Mohammed Valli Moosa, at 37 the youngest member of the Mandela Cabinet, walked into his office on the first day the democratic government took power his sense of awe at the historic moment was tinged with the unease of a personal dilemma. Valli, as he liked to be called, had been an anti-apartheid activist all his adult life and had many tough encounters with the hated Security Police. They had harassed and detained him without trial, first as a student leader then for a year-and-a-half during the great township uprisings of the 1980s when he was on the national executive committee of the United Democratic Front. It was an incarceration that ended only when he managed to escape with a comrade, Murphy Morobe, and seek refuge in the US Consulate in Johannesburg where he remained for five weeks until the Americans managed to negotiate his liberation. Now, as Valli slipped into his seat of power he contemplated the fact that the Director-General of his Department of Constitutional Affairs, the chief civil servant with whom he would have to deal in the closest of working relationships, was the former chief of the National Intelligence Services, Niël Barnard. The old regime's security boss. President de Klerk had moved him to this new post after the ANC had been unbanned.

"I simply couldn't do it," Valli told me later. "So I called him in and told him: 'I can't work with you. You've got to go.'" Barnard was gracious, saying he understood the minister's attitude and in his position would probably have done the same. After all a minister has to be able to work with a degree of intimacy and confidence with his Director-General. It was not a fiery confrontation. "We didn't shout at each other or anything like that," Moosa said." Still, it was pretty blunt, with Moosa putting Barnard on paid leave with immediate effect to get him out of the ministry until the formalities of his dismissal could be completed.

Next day Moosa told the President of his decision, which Mandela typically accepted without question. But after a brief discussion on other matters, Mandela said quietly to the young Minister: "You know, Barnard was one of those who was in a committee that P W Botha sent to me while I was in prison. I would like to invite him to dinner at my home in recognition of that." This was a reference to a series of 47 secret meetings that Mandela had over a period of three years while he was still a prisoner, where the initial negotiations began that eventually led to the unbanning of the black political organizations, Mandela's own release and the setting up of the Negotiating Council. Barnard was also the key organizer of the prisoner Mandela's secret meeting with President Botha in 1989. This did not mean that Mandela liked the man: he, too, told me he had found it difficult to sit down and talk with a "master spy", as he called the NIS chief. But Mandela was never one to let personal feelings stand in the way of making what he regarded as an essential gesture of reconciliation.

And so Mandela duly issued dinner invitations to Barnard, his successor as head of the NIS, Mike Louw, General Johan Willemse, the former Commissioner of Prisons, Kobie Coetsee, the former Minister of Justice – and Moosa. It was essentially a dinner for his old jailers. Slyly, the President also instructed his media spokesman, Parks Mankahlana, to have the media present for a photo opportunity after the dinner. As the guests filed out to face the cameras, Mandela had Barnard stand next to him. He made a short speech about Barnard's important contribution to the nation, then turned to Moosa saying: "Valli, I'm sure you have something to say." The surprised Moosa responded. "I don't really remember what I said, but it was quite a shock to my system," he told me. Then Mandela called on Barnard to say something in reply. All very gracious, if uncomfortable. "That's the sort of guy Mandela is," was Moosa's final verdict on this small but revealing incident. "He did it because he thought it was an important political leadership thing he had to do."

It was more than that. It was part of a carefully considered political strategy that Mandela pursued throughout his presidency, of trying to allay the Afrikaners' historic fear of majority rule. When in the dying days of the old republic P W Botha took to wagging his finger and warning repeatedly that one should "beware of the tiger in the Afrikaner", many were inclined to laugh him off. Max du Preez once mocked him openly by calling back from a group of surrounding reporters, "But there are no tigers in Africa." Mandela took the warning seriously, however. During his long years in prison Mandela had come face to face with the most brutal elements of the repressive regime and realized that behind the brutality and the strutting arrogance of the Afrikaner warders lay a deep-rooted fear of the black majority that outnumbered them so overwhelmingly. He learned, too, how best to deal with them: not with obsequiousness, but with a firmness that commanded respect and by showing a reciprocal respect for them, as individuals and for their language and culture. "When you are in prison," says Mandela, "you learn that it is not the prison commander who is important but the warder in charge of your section. When it is cold and you need another blanket, it is the warder you must negotiate with to get it." And so that, too, is where Mandela learnt the importance of negotiation. "Sit down with a man," he says, "if you have prepared your case very well, that man, after he has sat down to talk to you, will never be the same again."

The great advantage of prison, as Mandela is wont to say, is that it "gives you time to think". To think and to strategize. And it was during those years that Mandela came to realize that the greatest strategic challenge that would face the ANC if it ever came to power would be to strike a balance between black aspirations and white fears, especially Afrikaner fears. He understood the roots of those fears, the fact that unlike other colonial settlers, the British in India and the Dutch in Indonesia, the Afrikaners had no metropolitan home to return to come majority rule; or as one of Afrikanerdom's most elegant journalists, Schalk Pienaar, once put it in a justification of apartheid, the Afrikaners had "no central shrine of national existence to survive the death of the outposts".[1] Given Afrikaner dominance of the most powerful military in Africa and of a ruthlessly efficient police force, Mandela realized that unless those fears of cultural death could be allayed an ANC government would face the danger of a violent counter-revolutionary overthrow. So while still in prison he set about a diligent study of the Afrikaner mind, learning the Afrikaans language and reading Afrikaans history and literature. When he found there were no works of the Afrikaans poet D J Opperman in the prison library, he astonished his jailers by writing to the Minister of Justice requesting some.

Only two years after the bloody Soweto uprising of 1976, which was triggered by black students protesting against compulsory instruction in the Afrikaans language – the language of the oppressor, as they saw it – Mandela wrote: "Today South Africa has almost three million Afrikaners who will no longer be oppressors after liberation but a powerful minority of ordinary citizens, whose co-operation and good-will will be required in the reconstruction of the country."[2]

In the years leading up to and following his release, this strategy of meeting with Afrikaners and calming their fears became the hallmark of Mandela's political action. He used it to good effect during his secret meetings in prison with Botha's committee, where Barnard recalls that Mandela always greeted him in Afrikaans and allowed the NIS chief to conduct his side of the talks in his language. And after Mandela's release, he again entered into talks with the right-wing separatists and their supporters in the security forces whom he quickly identified as the most serious threat to his hopes of a transition to majority rule.

Fortuitously, the first contact that led to these talks took place in my own home. I had formed a friendship with Abraham Viljoen, a former theology professor turned farmer who was one of the first Afrikaners to meet with the exiled ANC and who happened to be the identical twin brother of Constand Viljoen, the recently retired chief of the South African Defence Force who had been persuaded somewhat reluctantly to assume the leadership of a broad alliance of right-wing groups called the *Afrikaner Volksfront*. When I bumped into Braam Viljoen, as he was generally called, in mid-1993 I found him to be a worried man. The right-wingers were talking of war, he told me, and were urging his brother to lead them in an operation to derail the negotiations for a democratic election and fight for the establishment of a separate Afri-kaner nation, or *volkstaat*. If Constand were to agree, said Braam, thousands of citizen force troops would likely join him and it was doubtful whether the Defence Force as a whole would act against them. There could be chaos. As we talked I suggested that Braam should use his contacts on both sides to try to arrange a meeting. It would be dif-ficult, we agreed, because neither side would want it to be known that it was talking to the other.

The upshot of our conversation was that Cyril Ramaphosa, the sec-retary-general of the ANC, and Z B du Toit, editor of the Conservative Party's official newspaper, *Die Patriot*, met secretly at my home where they agreed to persuade their respective leaders to get together. More than twenty secret meetings took place in the months that followed between Mandela, Mbeki and the commander of the ANC's guerrilla force, Joe Modise, on the one hand, and Constand Viljoen and two other retired generals, Tienie Groenewald and Kobus Visser, on the other. Again, as with Mandela's meetings in prison and the secret encounters between the government and the exiled ANC, the two sides surprised each other with their degree of mutual understanding. "They were much more reasonable than we had expected," Constand Viljoen told me later. "There was an honesty between us. In fact we agreed afterwards that we could get along better with the ANC than with the National Party." For his part, Mandela, too, warmed to Viljoen whom he saw as a straightforward, honest man whom he could trust. His message to the generals was simple. "If you want to go to war," he told them, "I must be honest and admit that we cannot stand up to you on the battlefield. We don't have the resources. It will be a long and bitter struggle, many people will die and the country may be reduced to ashes. But you must remember two things. You cannot win because of our numbers: you cannot kill us all. And you cannot win because of the international community. They will rally to our support and they will stand with us."[3] It was an incontrovertible argument.

Mandela went further still in reaching out to conservative Afrikaners. He called on the bitter old ex-President, P W Botha, at his retirement home appropriately located in a resort called The Wilderness and pleaded with him to urge restraint on the right-wingers. He tried to reassure the military and security leaders. He called on General George Meiring, head of the army, to offer him the job of Chief of the Defence Force, and on General Johan van der Merwe, the Commissioner of Police, to urge him to stay on under the new regime – even though he knew both had carried out violent operations against black activists only a few years before. Both accepted. Some of the ANC leaders thought Mandela was too trusting, but he was determined to bring anyone who might cause trouble on side. In Lyndon Johnson's famous phrase, he reckoned it was better to have them inside the tent pissing out rather than outside pissing in.

In the end the threat of a right-wing coup collapsed when an attempt by Viljoen to lead a group of 5 000 *Volksfront* combatants in to the nominally independent tribal "homeland" of BophuthaTswana to prop up its dictator, Lucas Mangope, ended ignominiously. Mangope was refusing to allow the people of his apartheid creation to participate in the first democratic election in 1994, and as his civil servants rebelled and the administration began to fall apart he appealed to the *Volksfront* for help. Foolishly Viljoen agreed, thinking no doubt that control of the territory would put him in a stronger negotiating position. But the simultaneous intervention of a wild bunch of much cruder racists from Eugene Terre'Blanche's *Afrikaner Weerstandsbeweging* (Afrikaner Resistance Movement) wrecked his plans. As the AWB men roared into the "homeland's" capital of Mmabatho yelling racist abuse at people in the streets and taking pot shots at them, killing and wounding many, the BophuthaTswana army, which was supposed to supply Viljoen's men with weapons, mutinied. The invaders had no option but to with-draw – and as they did so a hail of gunfire brought one of the AWB cars to a standstill. The wounded occupants tumbled out into the road. Then, as TV cameras rolled, an enraged black policeman walked up and shot each of them in the head.

The incident was appalling, and as the cold-blooded killing was shown on television news that night the whole nation shuddered. But the impact was salutary. Suddenly everyone could see, right there in their own sitting rooms, what all the Rambo talk of the right-wingers could lead to in reality. They had seen the loud-mouthed white men lying in the dust at the feet of the black police pleading for help. And they had seen them die like dogs. As I wrote at the time: "The bubble of adventure, the heroic re-enactment of historic Boer myths, was punctured in a day of blood and humiliation."[4]

Now all Mandela's patient placating of his ex-enemies paid off. Constand Viljoen, appalled at the BophuthaTswana fiasco, left the *Volksfront* and flew to Cape Town to register a right-wing party of his own, the Freedom Front, to fight the elections and campaign for his cause by constitutional means. He duly won seven seats in the election and took his place in a parliamentary front bench as a political leader. Mandela even appointed one of the Freedom Front hardliners, Thomas Langley, whom he felt had played a constructive role in the Negotiating Council, to the envied position of Ambassador to Václav Havel's Czech Republic.

As President, Mandela made reconciliation the central theme of his leadership, becoming a master of both the intimate personal touch and the symbolic public gesture aimed at winning the hearts and minds of those who feared him most. He was acutely sensitive not to trample on Afrikaner symbols. Statues and monuments remained untouched, street names commemorating events and heroes in the saga of Afrikaner his-tory were not changed. He was even sensitive when it came to changing names that honoured some of the more egregious creators of apartheid. I had experience of this when the Minister of Water Affairs, Kader Asmal, invited me to join a commission to rename the country's dams, many of which had been named after cabinet ministers of the apartheid era. When it came to considering the largest of these, the giant Verwoerd Dam on the Orange River, I proposed that it be renamed

Lake Luthuli, to honour the ANC leader of the 1960s, Chief Albert Luthuli, who had been South Africa's first Nobel Peace Prize winner and whom Verwoerd had banned and banished to a remote district of KwaZulu/Natal where he died in obscurity when, old and blind, he was knocked down by a train. Willem de Klerk, brother of "F W", seconded the proposal and it seemed certain to be adopted. But at the next meeting of the commission Kader Asmal whispered to me confidentially that "the old man would rather we didn't pursue this idea". Mandela was sensitive about replacing an Afrikaner politician's name with that of an ANC politician. And so we named the lake the Gariep Dam instead, after the original San, or Bushmen, name of the great river on which it had been built.

Mandela's most spectacularly successful gesture was his appearance, just one year after becoming President, at the final match of the Rugby World Cup in Johannesburg. Rugby had long been a sporting obsession among white South Africans, the physical expression of their self-image of rugged manhood and national toughness, and few things had pained them more than being shut out of international competition because of the government's insistence on apartheid in sport. By the same token most black South Africans spurned the game, preferring soccer. To them it was the oppressor's sport, and it still rankled with them that rugby's one-time chief administrator, Danie Craven, whom whites revered, had once vowed that "over my dead body will any black man ever wear the Springbok jersey".

Now after long years of isolation South Africa was back in international sport and as a reward for its remarkable transition to a non-racial democracy the World Cup tournament was played here. As the matches began there was apprehension in the land: after being out in the cold for so long our team was new, untested, and might be humiliated. Moreover, to the late Danie Craven's posthumous chagrin, it was racially integrated, with a black wing three-quarter, Chester Williams, included. The New Zealand All Blacks were the short-odds favourites with an apparently unstoppable human giant, Jonah Lomu, playing on their wing. But as the South African team progressed through the early rounds, excitement rose and by the time the team reached the final against the formidable New Zealanders the whole country was in a fever of excitement. Mandela, sensing the emotional intensity of the occasion, went to watch what was a nail-biting match. His attendance caused a stir of appreciation in the huge and overwhelmingly Afrikaner crowd. When South Africa won dramatically in extra time he walked onto the field wearing a Springbok cap and the captain, François Pienaar's, number six jersey to present Pienaar with the trophy. The crowd went wild with delight. "Nel-son! Nel-son!" they chanted as they waved the colourful new South African flag. As I drove home from the stadium that evening, crowds of cheering, dancing black people clogged the streets and jammed the traffic to a standstill. It was the new South Africa's euphoric high.

Other symbolic gestures followed. Mandela travelled to the little Northern Cape town of Orania, where some 600 diehard Afrikaner rightists are trying rather forlornly to establish the nucleus of what they hope may one day become a *volkstaat*, to visit Betsie Verwoerd, 94-year-old widow of the chief architect of apartheid and the man who outlawed the ANC, Hendrik Verwoerd. They chatted amiably as she served him tea and showed him a statue of her husband. Mandela followed this up by meeting with other widows of former apartheid Prime Ministers. One Sunday he joined a congregation at a Dutch Reformed Church service in Pretoria; he went to an Afrikaner cultural festival in the Karoo town of Oudtshoorn, and he addressed numerous gatherings of Afrikaner business and cultural organizations.

All responded viscerally to the old man with the ready smile and warm words. A remarkable number of Afrikaners not only voted for the ANC but joined it, ranging from academics and old party stalwarts to, most astonishingly, one of Verwoerd's grandsons, Wilhelm, and his wife Melanie. A year before the first democratic election Wilhelm Verwoerd, a young philosopher at Stellenbosch University who had undergone a searing transformation of his own that had involved estrangement from his entire family except for his frail granny Betsie, appeared before an excited crowd at an ANC rally in the Parow Civic Centre outside Cape Town to declare his membership of the organization his grandfather had outlawed. "Viva Verwoerd!" chanted the crowd. Of all the ironies in the changing value system of South Africa, none could have been more startling than that chant of black praise for a name which more than any other is identified with apartheid. As Mandela was to write in a foreword to a book by Wilhelm Verwoerd about his political conversion: "May this record of personal courage inspire us all to join hands with one another in building a nation in which each and every individual and community feels at home."[5] Melanie Verwoerd was duly elected a member of parliament for the ANC. Today she is South Africa's ambassador to Ireland.

Afrikaner businessmen, too, have fallen over themselves to shake off their past and identify with the new regime. In February 1999 more than 30 of them put their names to a statement praising President Mbeki's "vision and leadership" which appeared on the front pages of South African newspapers. They included Neil van Heerden, a former diplomat who served as Director-General of the Department of Foreign Affairs during the apartheid era and now heads the South Africa Foundation, a business organization which put out pro-South African propaganda during those years. Another was Paul Kruger, chairman of Sasol, the country's biggest fuel and chemicals company and a long-time supporter of the National Party. He told reporters he admired the black government's economic policies. "I believe one should give credit where credit is due," he said. "This isn't to say I'm going to vote for this government. This doesn't mean joining the ANC. But this government is on the right track. I am positive about the future, and I want to get that message of hope across, particularly to Afrikaans-speaking people."[6]

There is a sense among many blacks that Afrikaners are more committed to the country and have adapted better than the more liberal English-speaking community to the transformation. Archbishop Desmond Tutu, the Nobel Peace laureate, is one who believes this, although he is careful to pay tribute to what he calls "some quite outstanding people" in the English community. "You see the Afrikaners have no liberal tradition," he told me in an interview, "so that there is no middle ground. Once they are committed, once they make up their minds, then it's all or nothing. The English, on the whole, are more subtle. They are very good at saying we were not responsible for apartheid, but when you look at the statistics you realize how much they supported the National Party."

Carl Niehaus, a young Afrikaner who underwent his political transformation much earlier and paid the price of long imprisonment for his role in the anti-apartheid struggle, takes a less charitable view of some of these latter-day conversions. "There is a group of Afrikaners who have been opportunistic," he says. "They are making the move from one power relationship to another quite seamlessly."

Whatever the motivation, commitment or opportunism, one thing is clear. P W Botha's Afrikaner tiger has been tamed. Disgusted, the crabby old ex-president changed his metaphor and told an Afrikaans journalist that today's Afrikaners reminded him of "a car with four flat tyres – and the spare missing."[7]

* * *

Of all the changes that have taken place within the Afrikaner community, none has been more dramatic than the collapse of Afrikaner Nationalism and its supportive institutions. They were the driving force of South African politics for nearly the whole of the twentieth century, yet now they have collapsed within a decade. The party has shrunk from its gargantuan majorities of the seventies and eighties to 20,4% in 1994, 18,3% in the municipal elections of 1996, 13,3% in a 1998 opinion poll, to a miserable 7% in the 1999 general election, and now it stands to be decimated in 2004. The once all-powerful Broederbond secret society, which evolved the apartheid ideology, controlled the South African Broadcasting Corporation and exerted a pervasive influence on the whole of Afrikanerdom, has been reincarnated into a powerless talk shop called the Afrikaner Bond. The Afrikaans language has been officially downgraded. Afrikaans schools and universities are being integrated and are losing their ethnic character. The Dutch Reformed Church no longer asserts any political influence. The civil service, dominated for generations by Afrikaners, is being Africanized. The corporate Afrikaner banks and insurance companies are being subsumed into mergers and no longer serve an ethno-nationalist purpose.

Central to this, of course, has been the discrediting of the apartheid ideology – now officially classified as "a crime against humanity" by the Truth and Reconciliation Commission – which these institutions created and which sustained them in turn. As with communism and the ANC, the demise of the ideology led to the collapse of Afrikaner Nationalism's entire intellectual universe.

The result is that, however calm things may appear on the surface, however tame the tiger has become, the Afrikaner community has been plunged into a state of uncertainty. "It's like the earthquake of Lisbon," says Braam Viljoen, referring to the catastrophic eruption followed by a tidal wave and a fire which destroyed much of the Portuguese capital in 1755 and caused some intellectuals at the time to question the optimistic philosophy of the Age of Enlightenment.

For some it is nothing less than a crisis of identity. What does it mean now to be an Afrikaner? What becomes of the Afrikaners' national consciousness, of their self-identity as a people, a *volk*? Isaiah Berlin, the great Oxford philosopher, says national consciousness may be as old as social consciousness itself, and that nationalism is the extreme form of it "which usually seems to be caused by wounds, some form of collective humiliation usually animated by grievances."[8] Their thunderous history, from the Great Trek of 1836 to the Anglo-Boer War to the Great

133

Depression and poverty in the cities, provided that furnace of humiliation in which Afrikaner Nationalism was forged. To this was added an ideology and a theological justification for it. In my book *The Mind of South Africa* I outline how a new Afrikaner intellectual elite went to Germany and the Netherlands in the 1930s and extrapolated ideas from the writings of the German Romantics, Herder and Fichte, then being corrupted by the Nazis to give some intellectual veneer to their *Rassekunde*, and from the theological ideas of Abraham Kuyper at the Free University of Amsterdam, to evolve the concept of "Christian Nationalism", the concept that Afrikaners were not only a distinct national group with their own *Volksgeist*, but that they had a God-given right through the "ordinances of creation" to their own nation-state and had also been called by God – in a Calvinist sense of calling – to bring civilization to the African continent.[9]

Now all this was shattered. Afrikaners, who throughout their history had followed patriarchal leaders, suddenly found themselves bereft of country, ideology and leadership. With Verwoerd and Vorster dead, P W Botha, F W de Klerk and Constand Viljoen retired, Eugene Terre'Blanche imprisoned and discredited, Ferdi Hartzenberg disappeared, only *Kortbroek* van Schalkwyk remained, thrashing about trying to shake off the past and find a new identity for his grievously shrunken and renamed New National Party. What were they to do? What was their role to be in this new dispensation run by their erstwhile enemies, the communist-terrorists they had been taught to fear and hate but to whom their own leaders who had taught them those very sentiments had now handed over the country? What did their 350-year history amount to? Having been proud Afrikaners, they now found their very identity was a stigma.

Some want to reject such an identity. Jacques Pauw, a prominent Afrikaans journalist who covered the Truth and Reconciliation Commission's hearings, has said the revelations of atrocities he heard there filled him with such revulsion that he rejects the term Afrikaner. Antjie Krog, an Afrikaans poet who also reported on the TRC hearings, expresses the anguish of her own identity crisis in a uniquely literate way.

> "Was apartheid the product of some horrific shortcoming in Afrikaner culture? Could one find the key to this in Afrikaner songs and literature, in beer and *braaivleis*? How do I live with the fact that all the words used to humiliate, all the orders given to kill, belonged to the language of my heart? At the hearings many of the victims faithfully reproduced these parts of their stories in Afrikaans as proof of the bloody fingerprints on them."[10]

At the other end of the spectrum are some who are still unrepentant, unreconstructed racists. In May 2002 two members of a rugby club were found guilty of beating a black teenager to death on a farm in the northern Limpopo Province and throwing his body into a crocodile-infested dam. The rugby players were on the farm for a team-building weekend when they went for a drive and, on hearing there were black youths "trespassing" on the farm, set out to catch and beat them. The two players were sentenced to 18 years imprisonment. Yet other Afrikaners are in denial, claiming they knew nothing of apartheid atrocities and dismissing the TRC hearings as a witch-hunt, or simply saying they are sick and tired of guilt confessions and it is time to bury the past. Still others are eager to find a new basis for giving meaning and legitimacy to the concept of a discrete Afrikaner *volk* within the larger rainbow nation and to define a new role for it to play.

"Afrikaners are milling about like a flock of penned-up sheep," writes Willem de Klerk, the ex-president's elder brother, a theology professor, journalist and political polemicist who once edited two major Afrikaans newspapers, *Die Transvaler*, an official organ of the National Party, and the mass-circulation weekly *Rapport*. The community is in a state of shock, he says. Shock and depression and confusion. It is suffering from a cumulative sense of loss: "Loss of power. Loss of influence. Loss of prestige. Loss of security. Loss of privileges. Loss of credibility. Loss of language . . . We are suffering from a poverty of political, religious and cultural leadership . . . There is a question mark over our history . . . Our self-image has been damaged."

De Klerk, generally known by his nickname Wimpie, pours out this diagnosis in a book whose central purpose is an appeal to the *volk* to shake off its negativism and band together to save itself from committing "national genocide."[11]

The Afrikaans title of Wimpie de Klerk's book essentially divides Afrikaners into three categories: those who are morose and out of sorts, those who are scratchy and aggressive, and those who are positive or stout-hearted. His pitch is to the latter group, but in making it he is brutally critical of young Afrikaners particularly.

> "The following argument," he writes, "can be heard, with variations, among thousands of modern young Afrikaners: we are just a collection of materialistic or fugitive Europeans and degenerate adventurers. Actually a bunch of immigrants who, through the centuries of colonialism, seized South Africa and looted it. We speak a European dialect. Our history consists

mainly of a series of military and strategic incidents in the plundering of the San, the Khoi and the Africans. We have no clear profile of a binding self-existence and therefore we can hardly be called a people. The notion of an Afrikaner *volk* is a lie. The sooner we throw it in the rubbish bin the better."[12]

Such a denial of one's own identity, De Klerk warns, is the way to social isolation and rejection, for others will not accept you as one of them. It also carries the risk that the fountainheads of the *volk's* existence will begin to dry up – its education, art, literature, theatre, television, songs, even the language itself will wither away and within two or three generations Afrikaner consciousness itself may become extinct.

De Klerk is even more savage in his denunciation of those who leave the country to settle elsewhere, calling them "cowardly quitters". And he sails into Afrikaner political mythology with gusto, accusing his people of an "exclusivity neurosis" in their "anxious striving for separation", of distorting their history and misusing their Calvinist "divine calling" to justify that history. Afrikaners, he says, have been guilty of "naked chauvinism", and of developing a "chosen people fantasy" that was "a hypocritical presentation and a falsehood".[13]

More egregious still, he feels, is the plea by some Afrikaners that they did not know of the injustices committed during the apartheid years. This is nothing less than "arrogant and insensitive self-justification with racist undertones", De Klerk declares. The excuse that atrocities were committed by just a few "rotten apples in a big basket of healthy apples" is pusillanimous nonsense. "The whole apartheid-basket was contaminated," he thunders. "And even if some Afrikaners did not know this at the time, they should feel a deep shame now that they do know. The Truth and Reconciliation Commission's exposures of apartheid guilt, despite criticisms, are so painful, so gripping in their human grief, that all Afrikaners in biblical idiom should rend their garments and cover themselves with ashes."[14]

That said, do Afrikaners, and whites in general, deserve another chance? Yes, De Klerk replies to his own rhetorical question, because revenge and retaliation are also wicked: life is about mercy, forgiveness and restoration. What is required is for Afrikaners, from the individual to the institutions of politics, church, business and the professions, to acknowledge that they committed grievous injustices through apartheid – and then to undertake a new trek by entering into a co-partnership with all other South African groups to help build the new democracy and uplift the disadvantaged.

The 1999 election has finally killed the dream of an Afrikaner homeland, he says, but the thoughts and emotions and the right of Afrikaners to protect their interests and live their own communal lives can never be shut away. The critical thing is that it can be realized within a larger South African context.

> "The concept of being part of a rainbow nation is essential. That means precisely a nation with its own different colourations. To be a South African, white Afrikaner, mainly of European descent and an African, is the right formulation. The one does not exclude the other. All deserve a deep loyalty."[15]

To achieve this, De Klerk contends, new community structures are needed, headed by a central Council of Afrikaans Representatives, with new leadership and new vision, that over time can build a new sense of an Afrikaner community inclusive of all who use the Afrikaans language, regardless of race, creed or history, that can replace the old, contaminated one, and that can eventually bring about a rebirth, be the seed, of a new Afrikaner *volk*.

* * *

But if Wimpie de Klerk thought his impassioned appeal would elicit an enthusiastic response from fellow Afrikaners, he was in for a big surprise. Instead a fellow journalist who had worked for him while he was editor of *Die Transvaler* wrote an open letter, dripping with sarcasm and rage, accusing De Klerk of dishonesty and hypocrisy.

The thrust of this tirade, penned by journalist Chris Louw and published in the Johannesburg newspaper *Beeld*, was to accuse De Klerk and his older generation of misleading young Afrikaners with their apartheid rhetoric and sending them off to fight and die in a futile bush war against the ANC – only in the end to capitulate themselves in their role as the Afrikaner political establishment and hand over the country to the erstwhile enemy. And now he had the effrontery to berate this young generation, as it entered middle age, for not identifying more wholeheartedly with the new South Africa. "I am the hell in," Louw fumed in his letter. "The hell in for your arrogance, the self-justification, the rationalizations and for the lies."[16]

Claiming to speak on behalf of his disaffected generation, Louw protested that they had been raised in a culture of obedience. "We were brought up to be seen and not heard," he wrote, "to obey orders without talking back, to respect our elders. To say yes father, no father, right father, quite so father. To be prepared, if needs be, to give up our lives for country and the Great Cause.

"Your generation," he went on, was the first, and possibly the last, in Afrikaner history never to have fought in a war: born too late for the Anglo-Boer War, too young for World War I, too German-neutral for World War II, too busy thinking and wondering and planning national schemes and constellations and seeking justification for them to be involved in the border war (against the ANC).

"You were the first generation of Afrikaners who sent your children off to die for you. And those who didn't wish to defend your stupid dreams with the weapons that you issued to us were sent to prison, or, worse, declared insane.

"And you? Where were you?" he asked Wimpie de Klerk pointedly. "You withdrew into your shadowy office and coined comforting new words and ringing phrases."

Louw was even more scornful of the leadership generation's performance in the Negotiating Council, which he attended as a reporter.

"And then came your big chance ... your moment of truth arrived. To meet the ANC – the enemy – face to face across the battlefield of the conference table. The youth had held the fort for years. Now the kid's play was over. Now you would take up your weapons. You were battle ready. Your words had been sharpened by years of training.

"But all your grand plans were unmasked in a few months at the multiparty negotiations. Where were your seven-point plans, your five-point strategies, your minority guarantees, as you went to take up your position before the representatives of the entire country? Where were the boasts, the threats, the fiery speeches, the pledges? I was there. It was a pathetic sight to behold as your arguments – your delusions – were ripped out from under you.

"Now we sit with new questions. Apartheid is dead, the time for mourning is over. Things are being reformed and transformed. A new state is being formed at the snap of a finger. 'Come, come, little Boer, move your ass. The old black uncle has established his own state. Stand to attention. Don't talk back, your days are over. It's your duty to help establish the new state. You must transfer your skills to the new black elite to justify your existence.'"[17]

And in a final bitter jibe he challenged his former editor: "What is the finest achievement of your generation, the generation that never smelled blood or heard the whistle of bullets or experienced the fear of battle, who only thought Great Thoughts and brought forth philosophies of life? I confess my subjectivity, but didn't you devote all your energy to misleading the outside world and your own children? Wasn't your greatest achievement the manner in which you succeeded like word-artists in selling us dogmatic horse turds as moral figs?"

Louw's 2 000-word letter had a startling impact. It triggered an avalanche of responses that filled the letters pages of *Beeld* for months, constituting a massive national debate in which Afrikaners poured out their anger at their leaders and their anguish over their identity crisis. It culminated in a conference in the university town of Potchefstroom, presided over by Frederik van Zyl Slabbert, where dozens of the letter-writers came to vent their views verbally. And finally it emerged as a powerful polemical play that was the highlight of the Little Karoo Afrikaans Cultural Festival in June 2001 before going on a national tour to the acclaim of critics around the country. Seldom can a letter to a newspaper have created such a stir.

Many of the letter-writers identified passionately with Louw's accusations, others accused him of racism, some charged him with blind naivety. "Why couldn't you think for yourself?" wrote 35-year-old Annesu de Vos, an Afrikaans poet now living in self-exile in Canada. "I cannot understand why all those who now complain that they were 'brainwashed' found it so difficult to identify injustice at the time. It was there under your nose! It screamed in your face ... You are a shareholder in Lies (Pty) Ltd."

To a degree both attack and counter-attack contained a measure of unfairness. Wimpie de Klerk could hardly be categorized as a major apartheid ideologist. He was the quintessential Afrikaner *verligte*: indeed he coined the terms *verligte* and *verkrampte* to describe the rival reformist and diehard wings of the National Party in its heyday.[18] I knew him well and have no doubt that he was deeply troubled by apartheid but could not bring himself to denounce it openly. Instead he "worked within the system" to try to reform it, as the common rationalization of the *verligtes* put it. To liberalize, not abolish it, rather in the manner of Mikhail Gorbachev's *perestroika* – and ultimately with the same unintended consequences. That characterized his writing, and I have no doubt he can claim also to have played a role in persuading his brother to make his historic leap of faith in February 1990.

But it is also true that had Wimpie de Klerk published during the apartheid years what he has written now, the impact would have been seismic. He would have gone down in history as one of the great heroes and saviours of his country, far more even than his brother. As it is there is a slightly self-serving aura to his tract. The bold convert after the event. The trumpet call after the charge.

This, I think, is what riled Chris Louw. But there is more to it than that. There is also, I sense, a personal grudge. Louw was, in fact – as he told Annesu de Vos in an acerbic response to her criticism of him – quite an active dissident figure during the later apartheid years. He accompanied Afrikaner dissident groups to meet members of the ANC in exile, he met members of the Anti-Apartheid Movement in London and Amsterdam, signed a petition outside the South African Embassy in London calling for sanctions against the apartheid state, and spent nights in black townships to get a first-hand sense of what life was like for the policy's victims. And although he served in the military, he did not actually fight in the bush war against the ANC guerrillas. His outburst, he explained a little lamely in a second letter, was made as a collective charge on behalf of his generation. "I took up my pen," he wrote, "on behalf of members of my own peer group who cannot speak for themselves and who do not yet appreciate the full extent of what was done to them."

Yes, well, maybe. What I suspect is something closer to the bone, that Louw tried and failed while on the staff of *Die Transvaler* to persuade Wimpie de Klerk, his editor, to take a more outspoken editorial line in the newspaper, and that De Klerk put him down, perhaps a little paternalistically. "Do you remember," Louw challenges De Klerk in his open letter, "how you greeted me in the corridors of the newspaper office with, 'Good day, *Boetman*'?"– a slightly condescending salutation from an older person to a "young chap" that could have meant he regarded him as a politically immature upstart. Now, 20 years later, says Louw, the middle-aged *Boetman* "is the hell in".

The word became the catch-phrase for the whole tempestuous outpouring: "The *Boetman* Debate", it was called. And the title of the play simply, *Boetman is die Bliksem in!* (Boetman is the Hell in!) But whatever the personal motivation behind the letter that triggered it all, the debate itself was profoundly revealing of the turbulent state of the Afrikaner psyche as it grapples with its guilt-tinged past and its present crisis of role and identity. As a critic wrote of the play, its "masterful, brilliantly controlled stagecraft turns this dramatic curiosity into a major and traumatic sea change in cultural identity . . . *Boetman is die Bliksem in!* insists that if nation building is ever to have any meaning outside the comfortable platitudes of party caucuses, the kind of agonized guts baring we witness here is vitally necessary – for all of us."[19]

* * *

I first met Carl and Jansie Niehaus in court. They were both students, little more than kids really, boyfriend and girlfriend, he 23 and she 22. But they were on trial for their lives, charged with high treason. Both were Afrikaners from deeply rooted Afrikaner families and they had been studying at the politically select Rand Afrikaans University, but they had joined the ANC which made them ethnic traitors as well as subversive activists in the purely legal sense. The courtroom was packed with members of the Security Police come to gloat at their success in entrapping the young villains. The elderly Afrikaner judge, Willem Myburgh, draped in his crimson robes, glared down at them. The atmosphere reeked of hostility. There can be few things in this world capable of evoking such powerful emotions of confusion, hatred and total rejection as an Afrikaner who broke with family, tribe and party on grounds of political principle during the apartheid years. To make matters worse, Carl was a theology student and he had declared the policy, sanctified by the Dutch Reformed Church, to be unchristian.

The two had already walked a long, hard road before reaching this crisis in their lives. Carl's theological studies had brought him to the point where he was convinced that apartheid was morally wrong. When he voiced his misgivings on campus, he was howled down and denounced as a "communist". Other students shunned him and the university authorities warned him to abandon his political activities. When he refused, his room was ransacked and his books and papers were set on fire. Finally, when he distributed pamphlets on campus calling for equal education and the release of Nelson Mandela, he was expelled and his bursary was cancelled. His exasperated father, an old-fashioned conservative, ordered him to leave home. Angry and friendless, Carl describes in a brief autobiography how he stormed out of the family home in the western Transvaal town of Zeerust that night and caught a train to Johannesburg, where he slept on a park bench. He had rejected apartheid intellectually but had not yet joined any opposition organization, so he had no support network. Next morning, in something of a daze, the young Afrikaner Calvinist theologian wandered into the unfamiliar environment of St Mary's Anglican Cathedral in central Johannesburg, where he encountered the gentle African dean, Simeon Nkoane. The dean promptly telephoned the doyen of Afrikaner dissidents, the redoubtable Rev. Beyers Naude, and so began an odyssey that brought the young Carl into contact with anti-apartheid activists and finally to membership of the ANC. Through it all his girlfriend, Jansie, remained loyal and supportive.

Now here the two of them were standing together in the dock of this incredibly hostile courtroom. The Security Police had burst into their bedroom three months before and hauled them off for long, gruelling sessions of interrogation, beatings, humiliation and enforced sleeplessness. They had confessed nothing, but as the testimony began they quickly realized that they stood no chance. A fellow student, Robert Whitecross, had double-crossed them. He had shared student digs with Carl and Jansie, befriended them and joined the ANC with them, and finally accompanied Carl in reconnoitering the Johannesburg Gas Works to assess it as a possible target for attack by ANC guerrillas. But as the two discovered in court, he was really a Security Police officer who had been planted on them, and here he was to testify and show the court pictures of Carl inspecting the gas works taken by video cameras that Whitecross had planted there. There could be no defence in the face of that. The only question was what the sentence would be on this capital charge in a country which executed the third-largest number of people in the world, after China and Iran.

There was no point in trying to deny anything, but Carl wanted to explain himself, tell the world of his awakening to the evils of apartheid. All he had left was his day in court. But that meant exposing himself to the risks of cross-examination. When the questioning came, it was loaded. "So you are in favour of bomb attacks that can cause death and devastation?" the Afrikaner prosecutor, Jan Swanepoel, asked. Carl tried to explain that the ANC had tried for half a century to negotiate peacefully but had been met only with violent repression and ultimately with being outlawed, which left no alternative but to turn to an armed struggle in which they were doing everything possible to avoid loss of life.

"And where do you draw the line?" Swanepoel asked, his voice rasping with anger. "When, according to you, is a government so bad that violence against it is justified?"

"When innocent women and children are dying throughout the country as a result of the government's policies," Carl shot back at him, his own voice rising with indignation. It was a brave but foolhardy reply in this unequal contest, and Swanepoel spotted his opening.

"When you come out of prison," he asked, "will your attitude towards the use of violence be exactly the same?"

One could see the young man flinch and hesitate. How could he answer this one without either gainsaying himself or putting his life at risk? Carefully he replied that it was only with great hesitation that he had decided to become involved in the ANC's armed struggle and he hoped that in time the regime would come to its senses and abandon apartheid, but if it did not, then, yes, he would have to stand by his conviction that the armed struggle was morally justified.

It was enough to save his life, but his stubborn stand on principle probably added several years to his sentence. Judge Myburgh was harsh in his condemnation of the young man, accusing him not only of betraying his country and his people but of misleading his innocent young girlfriend. He sentenced Carl to 15 years imprisonment, and Jansie to four. As they filed out of the courtroom to begin their long incarceration, the young couple raised their fists defiantly and called out the ANC slogan, "*Amandla!*" (Power). It was 24 November 1983.

It was eight years before I saw Carl and Jansie Niehaus again. In a rare concession the two had been given permission to marry in prison, in a painfully brief 40-minute ceremony attended only by their parents, a priest and two witnesses, before being whisked apart again to their separate prisons. Jansie completed her sentence, then a year after Nelson Mandela's release and the unbanning of the ANC, Carl himself was freed, having been in Pretoria's bleak Central Prison for eight years and four months.

From then on life became a different kind of roller coaster for the couple. First, Carl became an official spokesman for the ANC in its run-up to the 1994 democratic election, then a member of parliament for the ruling party, and finally South African Ambassador to the Netherlands. His ambassadorial term completed, he returned to South Africa to work as a consultant for an international company, where sadly the couple's fairytale marriage withered on the vine and ended in divorce.

But however much Afrikanerdom rejected Carl and Jansie Niehaus, spewed them out as treacherous scum, they themselves never turned their backs on their families or on the *volk*. In his autobiography Carl recalls the pain he felt on reading a newspaper report during their trial which described them as having broken with their entire Afrikaner heritage. "How can you deny the blood in your veins and the marrow in your bones?" he wrote. He also recalls the advice Beyers Naude gave him, over and over again during those early years of counselling when he was trying to come to terms with his rebellion. "Whatever happens," the old dissident said, drawing on his own long experience, "don't ever try to deny your Afrikanerdom. Because you cannot."[20] And when I interviewed the couple again a decade after Carl's release and seven years into the new South Africa, they were still adamant. Whatever other young Afrikaners might be experiencing, they had no identity crisis.

Yet Carl Niehaus's role within the new black ruling establishment is not without its problems. Like some other left-wing whites in the ANC, he has found himself gradually sidelined. Their struggle credentials notwithstanding, they, too, are having to make way in the interests of affirmative action. When Carl's ambassadorial term in Holland ended there was no new diplomatic assignment: the once all-white, predominantly Afrikaner foreign service is being Africanized. Nor was there any redeployment offer to some new position in the government service. And so Carl slipped quietly into the private sector.

He is not bitter, but there are indications that he has gone through a phase of some confusion and introspection because of this. "Yes, I made a stand," he says, "but I have come to realize these last couple of years that that does not absolve me from what happened in this country and with white Afrikaners. It does not release me from that burden. The historical reality of this country, in terms of the way blacks were oppressed and whites privileged, is that there is now a demand for affirmative action. My first reaction may be to say, but dammit I'm different, I was part of the struggle, I sat in prison. But then you have to go beyond that and say, yes, I am white, I also benefitted from apartheid along with other whites, and I must accept that I am going to have to face part of the same reality as the other whites and see my opportunities limited because of it."

This has become a new article of faith in Niehaus's reincarnated existence, to the point where he launched a national campaign urging all whites to sign a declaration acknowledging that they had been beneficiaries of apartheid through the superior education, health services and other developmental opportunities they and their forebears enjoyed. It was a crusade that aroused almost as much emotional hostility as his original breach with ethnic protocol, and this time not only from fellow Afrikaners. The white leadership of the liberal Democratic Party, which is strongly opposed to affirmative action, was among those who refused to sign, holding that their long parliamentary opposition to apartheid absolved them of all blame for it.

But what does being an Afrikaner mean to such a couple who have been so far estranged from their people's fundamental philosophies and sense of national consciousness and self-justification? If they lost their sense of Afrikaner nationalism before, and now that nationalism itself is dead and there is no longer an Afrikaner state, what is left? What gives them their sense of identity as Afrikaners?

"The language," says Carl. "The fact that I speak Afrikaans. That is the core, I think. And with that goes some of the history, experiences such as the Anglo-Boer War and the impact those experiences had on the psyche of a group of people in this country. It's all part of understanding how I have been formed, how my parents brought me up and where I was brought up."

Jansie, too, feels the Afrikaans language lies at the heart of her own self-identity, a fact which ironically she feels she only fully appreciated while living in Holland as the ambassador's wife. "Precisely because the languages are so similar and yet as people we are so different," she says, "I developed a sense that being an Afrikaner has to do with being in Africa, of living with all these other people who, even though we tried to cut them off from us, somehow made us who we are." The language, she feels, with all its indigenous assimilations, from African tribes, from Khoi and San and Batavian slaves, is what epitomizes this. It is a trend she believes should be allowed to expand. The apartheid clinicians tried to purify the language, coining fancy new words to replace the alien influences; they hijacked it the way they hijacked Afrikaner history for their ideological purposes. "But a language is an organic, living thing, it is in people's mouths, not in dictionaries, and it must be allowed to absorb more from the African languages around it."

That, too, is their paradigm for the Afrikaner future in the new rainbow nation. "I think we are going to find that we'll muddle through," says Carl. "We won't have the melting pot model of America, nor will it be the kind of rainbow that has all the different strands of colour clearly defined. I think we'll have some people who still have some sense of ethnic identity, as being Zulu or Tswana or Afrikaner, but it will be watered down. We'll all end up speaking a kind of Africanized English, and we'll continue speaking our own languages, but rather badly I'm afraid, because they will lose their purity as all the other languages of South Africa influence them.

145

"In other words it will be a sort of frazzled rainbow, with the edges all blending into each other."

Frazzled rainbow or tamed tiger. Whatever the metaphor, the prospects seem good that the Afrikaner *volk* and their language will survive and find their place in the new multicultural society, and that the intense ethno-nationalism that drove them to the separatist and supremacist obsessions of apartheid will fade over time into a dim and guilt-ridden aspect of history whose own shame will serve to prevent its re-emergence, much as has happened with Nazism in Germany.

But the very concept of a rainbow nation forbids complacency. We need to take careful note of Isaiah Berlin's warning that the greatest defect in the Western political tradition, with its emphasis on rationality, individualism and universalism, has been to underestimate the power of group loyalty and its potential for embittered and aggressive self-assertion. Our own blood-soaked history is testimony to this, and history has a way of repeating itself. Group grievance is the danger. Berlin uses the German Romantic poet Friederich von Schiller's analogy of a bent twig to illustrate his point. You can bend the twig safely for a moderate distance, says Schiller, but bend it too far and it will lash back with painful consequences. Group consciousness can be tolerant and peaceful, says Berlin, but bend it too far with a sense of collective grievance or humiliation and it will react like Schiller's twig.[21] It is a warning every multicultural society on earth, and the world as a whole, should internalize.

As we set about building our new rainbow nation, frazzled as it may be around the edges, it is the twig not the tiger we must beware of.

CHAPTER EIGHT

OF CRIMES AND CONFESSIONS

By not dealing with past human rights violations, we are not simply
protecting the perpetrators' trivial old age; we are thereby ripping
the foundations of justice from beneath new generations.
— ALEXANDER SOLZHENITSYN

The deaths began within a few months of Prime Minister John Vorster introducing a 90-day detention law in 1963. The decision by the ANC 18 months before to resort to armed struggle after being outlawed by Vorster's predecessor, Hendrik Verwoerd, provided the tough new Prime Minister with the excuse he needed to bypass the rule of law and embark on an all-out campaign to try to smash all black resistance to apartheid. Vorster appointed his old buddy with whom he had been interned as a Nazi sympathizer during World War II, Hendrik van den Bergh, as Chief of the Security Police, trebled the size of that force and equipped it with draconian laws that enabled it to detain people without trial indefinitely. The 90 days could be repeated – "this side of eternity", as Vorster told Parliament. Two years later, to save paperwork, the initial detention term was doubled to 180 days, and in 1967 it was made open-ended. At the same time the Security Police were empowered to ban people – prohibiting them from meeting with more than one other person at a time and from speaking or being quoted in public – and to house-arrest them without trial; while acts of "sabotage" and "terrorism", both broadly defined, were made capital offences.

The first to die was Looksmart Ngudle, a young man who had joined the ANC's underground armed wing that was then planning acts of sabotage against strategic installations. He was arrested on 20 August 1963, and two weeks later was found hanged in his cell at a Pretoria police station. In a process that was to be repeated scores of times in the coming years, an inquest was held. There was medical evidence indicating that he had been tortured, but the magistrate hearing the case rejected it as unproven. There were no independent witnesses. Ngudle had been alone with his interrogators, and their testimony was that he had committed suicide to avoid betraying his organization. This the magistrate accepted. His finding, repeated over and over again during the next 27 years, was that no one was to blame.[1]

A year later Suliman Salojee, a 32-year-old apprentice attorney, fell to his death from a seventh-floor window of a building called The Grays, which then served as the Security Police headquarters in Johannesburg, where a notorious officer named Theuns Swanepoel – known as "Rooi Rus", or the Red Russian because of his red face and bull neck – had been interrogating him. Again the police claimed it was suicide and the magistrate accepted this. There was a repeat scenario in the case of Ahmed Timol, whom police said jumped to his death from a tenth-floor window at John Vorster Square, a new police headquarters building that replaced The Grays.

Gordon Winter, a journalist who had worked on my staff at the *Sunday Express* but later confessed to having been an agent for the Bureau of State Security (BOSS), an expanded body that incorporated the Security Police, subsequently claimed that both Salojee and Timol had been held by their ankles from the windows to terrify them into making confessions – and that the interrogators' grip had slipped.

Other improbable police explanations followed for the steady stream of deaths in detention. Interrogators claimed the 26 heavy bruises pathologists found on the body of Imam Abdullah Haron, a Cape Town Muslim leader and political activist, were the result of his having fallen down a flight of steps which they said had also induced a fatal heart attack. Nicodemus Kgoathe supposedly died after falling in the shower at a Pretoria police station, where Solomon Modipane, who was detained there with him, was said to have died after slipping on a piece of soap. In every case the magistrates accepted the police versions and found that no one was to blame for the prisoners' deaths.

Then came the big one. On the night of 17 August 1977 Stephen Bantu Biko, who must rank close to Mandela as one of the most remarkable figures in the whole long saga of black political resistance to apartheid, was stopped at a roadblock near the Eastern Cape city of Grahamstown and taken into detention for breaking a banning order which restricted him to his home district of King William's Town. Steve Biko was the founding spirit behind the Black Consciousness movement which had spread like a veld fire through the dry grass of black South African politics after the banning of the ANC and the Pan-Africanist Congress and Vorster's heavy crackdown on their lay membership. It had captured the imagination of the youth in particular and

148

ignited the massive black student uprisings that began in Soweto in June 1976 and shook the country for the next ten months. I did not know Biko personally but was aware of his burgeoning image and reputation for unflinching courage. My lifelong friend and fellow editor, Donald Woods, who lived in the Eastern Cape and knew Biko well, had given me glowing reports of this exceptional young man, describing him as "the most important political leader in the entire country and quite simply the greatest man I have ever had the privilege to know."

The news of Biko's death in detention staggered the country. Even the obsequious Afrikaans press seemed incredulous. More outrageous still was the callousness of the Minister of Justice, Jimmy Kruger, in announcing the news to the Transvaal congress of the National Party in Pretoria. Biko had died, he told the party members, of a hunger strike. To which he gratuitously added that he was indifferent to the black leader's fate. "I am not pleased nor am I sorry," he said. "It leaves me cold."

I was editor of the *Rand Daily Mail* at this time, and a few days after Biko's death I received a telephone call from Dr Jonathan Gluckman, a leading pathologist who had featured in many of the death-in-detention cases and with whom I had formed a close friendship. The call was terse and his voice sounded strained. "Meet me at my home this evening," he said, and hung up.

That evening he took me into his garden, away from any possible listening devices, and told me in confidential tones that Kruger had lied about the cause of Biko's death. "The family have engaged me as their private pathologist," he said, "and I have just attended the post-mortem examination. There was no hunger strike. Biko died of brain damage." Gluckman went on to explain that the back of the black leader's head had suffered a heavy blow causing the brain to jolt forward in an action known as a contra-coup and smash against the frontal part of the skull, causing the soft cells to break up and start bleeding. Clearly he had been attacked and killed by his interrogators.

It was a dramatic story of supreme national importance, but how to publish it was the problem. Gluckman had given me a copy of the post-mortem report signed by himself and the state pathologist, but he made me promise not to disclose that I had it or that he had revealed the findings to me. He explained that what he was doing in giving me this information was irregular and could lead to his exclusion from the inquest hearing, but he was so outraged by the Minister's untruthful statement that he felt ethically bound to expose the lie.

My problem was how to publish the story without disclosing the source. The English-language press was under tremendous pressure from the Vorster government, and faced with the threat of a severe new press control law had agreed to subject itself to the jurisdiction of a voluntary Press Council that would adjudicate on complaints against individual newspapers. I knew I would be hopelessly exposed to a charge before the council if I were to publish a story of such magnitude with no attributable source and no way of proving its accuracy. But I also knew the story was true and too important to suppress.

I briefed the paper's political correspondent, Helen Zille, whom I regarded as the most meticulous journalist on the staff, and sent her to confront the state doctors in Port Elizabeth who had attended Biko during his last days. She was to ask them whether they knew he had suffered brain damage. Not surprisingly, they refused to respond. But at least this gave us a source of sorts. On Zille's return we wrote a carefully crafted report, stating that she had met the medical specialists who had examined Biko in detention and confronted them with information in the newspaper's possession that he had not died of a hunger strike but of brain damage. It was still a defective report in that it did not explicitly cite the source of the information, but it was the best we could do and I decided to take a chance and publish.

Kruger was outraged. Or at least he feigned outrage. He demanded an immediate hearing of the Press Council that very day. I refused, claiming my right under the Press Council's rules to seven days to prepare my case which I hoped would allow time for confirmation of our report to emerge elsewhere. But the chairman of the Newspaper Press Union, the proprietors' body, and eventually even my own managing-director, Leicester Walton, put relentless pressure on me to accede, saying the whole government was in a fury and if I refused they feared Vorster would use that as a pretext to introduce his threatened press law. They inferred that I would be responsible for the destruction of what was left of press freedom in South Africa.

So we went to a hearing that night. The case was heard by a retired Appeal Court judge, Oscar Galgut, and I was represented by the prince of South Africa's many fine civil rights lawyers, Sydney Kentridge, now an eminent QC in Britain. Kruger, showing as much contempt for the process he had demanded as he had for the prisoner his police had killed, did not bother to attend. It was a farcical hearing. Kentridge made it clear that I had solid, irrefutable evidence of the true cause of Biko's death but was honour bound not to disclose the source, that we had confronted the doctors in Port Elizabeth with it and they had not denied it, and that what we had published would inevitably be vindicated when the inquest was held. But Galgut, like all those inquest magistrates, was unmoved. If a scalp was needed to keep Vorster at bay, here was one at hand. He found against the *Rand Daily Mail* and compelled me to publish an apology to Kruger in the next day's paper. To its shame that conviction by my own professional body still stands against my name – guilty of having published the truth in one of the most disgraceful cases of state murder in our country's history.

In due time, of course, as Kentridge had predicted, the facts about Biko's terrible death were revealed at the inquest. The facts, but not the culprits. Again, as in all the other cases of death in detention between 1963 and 1990, the interrogators and the torturers and the killers systematically denied their role and in the absence of other witnesses in those dark and secluded gulags the magistrate simply accepted their protestations of innocence.

In the Biko case, however, even the sanitized version the interrogators gave was horrifying enough to appall the whole world. For three weeks Biko had been kept, naked and manacled, on a mat in a suburban police station cell. Then on the morning of 6 September 1977 he was taken for interrogation to the Security Police offices in central Port Elizabeth. Five men, led by Major Harold Snyman, questioned him. There was a fight. A "scuffle", the interrogators called it, in which they claimed Biko "went berserk" on being confronted with incriminating evidence against him. In the course of this scuffle, the interrogators said, Biko had "bumped his head", but they were vague about what had caused the bump or what its effect had been. All they would say was that he had later been put in a cell, naked and manacled once more – which they insisted was on orders of their commander – and left for the night. Next morning the local Security Police chief, Col Pieter Goosen, noticed that Biko had not moved and his blankets were soaked with urine. Goosen said he thought Biko was "shamming" but called in a district surgeon, Dr Ivor Lang, who told him there was nothing wrong with the prisoner and made out a medical certificate stating this. Later the chief district surgeon, Dr Benjamin Tucker, advised that Biko be admitted to the prison hospital. For four more days Biko lay there in a comatose state while the interrogators pondered what to do. A specialist physician, Colin Hersch, ordered a lumber puncture which revealed blood in the spinal fluid. A neurosurgeon, Roger Keeley, was consulted by telephone and said the signs did not indicate brain damage. By 11

September Goosen decided to send Biko to a prison hospital in Pretoria. So the unconscious prisoner was bundled into the back of a Land Rover, still naked and manacled and lying on mats, and driven 1 200 km (750 miles) through the night to Pretoria. There he was put on a drip and left lying in the prison hospital. He died the following night.

Kentridge's cross-examination at the inquest exposed huge holes in the interrogators' story. It made no difference. In the most notorious finding of all, the Chief Magistrate of Pretoria, Marthinus Prins, took just three minutes to dispose of the case. "The available evidence," he said, "does not prove that the death was brought about by any act or omission involving or amounting to an offence on the part of any person."

The interrogators went back to work, and a year later Col Goosen was promoted to Deputy Commissioner of Police. One of the interrogation team, Capt. Daniel Siebert, became a general.

* * *

But if this was bad, worse was to come. The 1980s brought a sea change in the apartheid regime's approach to national security. Until then it had been seen as a police matter with at least a token effort to handle it within the framework of domestic law, however much that framework had been distorted by legislation that violated the rule of law. But 1980 saw the collapse of white rule in neighbouring Rhodesia and the growth of black regimes sympathetic to the ANC in the former Portuguese colonies of Mozambique and Angola. International pressure mounted on South Africa to give independence to Namibia, a former German colony then called South West Africa which Pretoria administered under an old League of Nations mandate granted after World War I. The apartheid regime felt itself to be increasingly under an external as well as an internal threat. It was becoming more deeply involved militarily in resisting the liberation struggle of the South West African People's Organization (Swapo), which was being aided by Angolan-based Cuban troops as well as the Angolan army equipped with Russian T-54 tanks, missile-firing helicopters and Mig jet fighters. Former Defence Minister P W Botha had succeeded John Vorster as Prime Minister, bringing with him a more militaristic mindset. The focus of Pretoria's perception of the security situation began to shift, to see it more in terms of a foreign war being waged against foreign foes on foreign soil. That meant the observance of domestic law was less of an issue. Killing the enemy in a foreign war was not murder. Moreover it was a terrorist war, went the rationale, and the prevailing military doctrine on counter-terrorist warfare was that the defending forces should use the same ruthless methods as the terrorists.

And so the use of death squads and dirty-tricks units arose.

The first of the death squads, or special force units as they were euphemistically called, was named *Koevoet*, an Afrikaans word meaning crowbar. It was a fearsome outfit that carried out assassinations, poisoned food supplies, planted booby traps and car bombs, and sometimes secreted incriminating evidence into the homes of targeted individuals to discredit or terrify them. In the field the unit moved with expert Ovambo and Bushmen trackers and fought ruthlessly, taking no prisoners and often executing men, women and children on a whim and keeping body parts as trophies.

Then as black militancy began escalating at home from September 1984, and South Africa began contemplating independence for Namibia to concentrate its defences on the home front, the strategies and attitudes that had evolved in the Namibian war were brought back – together with some of the *Koevoet* veterans. Death squads and dirty-tricks units were formed in South Africa as well: a special defence force organization called the Civil Co-operation Bureau (CCB), which described its own mission as "killing, infiltration, bribery, destruction and compromising (people)"; another called Strategic Communications, or Stratcom, which specialized in planting propaganda and disinformation in the media to "counter negative reporting on South Africa"; and, most fearsome of all, a special hit unit of the Security Police called C-1 which established its base on a farm north of Pretoria called Vlakplaas.

Alongside these structural changes in the defence apparatus, the Botha regime developed a new strategic doctrine that was to alter the administrative structure of the country. Underlying the doctrine was a belief that South Africa was the target of a "total onslaught" directed from Moscow to overthrow white rule and install the ANC as the Soviet Union's puppet regime and so give the communist empire a foothold in Africa's most resource-rich region. The concept of the "total onslaught", extrapolated from the writings of a French military strategist, General Andre Beaufre, and an American, Lt-Col John J McCuen, held that revolutionary movements waged their struggle at every level of society, aimed at undermining the authority of the regime at the social, political, economic, media, educational, religious, administrative and psychological levels. To counter this one required a "total strategy" that could meet the assault in all these sectors. And so was born an elaborate new

153

structure, called the National Security Management System, to give effect to Botha's "total strategy". At its apex was the State Security Council, headed by the President, and including the Ministers of Defence, Justice, Law and Order, and Foreign Affairs, the Chief of the Defence Force, the Commissioner of Police, and other members of the Cabinet and civil service whom the President chose to co-opt. The State Security Council was served by a Secretariat with a full-time staff headed by a defence force general.

At the regional level were a series of Joint Management Centres (JMCs) comprising regional political leaders and military and police chiefs, while at municipal and village levels there were sub- and mini-JMCs established in the same way and including fire services and civil defence units. All were dominated by Security Police and Military Intelligence representatives. Their job was to keep watch on every aspect of society for political agitators and activists, and at the same time be on the alert for community grievances, such as bad roads or a broken communal water tap, that the agitators might be able to exploit, and order the relevant government departments or local authorities to rectify them in the interests of national security. It was done in the name of "winning the hearts and minds of the people", but in reality it meant the establishment of a massive military-security government within the civilian government, and that Big Brother loomed large over the entire society.

"We were told that the enemy was 'everywhere', in universities, trade unions and cultural organizations," Eugene de Kock, a former *Koevoet* commander who became the head of C-1 and the country's most notorious hit-man, wrote in his autobiography. "They all harboured enemies of the state who were waging psychological and economic warfare against us."[2]

These enemies had to be rooted out. As we were to learn later, the system included weekly meetings of a select group of Security Police chiefs known as the *Sanhedrin* – a name taken from the rabbinical court in Biblical Jerusalem that found Jesus Christ guilty of blasphemy and handed him over to the Roman governor, Pontius Pilate, for punishment – which studied reports from the JMC network and literally decided who should live and who should die. Permission to assassinate was then sought from the State Security Council and the task assigned to one of the death squads. So began an altogether new level of political murders.

* * *

The first thing one noticed about Matthew Goniwe was his smile. A big, broad, Jimmy Carter smile that announced his arrival like a signature tune. I first encountered Goniwe, and his smile, when I visited the small Eastern Cape town of Cradock, where he lived, in November 1984. I had gone there to report on the remarkable phenomenon of a rural revolution that had effectively paralysed a chain of country towns in the old frontier region of the Eastern Cape where the first British settlers – including my own ancestors – had landed in 1820 and established a farming community on the edge of the lands of the Xhosa people with whom they then fought nine expansionist wars. The great black uprising that was finally to drive South Africa to its political epiphany had begun in the townships around Johannesburg three months before and quickly spread to other areas. Now, remarkably, it had caught fire in this rural area as well. The Eastern Cape had been an early growth point for the ANC, for this is where the first mission schools and Fort Hare University were located, which had given many of the older leaders, such as Nelson Mandela and Oliver Tambo, their education. Still, rural rebelliousness was unusual: the tribal folk were mostly uneducated and in their slow and amiable ways tended to be placid and apolitical. But here they were boiling with militancy in Cradock and a dozen other nearby towns as the young activists organized strikes, street demonstrations and consumer boycotts that brought administrative and commercial activity to a standstill. The government had already classified much of the region as "ungovernable".

The reason was Matthew Goniwe. This remarkable young school teacher had been imprisoned for four years in the nominally independent Transkei tribal "homeland" for political activism, after which he had moved to Cradock with his young family and taken up another teaching post in the apartheid government's segregated education system. He had kept a low political profile to begin with and been rapidly promoted to acting principal of the Sam Xhallie secondary school in Cradock's run-down black township of Lingelihle. The school was in poor shape when Goniwe took over, but he quickly inspired a spirit of pride and self-discipline among the students. Then as his local reputation spread and the great black rebellion began in the north, he reverted to political activism. With a fellow teacher at the Sam Xhallie school, Fort Calata, he formed the Cradock Residents Association, known as Cradora, which began campaigning for improvements to the wretched facilities in Lingelihle. As the rebellion burgeoned, Cradora's influence spread to neighbouring towns and Goniwe became first a regional and then a national figure. In desperation the government ordered him transferred to another school in a distant town, but a mass meeting of Lingelihle residents demanded that Goniwe refuse the transfer, which he did at the cost of his job. And so he became a full-time political activist and a major problem for the apartheid administration.

That was why I went to see him. We met in a sleazy hotel in a Coloured township adjoining Lingelihle, where he strode in wearing his smile and we talked for the entire afternoon. Just as Donald Woods had been riveted by the personality of Steve Biko, so was I by Matthew Goniwe. I found him charming, intelligent and wonderfully relaxed despite the fraught circumstances in which he was operating under the menacing surveillance of the local Security Police. When I left to make a quick drive around Lingelihle I was promptly arrested and taken to the police station for questioning. What was I doing there? What was my interest in Goniwe? What did I know about him? When I telephoned Goniwe that night to tell him what had happened, he laughed. "Now you know what it's like here," he said lightly.

We became friends and I telephoned him frequently after that for updates on what was happening in the region. The following May I drove back to Cradock with my wife and young son to introduce them to Goniwe. Next day he was due to attend a weekly meeting in Port Elizabeth of the United Democratic Front, a newly formed alliance of activist organizations that was really the local front for the outlawed ANC, and I offered him a lift. We chatted animatedly as we drove along the lonely country road. As I dropped him off at the UDF office we bade each other farewell. "Please take care, Matthew," I enjoined him. "I don't like this road. It's too lonely."

A month later he was dead.

At first all we knew was that he had disappeared. He had not returned home from one of his weekly trips to the UDF meetings in Port Elizabeth. His wife, Nyameka, was worried: colleagues at the UDF office told her next morning that Matthew had left after dark with three companions, Fort Calata, Sparrow Mkonto and Sicelo Mhlauli, but there was no sign of them. Then a road worker found a burnt-out car in the coastal shrubbery off the Port Elizabeth-Cradock road near a spot called Bluewater Bay. Its scorched registration plates indicated it was an old scrapped vehicle that had apparently been abandoned there. There the matter may have remained, the fate of Goniwe and his companions forever unexplained like the *desaparecidos* of Latin America, except that the killers had bungled. In fitting false registration plates to the car before setting it on fire they had dropped one of the originals in the shrubbery. This enabled the car to be identified as Goniwe's. A search began and over the next four days the bodies were found, dumped in separate spots up to 14 km apart. Their injuries were extensive. Mhlauli, the first to be found, had been stabbed more than thirty times and his throat slit, and his right hand was missing. The others had also been stabbed, and Mkonto had been shot in the head. All the bodies had been mutilated and burned to prevent identification. But for the registration plate they would have appeared to be just four more anonymous victims of the political violence then sweeping the country.

The inquest, held three years later, was as inconclusive as all the others of the apartheid era. The family's lawyer, Arthur Chaskalson – now the Chief Justice of South Africa – was able to note that all the circumstantial evidence indicated the killings were the work of a professional death squad that knew precisely what the victims' movements were, which had lain in wait for them, stopped them, killed them and sought to make them disappear. But the magistrate's finding was the same old refrain: "Their deaths were brought about by a person or persons or group of persons unknown."

Eight months later a startling new development brought more substantive evidence of state-sponsored death squads. A black member of the Security Police, Almond Butana Nofomela, was due to be executed at dawn on 20 October 1989 for the freelance killing of a white farmer – and as Samuel Johnson once noted, nothing concentrates the mind so wonderfully as knowing you are about to be hanged. So on the evening of the 19th, after the condemned man's commanders whom he thought would help free him had visited his Death Row cell to tell him instead that he would have to "take the pain" for killing a white man, Nofomela telephoned Lawyers for Human Rights in Johannesburg to say he wanted to make a statement. So it came about that on the night before he was due to die Nofomela made an affidavit in his cell to lawyer Shanks Mabitsela that blew the lid off the Vlakplaas death squads. He told of assassinations he had been involved in as a member of a Security Police death squad and named the commander of the squad as Capt. Dirk Coetzee. The statement saved Nofomela's life, for he was granted a stay of execution as an important potential state witness, then indemnity, and eventually amnesty.

Coetzee, meanwhile, had been tracked down by Jacques Pauw of that wonderful little Afrikaans newspaper, *Vrye Weekblad*. When Nofomela named him he panicked and fled the country. Pauw followed him and in the weeks that followed Coetzee gave the journalist a detailed account of what his death squad had done, which *Vrye Weekblad* published.

In the public outcry that followed, F W de Klerk, who had just succeeded P W Botha as President, appointed the Attorney-General of Natal Province, Tim McNally, to head an investigation into the allegations. It was the same old story: McNally found there was no evidence that Nofomela and Coetzee were telling the truth. As public pressure continued to mount, De Klerk appointed a judicial commission of inquiry under Judge Louis Harms. But the commission's terms of reference were severely restricted: it could neither subpoena witnesses nor grant them indemnity from prosecution. And McNally, despite his questionable record in the earlier hearing, was appointed to lead the evidence. Vital documents were withheld and several senior officers refused to testify. Some appeared in disguise and testified under false names. Many, it was later revealed, lied systematically. In the end Harms found that the Civil Co-operation Bureau had been involved in death squad activities, but he named no specific culprits and exonerated the police and the military.

The next glimpse into the cesspool of state-sponsored crimes came with a re-opening of the Goniwe inquest in 1992. By this time the ANC had been unbanned and the country was moving towards the negotiating table, with the result that some troubled consciences were beginning to twinge. Someone in the military-security establishment – thought to be Col Lourens du Plessis, secretary of the Eastern Province JMC – slipped a vital document to Bantu Holomisa, then president of the nominally independent Transkei "homeland", who in turn passed it to Zwelakhe Sisulu's *New Nation* newspaper, which published it. Holomisa was a maverick figure who became head of the "homeland's" army then seized power in a coup that took Pretoria by surprise, after which he gradually began to reveal his ANC sympathies.

The document was a signal message which Du Plessis had sent on behalf of the chairman of the Eastern Province JMC, Gen. Joffel van der Westhuizen, to the chairman of the strategy branch of the Secretariat of the State Security Council, Gen. Johannes Janse van Rensburg. It listed the names of three men, Matthew Goniwe, his cousin, Mbulelo Goniwe, and Fort Calata, then said simply: "It is requested that the above-mentioned persons be removed permanently from society as a matter of urgency." The date on the message was 7 June 1985 – 20 days before the Cradock Four were murdered.

It was a smoking gun pointing to the very apex of the country's political leadership, at the President and his most senior ministers on the State Security Council, but once again the old regime's protective reflexes went into operation.

A new inquest was ordered, this time heard by the Judge-President of the Eastern Cape, Neville Zietsman. Col du Plessis testified that he had prepared the signal message on Gen. van der Westhuizen's orders and transmitted it to the State Security Council. Goniwe, Du Plessis said, had become such a problem for the government that Van der Westhuizen risked losing his job if he did not resolve it. He said, too, that the general was quite explicit in briefing him to use the phrase "permanently removed from society", which he, Du Plessis, knew to be a common military euphemism for having someone killed. He certainly understood the message to mean that the general was seeking permission for the three activists to be assassinated. Van der Westhuizen himself, however, insisted that Du Plessis had misunderstood him: all he had wanted was for the Cradock activists to be detained. For his part, Gen. van Rensburg told the judge he could not remember ever having received such a signal message and did not know what had become of it. In any event, he insisted, the State Security Council did not authorize killings. If the signal had been sent there, it had been sent to the wrong address.

Dead end again. Judge Zietsman's finding went further than any before it, but still failed to find anyone responsible. The problem, he explained, was that there was no evidence of what had happened to the signal after it had been sent to Gen. van Rensburg, which meant there was no evidence that it had been passed on to a higher authority which had then acted on it. And while he did find that the murders had been committed by members of the security forces, "I am not able, on the evidence placed before me, to identify the murderer or murderers."

* * *

The problem that faced the new South Africa was how to set this grim history of atrocities straight. The long record of official cover-ups could not be allowed to stand, for that would not only serve to legitimize such actions and reinforce the sense of impunity of the security forces, it would also leave the victims filled with a sense of unrequited grievance that might fester over time and be mythologized into powerful ethnic hatreds. The history of the Balkans and of Northern Ireland offer stark warnings of this.

It seems clear, therefore, that if ever there is to be a true spirit of national unity in South Africa, the victims of oppression and its perpetrators must come to terms with one another. Equally, if ever there is to be a sound democracy based on respect for human values then past violations of those values must be exposed and purged from the national psyche. All the great religions call for conflicts to be resolved through reconciliation, which they say can come about only if there is first confession and atonement. The political scientists tell us much the same. Guillermo O'Donnell and Philippe C Schmitter, in their seminal comparative work on transitions from authoritarian rule in a number of European and Latin American countries, are emphatic in their advice.

"It is difficult to imagine how a society can return to some degree of functioning which would provide social and ideological support for political democracy," they write, "without somehow coming to terms with the most painful elements of its own past. By refusing to confront and to purge itself of its worst fears and resentments, such a society would be burying not just its past but the very ethical values it needs to make its future livable."[3]

How to achieve this was the problem. You cannot have Nüremberg trials after a negotiated settlement, with executions and imprisonment of the guilty. The prospect of that would ensure that you never reached a negotiated settlement in the first place. At the other end of the spectrum De Klerk and the National Party establishment wanted a general amnesty for everyone who had been involved in the political conflicts of the past. The liberation movements were not prepared to accept such a whitewashing of the past. So the matter went to the Negotiating Council where the parties eventually settled for a trade-off – the exchange of truth for amnesty. Those who had committed atrocities could make their confessions and be indemnified from prosecution. Thus was born the Truth and Reconciliation Commission, headed by that prince of compassion, Archbishop Desmond Tutu.

The commission was formed on 5 December 1995. Its role, set out in an Act of the new Parliament, was to compile as complete a picture as possible of gross human rights violations that had taken place between 1 March 1990 and 5 December 1993. To do this the commission divided its functions into two parts. Separate units of the commission would travel about the country taking testimony from victims and gathering information about atrocities that had been committed; while a specialist amnesty committee of five, with three judges, would receive applications for amnesty which separate units, each headed by a judge, would then hear and adjudicate. There was also a reparations committee given the task of recommending a system of reparation to the government.

The archbishop's commission thus became a series of travelling confessionals that investigated 31 000 cases of human rights abuses in three years and in the end presented President Mandela with a report of one million words. Unlike other truth commissions in countries such as Chile, Argentina and El Salvador which sat behind closed doors and kept their reports secret, South Africa's TRC was open to the public. Hearings were in community halls in cities and small towns, often in the black townships where the atrocities had been committed and the victims lived, which were packed with spectators. More than that, they were covered extensively by the media, with highlights broadcast to the nation on radio and television in all the country's 11 official languages. In addition to featuring key items in its nightly news bulletins, SABC-TV broadcast a special programme on each week's hearings in prime time on Sunday evenings, anchored by the former editor of *Vrye Weekblad*, Max du Preez. Another Afrikaner, the talented poet Antjie Krog, headed the SABC radio team whose special importance was that their broadcasts reached the poor and illiterate masses. And so this remarkable process of confession and catharsis, of victims and torturers and widows and assassins confronting one another and talking through their guilt and pain, became a truly national experience played out in homes and offices throughout the country

For the first six months the TRC heard evidence from the victims. The settings for these hearings were stark, far removed from the pomp and ritual of court cases with robed lawyers and stern-faced officials. The community halls where they were held were mostly sparsely furnished, with the commissioners sitting on hard-backed chairs on a small stage, the witnesses at little tables and the audiences on stools in their working clothes. But the action was charged with high emotion and the testimony often wrenching. As Alex Boraine, a former Methodist minister and liberal politician who served as Tutu's deputy on the commission, has written: "It was a ritual, deeply needed to cleanse a nation. It was a drama. The actors were in the main ordinary people with a powerful story. But this was no brilliantly written play; it was the unvarnished truth in all its starkness."[4]

The hearings began in East London on 16 April 1996, the commissioners having chosen an Eastern Cape city because they felt that was where the worst atrocities had occurred. One of the first to testify was Nomonde Calata, the widow of Goniwe's friend Fort Calata, whose display of raw, heartrending pain 14 years after her husband's death provided a defining moment for the entire TRC process. Nomonde was only 20 when Fort died, newly married and deeply in love, torn between admiration for her young husband and constant worry about the risks he was running. She talked about her fever of anxiety the night Fort did not come home. She lay awake growing more agitated by the hour. From time to time she would get up and peer out of the window, only, with bitter irony, to become even more anxious because the police in their distinctive yellow vans and big armoured Casspirs who had kept constant watch on their home for months were no longer there. Why weren't they there? Was it because they knew there was no need to keep watch any longer? Morning came and there was still no word. She went over to Nyameka Goniwe's home where she saw the other young woman weeping.

At that moment in the telling of her story Nomonde Calata disintegrated. She threw her head back and let out a terrible cry. "A primeval and spontaneous wail from the depths of her soul," is how Boraine, who was on the panel of commissioners hearing her testimony, described it. "It was that cry from the soul that transformed the hearings from a litany of suffering and pain to an even deeper level. It caught up in a single howl all the darkness and horror of the apartheid years."[5] It transfixed everyone who was present and was carried on radio and television throughout South Africa. For Krog, sitting in the reporters' gallery, it was "the signature tune, the defining moment, the ultimate sound of what the process is about. She was wearing this vivid orange dress, and she threw herself backwards and that sound … that sound … it will haunt me for ever and ever."[6]

Bit by bit, in town after town around the country, the truth came out about at least some of apartheid's worst atrocities. White South Africa, which had voted for the policy in ever-increasing numbers for half a century, was confronted with the appalling facts of the crimes committed in its name. And there could be no escaping them, for these were not reports that could be disbelieved or denied. They were confessions, by the perpetrators themselves.

White South Africans who for so long had refused to believe court testimony and newspaper reports of routine torturing of political prisoners saw on their television screens a burly Security Police torturer, Capt. Jeffrey Benzien, squat on the back of a black victim lying face

OF CRIMES AND CONFESSIONS

down on the floor and demonstrate how he pulled a wet bag over the man's head to suffocate him to the edge of death. They heard others testify how they "tubed" political prisoners, pulling a strip of rubber tubing over the prisoner's nose and mouth and sometimes keeping it there too long, so that the victim died. When the victims suddenly voided their bladders, one torturer explained, "then you knew they had gone to another place". They heard the Vlakplaas commander, Capt. Dirk Coetzee, confirm the allegations of Almond Nofomela and the reports in *Vrye Weekblad*. They heard him describe in ghoulish detail how his unit had "taken out" a young activist, Sizwe Kondile, then placed his body on a pyre and sat beside it on a river bank drinking brandy and enjoying a barbecue while it burnt to ashes. "It takes seven hours to burn a human body," Coetzee explained. "The buttocks and upper part of the legs had to be turned frequently to ensure that they were reduced to ashes."

They heard officers in a special chemical warfare unit explain how they developed special poisons that could be sprinkled on the clothing of black leaders, and how they tried to develop a pill that would render black women – only black women – infertile and so cut the black birth-rate. They even considered developing a drug that would give Nelson Mandela meningitis and render him mentally ineffectual before his release from prison.

The cascade of horror was numbing. "We listened to stories of betrayal, of informers, of dirty tricks, of cover-ups, beatings, stabbings, shootings, electric shocks, burning of bodies," writes Alex Boraine. "It was like a huge sewer spilling out its filth and stench."[7] And Antjie Krog again: "Week after week; voice after voice; account after account. It is like travelling on a rainy night behind a huge truck – images of devastation breaking in sheets on the windscreen."[8]

But the TRC was not the only place where the apartheid sewer was spewing out its filth. Almond Nofomela, Dirk Coetzee and *Vrye Weekblad's* disclosures of Security Police death squads operating from their base at Vlakplaas farm had at last prodded President de Klerk into action, if only as an attempt at damage control. The result was the arrest of Coetzee's successor as the head of section C-1 at Vlakplaas, Eugene de Kock, who had become the apartheid regime's chief assassin. His two-year trial, which began in February 1995 and resulted in his being found guilty of 89 charges, including nine of murder, and sentenced to two life terms plus 212 years imprisonment, yielded the most horrifying stories of all.

Aged 44 at the time of his trial, De Kock had been in the killing business all his adult life. He began in the 1970s, fighting in a South African police unit sent to Rhodesia to help Ian Smith in his futile bid to stave off black majority rule in that neighbouring country. After that De Kock transferred to the notorious *Koevoet* unit in Namibia. It was there that De Kock learned the skill of turning black guerrillas against their own kind by terrifying them with torture and the threat of a cruel death. Having perfected *Koevoet's* brutal fighting methods, De Kock returned to Pretoria in 1985 and was given command of the C-1 special unit, whose task was to undertake covert operations against "enemies of the state", meaning supporters of the ANC.

Over the next eight years De Kock's unique talent for violence earned him the nickname "Prime Evil" among his colleagues. He and his unit, consisting largely of turned ANC guerrillas called *askaris,* killed scores of people; De Kock told the court he did not really know how many. Senior police officers around the country would telephone him and give him the names of people they wanted "taken out". Some of the killings were wantonly savage. Once De Kock cleaved a victim's head open with a garden spade. On another occasion, in a fit of rage, he attacked one of his *askaris* with a billiard cue which he broke over the man's head, then beat and kicked him to death.

Members of the unit usually disposed of bodies by wrapping them around a stick of dynamite and blowing them to smithereens. They mailed poisons and booby-trapped bombs hidden in pens, manuscripts, tape recorders and radios to exiles living in Swaziland, Tanzania and Zambia. They blew up the headquarters of the South African Council of Churches and the Congress of South African Trade Unions in Johannesburg, as well as the ANC headquarters in London. And they were rewarded by the authorities. De Kock became one of the most highly decorated officers in the South African Police Force.

Its horrifying revelations aside, De Kock's trial triggered a rush of applications to the TRC's amnesty committee. Until then few had bothered to apply, thinking no doubt there was not enough evidence available to put them at risk of prosecution. But De Kock was an angry man, lashing out at his superiors and the political leadership for instructing men like himself to carry out covert operations and then leaving them to take the rap. He was pointing fingers and naming names, and many who had been associated with him panicked and ran for amnesty. At first five high-ranking Security Police officers applied for amnesty, owning up to 40 murders as well as several bombings, and since they would have to tell all at their hearings this triggered a further rush until nearly eight thousand made applications to the Amnesty Committee.

The amnesty hearings were more formal, more like a court trial, than those at which victims recounted their experiences. Applicants had to satisfy the committee that they had told the whole truth; that their offences had been associated with a political objective; and that they had been committed on behalf of a political organization. In other words they had to show that what they had done was part of the political conflict between the liberation movements and the apartheid regime, not simply the acts of individual racists. Moreover, victims or their families could oppose the applications, which meant their lawyers could cross-examine the killers and torturers and call their own witnesses to challenge their testimony.

Among the 8 000 applicants to the Amnesty Committee were the killers of Steve Biko and the Cradock Four. So finally, after 24 and 16 years respectively of systematic cover-up and official perversion of the legal process, South Africans learned at last who had committed these most heinous of all the state's many murders of its own citizens.

Five senior Security Police officers who constituted the "day squad" that had interrogated Biko on 6 September 1977 – Harold Snyman, Daniel Siebert, Gideon Nieuwoudt, Jacobus Beneke and Rueben Marx – testified about how the so-called "scuffle" had really begun, and how the next day they had all met and agreed to fabricate a different story that all would stick to at whatever inquiries ensued. This even included altering the date on which Biko was fatally injured.

What had really happened, they now said, was that far from Biko having "gone berserk" on being confronted with incriminating evidence, it was in fact Siebert who had become enraged when the Black Consciousness leader insisted on sitting on a chair during the interrogation. This assertion of human dignity was apparently too much for the white policeman, a passionate apartheid ideologue, who had rushed at Biko, grabbed hold of him and hauled him to his feet. That, they said, had started "a very violent struggle" during which, according to Capt. Siebert's deposition to the Amnesty Committee, "three of us grabbed Biko and moved with him in the direction of the corner of the office and ran with him into the wall." Biko fell, dazed, and according to Col Snyman "looked like someone who had been knocked out in a boxing match."

They were vague about the details of the fight and their versions differed. They also denied emphatically that they had beaten up their prisoner or tortured him, but admitted that Sgt Nieuwoudt had lashed him across the back with a length of hosepipe and that after Biko had been knocked out, and while he still looked semi-conscious, they had manacled him, crucifixion style with arms and legs spreadeagled, to a grilled door where they left him, naked and hanging, for three or four hours. Yes, Col Snyman agreed after relentless cross-examination by the Biko family's lawyer, George Bizos, that was inhumane treatment. It was torture. "But we were acting under instructions," Snyman insisted. Whose instructions he would not, or could not, say.

The committee denied the six interrogators amnesty. They were not satisfied the men had told the whole truth. A companion of Biko's, Peter Jones, who was arrested with him, testified that the same five-man interrogation team had handcuffed him and then, as he stood defenceless in the middle of the room, set about systematically beating him up, kicking him and lashing him with chain-filled lengths of hose-pipe until he collapsed in a groaning heap on the floor. Siebert, Jones said, was the most brutal of his assailants and he suspected he was the one who had delivered the fatal blow to Biko. But however inadequate their confessions, South Africa at last knew who Biko's killers were.

The leader of Biko's interrogation team, Harold Snyman, was also among six senior Security Police officers who applied for amnesty for killing the Cradock Four. By now Snyman was on his deathbed, stricken with terminal cancer, and could not appear at the hearing. The other five – Sakkie van Zyl, Nic van Rensburg, Hermanus du Plessis, Gideon Lotz and Eric Taylor – claimed they had acted under Snyman's command and did not know who had instructed him to carry out the assassinations. So the line to the top remained blurred, the destination of the signal message to the State Security Council requesting permission to kill Matthew Goniwe and his colleagues still undisclosed. And so the involvement of the political leadership, including President P W Botha and his top ministers and generals, remained wrapped in secrecy. Significantly Gen. Joffel van der Westhuizen, who had sent the signal, did not apply for amnesty. Presumably he, too, felt secure from prosecution for the same reason.

It was, however, an omission that cost the six policeman their amnesty. That and a deliberate lie they all persisted with about the reason for killing Sicelo Mhlauli. He was in fact not a known political activist but had simply been a passenger in Goniwe's car, getting a lift home to Cradock. The six police officers had obviously killed him along with the others because they could not let a witness to their crime go free, yet foolishly they would not admit this. In their testimony to the committee they insisted they had known him to be a dangerous activist. This was their undoing. George Bizos, that tenacious old warhorse who had fought so many civil rights cases throughout the apartheid era and who appeared here again for the victims' families, demolished their fabrication by producing a document from the Security Police's own files which stated simply: "*Mhlauli – onbekend*" (Mhlauli – unknown). The applicants had overlooked the fact that there was now a new regime in power, and new hands had access to police files.

It was poetic justice that Mhlauli turned out to be their undoing, for the killers had treated him with the most crass disrespect of all. As other testimony before the TRC was to reveal they had cut off one of Mhlauli's hands and kept it preserved in a bottle in their office to terrify other political prisoners during interrogation. "What kind of person, what kind of human being," asks Antjie Krog, "keeps another's hand in a fruit-jar on his desk? What kind of hatred makes animals of people?"[9]

It is difficult to judge how this outpouring has affected the South African public. For some black people it seems to have been cathartic to be able to tell their stories and to hear the confessions. Boraine quotes Lucas Sikwepere who had been shot in the face by police and blinded, then later badly tortured, as saying at the end of his testimony: "I feel what has been making me sick all the time is the fact that I couldn't tell my story. But now it feels like I got my sight back by coming here and telling you the story."[10] For others, it has been infuriating to see the guilty get amnesty and walk free – although I would argue that the shame of exposure has been a punishment in itself. Many whites accused the TRC of being a witch-hunt and of stirring up hatreds that they said would make reconciliation impossible. Some reacted with fury and sent death threats to Tutu and the other commissioners. At one point the New National Party threatened to take the commission to court for bias. Yet others tried to ignore it with a sullen withdrawal. But for a few, mainly white Afrikaners, there is a deep sense of guilt and soul-searching, for theirs was the ruling group and these confessing monsters are their own people. Krog speaks for them when she writes: "In some way or another all Afrikaners are related. From the accents I can guess where they buy their clothes, where they go on holiday, what car they drive, what music they listen to. What I have in common with them is a culture – and part of that culture over decades hatched the abominations for which they are responsible."[11]

At her book launch in mid-1998, Krog offered some further reflections on what her prolonged exposure to the Truth Commission's revelations had meant to her as an Afrikaner. "Some of us may deny it," she said, "but deep down Afrikaners know the truth. We are embarrassed, we are deeply ashamed and isolated in our clumsy, lonely attempts to deal with our guilt." Saying the Truth Commission had shattered the self-image of Afrikaners, she added: "We now know exactly what we as Afrikaners are. A people capable of indescribable evil. But also a people of an honesty to walk the road of this country and this continent."

For me, the importance of the TRC is that it placed the truth on record. Not the whole truth, to be sure. Many cases, perhaps hundreds, were not dealt with, and in others key witnesses were dead or testimony was otherwise unsatisfactory. Worst of all, the political leaders responsible for the whole wicked system have evaded accountability. But for all these shortcomings, the TRC was able to reveal enough to establish the essentials of the apartheid regime's evil doings – the fact of the systematic torturing of prisoners, of state-sponsored death squads, of dirty tricks, official lies and cover-ups and the systematic corruption of the justice system.

It has done so to a degree unequalled by any other post-conflict inquiry. Enough, certainly, to put our historical record straight so that all future generations of South Africans can be taught a history that is based on fact and not on some mythologized or sanitized version of our past. And the facts of that history are not deniable because they came from the mouths of those who committed the deeds. That has been the supreme value of the archbishop's confessional.

What about the TRC's other role, of national reconciliation? This is harder to answer. There have certainly been some individual cases of forgiveness and reconciliation, and these have been remarkable and uplifting. It is significant, too, that there has been no single instance of private revenge as a result of the hearings.

But whether there can be the same kind of cathartic relief and reconciliation at a group or national level as there has been at individual level is questionable. Desmond Tutu and Alex Boraine believe there can be and express regret that the leaders of the National Party have not tried to achieve this through expressions of repentance – but both are men of religion whose faith leads them to such a belief. I am less certain. What I am sure of is that a process of slow, incremental reconciliation is taking place in South Africa as people adjust to the realities of living under a majority government and working and playing more intimately together. It may be that the truths the TRC revealed have played a role in this.

Towards the end of the commission's hearings a minister of the Dutch Reformed Church, Dr Ockie Raubenheimer, invited Archbishop Tutu in his capacity as TRC chairman to preach in Raubenheimer's suburban Johannesburg church. It was a significant invitation: the Dutch Reformed Church, the main denomination of the Afrikaner community, was a pillar of support for the apartheid system, earning for itself the sobriquet of "the National Party at prayer". Raubenheimer, moreover, was a chaplain in the defence force and thus an integral part of the regime's repressive machinery, while Tutu was a symbol of enmity to Afrikaners throughout the apartheid years. Now the two were together before a congregation of Afrikaner notables.

The service began cautiously enough, with Raubenheimer speaking of the Afrikaners' role in the past, saying there was much to be proud of but there had also been some mistakes. But after Tutu's sermon, in which the little archbishop referred to the "evil deeds" of the past and the need for a leader to step forward and help the people come to terms with what had been done, Raubenheimer unexpectedly stepped forward. "I am not scheduled to speak now and actually I am not sure what I am going to say," he began. Then, turning to Tutu, he said: "As a minister in the Dutch Reformed Church for 20 years, as a chaplain in the defence force, I want to say to you we are sorry. For what we have done wrong we ask the Lord for forgiveness." He ended in a whisper, choked by tears. Tutu got up, put his arm around the distraught minister, and for an emotion-charged moment the two men stood there hugging each other as the congregation rose to its feet and applauded.

Perhaps this was a beginning.

CHAPTER NINE

THE GREAT U-TURN

"It has been remarkable to see how these former ideologues became pragmatists. As the world changed, they changed."

— JAMES JOSEPH, FORMER US AMBASSADOR TO SOUTH AFRICA

The African National Congress has undergone an astonishing about-turn in the formulation of its economic policy, from a left-wing socialist position that envisaged large-scale nationalization to a position where it has now embraced free-market orthodoxy that involves large-scale privatization.

This presents one of history's great paradoxes. The old apartheid regime, which proclaimed itself one of the most vehemently anti-communist on earth, ran an economy that established the largest amount of state-owned industry outside the Soviet bloc. Now the ANC, long portrayed by the old regime as a surrogate of Moscow and which is in a formal alliance with the South African Communist Party and the big trade union federation, Cosatu, is embracing the free market and privatizing those para-statals. What is more, it is communists and trade unionists in the new Cabinet who are spearheading this capitalist charge.

In January 1990, a month before he was released from prison, Nelson Mandela issued a press statement in which he declared: "The nationalization of the mines, the financial institutions and monopoly industry is the fundamental policy of the ANC and it is inconceivable that we will ever change this policy." Yet four years later, when the ANC assumed power, it had indeed done the inconceivable and dumped the policy of nationalization in favour of the free market. And four years after that Mandela and his chosen successor, Thabo Mbeki, both issued stinging rebukes to the SACP and Cosatu at their congresses for publicly criticising the ANC's change of tack and telling them in effect either to toe the line and accept the new policy or quit the alliance.

There are few parallels anywhere of such a startling U-turn, undertaken it must be noted in a volatile international economic climate and in the face of mounting unemployment, yet without producing a split in the ruling alliance. At least not yet. It has indeed caused serious tensions, but at the time of this writing the alliance is still holding together, which says much for the skills of the political leadership.

The origins of the commitment to nationalization go back to June 1955 when the ANC, then not yet outlawed, convened a "Congress of the People" to formulate a vision of a South Africa beyond apartheid. The ANC had formed an alliance with the Indian National Congress (originally formed by Mohandas Gandhi in the early part of the century), the Coloured People's Congress, a white organization called the Congress of Democrats which contained many members of the Communist Party that had been outlawed five years before, and with the trade union movement, then called the South African Congress of Trade Unions (SACTU). They all participated in the event. The ANC invited others as well, the Liberal Party, later led by author Alan Paton, and the United Party which was then the rather effete opposition in the whites-only Parliament. Although these predominantly white parties did not attend, the invitations were a significant indication of the ANC's commitment to the principle of nonracialism.

Three thousand delegates turned up at the gathering, held on a battered stretch of *veld* under some eucalyptus trees at a place called Kliptown, in what is now part of Soweto. There, despite some provocative interventions by the police, the gathering drafted and adopted a Freedom Charter, an inspired declaration setting out the liberation movement's fundamental ideals that was to acquire the status of holy writ in the years ahead. Composed in sonorous language the Charter begins: "We, the People of South Africa, declare for all our country and the world to know: that South Africa belongs to all who live in it, black and white, and that no government can justly claim authority unless it is based on the will of the people." Then follows a manifesto of human rights and equality combined with a vision of radical political transformation, including the following critical passage:

> The national wealth of our country, the heritage of all South Africans, shall be restored to the people;
> The mineral wealth beneath the soil, the banks and monopoly industry shall be transferred to the ownership of the people as a whole;
> All other industries and trade shall be controlled to assist the wellbeing of all the people;
> All people shall have equal rights to trade where they choose, to manufacture and to enter all trades, crafts and professions.

There was also a passage which declared that the restriction on land ownership, which had been introduced with the Land Act in 1913 that prohibited blacks from owning land outside the tiny reserves which later formed the bantustans, would be ended, and that "all the land shall be re-divided amongst those who work it".

The Freedom Charter was adopted at a special congress of the ANC the following year and so became formal policy of the organization.[1] There was much debate in the years that followed about whether or not the charter was a blueprint for a socialist state. Particularly during the four-year Treason Trial in which 156 ANC leaders, including Mandela, were accused of participating in a conspiracy inspired by international communism to overthrow the state by violence, the defence made strenuous efforts to show that it was not. Thomas Hodgkin, a distinguished British scholar of African politics, likened its language to that of the British Fabians of the late nineteenth century, while Jack Simons, a Marxist academic who had been a member of the Central Committee of the SACP, stressed the omission of any reference to the abolition of classes which, he said, was "inexcusable" for a Marxist.[2] Nevertheless the principle of nationalization was certainly strongly implied, and in later years ANC leaders in exile spoke freely of a commitment to "nationalize the commanding heights of the economy".

Mandela's statement from prison reaffirming the ANC's commitment to nationalization was intended to quash rumours that had been published in the newspapers suggesting he had undergone a change of mind in recent years. The rumours were false. The prisoners on Robben Island had debated nationalization for years, and Mandela had always been convinced it was the right policy. He had seen how Afrikaner leaders had used it to advance, empower and enrich their own people, and he had argued during the Treason Trial that it would enable blacks to own their own mills and factories. He had been an admirer of the British Labour Party and taken note of how it had included Clause Four, providing for nationalization, in its constitution shortly before he went to prison. Prison, moreover, had kept him in something of a time capsule: he was not exposed to the general disillusionment with state-ownership that had set in around the world from the seventies onwards.

Mandela stuck stubbornly to his views after his release, arguing with Western diplomats that countries like Britain, Germany and Japan had all made use of nationalized industries to revive their economies after World War II. Apartheid had been the equivalent of a war against black South Africans, he reasoned. His words went down well in the townships, but business leaders became increasingly worried. The *Financial Mail* railed at the ANC for being "muddled and confused" and, with a paternalism counter-productive to its purpose, advised business to "patiently and systematically educate blacks into the realities of the world".[3]

After Mandela made yet another public statement affirming the ANC's commitment to nationalization and two of his oldest colleagues and advisers, Walter Sisulu and Ahmed Kathrada, made statements of their own backing him up, I wrote a column in a Johannesburg newspaper on 15 August 1990 saying nationalization would be a serious mistake. I cited the example of Zambia's unhappy experience in nationalizing its copper mines soon after gaining independence from Britain in 1964. President Kenneth Kaunda, I noted, had to raise a large loan to pay compensation to the mining companies, Roan Selection Trust and the Anglo American Corporation. He then had to enter into a management contract with those companies, paying them to continue running the mines because the Zambian government did not have the expertise to do so.

That done, the copper price crashed, leaving Zambia with an enormous debt to service from depleted copper earnings, while Anglo American took the compensation money and established a hugely successful offshore subsidiary called Minorco. Many things had gone wrong in Zambia, I said, but its slide from copper-bottomed prosperity to worst-case penury had started with this ill-considered nationalization.

Gold mining in South Africa, I warned, was similarly an industry in decline, with both the gold price and production falling steadily. Taking over the mines would be hugely expensive: the market valuation of South African gold shares at the time was about R55 billion, which would mean adding that sum to the country's existing R88 million foreign debt that was already proving difficult to serve. At 15% interest, servicing the additional R55 billion debt would cost more than R8 billion a year.

"To achieve what?" I asked. "Last year, after tax, the gold mining companies paid a total of R2,1 billion in dividends. Since the state gets the tax anyway, that is the additional amount it would gain by nationalising the mines. An outlay of R8 billion a year to gain R2,1 billion! It makes no sense."[4]

Next morning my telephone rang and Mandela was on the line. "I've read your article and I'd like to talk to you about it," he said. "Won't you come and have lunch with me?" So I drove to his home in Soweto where we lunched and talked for three hours. I went through all the arguments in the article once again, stressing that the uneconomic figures aside, it seemed to make little sense for a new majority government to take on such a huge burden at the cost of other, more pressing priorities such as education and housing. Other ways should be found to compensate for the past and bring blacks into the economy as well as the political system.

He listened carefully but still seemed unconvinced, harking back repeatedly to the National Party government's success in helping its people advance through state-owned industries. Then in a moment of candour he turned to me and said: "But I don't know very much about economics. I must go and talk to some businessmen about this." It was the first hint that there might be room for a rethink.

One of the first businessmen Mandela talked to was Chris Liebenberg, the chief executive of Nedcor, a major banking corporation, whom he later appointed as his Minister of Finance. Like most of the business community Liebenberg was becoming increasingly worried about the ANC leader's repeated statements on nationalization, each of which caused the Johannesburg Stock Exchange to shudder, so he eventually telephoned ANC headquarters and asked for an appointment. To his surprise, Mandela agreed.

"I went across to Shell House (the ANC's headquarters building in downtown Johannesburg, now called Luthuli House) and spent an hour or so talking to him," Liebenberg told me later. "I told him why I thought nationalization was a bad idea, and he asked me to write a memorandum that he could study at his leisure."

Some time afterwards Mandela called Liebenberg to say he would like a further discussion. Liebenberg invited him to have dinner at the bank, where they were joined by Nedcor's chairman, John Maree, and its chief economist, Merton Dagut, who had been Head of the Department of Economics at the University of the Witwatersrand in Johannesburg. Mandela brought Trevor Manuel, the newly appointed head of the ANC's Department of Economic Planning. "We reinforced what I had put to him in the memorandum," Liebenberg recalls.

It was the start of a relationship of mutual trust and respect. The two met many times on a number of issues. Mandela met with other business leaders, too, notably Harry Oppenheimer, patriarch of the founding dynasty of the giant Anglo American Corporation. Oppenheimer put together a small forum of business leaders that became known as the Brenthurst Group, which met periodically with Mandela and other ANC leaders at the tycoon's mansion in Johannesburg to discuss economic issues. The British and American ambassadors, Robin Renwick and Princeton Lyman, also put pressure on Mandela.

But as Anthony Sampson has noted, it was not until February 1992 when Mandela went to the World Economic Forum in Davos, high in the Swiss Alps, that he finally turned against nationalization.[5] In that rarefied atmosphere to which, in the words of Lewis Lapham, the sardonic editor of *Harpers Magazine*, the upper servants of the global economy make their way each year from the low-lying places of the earth to brood upon the mysteries of capitalist creation, Mandela underwent his epiphany. The routine at Davos is that the world's top politicians, bankers and industrialists mingle together at a series of presentations, lunches and dinners. As Mandela later confided to Ambassador Lyman, the ANC leader found himself being lionized by everyone, but as he went from table to table he found they all wanted to know about his position on nationalization. And when he told them, the message was the same: there was no way the new South Africa would be able to attract foreign investment if it stuck to its old philosophy.[6]

Mandela was finally turned, according to Sampson, by three sympathetic delegates from the left. "The Dutch Minister of Industry was sisterly and understanding, but smashed his argument. 'Look, that's what we understood then,' she explained, 'but now the economies of the world are interdependent. The process of globalization is taking root. No economy can develop separately from the economies of other countries.' Leaders from two Asian socialist countries – China and Vietnam – told him how they had accepted private enterprise, particularly after the Soviet Union collapsed."[7]

They changed his view entirely. That night Mandela struck out the passage on nationalization in a prepared speech he was due to deliver the next day and wrote a brief new paragraph in its place:

"We visualize a mixed economy in which the private sector would play a central and critical role to ensure the creation of wealth and jobs. Side by side with this, there will be a public sector perhaps no different from such countries as Germany, France and Italy where public enterprises constitute 9, 11 and 15 per cent of the economy respectively, and in which the state plays an important role in such areas as education, health and welfare."[8]

It was an enigmatic statement, in that the economy he would inherit when he came to power already contained a much larger public sector than that, which meant that in the haste of the moment he was actually implying a significant degree of privatization. Whether he realized this at the time is doubtful, but his change of mind was firm. He went on to make similar statements in Copenhagen and Paris, then returned home where, he told Sampson, he summoned other ANC leaders and told them: "Chaps we have to choose. We either keep nationalization and get no investment, or we modify our attitude and get investment."[9]

* * *

While Mandela was undergoing this slow but ultimately emphatic change of mind, the ANC as a body was experiencing a more incremental and uneven transformation of its own. The ANC had never been an ideologically homogeneous organization. From its inception in 1912 when its founder, Pixley ka Seme, summoned "African leaders" of all kinds to fight the iniquitous Land Act, from the small educated elite of the day to an array of tribal chiefs and elders, it has been an alliance of disparate elements drawn together for the common purpose of fighting racial oppression. When later it drew in white, Indian and Coloured leftists and formed its alliance with unionists and communists, it became even more eclectic and developed a tradition of robust internal debate, an organization which the young Nelson Mandela once aptly described as "an African parliament". In exile the range of nuanced ideological views widened still further as members became scattered across a global diaspora subject to a variety of local experiences. Some studying in Britain drew close to the British Labour Party, even working for it at constituency level, others became enamoured of Scandinavian social democracy, yet others studying in the Soviet Union and Eastern Europe became committed to – and ultimately disenchanted with – Soviet communism. Overall, the centre of political gravity was firmly to the left, but there was no agreed economic policy blueprint. When the ANC came home in 1990, the Freedom Charter of 35 years earlier was the only official statement of economic intent it had.

Indeed there was little discussion of economic policy, or any other post-apartheid policy issues, during the exile years. The struggle against apartheid was such an all-consuming subject that it excluded almost everything else. Only in the mid-1980s, when the great uprising in the black townships began to attract international attention and rattle the apartheid regime, did the exile leadership begin to focus a little more on policy issues inside the country.

I first became aware of this shift when I interviewed the ANC President, Oliver Tambo, in Lusaka in February 1986. After the interview he began questioning me about what was happening within

Afrikaner Nationalism, then asked me if I would talk to some of his colleagues on the subject. Next day I addressed 12 members of the ANC leadership group on the conflicts I could see developing in the ruling establishment and the growth of a reformist movement at its core. Their interest intrigued me, for until then the ANC leaders had seemed indifferent to the inner machinations of white South African politics, regarding it as irrelevant.

The reason for this sharpened interest only became clear to me much later when I eventually learned that Mandela's lawyer, George Bizos, had seen Tambo only a few days before my visit to inform him about a secret meeting that had taken place between Mandela and the South African Minister of Justice, Kobie Coetsee, in a Cape Town hospital three months earlier. The ANC leadership had heard rumours of the secret meeting and were understandably anxious about it, so Bizos had flown to Lusaka bearing a message from their imprisoned colleague to reassure them he was neither selling out nor being duped by the government but that he believed there might be the possibility of beginning a negotiation with the apartheid regime. Obviously the exiled leadership were intrigued by this remarkable turn of events and eager to gain some insight into what political forces in Afrikaner politics may have given rise to it and what it might portend. As we now know that secret meeting in the hospital led to others and in fact marked the start of the remarkable negotiating process that eventually culminated in South Africa's political transition from apartheid to democracy.[10]

As the number of clandestine contacts picked up, the first meeting between ANC economists and others from inside South Africa took place in 1986 at York University in the north of England. Professor Pieter le Roux, Director of the Institute for Social Development at the University of the Western Cape, which was later to become an economic think-tank for the ANC, was among those who attended. Le Roux recalls that the ANC and SACP members were eager to avoid conflict and present a moderate and reconciliatory image to the people who had come from South Africa. "I presented a paper in which I suggested that a social democratic dispensation was the most likely outcome in a post-apartheid South Africa," he says, "and they gave me a warm reception, telling me it was most interesting, even though some of the left-wing English academics were scornful of it. In their own presentations the ANC people said nothing about nationalization, but in private conversations it was quite clear they were still committed to the Freedom Charter." A second meeting in Amsterdam a few months later followed a similar pattern.

The most important of these early meetings took place in Lausanne, Switzerland, nearly three years later, in June 1989. The hawkish old President P W Botha was still in power and the ANC was still a banned organization, yet several of his senior government officials attended and interacted with the outlaws. They included Jan Lombard, Deputy Governor of the Reserve Bank, and Estian Calitz, Deputy Director-General of the Department of Finance and soon to become DG, who met up with Tito Mboweni and Maria Ramos, future heads of the Bank and the Treasury. Rudolph Gouws, Director-General of the Department of Manpower, together with members of the South African Chamber of Business and other leading business figures, including the heads of a major bank and a building society, Conrad Strauss and Bob Tucker, also attended. It was the first time economists from the ANC and the government met face-to-face and so marked the start of the real economic debate. It was also one of the most striking examples of the extraordinary process of secret talks that paved the way to South Africa's negotiated transformation.

Pieter le Roux organized the Lausanne meeting. "I thought it was important to get government and ANC economists together," he says. So he approached the Vice-Chancellor and Principal of his university, Jakes Gerwel, whom he knew had close contacts with the ANC, and an enlightened and innovative civil servant, Simon Brand, then head of the Development Bank of South Africa, who was well connected to key government officials. Gerwel reported back that Thabo Mbeki favoured the idea, and Brand gave Le Roux the names of senior civil servants he believed would be willing to attend – provided the meeting was billed as an international conference and not specifically a meeting with ANC economists. Le Roux also raised Swiss funding for the colloquium, as it came to be called.

And so it came about that these major figures from both sides of South Africa's bitter political battlefront came together for four days to talk about the economic future of their country in the company of an array of academic economists from Britain, the United States, Western and Eastern Europe and the Soviet Union. Lesser ANC figures and members of the internal United Democratic Front, essentially a front for the outlawed liberation movement, were also there. Ramos believes the encounter was an important wake-up call for the old adversaries who had disparaged one another for so long. "We disagreed about a lot of big things," she recalls, "but there was a good atmosphere with a lot of intellectual engagement on all the issues. I think it made the government and

The day of liberation – 26 April 1994. *(Sunday Times)*

The opulent Beau-Rivage
Palace Hotel, in
Lausanne, Switzerland,
where ANC economists
met secretly with
government officials in
1989, while the ANC was
still banned.

Above: Sandton *(Sunday Times)* and *(left)* Alexandra township *(PictureNet).* One city, two worlds.

An unemployment queue in Johannesburg, one of many as the transforming economy hits the unskilled particularly hard. *(Sunday Times)*

A cargo of cars for export. The booming motor industry is the most successful sector of South Africa's transforming economy.

Above: Multiple murderer Eugene de Kock *(second from left)* at Vlakplaas, where he and his assassination unit planned the 'elimination' of anti-apartheid activists. *(Sunday Times)*

Left: F W de Klerk. Ex-president. He withdrew too soon from the Government of National Unity. *(PictureNet)*

Above: Tony Leon, leader of the opposition in Parliament, smart and articulate, but the chemistry between him and President Mbeki is unfortunate. *(Sunday Times)*

Left: Marthinus van Schalkwyk struggling to shed the NNP's albatross of apartheid. *(Sunday Times)*

Above left: 'Taddy' Blecher, founder of CIDA City Campus, a business school for the poor that is in effect the world's first free university. *(Sunday Times)*

Above: Thabo Mbeki, a brilliant mind, with some inexplicable failures. *(Business Day)*

Left: Govan Mbeki, veteran of the struggle and father of the president. *(Sunday Times)*

Above left: Vella Pillay, chairman of the Macro Economic Research Group (MERG), whose report to the ANC was shelved. *(Sunday Times)*

Above: Bobby Godsell, chairman of AngloGold, which was then the biggest gold mining company in the world, at the march of the National Union of Mineworkers, protesting against plans for the sale of gold stocks. *(Sunday Times)*

Left: Helena Dolny, Joe Slovo's second wife, who became the victim of back-stabbing politics and bad journalism. *(Business Day)*

Carl Niehaus – he paid the price of dissidence. *(Financial Mail)*

Bottom left: Peter Mokaba *(PictureNet)* and *(right)* Parks Makahlana *(Sunday Times),* both AIDS victims who died in denial.

Below: Trevor Manuel, the Minister of Finance and Maria Ramos, his director-general – the developing world's most effective financial team. *(Sunday Times)*

Top: Mohammed Valli Moosa – Nelson Mandela gave him a lesson in the diplomacy of reconciliation. *(Business Day)*

Centre: Frederik van Zyl Slabbert, white liberal leader and a key agent of change. *(Financial Mail)*

Bottom: The ultimate gesture of reconciliation, Nelson Mandela visiting Percy Yutar, the venomous prosecutor who sent him narrowly past the gallows to prison for 27 years. *(Sunday Times)*

Top left: Max du Preez, founder/editor of the courageous *Vrye Weekblad,* which exposed the hit squads. He later became a prize-winning broadcaster, until he was fired by the SABC for 'insubordination of management'. *(Financial Mail)*

Top right: Ivy Matsepe-Casaburri, pitched into the role of the first black chairperson of the SABC. *(Financial Mail)*

Left: Zwelakhe Sisulu, first black CEO of the SABC. *(Financial Mail)*

Above: The Rev Hawu Mbatha, the 'smiling reverend', whose ineffectual tenure as CEO of the SABC saw the public broadcaster spin into decline *(Sunday Times)*

Top: Nelson Mandela, Allister Sparks and Anton Harber, who was then the ground-breaking editor of the *Mail & Guardian.*

Bottom: Former editors Laurence Gandar, Raymond Louw, Allister Sparks and Rex Gibson at the party for the closure of the *Rand Daily Mail* in 1985.

Top left: Sydney Kentridge QC, the country's top defence lawyer and champion of the media. *(Business Day)*

Top right: Arthur Chaskalson – from civil rights lawyer to chief justice. *(Financial Mail)*

Left: Justice Johan Kriegler of the Constitutional Court. First a brave landmark judgement, then a slight disappointment. *(Business Day)*

Above: Nomonde Calata, whose cry of anguish as she told the first TRC hearing of the night her husband was waylaid and murdered as one of the 'Cradock Four' provided the defining moment for the Truth Commission process. *(Sunday Times)*

Above right: Matthew Goniwe, the dynamic young activist, who led a movement that rendered a chain of country towns in the Eastern Cape Province 'ungovernable' in the 1980's, photographed in Lingelihle township shortly before his murder on 27 June 1985. *(Sunday Times)*

Right: Captain Jeffrey Benzien gives the TRC a live demonstration of the 'wet bag' torture that he used to suffocate political prisoners to the edge of death. *(Die Burger)*

Top: Phillip van Niekerk, the then editor of the *Mail & Guardian,* testifying at the Human Rights Commission's controversial press inquiry. *(Sunday Times)*

Bottom: Allister Sparks, Nelson Mandela and the late Sue Sparks.

business people realize we weren't just a bunch of people who didn't have the ability to think through these things, while on our side we felt the same about them."[11]

It was a remarkable gathering in a remarkable place. The colloquium was held in one of Europe's grandest hostelries, the Beau-Rivage Palace Hotel, a 150-year-old neo-baroque confection set in 11 acres of parkland in the grounds of Lausanne's Olympic Centre with panoramic views across Lake Geneva to the spectacular Swiss Alps beyond. This opulent pile, recently renovated to the full splendour of its glory days, was a favourite retreat of the rich and famous of the *Belle Epoch*: its leather-bound guest book contains the names of Coco Chanel, Noel Coward, Somerset Maugham, the Duke and Duchess of Windsor, and other faded European royals and Russian archdukes. With its spacious suites and magnificent reception rooms, the hotel must have presented something of a culture shock to the young "comrades" fresh from the street battles in South Africa's bleak black townships.

Le Roux's impression at the colloquium was that ANC interest in nationalization had declined compared with the York and Amsterdam meetings. The Berlin Wall had not fallen yet, but Soviet bloc economies were clearly in trouble and Mikhail Gorbachev's *perestroika* reforms were whittling away at the old ideology. Once again it was the British left-wingers, particularly from the School of Oriental and African Studies at London University, who were the strongest advocates of central planning while, ironically, it was an East German economist, Gerard Wittich, who offered the strongest warning against nationalization. When the ANC took over the country, Wittich noted with remarkable prescience, it would have difficulty finding enough qualified people to run the existing para-statals never mind additional nationalized corporations.[12] Even some of the advocates of nationalization warned that state ownership could be problematic. The huge cost of compensation was raised, and one suggestion was that the state could cut these costs by acquiring only 51% of shares or even less to have a state veto over decisions. Professor Rafael Kaplinsky, of Sussex University where Thabo Mbeki and other present-day leaders had studied, warned with keen foresight that the new South Africa would run into a skills problem since, as he put it, the days of "Fordism", or simple routine production-line work, were over and modern industries now required highly trained multi-skilled workers.

Six months later the ANC and its allied organizations were unbanned, and in April 1990 economists from all three alliance partners met in the Zimbabwe capital of Harare to prepare a draft economic policy document. It was a significant event: not only was this the first statement of economic policy since the Freedom Charter, but as Ramos recalls: "While nationalization was still very much part of the thinking, it was already being tempered by the reality of the world we were living in, by the realization that economies had to globalize, that South Africa had to come out of a long period of isolation and become globally competitive." And so there began a shift away from the Charter's call towards the Asian model of a "developmental state". The state would still play a central role, but not in a socialist manner. Instead it would intervene to direct economic activity in a way that would bring about "growth through redistribution". The state would do this by redistributing income to the black poor, which would increase demand, production and job-creation, all of which would generate growth. The private sector would have to obey the government's directives. "The ANC would prefer that these essential reforms were carried out in co-operation with business," the document said, "but if such co-operation were not forthcoming, a future democratic government could not shirk its duty."

Not surprisingly, the business community was not happy with this formula for macro-economic populism. Even some pro-ANC economists warned that several Latin American countries, notably Peru under Alan Garcia in the 1980s, had tried such policies only to find that the swelled demand soon outstripped the country's capacity to produce, causing prices to rise, imports to rocket and exports to fall. The result was that they achieved spectacular growth to begin with but then ran into crippling foreign exchange shortages, runaway inflation and ultimately a debt trap. Peru ended up in 1989 with a 20% contraction in gross domestic product, a 50% fall in real urban wages, and 2 775% inflation. "For countries like South Africa, playing around with demand is risky," warned economist Terence Moll. "The danger is that errors in controlled aggregate demand can lead to all kinds of nasty developments."[13]

The criticism made an impact. A redraft of the policy document was submitted to the ANC's National Conference in Durban in July 1991, but it was not formally adopted. Instead the document was extensively discussed throughout the ANC's regions and eventually a modified version was produced. But essentially it remained a growth through redistribution model.

Nearly a year later, in March 1992 – just one month after Mandela's critical meeting in Davos – a new think-tank exercise saw the start of another fundamental shift in ANC economic thinking – this time away from the growth through redistribution model and towards economic reforms aimed at attracting fixed investment. Again Pieter le Roux was the organizer. He invited a large group of academic economists, and representatives of all political organizations as well as trade unions, business and civic organizations, to spend three weekends over four months at a conference centre in the Western Cape winelands called Mont Fleur, playing out a series of possible scenarios for a post-apartheid South Africa.

The sessions began with a presentation by Derek Keys, the former mining house chief executive who by then had become De Klerk's Minister of Finance, of the grim state of the South African economy. Since 1980, Keys told the gathering, there had been "a cancerous growth of government consumption expenditure at the expense of investment". Economic growth and per capita GDP had declined. Now the country's traditional growth path was under threat because the technological revolution was shifting the terms of trade against primary product exporters. The long racial conflict, combined with labour militancy, had undermined business confidence. A massive rise in unemployment lay ahead. Rapid urbanization was overwhelming the cities, rural areas were collapsing, political and criminal violence was exploding, black schools were often not functioning, the health system was not coping with increasing demands, and the social fabric of the black majority population was being torn apart. The conclusion of Keys's presentation was that if trends of the past 10 to 15 years could not be reversed, "all problems will become insoluble well before the end of this decade."

Sobering stuff indeed for the liberation movements, who had dreamed for years that when eventually they came to power they would inherit a well-developed and healthy economy that would enable them to launch a range of social welfare programmes to uplift their people who had been oppressed and discriminated against for so long. It focussed their minds on the limited possibilities that lay ahead of them, and was an important preparation for the scenario games they were about to play.

Initially 32 future scenarios were put on the table, which were then boiled down to four which separate groups had to study and play out before the full audience. The scenarios were given colourful names – The Ostrich Act, in which the old regime refused to settle in the face of liberation movement demands it regarded as too radical and decided to use its military-security strength to hold on to power for at least another decade; The Lame Duck, in which a constitutional settlement was reached which tried to allay white fears by ensuring a long transition of five to eight years with many "sunset clauses" giving the old regime a veto right on economic policies; Icarus, in which the new government embarked on a policy of macro-economic populism, trying to prime-pump the demand side of the economy with big increases in wages and government spending; and The Flight of the Flamingos, in which the parties negotiated a political system with a high degree of legitimacy and the new regime made a lot of social investment within a framework of fiscal discipline and adopted balanced economic policies aimed at creating conditions to attract fixed investments and a reorientation of the industrial sector towards the export of manufactured goods.

Trevor Manuel, the future Finance Minister, and Tito Mboweni, the future Governor of the Reserve Bank, both participated in the team which presented the Flight of the Flamingos scenario and which was acclaimed the preferred course to follow. For Manuel especially it was a watershed experience. He arrived at Mont Fleur a convinced supporter of the "growth through redistribution" model, but in the course of the scenario playing came to see its high risks. "Mont Fleur was actually quite profound in my thinking," he told me some years later.

It was not only the scenario itself that influenced him, but Keys. The scenario players took a break one Saturday afternoon when some went to watch a key rugby match in Cape Town. Keys stayed. "Derek sat around and chatted with us, and it was very important," Manuel recalls, "because we were trying to understand the Icarus scenario and the dangers of macro-economic populism. That was certainly profound for me." It was the start of a friendship and a mentoring relationship across the political divide that Manuel and others admit was important in preparing the young team for the tough task that lay ahead.

Two months later the ANC held a major policy conference and drafted a comprehensive set of policy guidelines called *Ready to Govern*. The section on economic policy was a watershed. Firstly, the threats to business were gone. "We envisage a dynamic private sector," the document declared, "employing the skills and acumen of all South Africans, making a contribution to the provision of good quality, attractive and competitively priced goods and services for all South Africans."[14] It downplayed the role of the state, saying that while it would still oversee the general direction of the economy the state's role would be primarily to provide infrastructure and welfare payments. Most important of all, for the first time it held out the possibility of privatization. It did not use the dread word: as Manuel explains, Mandela in his inimitable style drew them aside saying: "Come, boys, I need to talk to you. Look, there's Joe Slovo (the Communist Party leader). He can handle the concept but the word privatization is going to be very difficult for him." So while the word was struck out, the concept remained clear enough. In assessing "the balance of evidence in restructuring the public sector", the document says, the new democratic state would consider:

> "*Increasing the public sector in strategic areas through, for example, nationalization, purchasing a shareholding in companies, establishing new public corporations or joint ventures with the private sector;
>
> * Reducing the public sector in certain areas in ways that will enhance efficiency, advance affirmative action and empower the historically disadvantaged, while ensuring the protection of both consumers and the rights and employment of workers.
>
> Such a mixed economy will foster a new and constructive relationship between the people, the state, the trade union movement, the private sector and the market."[15]

So the door for a complete about-turn on economic policy was open. As William Kentridge noted soon afterwards: "Three years and three generations of policy positions have wrought a sea change in ANC economic thinking, indicative of a growing pragmatism in policy-making and a willingness to engage with, and accommodate, supporters and critics alike."[16]

* * *

But before that gap was taken there was one more twist on the road to free-market capitalism. On a trip to Canada not long after his release, Mandela elicited a promise from Prime Minister Brian Mulroney to help the ANC improve its understanding of economic matters. This led to a Canadian aid agency visiting South Africa in July 1991, where it concluded that the ANC's Department of Economic Policy (DEP) was far too small and inexperienced to cope with the mass of diverse issues confronting it. The agency proposed a new body to help co-ordinate research and construct a comprehensive macro-economic model for the ANC, taking the *Ready to Govern* document as its starting point, while the DEP formed itself into shadow ministries. The result was that in mid-1992, shortly after the *Ready to Govern* document was adopted, a high-powered unit known as the Macro-Economic Research Group, or MERG, was established. It drew on 100 economic specialists, most of them foreign academics, and included leading ANC, Cosatu and SACP figures together with local academics, who worked under the co-ordinating chairmanship of a long-time ANC economic adviser, Vella Pillay, a consultant to the Bank of China based in London.

Significantly the four people who today are at the heart of managing the South African economy, Trevor Manuel and Maria Ramos at the Treasury, Tito Mboweni at the Reserve Bank, and Alec Erwin, the Minister of Trade and Industry, were all part of MERG.

The group worked for 16 months, then presented its report, a glossy bound volume of 300 pages entitled *Making Democracy Work,* to the ANC and the business community at a ceremony in Johannesburg's Rosebank Hotel in November 1993 – just six months before the ANC came to power as the leading partner in the Government of National Unity. But the report never saw the light of day. It was stillborn. Even before it was published, Mandela withdrew his offer to write a foreword, and when I sought a copy at ANC headquarters some years later there was none to be found.

Indeed even as Pillay presented his report that November, the ANC's two key economic specialists, Manuel and Erwin, were drafting a secret letter of intent to the International Monetary Fund on behalf of all parties involved in the Negotiating Council seeking an $850 million loan, ostensibly for drought relief. The letter committed the incoming government to cut the budget deficit by 6% of gross domestic product in the coming financial year, maintain a high interest-rate policy and continue to open the economy to competition from other countries – all steps that flew in the face of MERG's proposals. Moreover, by then the ANC had already adopted clauses in a new Bill of Rights entrenching property rights which drew them still further away from nationalization.

There were two interrelated reasons for the rejection of the MERG report. Firstly, members of the DEP felt their work was being usurped by outsiders and they resented this. Some local economists felt the preparation of the report was being driven by the overseas academics. As one observed sourly, not since colonial days had South Africa's economic policy been driven by foreigners.[17] But more important, by then ANC thinking was already beginning to move in a free-market direction while MERG advocated heavy state intervention in the economy, not so much for orthodox socialist purposes but in line with the Asian developmental state model. The MERG team contained some heavy-weight economists from the School of Oriental and African Studies at

184

the University of London who were strongly influenced by the success of the emergent "Asian Tiger" economies – particularly Japan, Taiwan, South Korea and Singapore – all of which featured systems of heavily managed capitalism.

What MERG presented was a ten-year reconstruction plan, divided into two five-year phases. The programme did not recommend any large-scale nationalization of industry: indeed its only concession to the Freedom Charter's pledge was a proposal to make a token transfer of the ownership of wealth to the black majority by establishing "compulsory funds" that could buy shares in listed companies.[18] The basis of its recommended programme was an acceptance of capitalism with a vigorous private sector and a strong drive to encourage local and foreign investment, but combined with heavy strategic intervention by the state to direct the economy. Significantly, no representatives of business were included in the research group, otherwise some might have pointed out the inherent contradiction between these two aims.

Meanwhile, the De Klerk government with Keys at the Ministry of Finance was itself beginning to reconstruct the economy, away from the isolationist "national socialism" of the apartheid era towards a more orthodox free-market policy called the Normative Economic Model. It advocated privatization, deregulation and competition to stimulate private sector investment, higher growth and employment. This policy MERG proceeded to trash, arguing that it would perpetuate white privilege and leave the poor to benefit only from dubious "trickle-down" effects, whereas MERG wanted to target the poor directly. "MERG is convinced that a sea change in economic policy is essential," the report declared.[19] This sea change, essentially a classic growth through redistribution formula, was embodied in the ten-year plan.

Phase One of the plan consisted of a programme of heavy state investment in human development and physical infrastructure, with public works projects focussed on housing, rural water supply, road development, health services, electrification and, above all, a massive educational and training programme to uplift the skills level of the labour force. Strategies were also proposed to encourage savings and channel these into domestic investment to boost demand.

More controversially, the programme called for a national minimum wage double that paid to millions of farm workers, domestic servants and participants in public works and drought relief programmes.[20] In an interview some months later MERG's chairman, Vella Pillay, advocated an immediate 30% to 40% increase in black wages, funded by a decrease in corporate profits, which he said would boost demand and "provide the spurt to secure the economy's long-term growth and expansion".[21] This was pure macro-economic populism, the high-flying Icarus of the Mont Fleur scenarios. As Nicoli Nattrass, then a pro-ANC economist at the University of the Western Cape, warned in a sharp criticism of the MERG report which she described as "uneven and schizophrenic", this would almost certainly increase unemployment as employers retrenched to cut costs. Maybe not in Singapore with its highly skilled labour force, but in South Africa certainly. "Given South Africa's huge surplus of desperately poor unskilled people, it seems better to provide as many jobs to the poor as possible than it is to provide the lucky few with over double the going wage in agriculture," Nattrass added in an observation that was to resonate in the years ahead.[22]

This initial five-year phase of the MERG programme envisaged a rapid increase in corporate sector investment that would put the economy into a "sustained growth phase", boosting the growth rate to 4,5% and creating 300 000 new jobs a year by 2004. However, the anticipated private sector investment would have to take place in the face of pervasive state intervention in the economy. The MERG planners were sanguine about this, brushing aside the possibility that investors might be put off by the prospect of so much bureaucratic regulation and simply decide not to come – in which case the whole growth phase would be stillborn. As Nattrass noted: "The weak link in MERG's strategy is its failure to address the issue of business confidence."

The recommendations included intervention in the output and pricing decisions of the minerals sector; regulation of the housing and building supplies market; extending controls over mergers and acquisitions; monitoring the behaviour of participants in oligopolistic markets; creating supervisory boards with bank and trade union representatives to oversee the making of big companies; and, most controversial of all, a Capital Issues Commission to examine and authorize company plans for new investments. The commission's purpose, the report said, would be "to channel funds into private sector investments which have a high national priority (and) … to ensure that companies raising capital conform with national policy on ethnic and gender employment and other policies." MERG also advocated placing the Reserve Bank under political control.[23]

The proposals to boost education and raise the skills level of the labour force were imaginative and ambitious. Whether they were affordable is another matter. The starting point was to ensure that all children were given ten years of schooling. Under the apartheid regime schooling was not only racially segregated but grotesquely unequal. While it was compulsory and free for white children, black children were required to pay school fees, school facilities were appallingly inadequate, more than 60% of teachers were themselves under-educated, and schooling was not compulsory, which meant more than half the black children of school-going age were not in school at all.

But it was in adult education than the MERG proposals were most radical and ambitious. Noting that the vast majority of economically active black people were neither literate nor numerate – less than 2% matriculated with mathematics between 1990 and 1993, and 0,2% matriculated with both science and maths – the report nevertheless argued that "behind the label of unskilled (black) work there exists a large pool of unrecognized skill and a poorly motivated labour force."[24] Those talents, it reckoned, could be rapidly developed by an ambitious education and training programme.

Beginning in 1994, 50 000 lower-skilled employees should enter a programme that would see them in school one day a week. Each year another 50 000 would enter the programme which would last four years, thus bringing 200 000 under-educated workers up to the level of Standard Eight, or Grade 10. Those who achieved basic literacy and numeracy should then enter a further two-year course, taking them to matriculation.

Meanwhile, 100 000 unemployed people should be taken up each year in public works projects, embarking at the same time on a similar one-day-a-week training programme lasting four years.

In addition, private sector firms should be required to take on a number of new workers from the pool of unemployed – the numbers being determined according to the firms' staff complements and skills bases. Once taken on, these new employees would also embark on a one-day-a-week, four-year training programme. To encourage private firms to participate, the government should pay a subsidy of 20% to 30% of the training costs. To coerce them, only firms that participated should be allowed a role in the wide range of state infrastructure projects that would be launched.

Overall the MERG report was an elaborate document that involved much detailed hard work, and many of the foreign participants who contributed time, effort and expertise into compiling it, especially chairman Pillay, were bitter that it was brushed aside. But the reason it was so unceremoniously dumped is one of the most instructive chapters in the ANC story. Planning in the abstract is one thing; confronting the realities of power in the new globalized world is quite another.

* * *

The ANC confronted those realities within days of being sworn in to power on 11 May 1994. As they moved from Pretoria to the legislative capital of Cape Town, into what was still called the Hendrik Verwoerd Building opposite the gracious old Victorian red-brick Houses of Parliament, the new administrators found they had inherited not only the horrendous social distortions inflicted by 342 years of racial oppression, but also a legacy of massive fiscal and administrative incompetence as well.

Despite Derek Keys's pre-election warnings, at Mont Fleur and later at a *bosberaad*, or bush conference, with De Klerk's Cabinet at a game reserve called D'Nyala near the small town of Ellisras in what is now Limpopo Province, the ANC leadership had been massively preoccupied during the last stages of the negotiations and in the run-up to the first democratic election with the task of warding off a violent counter-revolution by white right-wing extremists and Chief Mangosuthu Buthelezi's Inkatha Freedom Party and bringing them into the transition agreement. Economic policy had become increasingly important in ANC thinking after the unbanning, but now in this last phase before the transition and with the excitement of the election itself, it had been somewhat eclipsed. Many in the ANC also had romantic ideas of what governments could do, ignoring both economic constraints and the cumbersome nature of bureaucratic procedures. Now as they settled in to their new offices with wide picture windows looking out on the glorious vista of Table Mountain, they were in for a shock.

Their first task was to prepare for a new national budget, and as the vital statistics of the economy landed on their desks they realized the country was close to bankruptcy. It was down to three weeks of foreign exchange reserves, in the last days of their putative independence the bantustan leaders had run up staggering debts of more than R14 billion, and the economy as a whole was in distress. "It hadn't been growing since 1984," says Iraj Abedian, an Iranian-born economist who was then one of the key advisers to the ANC leadership.[25] "The tax base wasn't growing, there had been disinvestment and boycotts, all of which meant the economy had gone through ten years of fiscal crunch. Now the ANC inherited that crunch."

From the inside Mac Maharaj, who had been part of the Transitional Executive Committee that had effectively run the country in the final run-up to the election, saw this as the defining moment in the ANC's great U-Turn. A change of direction brought about not by a Damascus Road conversion, he says, but by force of circumstances. "It was driven by necessity, very harsh necessity. By the time the figures started to emerge, it was clear there were no funds to run any kind of socialist experiment."

Quite apart from MERG's disincentives to investors, the economic figures made that report's proposals for lavish spending and wage increases look like a Christmas wish list. Even if the ANC had adopted the recommendations they would have had to be abandoned. And so the report was thrown out in its entirety – which, unfortunately, meant some of its better proposals, in adult education and skills training and for public works projects, went out with the bathwater. But more of that later.

Nor was it only an economy in stress that the new regime found it had inherited. Its dowry included a shambles of mismanagement. Most white South Africans thought – and many still think – that, apartheid aside, South Africa had been efficiently run by the white regime and that now, like the rest of Africa, it was going to the dogs under a black regime. The reverse is the case.

The most startling example of this was the discovery, early in the new regime, that the giant Electricity Supply Commission, Eskom, the world's fourth-largest power generator and the R150 billion jewel in South Africa's crown of state-owned corporations, had no legal basis for its existence. For years Eskom had been regarded as the most solid of national institutions. It had issued bonds inside the country and abroad, to investors in Britain, Germany, Switzerland and elsewhere. Yet what none of the investors knew was that, in Abedian's words, "it was basically a non-existing legal entity". The apartheid government had enacted legislation which regulated Eskom's service provision but it did not cover ownership. There was nothing to establish who owned it.

As politicians, the ANC could have made a meal of this discovery. They could have trashed De Klerk's National Party and exposed its administrative incompetence. But they took fright: public disclosure of such a gross dereliction of administrative diligence involving such a huge institution could, according to Abedian, "have sunk the country into a financial chasm". So the new regime decided to keep mum and fix the legal bungle quietly.

Ramos, who discovered the legal flaw soon after joining the Department of Finance which she now heads, regards it as symptomatic of wider incompetence on the part of the old regime. One of five sisters of Greek immigrant parents, Ramos trained in Britain, lectured at the London School of Economics and worked for ten years as a risk analyst at a bank. Young, smart and energetic, she pitched into her speciality and, noting that the new government had taken over the national debt, set about checking what these liabilities were. With talk of privatization now in the air, Ramos also began checking on the covenants covering the parastatal corporations that might be sold. Who owned them? What were they worth? How did one determine value? It was then that she hit upon the absence of any legal basis to Eskom's ownership.

It was then, too, that Ramos uncovered the huge liabilities incurred by the bantustans. Their leaders had been on a spending spree in the dying days of apartheid and there were no records of what they had squandered. Finding out was a massive task. In one instance the BophuthaTswana government of Chief Lucas Mangope had bought shares in a foreign company called Ininco, which Ramos discovered had never existed. "We spent tens of thousands of rands in lawyers' fees trying to track that one down," she recalls. The apartheid regime had also established 158 so-called financial development institutions at national level, in the provinces and in the bantustans, all of which had run up heavy liabilities. Again there was no proper data. As far as Ramos could see, there had been no financial management systems in place under the old regime. "These guys never bothered to do any of that," she told me. "Debt management was not a concept I found in the Department of Finance.

"There was an administration, pretty junior people, whose job of debt management involved simply ensuring that every six months people would pay the interest on the bonds they were holding. There wasn't a sense of maturity, of deficit, of managing an enormous portfolio of liabilities, of deciding when you want to borrow, for what maturities and for what reason, and trying to determine what risks you were prepared to take. There was nothing of that."

Compounding the problem of administrative incompetence was one of delivery. The rookie regime, eager to get cracking with transforming the country, ran up against an ossified bureaucracy of mostly white Afrikaner males who had served a white population under siege all their lives and had neither the mindset nor the policy-making capacity to develop strategies that would meet the objectives of the new regime. Journalist John Matisonn quoted one eager new technocrat as likening his work in government to standing in front of a long piece of string. "You want to do something. You can't do it yourself, because it's too far away. So you push the string – and all that happens is that your end compresses a few centimetres. Nothing else moves."[26]

Ramos puts a more domestic touch to her imagery. "Arriving in the department was like arriving in a place that has been closed up for a very long time and you open up all the windows and pull down the old curtains and you start to spring clean and fumigate. It was an old environment, it was male, it was white, it was closed and fetid."

But not all the problems can be laid at the door of the old regime. The newcomers were not well equipped either for the huge task they faced. Having thrown out MERG, the ANC had no detailed economic programme to begin putting into effect from day one. The nearest they had was a document called the Reconstruction and Development Programme, or RDP, which had been hastily crafted in preparation for the election campaign. But it was an inadequate and problematic document.

As the ANC's economic thinking had begun to shift from 1990 onwards, differences became increasingly apparent between it and its alliance partners, Cosatu and the SACP, both of whom were more wedded to the socialist ideal. Cosatu in particular was much more taken with MERG's proposals than the ANC leadership was, so that when it came time to draft an election platform Cosatu decided to put its proposals on the table early to ensure maximum input. Its General Secretary, Jay Naidoo, prepared the first draft of the RDP, which then became the alliance's basic working document. Later Manuel and Ramos became involved in the economic section. In all the RDP document went through six drafts, and what eventually emerged was a wordy compromise between the two positions, strong on rhetoric with many pledges to deliver "a better life for all", but weak on how actually to deliver on those promises.

The RDP set ambitious targets: in five years it would redistribute "a substantial amount of land" to the landless black population, it would build a million houses, provide clean water and sanitation for everyone, electrify 2,5 million houses and provide access for all to education, health care and telecommunication facilities.

But the economic section was riddled with ambiguities. While promising all these things, the RDP also pledged the government to "avoid undue inflation and balance of payments difficulties". It would redirect government spending rather than increasing it as a proportion of the gross domestic product. And while pledging to "pay attention to macro-economic balance", the RDP also promised to "meet the basic needs of the people – jobs, land, housing, water, electricity, communications, health care and social welfare."

It was really an election manifesto rather than a systematic set of policy programmes, and even though the new regime has in fact achieved a commendable number of these goals and come close on others, the RDP as it was structured was an impossible administrative instrument. With such ambiguities it was not clear what it meant, or how to implement it. There was no operational plan to put it into effect.

President Mandela put Jay Naidoo in charge of the RDP, as Minister Without Portfolio. It was an administrative disaster. Naidoo had no department or proper budget of his own and no clear line of authority within the administration. It meant that to pursue the RDP's objectives he was constantly parachuting into the territory of other ministers. This caused confusion and resentment. All kinds of co-ordination problems arose.

With the RDP proving an inadequate tool for the tough job at hand, other economic problems arose. While significant foreign exchange did flow into the country during the first year of the new administration, it soon began to tail off. At the same time a conflict of strategies between the Reserve Bank and the government arose. Alec Erwin at Trade and Industry began opening up South Africa's isolated economy to greater world trade by cutting subsidies and slashing through the country's hideously complex web of tariffs and industrial regulations. At the same time the conservative Chris Stals, held over from the old regime as Governor of the Reserve Bank and no doubt nervous about what these rookies were doing, focussed on protecting the rand currency by raising interest rates. It was a deadly combination. If you cut subsidies and import tariffs while keeping the currency hard, you kill local industry. The hard currency stifles exports and if the government no longer helps manufacturers with subsidies they are at the mercy of importers who, with import tariffs gone, can undercut them.

This began to happen in 1995, which became a watershed year for the new regime. As the economy sputtered, Erwin, travelling abroad with Ramos and Naidoo to launch an international dollar bond, also found that the international finance markets in Frankfurt, Milan, London and New York had one overriding concern: they wanted to know whether this new team would be able to get the country's macro-economic balances right. "They weren't interested in hearing you waffle on about all sorts of other things," says Erwin. "The RDP talks of macro-economic balance, but we had such imprecise answers we couldn't deal with their questions properly because they'd know we were talking crap."[27] The government realized it needed a new growth strategy with a more precise macro-economic framework to guide it.

So in mid-1995 Erwin set up a team to develop such a programme, with Abedian as technical co-ordinator. The team worked for nine months, then produced a policy document called Growth, Employment and Redistribution, or GEAR, which Manuel presented to Parliament on 14 June 1996. The government has insisted ever since that GEAR did not replace the RDP, that, in Erwin's words, "the RDP is embedded in GEAR" which is simply "a strategy to finance the programme". But in fact the RDP disappeared as a political slogan which had acquired talismanic importance to the alliance partners, and Naidoo's job went with it. The former Cosatu Secretary-General became Minister of Posts, Telegraphs and Broadcasting in the Mandela Cabinet, the RDP office was closed, and the programme's goals were assigned to the various government departments.

More than that, GEAR was an unvarnished free-market programme, directly in line with the neo-liberal agenda, or what is known as the "Washington consensus", a combination of relaxed exchange rates, privatization, fiscal discipline and collaboration with the private sector to produce export-driven growth.

The irony is that Erwin, GEAR's initiator and now as Minister of Trade and Industry its key driving force, is a member of the Communist Party who came to government from the most radical of South Africa's trade unions, the National Union of Metalworkers. I also recall a conference in Paris in 1991 when Erwin froze the room with an outburst at a group of businessmen who had riled him, telling them: "You guys have had your turn. When we come to power we will capture the commanding heights of the economy, the state will nationalize the private sector." But Erwin was no conventional leftist. He only joined the SACP in 1990, when international communism was collapsing. When I suggested to him once in a moment of levity that he must surely be the only rat ever to have joined a sinking ship, his serious reply was that he had always been a Marxist but had shrunk from joining the party because it was too doctrinaire. With the collapse of Soviet communism he believed the SACP could democratize and become more pragmatic. Today the business community, at home and abroad, admires Erwin enormously, regarding him as perhaps the most enlightened and competent member of the Cabinet, but he insists he is still a Marxist. "It's a system of analysis," he says. "When I approach an economic problem today I approach it from a Marxist perspective. We all do. But that doesn't stop us from recognising the power of the market.

"The most important thing," he adds, "is that we are not utopian. If the capitalist system is dominant, if powerful global forces are there and they are real, then it's pointless trying to implement a programme that has no bearing on the present."

With the change of GEAR there also came an awareness that privatization, far from being a selling-off of the family silver, could have important developmental advantages. It could mean considerable injections of investment capital as well as modern technology and skills which the state itself could never afford. Moreover the sale of these major assets could bring in substantial capital sums to help fund social spending. Imaginatively managed, privatization could also further black advancement in the private sector by favouring buyers who included black partners in their consortia. Ways could even be found to deal with the main worry about privatization, which is that private companies would not provide essential services to uneconomic sectors of the country. The state could maintain an effective controlling share, or offer incentives to the private companies to provide the essential services. Thus, for example, when 20% of the telecommunications parastatal, Telkom, was sold to South-Western Bell and Malaysian Telecom, it was granted a five-year monopoly in the fixed-phone business on condition it provided a specified number of lines to poor rural areas and connected every school, police station, clinic and community centre in the country in that time.

Of course, as Mandela had warned the comrades when that critical enabling clause was included in the ANC's *Ready to Govern* document back in 1992, ideological fixations die hard and trigger words can detonate them, so the word "privatization" is never used in the new South Africa. What is happening is "a restructuring of state assets".

Thus GEAR marked the completion of the ANC's astonishing ideological U-Turn. The verbal camouflage notwithstanding, it also caused great acrimony in the alliance, with Cosatu and the SACP feeling their socialist concerns had been roughly cast aside. What rubbed salt in their wounds was that they felt the policy change had been foisted on them without consultation. The ANC had presented GEAR without

194

even a debate in its National Executive Committee. Some disgruntled alliance members accused the political organization of having betrayed the revolution.

* * *

The gap between Cosatu and the ANC began to appear soon after the unbanning. Cosatu economists joined in the Harare conference in April 1990 and its report was accepted as representing both organizations. But soon after that the business community, realising that economic transformation was going to be inevitable, began producing a series of policy documents and scenario shows of their own, all extolling the merits of the free market, to which Cosatu felt obliged to respond with its own socialist-oriented ideas.

Cosatu was also intent on maintaining its own line of thought and action, allied to but independent of the ANC. It had watched other trade union movements in Africa get absorbed into government after independence and become emasculated, and it did not want to suffer the same fate. So it wanted its own distinctive policy, and in May 1991 convened a conference to begin discussing it.

This led to another meeting a year later which yielded a policy document called *Economic Policy in Cosatu*. By happenstance this second meeting took place at the same time as the Mont Fleur scenarios, and so Cosatu missed what proved to be such a seminal experience for Manuel and other members of the ANC's economic team. It was a precursor of their widening differences. Ironically the document Cosatu produced plumped for a policy of growth through redistribution – precisely the Icarus scenario the ANC members were abandoning at that very moment. Cosatu's plan was based on expanding demand through higher wages and an inward-looking industrial policy, rather than an export-oriented one, designed to produce basic goods for the poor. In time this policy document flowed into another, the Industrial Strategy Project (ISP), then being prepared by a pro-Cosatu team called the Economic Trends Research Group. The ISP report in turn was heavily drawn on by the MERG researchers – so that in the end Cosatu was much more enamoured of the MERG report than the ANC was, and was pained when it was dumped.

So the tensions increased. Cosatu was trying to walk a tightrope, to be part of the ANC alliance but with its own identity and policy. It wanted to be part of the decision-making process, to be consulted in depth on policy matters and to have its views incorporated in the decisions. This was feasible while the alliance was still a liberation movement, but became increasingly impractical when the ANC became the government. Then the unionists began complaining that when they were consulted it was merely a token gesture and their views were ignored, while the ANC replied testily that "government must govern". The executive had to take decisions and act in the national interest.

More fundamental still was that the two groups had different vistas of responsibility which gave them different perspectives. The government's concern had to be the national interest, that of all South Africans, while Cosatu's focus was inevitably on a much narrower constituency, its own members of the working class. Not only did the government have to take a broader view on every issue, it was exposed to a much wider range of influences and experiences at home and abroad. As one senior member of the ANC put it: "Everybody in the executive, and even in Parliament, was grappling with a huge range of complex issues and they grew enormously as a result. Those in the unions were locked in their own paradigm, which is the union-management dichotomy, and were not growing at anything like the same rate."

Compounding this was the fact that the top Cosatu leaders have been repeatedly creamed off into senior jobs in the government and the ANC. The unions have in fact been a wonderful training ground for the country's new political leadership, which may well have been their most important contribution to the building of a new South Africa. But the repeated co-option of their best leaders, beginning with Cyril Ramaphosa and Jay Naidoo, has weakened them. It has also annoyed some Cosatu members as President Mbeki in particular, with machiavellian craftiness, has used ministers drawn from the unions and the Communist Party to enforce the most unpopular decisions on their former colleagues.

Cosatu faces some structural problems too. As the South African economy transforms, with the primary sector losing importance and the secondary and service sectors gaining, the power base of the work force is shifting away from Cosatu's traditional strength among mineworkers and other less-skilled people to those with higher skills levels. And many of these higher-skilled workers, in the words of one labour analyst, "are not nearly as receptive to the kind of arm-wrestling that Cosatu is used to."

Business, meanwhile, has undergone its own transformation. South Africa used to present an unhealthy picture of monopoly capitalism, with only about a hundred white men, a brotherhood of company directors, effectively controlling nearly the whole of big business through a maze of interlinking shareholdings. At one time McGregor BFA, a business information provider, calculated that the Anglo American Corporation effectively controlled nearly half the capitalized value of the Johannesburg Stock Exchange. Now the behemoths are restructuring and unbundling. When many foreign companies disinvested under anti-apartheid pressure in the 1980s, some of the larger South African companies snapped up their operations at bargain-basement prices, turning themselves into multi-enterprise conglomerates. Now, under the different pressures of globalization, the emphasis is on core businesses. Many enterprising firms are also breaking out of the old laager of isolation, listing in London and reaching into Africa, Latin America, Asia and North America, to join the new game of playing in the global marketplace.

Business, being always eager to curry favour with governments wherever they are, has also actively helped draw blacks into the private sector, offering directorships to individuals and encouraging the development of new "black empowerment" companies. Not all have been successful but some have, and the experience has been transforming for many white businessmen who once bent over backwards to please – and thus win contracts from – the apartheid regime.

Overall there has been a massive transformation of the private sector as well as of the government and its state apparatus. Given where they came from, there has also been a surprising degree of convergence in the economic thinking of government, business and labour. There are still differences, primarily around the emphasis to be placed on the two main aims of restructuring – redressing social imbalances, or promoting international competitiveness. Business complains about inflexible labour regulations, affirmative action and an employment equity law which requires employers to report to government on the racial composition of their work force. Government counter-accuses business with charges of negativism. At times the differences become acrimonious, as when business protested aggressively in June 2002 against the Minerals and Petroleum Resources Development Bill aimed at ending the big mining houses' perpetual monopoly over the country's mineral rights. But for the most part pragmatism prevails, and there is a considerable degree of discussion and collaboration in joint bodies such as a National Economic, Development and Labour Council (Nedlac) where Cosatu, government and business are represented.

In the long term the most significant differences are between Cosatu and the government. What has aggravated the relationship is that GEAR has fallen well short of the optimistic targets the government set for it in July 1996. GEAR's begetters predicted a GDP growth rate that would reach 6% by 2000 and the creation of 810 000 jobs by 1999. Instead growth fell from 4,3% to 3,4% by 2000 and to 2,2% in 2001, while half a million jobs have been lost.

The following year saw a marked improvement with growth back to 3% despite a grim global recession and with the rand recovering 40% against the dollar. This enabled Mbeki to claim in his State of the Nation speech to Parliament on 14 February 2003 that "the tide has turned". A week later Finance Minister Trevor Manuel presented an upbeat budget, relaxing exchange controls and cutting taxes for the second year in a row, while at the same time increasing capital expenditure on infrastructure development and giving a significant boost to social services for the poor. The implicit message was, after going through a valley of austerity GEAR's macro-economic restructuring is beginning to pay off, exports are on the increase and better days lie ahead.

There is every reason to believe this is true, but the payoff in job creation is still not there to any significant extent and this is what distresses Cosatu. The government's critics in the union movement see the massive loss of jobs over the past nine years as a vindication of their belief that the ANC chose the wrong ideological route and that it not only betrayed the revolution but its own people as well by inflicting such hardship on them.

Internal debates in the alliance have become steadily more rancorous over the years and it is clear that the ideological differences are deepening. What this means is that South Africa now effectively has two parliaments – the elected Parliament in which ANC and Cosatu members sit together on the government benches facing an Opposition, which, with the exception of two members of the PAC and one of the Azanian People's Organization (AZAPO), is uniformly to the right of them; and the alliance itself where Cosatu and the SACP form a left-wing opposition to the government.[28]

The debates in the two "parliaments" are quite different. The Opposition in the elected Parliament is constantly demanding greater concessions to the interests of business and the free market to make South Africa more globally competitive, particularly by speeding up privatization and making the labour regulations more flexible; while the opposition in the alliance is constantly demanding more state intervention to redress social imbalances, boost social welfare payments, uplift the black working class, and to end privatization which leads to retrenchments.

The intriguing fact is that this second opposition is obviously the real one. The official Opposition in Parliament, the Democratic Alliance, is predominantly white and has little growth potential beyond the white community and other minority groups. It may pick up a smattering of black supporters who have fallen out with the ANC, but it is inconceivable that an overwhelmingly black electorate is going to vote a white-dominated party into power any time soon after the end of apartheid. This means that while the Democratic Alliance can play a useful role as a watchdog on government, criticising policies and exposing corruption and maladministration, it is not a true political opposition in the sense that it is not a realistic alternative government.

The only realistic alternative government lies within the alliance, in the form of Cosatu and the SACP and some individual ANC members, such as Mandela's ex-wife Winnie, who are sympathetic to the populist line. Not only is it an overwhelmingly black opposition and therefore one with growth potential, but it also has a potent potential platform in championing the cause of the have-nots who have suffered the consequences of the government's U-Turn and would be receptive to a populist election campaign. The real opposition is to the left, not the right, of this turnaround government.

* * *

The big question then is: Can the alliance hold? The internal conflict reached a new peak in September 2002 when Cosatu, backed by the SACP, launched a series of bitter attacks on the government's privatization policy that culminated in a two-day national strike backed by protest marches around the country. Mbeki was outraged and at a big ANC policy conference launched an angry counter-attack, accusing "ultra-left sectarian elements" of trying to "capture control of our movement and transform it into an instrument for the realization of its (socialist) objectives." Which, he insisted, had never been ANC policy; the ANC had always been a national liberation movement with no inherent mission to fight for socialism. Although Mbeki never mentioned Cosatu or the SACP by name, he sent out a thinly veiled warning to both that he was prepared to consider ending the alliance with them. "We are permanently interested in increasing the size and strength of our movement," he said. "Nevertheless I am convinced that we must also pay particular attention to the principle – better fewer, but better!"[29]

Despite these growing tensions, I do not believe the alliance has reached breaking point yet. Eventually, yes, I believe a break-up will take place. For the moment, though, Cosatu has too much to lose by breaking away, in the form of patronage and job advancement opportunities for its members and at least some insider influence on policy formation. Scores of Cosatu members hold well-paid positions in the national and provincial cabinets, the legislatures, the civil service and even in the diplomatic corps, which few would want to surrender. Nor would others who hope they are in line to climb the same ladder. Cosatu is an important recruiting ground for the government which serves as a powerful inducement to even the most disgruntled members to remain inside the tent. And even though Cosatu complains that it is not properly consulted and that its views are ignored, the government does periodically throw it a bone in the form of an amendment to labour legislation or some other such concession. Outside the tent it would get nothing.

Equally dissuasive is that Cosatu at this stage would likely suffer heavy defeat if it were to break away and oppose the ANC. It is not a political party and does not have either the image or the campaigning skills of one. And although it has a substantial membership of almost two million, the numbers are declining and Cosatu's structures do not extend beyond that. Nor does its natural constituency. The unemployed may identify with some of Cosatu's criticisms of government, but they are not enamoured of the trade unions whose members represent an economic elite and whose pressures for higher wages and other protections shrink the job market and make it harder to find low-paid work below the minimum wage. There may be a lot of potential support there, but it remains to be mobilized and that will take time, money and a lot of political skill. Until that happens, in Frederik van Zyl Slabbert's experienced political judgment Cosatu would be "eaten for breakfast" in an election.[30] And its leaders know well enough that opposition politics is not a profitable game in Africa, at least not in the early years after independence or liberation. The *uhuru* parties tend to have a long momentum of popularity.

But in the long run I believe a split is inevitable. As a new class stratification begins to overlay the old racial one, different constituencies will take shape and this will eventually result in a political realignment to match them. It is constituencies rather than politicians that give rise to viable political parties. Cometh the constituency, cometh the party – and it is the smart political leader who spots the opportunity and takes advantage of it.

I foresee three parties emerging to serve three new constituencies – the ANC rooted in a fast-growing multiracial middle-class constituency and evolved into something like Tony Blair's New Labour or the German Social Democratic Party; a socialist workers party led by the labour movement and the intellectual leftists now in the SACP serving the working class; and another party making its pitch to the underclass, the poorly educated and the tribal traditionalists who find themselves outside the economy and whose tribal institutions and cultures are being eroded by modernism. Unlikely though it may appear now, this third party may be an alliance between a reformulated PAC, the Inkatha Freedom Party and other traditionalist elements.

But all of this will take at least another five to ten years.

CHAPTER TEN

FOR RICHER, FOR POORER

"We can no more reject globalization than we can reject gravity.
The question is how do we deal with it?"
— JEREMY CRONIN, DEPUTY SECRETARY-GENERAL OF THE SACP

For whosoever hath, to him shall be given,
and he shall have more than abundance:
but whosoever hath not, from him shall be
taken away even that he hath.
— MATTHEW 13:12

There are few things in the modern world that whip up such intense emotions as the new phenomenon of globalization. There are the theological free-marketeers who believe this is the one true faith, the ultimate solution to the eternal happiness of the human race, the end of history as American political scientist Francis Fukuyama has put it, with free-market capitalism now triumphant and standing alone as the only system to be pursued and perfected for the rest of time. And there are the equally passionate opponents to whom globalization is an epithet for a new form of capitalist colonialism that enables the rich countries and companies to exploit the poor, an eclectic coalition of environmentalists and socialists, radicals and anarchists, who have mobilized their forces to launch violent demonstrations against those they see as its demon creators at meetings in Seattle, Washington, Prague and Genoa.

The truth, of course, is that globalization is neither of these things. It is not a panacea and it is not a conspiracy. Like the industrial revolution of the early nineteenth century, it is a phenomenon of technical advancement, a great leap forward in the long story of international trade and communications that is reshaping the world in ways both productive and disruptive. It is creating exciting new vistas of opportunity, but it is also recreating the bleak world of Charles Dickens as a rampant capitalism, unrestrained by the competition from communism which tempered its avarice before, pursues those opportunities with

202

scant regard for those who get trampled on or left behind. Once again the poor are held to be responsible for their own misery, and welfare services are being cut.

The new globalized economy is ruthlessly competitive, with a spirit captured in the language used by some of its proselytes who talk of "creative destruction", meaning the process of destroying old and less efficient enterprises and replacing them with new, more efficient ones. To be globally competitive one must cut costs, which means downsizing staffs and raising productivity. It places a premium on skills, particularly the multi-skilled worker who can perform the tasks of several and therefore commands a higher wage, while the unskilled – of whom there are many in the developing countries – become not only unemployed but unemployable. It places an even greater premium on modern, high-tech equipment that can replace workers altogether and which doesn't go on leave, get sick or belong to trade unions that demand higher wages and go on strike. All they require are a few highly trained technicians to make and maintain them: a new breed of white-coated workers who are paid a great deal but whose services cut the wage bill massively. Thomas L Friedman, in his seminal book on globalization, *The Lexus and the Olive Tree*, recounts how he went to the Lexus luxury car factory in Japan where he saw 300 cars being produced each day by 66 human beings and 300 robots. "From what I could tell," he writes, "the human beings were there mostly for quality control. Only a few of them were actually screwing in bolts or soldering parts together. The robots were doing all the work."[1]

Globalization is certainly generating much greater wealth worldwide, but it is distributing that wealth unequally so that the rich are getting richer and the poor poorer, within nations and between them. As Anthony Giddens, Director of the London School of Economics, has pointed out, the share of the poorest fifth of the world's population in global terms dropped from 2,3% in 1989 to 1,4% in 1998, while the proportion taken by the richest fifth has risen. In sub-Saharan Africa, the world's poorest region, 20 countries have lower incomes per head in real terms than they had in the 1970s.[2]

This expanding inequality is the most serious problem facing the world today. For all its wealth-creating benefits, globalization is causing rising inequality and perilous instability in too many parts of the world. As one of its more articulate critics, American labour leader Jay Mazur, warns: "A world in which the assets of the 200 richest people are greater than the combined income of the 2 billion people at the other end of the economic ladder should give everyone pause. Such islands of concentrated wealth in a sea of misery have historically been a prelude to upheaval." Mazur points out, too, that the average CEO in the US earns 416 times more than the average worker.[3]

The United Nations Secretary-General, Kofi Annan, made much the same point in his wide-ranging *Millennium Report*. "The benefits and opportunities of globalization remain highly concentrated among a relatively small number of countries and are spread unevenly among them," the report noted, while elsewhere "globalization has come to mean greater vulnerability to unfamiliar and unpredictable forces that can bring on economic instability and social dislocation, sometimes at lightning speed."[4] The *Millennium Report* also gave a graphic picture of what Marshall McLuhan's "global village" would look like as an actual village at the turn of the century:

"Say this village has 1 000 individuals, with all the characteristics of today's human race distributed in exactly the same proportions ...

Some 150 of the inhabitants live in an affluent area of the village, about 780 in poorer districts. Another 70 or so live in a neighbourhood that is in transition. The average income per person is $6 000 a year, and there are more middle-income families than in the past. But just 200 people dispose of 86% of all the wealth, while nearly half the villagers are eking out an existence on less than $2 per day.

Men outnumber women by a small margin, but women make up a majority of those who live in poverty. Adult literacy has been increasing. Still, some 220 villagers – two-thirds of them women – are illiterate. Of the 390 inhabitants under 20 years of age, three-fourths live in the poorer districts, and many are looking desperately for jobs that do not exist. Fewer than 60 people own a computer and only 24 have access to the Internet. More than half have never made or received a telephone call."[5]

People and countries and companies. Of all the beneficiaries of globalization, none is prospering more than the multinational corporations which can now manufacture their products wherever they choose, even splitting their production processes between various countries to reduce costs and increase productivity, while marketing them globally in swelling amounts to reap ever larger profits. Some of these companies have grown to the point where their economies exceed the GDP of many counties. I attended a colloquium on Robben Island in March 2000 of the Young Presidents' Organization, an international club of CEOs under the age of 50, at which those present boasted that if the collective corporate value they represented were a country, it would be the third-largest nation on earth. Yet despite the power these economic behemoths wield in the new globalized world, no one elects those who control them in an age when democracy is supposed to be the corollary of capitalism.

Nor is globalization's impact only economic. It is political, technological and cultural as well.[6] It is homogenizing the world with the spread of the English language and American pop culture. It is melting down the nation-state with the emergence of international regulating bodies such as the World Trade Organization and large trading blocs such as the European Union, Nafta (North America), Mercosur (Latin America), Seato (Southeast Asia), and our own 14-nation Southern African Development Community (SADC) – with the EU already having a uniform currency and a joint central bank, while it is increasingly developing a federal political structure.

It is placing stresses and strains on traditional ways of life and cultures, on sexuality, marriage and the family, even on religious traditions, as women stake a claim to greater autonomy than in the past. All this, says Giddens, is dividing the world between cosmopolitans and fundamentalists. Here, he warns propitiously, lies the battleground of the twenty-first century, as the fundamentalists find these developments disturbing and dangerous and take refuge in a new and purified tradition – and sometimes lash back violently.[7] Here indeed lie the roots of not only Osama bin Laden and his Al Qaeda movement, but also of Jewish and Christian fundamentalism, all of which jointly and severally pose an ongoing threat to world peace – particularly when their cultural fears and fantasies coincide with the mass economic misery of their followers.

* * *

But before going further, let us pause to consider what globalization is. Something that has been so emotionally lauded and damned requires clarification before it can be more rationally assessed.

Strictly, globalization can be said to have started the first time a cave man traded a skin with another in the next valley. University of Cape Town economist Francis Wilson likes to say it came to South Africa in 1486 when the Portuguese navigator Bartholomeu Dias rounded the Cape, pointing the way for Europe's sea route to the East to be opened 11 years later and so drawing this country into the ambit of world trade as it then was. A slowly expanding process of global integration, in other words, but technology has speeded up that process.

The first great leap forward came with the industrial revolution and the invention of steamships, railways, the automobile and the telegraph. The latter half of the nineteenth century and the beginning of the twentieth saw a tremendous expansion of international communication and trade. But a 75-year interregnum followed as World War I, the Russian Revolution and the Great Depression brought international trade to a standstill and divided the world into two separate ideological and economic camps – a situation that was then frozen in place by World War II and its Cold War aftermath.

Today the word globalization really applies to the second and much greater leap that has taken place since the end of the Cold War: an incredible acceleration brought about by the convergence of two powerful new revolutions – the collapse of communism and with it the bipolar global divide, and the information revolution with its digital and satellite technology which has brought about the greatest and fastest advance in human communication in the history of the world. As Annan's *Millennium Report* notes, it took 38 years for radio to reach 50 million people, and 13 years for television. The same number of people adopted the Internet in just four years. In 1998 143 million people logged on to the Internet; by 2000 the number was approaching 700 million.[8]

It was not only the Berlin Wall that came down in 1989, all manner of other walls fell with it, from travel restrictions and news censorship to trade barriers and the end of fixed rates and capital controls. Suddenly the whole globe was open to free trade, and at the same time information, finance and investment capital could be flashed around the world at the speed of light. People could trade anywhere and everywhere instantaneously. Moreover the world had become a much bigger stage for all these players: 51 nations formed the United Nations at the end of World War II, but the end of colonialism has swelled that number to 192 today.

Inevitably the implications of such an immense and rapid change have been enormous and will continue to be so. Not all the ramifications are fully understood, but one thing seems certain. Globalization cannot be reversed, any more than the industrial revolution could be. Individual countries may opt out of it if they wish, and many are being left behind by the process – to their great cost. But the process itself is irreversible.

* * *

The way the system works is both simple and bewildering. Everything depends on the instincts and behaviour of millions of investors around the world whom Friedman calls "the Electronic Herd" and who tend to be concentrated in the great financial capitals of New York, London, Frankfurt, Zurich and Hong Kong. Like any herd of animals on the great plains of Africa they may sniff the air, fancy they have caught the scent of a likely place to feed and begin moving there, to the great benefit of the country they converge on. But just as likely they may sniff danger, take fright and stampede away leaving financial devastation in their wake, even to the point of collapsing governments.

No one is in control of the herd. It operates entirely by its own instincts, based on the information it receives and how it interprets it. No sentiment is involved, no special circumstances are heeded; the herd is impersonal and is driven only by its instinct for profit. It does not always operate collectively: individual investors may follow their own hunches or seek out niche markets that take their fancy. But if one suddenly moves the others take note, and if a stampede begins the mass tends to follow.

Friedman, who is given to colourful metaphors, divides his Electronic Herd into two categories – the short-horned cattle, or portfolio investors, who buy and sell equity stocks, bonds and currencies; and the long-horned cattle, or foreign direct investors, who build factories or enter into production contracts with local manufacturers around the world.

It is the short-horned portfolio investors who are the more disruptive. It is they who are prone to sudden stampedes that can annihilate economies. They can move large sums of money around more quickly and easily than the direct investors, who have a longer-term commitment to the countries they locate in. But both can move more swiftly than ever before, and both have the ability to shape the behaviour of nations the world over as everyone tries desperately to capture and keep the herd's attention.

Among the most disruptive of the short-horned players are the currency speculators, mostly hedge-fund managers who have vast sums of money at their disposal. One of their favourite games is what is known as "selling short". If a speculator senses that a particular currency is showing signs of weakness he may decide to gamble on its pending decline and sell substantial amounts on the currency markets. If he sells enough he can actually create a self-fulfilling prophecy, driving down the value of the currency by his action. The trick is that the speculator does not have to deliver the currency he is selling right away, so that in fact what he does is to sell, say, South African rands which he does not have. He then waits for the price of the currency to fall, at which point he buys up what he needs at the lower price to deliver to the buyers – who of course have to pay the speculator at the dollar price the rands were at when they bought them. The speculator makes a killing, the buyers lose out, and the country concerned can be plunged into a currency crisis. In the globalized marketplace there are no rules to govern such currency trading, nor can a targeted country easily see what is happening until it is too late. In a single day which became known as Black Wednesday in 1992, George Soros, the king of hedge-fund traders, shook Britain's sterling currency and made a billion pound profit.

But if the perils of globalization are great, so are the benefits for those who are able to attract the huge and ever-growing herd of investors. How to do that, then, is the key to faster economic growth and the ability to provide a higher standard of living for a country's people. This is where the greatest controversy arises. In the heady triumphalism that now prevails in the capitalist West after the collapse of communism, there is an almost unchallengeable degree of consensus on what is required. Known as the "Washington consensus", it amounts to a formula that has been adopted by the main international agencies charged with the task of helping developing countries get on the high road to greater prosperity, the World Bank and the International Monetary Fund, both of which are headquartered in Washington DC. Friedman, in his swashbuckling way, gives it another name – the "Golden Straitjacket". Whatever the name, the formula is the same. To fit into this uncomfortable garment, Friedman says, a country must either adopt, or be seen as moving towards, the following:

"Making the private sector the primary engine of its economic growth, maintaining a low rate of inflation and price stability, shrinking the size of its state bureaucracy, maintaining as close to a balanced budget as possible, if not a surplus, eliminating or lowering tariffs on imported goods, removing restrictions on foreign investment, getting rid of quotas and domestic monopolies, increasing exports, privatizing state-owned industries and utilities, deregulating capital markets, making its currency convertible, opening its industries, stock and bond markets to direct foreign ownership and investment, deregulating its economy to promote as much domestic competition as possible, eliminating government corruption, subsidies and kickbacks as much as possible, opening its banking and telecommunications systems to private ownership and competition, and allowing its citizens to choose from an array of competing pension options and foreign-run pension and mutual funds."[9]

No variations are permitted. No concessions may be made to local circumstances. The Golden Straitjacket, says Friedman, is "pretty much one-size-fits-all", an injunction with which the economists at the World Bank and the IMF essentially agree. It may pinch and it may hurt, they say, but those countries which put it on and keep it on will be rewarded by the Electronic Herd with investment capital to grow.

* * *

Well, not always. Ironically, Friedman himself gives some insight into why some countries simply do not figure in the Electronic Herd's calculations however much they obey the orthodoxy. In yet another of his colourful metaphors, Friedman likens the global competition for strategic advantage between the two superpowers during the Cold War to a chess match. Citing a foreign affairs specialist who first put the analogy to him, Friedman points out that in the Cold War chess game the United States had to counter every move the Soviet Union made. Thus every pawn was important because it protected one's king. "If they took a pawn, they were that much closer to your king and therefore you were that much closer to defeat. And that is why you had to protect every pawn. Defending pawns was a way of defending your king. And that is why we ended up getting involved in places of no intrinsic importance to us, such as Vietnam, Angola or El Salvador."[10]

Quite so. But now the chess game is over and the pawns are no longer important, whether they are wearing straitjackets or not. That is why foreign aid to the developing world has shrunk. And it is not only the governments of the developed countries that have lost interest in the world's pawns, but the multinational corporations too. As Friedman notes wryly, the Electronic Herd doesn't play chess: it plays monopoly. And in that new game only the big properties are worth investing in; the minions don't matter; they are not worth bothering about. Indeed in my own frequent travels in the developed world, I have found there is not only less and less interest in the affairs of Third World countries but less and less awareness even of their existence. In this new age of fast action, short attention spans and snap judgments, there is no time for anything but the most important issues and places. And so the pawns of the world have simply disappeared from the Electronic Herd's radar screens. In investment terms, they don't exist.

For many, moreover, the straitjacket has meant penury and hardship for their people, because it simply does not fit all circumstances. How do you make the private sector the primary engine of growth in a country that has no meaningful private sector, or a skills base that is too small to stretch beyond an already thinly-staffed public sector? How do you attract foreign direct investors to a country that has no resources to exploit and is populated by people with no industrial or entrepreneurial expertise and next to no purchasing power? How do you increase Lesotho's exports, for example, when all it has to export is water from its high Maluti Mountains which can be gravity-fed to South Africa's industrial heartland around Johannesburg; or Malawi's when all it has to offer is a little home-grown tea and coffee and a pretty lake which may be of some interest to tourists who happen to be visiting other parts of southern Africa anyway? When the IMF prescribes austerity measures for some desperate countries seeking its loans to escape a debt trap, it means health budgets are cut and children are forced to leave school – yet public health and education are supposed to be essential requirements for getting going in the globalization era.

There is a sharp irony in the fact that capitalism, always so scornful of communism's central planning and command economics, should imagine that it can produce a centrally planned economic formula at the IMF in Washington, impose it on distant countries, and expect it to work. Like the conservative critics of the Age of Enlightenment, who began by attacking the danger of social theories presented as universal truths and then went on to become dogmatic social theorists themselves, so have the capitalist critics of Marxist Utopianism themselves become teleological evangelists.

These central planners, whom Joseph Stiglitz, former chief economist at the World Bank, has famously described as "second-rate economists from first-rate universities", often lack experience of the countries they are advising. "They are more likely to have first-hand knowledge of its five-star hotels than of the villages that dot its countryside," Stiglitz wrote in *The New Republic* in April 2000. "They work hard, poring over numbers deep into the night. But their task is impossible. In a period of days or, at most, weeks, they are charged with developing a coherent program sensitive to the needs of the country. Needless to say, a little number-crunching rarely provides adequate insights into the development strategy for an entire nation ...

"Critics accuse (the IMF) of taking a cookie-cutter approach to economics, and they're right. Country teams have been known to compose draft reports before visiting the country concerned. I heard stories of one unfortunate incident when team members copied large parts of the text for one country's report and transferred them wholesale to another."[11]

Stiglitz even blames the "Washington consensus" formula for the Asian crisis of 1997. At the time, he says, Thailand and the other Asian countries were coming off a miraculous three decades: incomes had soared, health had improved, poverty had fallen dramatically. But these countries then liberalized their financial and capital markets. Not because they needed to, Stiglitz contends. Their savings rates were high and they were attracting all the funds they needed, but the international organizations pressured them into it. The dogma required it. The result was a flood of short-term capital that fuelled an unsustainable real-estate bubble, which then burst with disastrous results. "Even as the evidence of the policy's failure mounted, the IMF barely blinked, delivering the same medicine to each ailing nation that showed up on its doorstep." The crisis was not caused by imprudent governments, as the doctrine routinely contends, but by imprudent private sector bankers and borrowers who gambled on the real-estate bubble.

George Soros, an enigmatic figure who is sharply critical of the system he exploits to make his money, is also worried that the global financial structure is loaded against the poor countries and in favour of the rich. "The trend of globalization is that surplus capital is moving from the periphery countries to the centre, which is the United States," he told reporters at an international conference on poverty in Monterrey, Mexico, in March 2002.[12] Soros believes a new global financial architecture is needed to control destructive surges in capital flows and bring about greater equilibrium in the world.

None of this means that the basics of macro-economic prudence, privatization and a quest for export-driven growth are not sound objectives to pursue. But it does mean one must beware of one-size-fits-all doctrines. There are no automatic formulae, no ultimate solutions, for achieving political and economic success or creating the perfect society, and any claims that there are carry the taint of totalitarianism. Soros calls such proselytes "capitalist fundamentalists" and says they are a threat to his vision of an open society. The fact is that all countries, like individuals, are different. Programmes need to be tailored to fit their circumstances, not force-fed from the dogma of a capitalist manifesto. And new international institutions need to be established to help small and poorly developed countries withstand the destabilizing winds of the new global environment. They cannot be left to fend for themselves on the assumption that if they simply do as they are told and don that straitjacket, all will be well.

* * *

Nor is it only the small and the weak who find the formula does not always produce the automatic benefits they have been led to expect. Trevor Manuel, emerging from the Monterrey conference, told reporters: "You can subject South Africa's policies to the tests of salt water and fresh water economists and we will pass those tests. But that has not translated into a great flow of investment."[13]

Why not? There are a number of reasons, of which the first and perhaps the most detrimental is the fact that Africa is a bad neighbourhood in the eyes of the investor community, a continent of pawns and political disaster that they feel is best avoided. But the condition of the African neighbourhood is a subject on its own that I shall return to later in this book.

Close behind is the fact that South Africa entered the competitive field of emerging economies late, after Asian and Latin American countries already had a head start. How the "Asian tigers", as the first highly successful developing economies became known, did it is instructive, for what they revealed is that countries do not grow because they get foreign investment; they get foreign investment only *after* they start growing. Investors do not look around the world for countries that are implementing the rigorous dictates of the Washington consensus; they look around the world for countries that are growing, where they reckon they can make a fast buck. It is growth that is the magnet, not economic orthodoxy.

The Asian tigers got started with very little in the way of economic orthodoxy. Countries such as Japan, Thailand and South Korea, which led the way, all had heavy state intervention in their economies. Their governments identified industrial sectors to be boosted, gave those industries low-interest loans from state-controlled banks to help them acquire the technologies and capital equipment they needed to develop, and at the same time used red-tape entanglements to discourage foreign competition. The result was that the local industries grew rapidly, opened up export opportunities in those fields and generated capital for further investment. As their economies boomed, showing spectacular growth from their low starting bases, foreign investors fell over themselves to get in on the act. They were not put off by the fact that several of the "tigers" ran up inflation rates of more than 20% and 30% during their take-off phase, or that Singapore, one of the most admired, still has more than 60% of its industries controlled by the state. It mattered not a whit that most were wearing loose-fitting smocks instead of straitjackets. It was the raw smell of growth that attracted the investors to these honeypots.

It is interesting to note that the MERG report included many of the features of these Asian success stories, underlining the point I made in the previous chapter that the report contained some sound advice which the ANC should have been more careful not to throw out with the bathwater. One of the worst errors was the obsession of Chris Stals, the Reserve Bank governor who was a hold-over from the old regime, with pushing up interest rates to an astronomical 25% in his efforts to bring down the inflation rate, which in fact was never out of synch with what the Asian tigers had tolerated during their take-off years. The purveyors of economic orthodoxy all applauded Stals, but what he did stopped South Africa's growth in its tracks at that crucial moment right after our miraculous transition when the admiring eyes of the world were upon us and we had a window of opportunity to produce a spurt of growth that might – just might – have caught the attention of the foreign investor community. By the time we had all our orthodox ducks in a row and were able to bring down both the interest rate and the inflation rate, the magic moment was gone. We were just one more developing country struggling to make it onto the Electronic Herd's radar screens. Some of the young whizz-kids who are making the herd's snap decisions today were at high school when we made our great transition, and to them the word "apartheid", if they have heard it at all, belongs in history books.

It must be noted, too, that South Africa could not have implemented all those Asian-inspired recommendations contained in the MERG report even if the new regime had wanted to do so. Apart from the ANC leadership's fears of macro-economic populism – and the excessive prime-pumping of the demand side of the economy that MERG advocated certainly justified those fears – the rules and regulations of the World Trade Organization that apply today would not have allowed it. The advanced economies, which watched the rise of those Asian companies with a mixture of admiration and alarm, moved to declare the methods they used protectionist and unfair. Domestic subsidies and high protective tariffs are no longer permitted if you wish to be a member of the WTO, and if you do not become a member your economy will surely wither and die in its isolation. There may be a great irony in the fact that the one proven method of generating growth in under-developed countries has been disallowed by the organization whose prime role is to help bring that about, but as we shall see in a moment that is not the only inconsistency in this lopsided world.

The fact that South Africa was late into the field of developing nations competing for the attention of foreign investors put us at a dis-advantage. By the time we got there the field was already crowded, and some of the early starters who were already in the tiger class were cap-turing all the attention and all the money. Investors who wanted to play in the emerging market chose them; there was no point in choosing second best and even less in gambling on a newcomer like South Africa.

There is another feature of the new global economy that comes into play here – winners, from sports stars to movie stars and from techno-logical innovators to heart surgeons to developing economies, take a disproportionate share of the prize money. Those who come second lag far behind them, and those who rank tenth hardly feature at all. Two American economists, Philip J Cook of Duke University and Robert H Frank of Cornell, explain why in a fascinating book called *The Winner-Take-All Society*, in which they point out that during the last two decades the top 1% of US earners have captured 40% of the country's total earnings growth. Nor is this growing disparity confined to the US. In Britain, the authors note, the richest 20% earned seven times as much as the poorest 20% in 1991, compared with only four times as much in 1977. "The British gap between males with the highest wage rates and those with the lowest is larger now than at any time since the 1880s."[14]

The reason is that in this modern age of mass production for mass global markets, a top tenor such as Luciano Pavarotti will make mil-lions more than those who are only fractionally less talented than he, because huge numbers of buyers the world over are prepared to pay a little more for his mass-produced compact discs rather than those of the second best. The local soprano who used to make a decent living performing for home-town audiences has had her moderate giftedness rendered worthless because modern communications technology has put her into daily competition with the world's top stars like Joan Sutherland or Kathleen Battle, whose CDs cost no more to stamp out than those of any other singer. In every field, Frank and Cook point out, globalization has meant that "rewards tend to be concentrated in the hands of a few top performers, with small differences in talent or effort often giving rise to enormous differences in incomes."[15] The world's top ten tennis professionals earn a fortune in prize money and lucrative endorsements, whereas a competent player like Australia's Wally Masur, who was ranked among the world's top 50 for many years and reached the US Open semi-finals in 1993, never had manufacturers selling tennis shoes and racquets bearing his name. His earnings were a fraction of those fractionally better than him. Likewise in Olympic competition. Only hundredths of a second separate the top performers in swimming, sprinting, downhill skiing and scores of other events. "Yet the gold-medallists in these events," the authors note, "often go on to earn millions in endorsements, while the runners-up are quickly relegated to footnotes."[16] The same applies to best-selling authors, top fashion models, movie stars, lawyers, surgeons, researchers, corporate CEOs.

And countries. "As the explosive growth of international trade and commerce has made national borders more permeable," write Frank and Cook, "more and more of the world's most talented professionals work outside their home countries. Many of these people eventually emigrate, to the substantial economic and cultural benefit of their new countries."[17]

In the same way, investors choose the most profitable emerging economies in which to locate their factories or place their portfolio investments, while those countries which are marginally behind in the economic rankings lose out. The winning tigers take all. And you have to grow first to be recognized as a tiger. A Catch 22 situation.

The dice are loaded in other ways too. The free-market ideologists claim the system's great virtue is that it offers everyone a level playing field. That may be true in theory, but in practice the field is anything but level. Just as the winner-take-all society favours the top performers, so does the global playing field favour the already rich and powerful. The G-8 nations lay down the rules of international behaviour through organizations such as the IMF, the World Bank and the World Trade Organization, which they control, but they do not themselves always abide by those rules. The developing countries are required to open themselves to free trade by lowering tariffs on imported goods and ending subsidies, which of course is great for the big exporters of the developed world, but those developed countries, especially the US and the European Union, maintain their own fat farm subsidies and high tariff walls to protect their agricultural and textile industries from Third World imports. The rich club of 30 Organization of Economic

Cooperation and Development (OECD) countries subsidize their agricultural sectors to the tune of an outrageous $1 billion a day, which is more than the combined gross national product of all Africa's 54 countries. As Trade and Industries Minister Alec Erwin has pointed out, if they were to drop those subsidies and remove non-tariff barriers, the benefit to the developing world would be three times annual aid flows – and aid itself would become unnecessary.[18]

When South Africa sought to negotiate a trade agreement with the European Union, the Mediterranean countries fought a fierce rearguard action to protect their agricultural industry, their fruit and their wines, from open competition with South Africa's despite the natural safeguard of seasonal difference between the northern and southern hemispheres. And opposition to America's imports of African textiles from a paltry 0,8% of all textile imports to 1,6% stalled the African Growth and Opportunity Act in Congress for more than a year.

Like equality, playing fields are more level for some than for others. In February 2002 President George W Bush suddenly slapped a 30% tariff increase on all steel imports into the US. Although he exempted a few Third World producers, South Africa included, it was a unilateral action in blatant violation of World Trade Organization rules that outraged the Europeans particularly. The motive behind it was patently to protect what has become an antiquated and inefficient industry in the US, precisely what the new ideology of global competition is supposed to rectify through elimination, the process of "creative destruction" so strongly advocated by the Republican Party particularly, but in this instance Bush was more concerned about the political kudos it would earn him in the traditionally pro-Democratic labour movement. Had a pawn country acted as he did, it would have suffered sanctions under WTO rules and forfeited any prospect of IMF aid until it rescinded the decree, but can anyone imagine the rest of the world refusing to trade with the only superpower? America's military and economic might enable it to act with impunity, hence the paradox of its growing unilateralist tendencies in this age of globalization which it is supposed to be leading.

But talk to the business community and you will hear another reason why South Africa has failed to attract as much foreign investment as it had hoped for, and which Manuel feels its economic good behaviour warrants. They will speak of "labour flexibility". It was a phrase that puzzled me when I first heard it, for it sounds like some form of multi-skilling on the factory floor. Then I realized it was globalization-era newspeak for something very different, a euphemism in fact for cheap labour and the right to hire and fire at will. It is a measure of the extent to which globalization is bringing back the spirit of primitive capitalism before the challenge of Karl Marx and the emergence of trade unions and collective bargaining.

Faced with the pressures of global competition, manufacturers strive for marginal advantage by cutting production costs, which means they want cheap but still highly productive labour, and by cutting inventory costs with just-in-time delivery schedules. They also want to be able to expand and shrink their labour forces in line with the boom and recessionary phases of the economic cycles, which means being able to hire and fire at will. Business people like to explain that this is really in the interests of the workers, because if they know they will not be able to retrench staff when the lean times come they will not hire extra people in the good times; so, you see, over time "labour flexibility" really means more employment. Not surprisingly, workers themselves see it differently. To them it means they are in no position to pressurize for job security, pension rights, standard hours and a minimum wage.

What it means in practice is that big multinational corporations want to break out of the constraints of labour legislation, workers' rights and collective bargaining in the old-established developed economies. Trashing the trade unions at home is one way, as Margaret Thatcher did in Britain, but easier still is to move abroad to a developing country where these constraints do not exist or are very weak. And the weaker they are the more "labour flexibility" there is reckoned to be. The opportunities range from sweatshops and the kind of dirt-cheap, regimented labour that is available in China, to Singapore's high-tech, high-pay workforce that nonetheless works under authoritarian conditions.

The point is that multinational corporations no longer choose their venues to serve local markets alone, but as bases from which to serve the global market – the availability of skilled but "flexible" labour being a major attraction. The multinational company may set up its own factory in the country of its choice, or it may enter into production contracts with manufacturers in developing countries. An international banker explained to me how the latter system works. A clothing manufacturer with a fashionable label will put out a tender for, say, a large order of stylish tee-shirts to be marketed world-wide, and manufacturers in developing countries bid for this order. "Depending on the

217

bids that come in," the banker explained, "the order may go this year to Malaysia, next year to Pakistan and the year after to Indonesia. It becomes a race to the bottom."

Thanks to the speed of modern communications technology, a multinational corporation can also slice up its production process and outsource each segment to whatever country can do it cheapest and most efficiently. A computer company can design its equipment at home, have it manufactured in, say, Taiwan, have the software written in Bangalore, India, and even have the company's accounting done in Bangladesh.

All this does indeed amount to the exploitation of cheap but skilled labour. It does indeed mean taking advantage of workers who are not protected by strong labour legislation. It does indeed bring back some of the aspects of primitive capitalism. But on the other hand it is also true that even a poorly paid job is better than no job at all, and that countries which open themselves up to this kind of low-wage, high-volume economic activity lay the basis for skills development, technology importation, capital accumulation and future growth. It is a process that gives substance to the crass words of Gordon Gekko in the satirical movie *Wall Street*: "Greed is good. Greed is right. Greed works." And to the old saw that, if you are poor, the only thing worse than being exploited is not to be exploited at all.

But South Africa has decided otherwise. Politics is the art of the possible, and it is simply not possible either morally or politically for a liberation movement that has come to power to free its people from the indignities of apartheid and 352 years of economic exploitation to tell them they must now join the race to the bottom and subject themselves to yet more exploitation. It has been tough enough navigating the great U-Turn without splitting the ruling alliance, but this would surely do it – and such a split would alarm the investment community far more than the country's present labour regime. When it comes to a choice between labour flexibility and political stability, the latter must win.

Instead South Africa is trying to exploit what Erwin calls its "dynamic competitive advantage over anything the G-8 countries can achieve". South African workers, he reasons, can achieve skills levels equal to or very close to those of the developed countries. This makes them "structurally cheaper". If that can be combined with "well-oiled industrial relations" that solves problems through mediation and conciliation rather than through strike action, there will be a competitive advantage that should attract foreign investors.

218

Taking that as the starting point, Erwin foresees a growth path through what he calls "multiplier effects", with the growth of small and medium-sized enterprises, and "accelerator effects", when a sufficient number of people with high-value jobs stimulate the economy through increased consumer demand. "It means you start your growth path slowly, around 3%," says Erwin, "and then climb to 4% and higher, up to 7%, before you start tailing off again. But we need that sustained growth above 4% for five or six, up to ten years, to get the structural changes in wealth that we need for a stable society."[19]

But the winds of globalization, the international financial crises and the slowdown in the world economy keep blowing South Africa off that track. And it remains to be seen whether international investors really are attracted by the competitive advantage Erwin says our labour force offers them.

CHAPTER ELEVEN

A BITTER INHERITANCE

"I owe much. I possess nothing.
I give the rest to the poor."
— FRANCOIS RABELAIS, FRENCH WRITER 1494-1553

Two factors in particular are making foreign investors sceptical about locating in South Africa. One is apartheid's legacy of poor education for the majority of the population and the way the job reservation laws favouring whites truncated the skills base of our working class. The other, also a legacy from the past, is South Africa's high crime rate. Foreign investors are reluctant to send management staff and their families to dangerous places where they may come to harm; and while the poor education system is slowing the production of new skills, the crime wave is hastening the departure of old skills as it drives the brain drain. Thus the two interact to destructive effect. Of all the old South Africa's wretched bequests to the new, these were the worst.

Of the two, the education system is the harder to remedy, for there is no way education can be speeded up. In the best of circumstances it takes 21 years and nine months to produce a new skilled worker. And before you can do that you must first produce a corps of skilled and dedicated teachers. As the ANC government came to power in 1994, it had to start that daunting task from scratch – and sadly it stumbled and wasted time at the beginning.

What the new regime inherited is what education minister Kader Asmal calls "a dysfunctional system". To begin with it was not only segregated but hopelessly unequal. White public education was equal to the best in the developed world, while black education was poorer than many in the Third World: buildings were derelict, 30% had no electricity, 25% no water, 50% no sanitation and one-third of the teachers were unqualified and many more were underqualified. Education for the Coloured and Indian minorities, also segregated from both the whites and the blacks as well as from each other, fell somewhere in between. And while education for whites was free and compulsory, for blacks, Coloureds and Indians it was neither.

Administratively, the system was fragmented to an unmanageable degree. Each of the four race groups had its own education department, as did each of the ten tribal bantustans and each of the four supposedly white provinces, while over them all was an umbrella Department of National Education. It made for 19 education departments altogether, all theoretically autonomous yet bound by the overriding doctrine of apartheid with its separate syllabuses for the different races so that, in the doctrine of the system's founder, Hendrik Verwoerd, none would be educated "to have expectations in life which circumstances in South Africa do not allow to be fulfilled".[1] In other words a hierarchical ladder of superior education for superior races. There were also superior budget allocations and superior facilities for the superior races.

All of which made education the explosive frontier of black anger and political resistance. It was black students in Soweto who rose up in 1976 to protest a decree requiring them to study in the Afrikaans language, so setting off a national uprising that kept the country in flames for 17 months and left 600 people dead and thousands imprisoned, and sent 14 000 into exile. It was the penultimate crisis of apartheid. The final crisis, which erupted in September 1983 and led eventually to apartheid's demise, was also joined by large numbers of student activists and raged for three years during which 3 000 people were killed and 30 000 were imprisoned without trial.

Black students, indeed the whole education system, became highly politicized and the culture of learning disintegrated. At the height of the conflict students coined the slogan: "Freedom now, education later." For many, that meant education never came, and for the system as a whole the ethos was lost in a nihilistic maelstrom. I remember visiting Fort Hare University in 1991 for the installation of the ailing ANC President Oliver Tambo as Chancellor, and as I strolled around the campus with a senior staff member I asked about the mood of the student body following a spate of campus disturbances. "You must remember," the staff member remarked matter-of-factly, "that some of these students murdered their headmasters before they came here." It was a conversation stopper, but no exaggeration. In the course of the great 1980s revolt, blacks who were seen as servants of the oppressive apartheid regime, particularly school principals, police officers, and township and bantustan officials, became the objects of a special hatred. They were derided as "system blacks" and many were singled out for the cruel assassination ritual known as "necklacing", in which the victim had a tyre filled with gasoline pulled around his body and set on fire.

Setting such a derelict system right is an awesome task. Unfortunately it got off to a slow start under a minister who was not up to the challenge. Sibusiso Benghu was a well-meaning man but he lacked the breadth of vision to see what South Africa needed to meet the challenges of global competition, and the political drive to seize the elan of the moment after the transition. In Chapter Three I outlined how Benghu actually worsened the chronic shortage of skilled teachers by trying to compel them to relocate to poorer regions or take retrenchment, which resulted in hundreds of long-serving teachers with valuable experience grabbing the fat golden handshakes and going off to start second careers.

Despite this a good deal was achieved in those first five years. Not only were all schools racially integrated by law (although many in black areas remain all black), the entire system was administratively integrated as well. The 19 different education departments of the apartheid era were restructured into one national and nine new provincial departments. It was a mammoth task that involved integrating 10 million students and teachers into a new system without interrupting school programmes.

Compulsory schooling was introduced for all children between the ages of seven and 14; the number of underqualified teachers was reduced from 36% to 26%; and the national education budget was increased from R31,8 billion in 1994 to R54,1 billion in 2000. That is 6% of the country's gross national product, one of the highest rates of government investment in the world. But education standards continued to lag behind those of other middle-income countries.

The appointment of Kader Asmal as the new Minister of National Education after the 1999 election saw a significant improvement. Asmal had been the star of the Mandela Cabinet. As Minister of Water Affairs he brought clean water to millions of households around the country and he stood out as a man of action. His energy soon galvanized the education scene: in his first year he called for a 5% improvement in the matriculation pass rate, and achieved a remarkable 9%. He also brought considerable educational and academic experience to the task. He had worked as a schoolteacher in Natal during his early years, then after joining the ANC and going into exile he studied at the London School of Economics before becoming a lecturer in law at

Trinity College, Dublin. He qualified as a barrister at both the London and Dublin bars, and on his return to South Africa became Professor of Human Rights Law at the University of the Western Cape.

But Asmal, too, has not found the job easy. In an interview soon after taking over he told me the most difficult part was getting things done through the system of delegated authority to the provinces. The law gives the minister the power to determine national norms and standards for education planning, but there is no way he can ensure the implementation of those plans in the face of provincial administrators who are sometimes incompetent or want to assert their independence. "The only part of the budget I control is the allocation of funds to the universities," he explained. It means trying to direct the system by remote control. One of Asmal's techniques is to submit regular reports to the President. "It is an enormously powerful thing," he says wryly, "because the political futures of the people involved are tied up with the extent to which they perform."

Worse still is the legacy of demotivation among the staff. There are headmasters who give no leadership and frequently don't even turn up for work; some teachers come to school drunk; there have been cases of teachers sexually harassing and even raping students; schools don't start on time, and there is a general air of disinterest and disorganization. Helen Zille, the former *Rand Daily Mail* reporter who exposed the truth about Steve Biko's murder in detention while I was editor of the newspaper, and who later became the Democratic Alliance's provincial education minister in the Western Cape for a time, told me of a survey taken in the province which showed that so much time was being wasted that some schools were delivering only 45 minutes of teaching a day. "Some teachers see their job simply in terms of a salary and perks," Zille said, "not as a set of responsibilities, not as a service role to students, and they don't see themselves as publicly accountable."

Asmal agrees. He has repeatedly complained about a lack of accountability on the part of school principals particularly. It is a factor that is as easy to see as it is hard to rectify. While I was in charge of SABC Television News I became aware of a school in a settlement called Bochum in what is now Limpopo Province which delivered a zero pass rate in the matriculation examinations for three years in succession. I twice sent reporters to the school to investigate. They were unable to locate the headmaster.

Asmal complains, too, about the teacher unions, especially the

Cosatu-allied South African Democratic Teachers' Union (SADTU), which are highly politicized, radicalized and confrontational. They defend these malingering, defaulting teachers and show scant concern for poor educational standards. "They don't differentiate between professional and union issues, and everything is dealt with by confrontation," says Asmal. Worst of all they often time their strikes to coincide with examinations, so that hurting their students becomes part of their collective bargaining pressure.

It is hard to understand this lack of commitment and the general insouciance among people who have suffered oppression, who have yearned for liberation, and who now literally have the future of the liberated country in their hands. Yet the couldn't-care-less attitude is widespread. Many senior officials in the new administration are baffled by it. Some attribute it to "a culture of entitlement", an attitude which says, in effect, that I have suffered and therefore the world owes me a living: I am entitled to be given pay and perks, I do not have to earn them. At least one senior ANC figure puts it down to the narrow career choices that were available to black people, women especially, during apartheid and which resulted in many square pegs going into round holes. "Jobs like teaching and nursing are a calling," she suggests. "They require people who feel a special dedication to that kind of work. But under apartheid these were the only status jobs open to black women, so that many who didn't feel that special commitment went into them."

My own assessment is that the apartheid regime, in the first instance, deliberately staffed black schools with servile personalities. The last thing it wanted, given the kind of truncated education for truncated opportunities that Verwoerd had prescribed, was strong-minded teachers who would awaken young black minds with inspiring ideas and ambitions. So the best teachers left or were fired and the Uncle Toms came in. Archbishop Desmond Tutu was among the many who quit teaching when the Bantu Education system was introduced. He changed career and became a minister of the Anglican Church, going on to be ranked alongside Nelson Mandela as a champion of his people's liberation and a winner of the Nobel Peace Prize.

Thereafter the intense radicalization of student bodies that swept through the black schools in the seventies and eighties, turning the schools into platforms of revolution and centres of flaming rhetoric, stripped these flaccid teachers and administrators of what little authority and respect they had. It alienated them from their communities, and to a degree that alienation has remained. Worst of all, it destroyed all sense of discipline and effectively broke down the culture of learning to such an extent that it has not yet been able to recover. The legacy lingers. High school students are still highly politicized and teachers are still demoralized and demotivated. The culture of learning is still not there.

Of course I generalize, which is unfair. There are wonderful, dedicated teachers all over the country, committed people battling against adversity. I know a farm school in Limpopo Province, not far from delinquent Bochum, that regularly produces 100% matriculation passes with excellent results in mathematics and science, and another in the desperately poor Transkei region of Eastern Cape Province that does equally well. Helen Zille tells me of members of a Cape Malay community who sought her permission to use a condemned building in a run-down area of the Cape Flats, outside Cape Town, and in those improbable conditions have created a school alive with the buzz of vibrant education; while another in a more salubrious neighbourhood with fine facilities has a bored and demotivated staff and library shelves with no books. It is, as Asmal says, a dysfunctional system but with these remarkable pockets of excellence and dedication.

Asmal's focus, as I write this, is on restructuring the higher education system. Here again the apartheid system produced a wicked and wasteful distortion. Instead of building universities where they were most needed to produce the skills South Africa requires to be competitive in the globalized environment, it built them for ideological reasons, as status symbols for the bantustans. As Asmal puts it scornfully: "Every 'homeland' wanted a technical college, an airport and a university." The result was a chain of little tribal universities stuck out in the bush, all of which have become sinkholes of squandered funds. Together they owe more than R2 billion, and their students owe some R150 million in arrear fees which they can never pay. They are poorly led and poorly staffed, delivering inferior education at enormous cost. Yet they cannot simply be closed, for what could then be done with their elaborate status-symbol buildings which are not sellable in such remote regions?

The obvious solution, which Asmal is now implementing, is to incorporate them as regional campuses of South Africa's major established universities, which are among the world's best. And so the country's 36 universities and technikons will be consolidated into 21. It makes every kind of administrative and educational sense, yet even so positive a step is encountering resistance from the educationists involved, for it means a loss of top jobs, a reduction in the number of vice-chancellors with their pay and perks and status. Greed, you see Mr Gekko, is not always good. But in this, as in the Great U-Turn itself, the government is showing determination in the face of resistance within its own ranks.

This will upgrade the standard of higher education generally, in the technical training institutes especially. "That," says Asmal, "is where we have got to get our computer people, our actuaries for planning purposes, our economists, our applied scientists." The globalized economy needs them all, and the need is becoming ever more urgent. South Africa is not only producing them too slowly, it is losing them at an alarming rate in the brain drain. A University of South Africa study conducted in mid-2002 estimated that 70% of skilled South Africans consider emigrating, and an estimated 20% have already left.[2]

The reasons are many. The greater mobility of labour that is part of globalization and the opportunities thrown up by South Africa's integration into international business after years of isolation are part of it. But so, too, is widespread fear of South Africa's high crime rate. This is not only keeping investors out, it is driving our own skills away.

* * *

The basis for the crime wave that engulfed the new South Africa almost from its inception was in fact laid a decade earlier when the old regime, massively preoccupied with trying to repress the great black uprising of the 1980s, failed to heed a significant shift that was taking place in the pattern of crime throughout the southern African region.

Two things were happening. A swift increase in the use of narcotics in South Africa meant that profits from the drug trade were increasing dramatically. At the same time there was a sharp rise in the number of white fortune hunters from various parts of Europe as well as Lebanon, Israel and India who were moving into resource-rich countries to the north of us, such as the Democratic Republic of Congo (then called Zaire), Angola and Zambia, where they were able to take advantage of corrupt governments and poor policing to establish lucrative smuggling operations in commodities such as gold, diamonds, emeralds, cobalt, ivory, rhino horn and particularly drugs.

The ballooning drug trade in South Africa became an obvious target market for these northern operators, and throughout the 1980s huge quantities of illegal drugs, particularly Mandrax (methaqualine), were smuggled into the country. Profits were enormous. Peter Gastrow of the Institute of Security Studies, which has done much valuable research into the growth of crime in South Africa, notes that a single Mandrax tablet which once cost 5 cents at a pharmacy acquired a street value of R15 in South Africa after it was declared illegal in the early 1980s; while pure cocaine, obtained for $2 500 from sources in Latin America, was diluted and sold for $50 000 in South Africa.[3]

The burgeoning South African crime gangs often ran into cash-flow problems in their dealings with these suppliers from the north, and so they resorted to barter transactions. Motor vehicles, especially luxury cars which were scarce in countries to the north, became key items in this barter trade.

And so there was an explosion of vehicle hijackings. Motorists were held up at gunpoint – sometimes in broad daylight, at traffic lights in city centres, even in their own suburban driveways as they returned home from work – and their cars were taken from them. Some motorists were beaten up and some were murdered, shot dead in cold blood or in panic by the young hijackers who were hired by crime syndicates to supply them with vehicles. Probably no other factor has done so much to drive the brain drain as the pervasive fear caused by the spate of vehicle hijackings and accompanying violence that hit South Africa soon after the transition.

Burglaries, bank robberies and big cash-in-transit heists, in which gangsters shot up security vehicles carrying large sums of money across the country, or stopped them with spiked chains thrown across a highway, also hit the headlines and intensified the fear.

Meanwhile crime syndicates from other parts of the world also began converging on South Africa, bringing with them new levels of sophistication and contacts with international criminal networks. Chief among these have been Nigerian syndicates that have gained a virtual monopoly over the hugely profitable cocaine trade. Chinese gangs have specialized in smuggling endangered marine species, particularly abalone and crayfish, to Hong Kong, Singapore and China.

A friend of mine, Michael Robinson, who works for BBC Television's Money Programme, discovered the extent of this growth in sophistication and internationalization of the networks operating in and through South Africa with a remarkable piece of investigative journalism in 1999. Robinson traced the path of a Rolls Royce Silver Cloud stolen in the English midlands, shipped to Durban by a Russian shipping company with false papers giving the car's destination as a non-existent automobile dealer in Lesotho, but in fact it was delivered to an Indian trader in South Africa's KwaZulu-Natal province who

227

changed the engine number and sold it to a Pretoria businessman, who now has it. The Russian ship, meanwhile, sailed on with a new cargo of right-hand-drive cars stolen in South Africa to be delivered in Australia.

The core problem was that the old regime never saw any of this coming, as the Commissioner of Police's annual reports to Parliament during those critical early years showed. Even when crime statistics showed that the number of vehicles smuggled across South Africa's borders had increased by a staggering 22% in a single year, the Commissioner's 1987 report sanguinely suggested this was probably due to the increased number of vehicles on the country's roads.

Throughout that critical time in the 1980s when the volume of criminal trade across the country's borders was growing exponentially and South Africa's street gangs were growing richer and turning into more sophisticated crime syndicates, the apartheid government's full attention was focussed on trying to quell the political revolt in the black townships. The Special Branch, the political police who spearheaded the counter-revolutionary operations, were the regime's blue-eyed boys who received the bulk of the resources and all of the special training. The regular detectives, who were aware of the incipient crime problem, were neglected and largely ignored. Some were even seconded to do border duty between what was then South West Africa and Angola in the war against the ANC. "We had to walk patrols and were not allowed to focus on people who were smuggling drugs, cars and guns through border posts," said one. "We suggested this, but it was rejected." As another put it: "Organized crime took the gap and expanded."[4]

Not until 1990, the year in which President de Klerk unbanned the ANC and the process of negotiation and transformation began, did the authorities wake up to what was happening with organized crime. The Commissioner of Police, General Johan van der Merwe, noted for the first time that "the confiscation of astronomic quantities of heroin, cocaine and methaqualine suggests that international drug cartels have identified South Africa as an important market." He also noted that 45% of vehicles stolen in South Africa were smuggled into neighbouring countries in that year. That works out at 30 890 vehicles – yet neither he nor his predecessors had noticed the steady build-up to that staggering figure over the previous ten years.

But by the time the authorities woke up it was too late. The crime syndicates had already established themselves and grown in sophistication. They had built up their international contacts and developed their money-laundering systems. And now a new factor kicked in – the virtual collapse of policing in South Africa.

Like teachers only more so, the police – half of whom were black – were despised in the townships as "system blacks" and the instruments of apartheid brutality. They were its front-line troops, the defenders of the status quo and the enforcers of its oppressive laws. They were the people who stopped anyone and everyone in the streets and sent them to jail under the hated pass laws; who broke down front doors to invade family homes in the middle of the night in their search for political activists; who joined in the torturing and even the killing of detainees; who infiltrated organizations and informed on people; who were in every respect the sharp end of apartheid oppression. And they were roundly hated for it. During the late 1980s they had lived in armed compounds for their protection, and every police station was a fortress surrounded with high security fencing and protected by armed personnel carriers.

Now suddenly everything was turned on its head and these selfsame police were supposed to be the defenders of the ANC, of the enemy they had been fighting. It was too much, too soon. Not only did the police lack the confidence of the communities they were now supposed to serve, but for the police themselves it was a bewildering experience. They had been required to do the apartheid regime's dirty work for it; they had been indoctrinated to believe they were engaged in a holy war to protect the fatherland against bloodthirsty communist terrorists who were bent on its destruction. Now the very people who had told them this were striking a deal and jumping into bed with those selfsame terrorists and leaving the police to twist in the wind before the courts and the Truth and Reconciliation Commission. Small wonder they felt disillusioned, demotivated and demoralized, and that in their disillusionment many simply crossed the line to become criminals themselves. Some left the police service to join the criminal syndicates or form new ones of their own. Others remained in the service but provided crucial services to the criminal syndicates in the form of documents for forging and changing the serial numbers of stolen vehicles, and even the destruction of police investigation dockets to abort prosecutions. As Gastrow and other researchers at the Institute for Security Studies have found, "serving members of the police play an important and direct role in the activities of indigenous crime syndicates and criminal networks ... (while) state officials from other government departments are also part of most of the operations of crime syndicates."[5]

Yet even this is not enough to explain the extraordinary lack of any visible police presence on the streets of South Africa. Police men and women are ubiquitous on the streets of New York, usually patrolling in pairs, and their high visibility is widely recognized as a major factor in the dramatic reduction of that city's once-notorious crime rate. But walk the streets of Johannesburg and you will rarely see a patrolling policeman. I once had cause to enter the Hillbrow Police Station, located in that inner high-rise suburb of Johannesburg which is now rated one of the most crime-ridden places on earth, and I found it packed with police staff behind desks, many lounging about smoking and chatting, while outside on Hillbrow's dangerous streets I failed to see a single patrolling policeman.

The reason for this lopsided deployment is an extraordinary distortion in the ranking structure of the police force, which now has five-and-a-half times more inspectors than sergeants and constables. Ted Leggett, another senior researcher at the Institute of Security Studies, who discovered this classic case of too many chiefs and not enough Indians, says it has distorted the whole structure and with that the efficiency of the South African Police Service.

Whereas sergeants and constables form 94,5% of the police force in Australia and 91% in Britain, they make up only about a third of South Africa's police force. The result is twofold. It has blurred the meaning of rank and the whole line of command and responsibility, with inspectors commanding whole squads of other inspectors while there are not enough sergeants and constables to send out on patrol. And secondly, as Leggett puts it: "New management positions have to be created to accommodate an ever-growing pool of commissioned members, whether these desk posts are needed or not."[6]

This phenomenon is startlingly apparent at police headquarters in Pretoria with its gargantuan staff complement of 14 000 – while the streets of the capital are bare of patrolling cops.

The reason for the distortion, according to Leggett, is again partly the integration of the ten bantustan police forces and the national force into a single unit. In the process many poorly trained bantustan police officers as well as thousands of inexperienced *kitskonstabels* (Afrikaans slang for instant constables, in the sense of instant coffee) and security guards who were recruited during the unrest of the 1980s became ranking members of the integrated South African Police Service. At the same time many members of the old force left, either through political disillusionment or to take advantage of golden handshakes offered to make room for affirmative action appointments. A wealth of policing experience departed with them.

Coupled with this is a promotion system that rewards length of service rather than performance. Thus a policeman has only to wait out the years to become an inspector, whether he is good at the job or not, while recruitment of new constables at the bottom of the ladder is hampered by miserable pay since all the money has gone to the chiefs. The result, in sum, is not only a badly lopsided force but a poorly qualified one whose members were often recruited with little regard to educational qualifications. More than 30% of the 120 000-member national force are illiterate, and more than 11 000 officers do not have driver's licences. Few have been trained in such vital policing skills as fingerprinting, ballistics and forensics.

Poor policing, which also results in the frequent acquittal of arrested criminals because of defective gathering of evidence, has had a further negative consequence – the growth of vigilante groups formed to exact their own vengeance on criminals who plague their communities. There are not many, but their emergence undermines community support for the rule of law and so represents a potentially serious threat to the development of an efficient criminal justice system.

The biggest of these vigilante groups is one called Mapogo-a-Mathamaga, which was formed in Limpopo Province, north of Pretoria, in August 1996 and now has 72 branches in five provinces with 70 000 members who buy its services.

Mapogo, as it is commonly called, was founded by a tough and charismatic figure, Montle Magolego, who decided to cash in on the growing distress of the region's business community following a spate of murders, robberies and burglaries. For a membership fee, Magolego offered not only to protect the business people but to recover stolen goods and to catch and punish the culprits. This his vigilantes do by flogging those they arrest with a *sjambok*, or rhino-hide whip, which has been soaked in salt and traditional herbs. According to community sources, Mapogo's vigilantes sometimes use more violent methods. More than twenty people have reportedly died after being beaten with rods, shot, electrocuted or thrown into crocodile-infested rivers.[7]

Magolego claims success for his swift and rough justice. He gives his clients placards bearing Mapogo's symbol of two leopard heads to fix to their premises, and even police in the region agree that these premises tend to be left untouched. But obviously Mapogo's activities are themselves sometimes illegal, and several of its members have been arrested on charges of kidnapping and torture.

Another, more complex, organization was formed in Cape Town in 1995, mainly by members of the city's Muslim community, in response to high levels of crime and drug trafficking in the Coloured townships on the Cape Flats. Calling themselves People Against Gangsterism and Drugs, with the acronym of Pagad, the organization contained both Islamic militants who had played an active role in the political unrest of the 1980s and more moderate Muslim organizations and neighbourhood watch groups. These two elements soon came into conflict, and in September 1996 there was a split which saw the militants effectively take over the leadership of Pagad. Prominent among these militants were members of a small pro-Shi'ite fundamentalist group called Qibla, which had been formed some years before to promote in South Africa the aims and ideals of the 1979 Iranian revolution.

From then on Pagad acquired not only a more militant character but also a more explicitly political agenda. Instead of simply criticizing the ANC government for its inability to deal effectively with crime and drugs, it began a campaign aimed at turning South Africa into a fully-fledged Muslim theocracy under the slogan "One solution, Islamic revolution". The idea may have been absurd, given that Muslims make up only 2,5% of South Africa's total population and 33% of those in Western Cape Province – of whom only 1% are Shi'ites – but Pagad has nevertheless become a chronic security problem in the Cape Town area and beyond.

Through an armed wing called the G-force, Pagad has continued its vigilante actions against those it claims are gangsters and drug dealers, adding hugely to endemic gang warfare on the Cape Flats, but Pagad is also the prime suspect in 42 unsolved cases of urban terrorism. These have included attacks on police stations in apparent retaliation for the arrest of G-force members, as well as attacks on Muslim businessmen, academics and clerics who have criticized Pagad's tactics. Most conspicuously, when the United States launched missile strikes on suspected Al Qaeda bases in Sudan and Afghanistan following the 1998 bombing of American embassies in Nairobi and Dar es Salaam, several businesses associated with the US, notably a Planet Hollywood restaurant, were bombed. In August 1999 a car-bomb was detonated near the US Consulate in Cape Town, injuring seven people. Other attacks have been on restaurants and places of entertainment, apparently with the aim of harming the tourist industry. There is also a widely held belief that Pagad members are themselves involved in drug-related activities and in fact much of the fighting is about a turf war. Initial popular support for Pagad has shrunk in the wake of its terrorist attacks, yet the organization continues its destabilizing activities and at the time of this writing the police have been able to make little headway in cracking it.

This is not to say that policing in South Africa is not improving. It is, slowly, although it is difficult to quantify this: analysts believe more recent crime statistics are being inflated by a growing public confidence in the police which is resulting in more crimes being reported. One significant figure, however, shows that the murder rate dropped by a third between 1994 and 2001 – and, according to the Minister of Safety and Security, Charles Nqakula, by 17% between 1999 and early 2003.[8] "That is the best index there is," says Leggett, "because murders have to be reported. Bodies have to be accounted for."[9]

One step that has helped has been the formation of an elite special investigating squad called the Scorpions, made up of skilled detectives who work closely with prosecutors to ensure successful prosecutions. It is assigned to tough, high-profile cases nationwide, and its successes have done much to raise the public image of the police force and to establish a benchmark of performance that other units can aspire to. Building up the morale and self-image of the police is obviously fundamental to instilling a new spirit of professionalism that has hitherto been lacking.

Looking back at how the crime wave began also raises the controversial issue of the effect of criminalizing drugs. Mind-altering substances are obviously harmful to people's health and may induce irresponsible behaviour, but that includes liquor which is consumed legally throughout most of the world. The point is that relatively few people die from consuming drugs, fewer by far than the number who die from alcohol abuse and an infinitesimal number compared with the millions who die annually as a result of smoking cigarettes. In terms of damage done to individuals, communities and particularly the nation as a whole, the harm done by the criminal activity that goes with the illegal drug trade is overwhelmingly greater than the harm done by the consumption of drugs.

Moreover, it is surely self-evident by now that all attempts to stop the use of drugs are both hugely expensive and utterly futile. Nor is there anything novel about this observation. America's attempt to enforce prohibition in the 1920s was a famous exercise in futility: all it produced was busthead liquor and the growth of the mafia. Now the same is happening with the prohibition of narcotics: adulterated drugs like crack and the growth of the drug cartels.

The logical thing for a progressive-minded country like South Africa, which has recognized the rights of individuals to have sovereignty over their own lives, which has legalized abortion and consensual sodomy, would surely be to legalize drugs and bring their commercial distribution under legalized control as with liquor and tobacco, so ending the criminal activity that goes with the criminalizing of an unstoppable trade. Logical yes, but practical no. For as long as the rest of the world, at least the developed world, does not follow suit, that would turn South Africa into the distribution base for all the world's cartels, which would make us a global pariah once again. But at least as a nation we should start preaching the logic of this obvious truth in the hope of eventually being able to bring an end to one of the globalized world's more insane obsessions, which has done more than anything else to proliferate organized crime to our own grievous cost.

* * *

Bitter though this twin legacy of South Africa's dysfunctional education and criminal justice systems is, not all is gloom and doom. As so often in this land of contradictions, even in its darkest corners there are inspiring rays of light. Many individuals have pitched in to help on both issues, often making considerable sacrifices in terms of time, money and commitment, and big business, which for years stood accused of profiting from apartheid and silently supporting it, has contributed heavily to the fight against crime and to setting up in-house training courses. Precisely because the issues are so challenging, there are heroes to be found here.

Adam Paul Blecher was 28 years old when he had his moment of epiphany. Until then he was a rip-roaring young business success, an actuary earning more than a million rands a year who loved the world of business and big corporate finance. Taddy, as he is known to everyone (his parents nicknamed him "the little tadpole" while he was still an unborn foetus, then become so attached to the name they gave him the closest phonetic equivalent they could think of, which was Adam Paul, but it was "Taddy" that stuck), grew up with six siblings. All were passionate liberal activists during their student years, out on the streets demonstrating against apartheid and confronting the police, while Taddy had his head down crunching numbers and thinking big business deals. He qualified as an actuary, joined a big international management consulting firm and began earning that big salary.

Then came his epiphany. Despite their earlier liberal zeal five of his siblings had become pessimistic about the new South Africa and left the country, and Taddy, the political agnostic of the family, was about to follow them. He had dazzling job offers from the United States, Australia and New Zealand, a girlfriend who had already left for the US and whom he planned to marry, and he had already packed up and bought his air ticket. There were just two weeks to departure when it happened.

"I lay awake all night," he recalls. "I felt sick, like I was running away from this country which I love so much. I felt I was just being weak, a sheep following the others. By morning I decided that I would not go, that I would stay and try to do something, something big, something meaningful, that would bring about real change." He has not married. "I was very much in love with the girl," he says wistfully, "but we are both strong characters and we wanted to go separate ways." He has not even unpacked his luggage, leaving it stored in his mother's cellar as an idiosyncratic symbol of another lifestyle put behind him. "Forty-two packing cases," he muses. "When I look at them now I am amazed at all the stuff I possessed that I don't need."

That was in 1995. What Taddy Blecher has done since then is to establish the world's lowest-cost university which offers a four-year course in business administration to some of South Africa's brightest but poorest black students at fees of only R350 (or $35) for the first year and R1 000 ($100) for each subsequent year – all of which is covered by scholarships. In effect it is the world's only free university.

It is a revolution in both the costs and techniques of higher education which Blecher believes can be a prototype for the transformation of South Africa.

Blecher's first step was to join up with three young black professionals, Conrad Mhlongo, Richard Peycke and Mburu Gitonga, who were running a small NGO that did community work in the townships, called the Community Individual Development Association (CIDA). From his million-rands-a-year job he began drawing a salary of R3 000 a month, which has since risen to R5 000. With his three new colleagues he went into the old and badly run-down township of Alexandra on Johannesburg's northern fringes for the first time in his life. It marked the beginning of a profound personal experience.

"I met the most incredible, dignified people, filled with a deep sense of caring for their community," Blecher told me in an interview. He immersed himself in the community, going to funerals, weddings and community functions and meeting thousands of people. He was especially impressed by the children, who responded to his efforts to help them with great warmth and enthusiasm so that he quickly decided to concentrate on education. "Working with the young kids was the most wonderful experience of my life," he said. "They would hug me and write me letters. They had so much heart and were so bright. I realized that these kids could be world beaters if they were given a chance."

It wasn't all easy. There was little discipline in the schools and lots of wasted time. So with the support of the headmasters he was working with, Blecher decided to crack down on lateness. After the morning bell rang, the school gates were locked and late-comers could not get in. They were outraged. They did the aggressive toi-toi dance of the black rebellion outside the gates to show their protest, and some even tried to cut their way through the security fence. But after a month all were arriving on time, and at year's end their examination results showed a 25% improvement. "Discipline and caring are the keys to education," says Blecher. "You must know people's names, you must know about their lives, and you must care about them. It is about hearts and minds, not buildings and equipment."

As Blecher built closer relationships with the Alexandra school-children, they would complain to him that after matriculating they would not be able to afford to go to university, and without that they could not get jobs. He started thinking about a free university.

His old firm, Monitor, which had given him their blessing, an office and lots of help when he told them what he was going to do, also provided two researchers to study the South African education system and its relationship to the economy. What the researchers found was a high correlation between levels of higher education and national wealth in all developed countries. While high-school education made little difference, tertiary education gave a major boost to a nation's economic performance. That noted, the researchers then found that only a dismal 6% of all South Africans, and 3% of blacks, had a tertiary qualification. "I realized this was a major crisis, a train that was going to crash," said Blecher. That was when he decided to establish what is now known as CIDA City Campus.

He put his plan to business leaders he had met during his career as an actuary, and the response was remarkable. Investec, a major finance house which had just moved into new premises in suburbia, donated its old building in downtown Johannesburg to the proposed new university, rent free. Dimension Data, an information technology company, installed a R5-million computer network system and also provides lecturers to run the university's computer courses. Pricewaterhouse Coopers handles the accounting courses. "All the lecturing is done by corporations, free of charge," Blecher explains. Other companies provide scholarships. Woolworths, a retail chain, provides the food to give the students free lunches every day. McGraw Hill, the publishing company, has donated the bulk of the university library's 80 000 books.

CIDA City Campus has been running for three years as I write this. When I visited the campus in August 2002, I found it buzzing with activity. Lecturers were using closed-circuit television to talk to students clustered about the building in groups of 35, each with a facilitator to help explain points and transmit questions to the lecturers through an intercom system. There were just under 2 000 students enrolled, from rural areas and townships throughout the country, all lodging in city apartment blocks at discount rents that Blecher has negotiated with the landlords. The first graduates will get their degrees in 2003. All have already been head-hunted by companies eager for black graduates to fill their black empowerment obligations. The drop-out rate so far has been only 15% – compared with a dismal national average of 85%.[10]

But this university's value reaches far beyond what is happening within its walls. An added dimension to Blecher's vision is a requirement that every student must undertake a community upliftment project back in his or her home area as part of the curriculum. The student must write up the project, which is graded for credit. Blecher explains: "We try to select students from townships and rural areas all over the country. More than a thousand communities are represented here. That means we can teach the whole country how to manage money, for example, or start small businesses."

Some students have undertaken projects to teach the thousands of hawkers who throng the sidewalks of Johannesburg how to manage their finances. Others have taught the mini-bus taxi owners of Pretoria about the importance of vehicle insurance. Sibungile Mndebele, a 21-year-old third-year student, spends every Saturday morning running a course in entrepreneurship for a group of 40 pupils at her old high school in Duduza township, east of Johannesburg.

Blecher calls this outreach programme the university's extra-net – "the human internet for people who have no computers and no electricity". He points out that between 55% and 65% of his students come from homes where neither parent got beyond primary school, and no one in the family has ever touched a computer or bought a stock exchange share or held a mid-level position in a bank, so they know nothing about how the world of business works.

Thanks largely to the massive corporate contribution, the economics of CIDA City Campus are as remarkable as the results promise to be. The fees for its four-year business degree course total only R3 650 (or $365), compared with R51 000 ($5 100) for a three-year BCom course at the University of Cape Town or Johannesburg's University of the Witwatersrand – and at least R1,3 million ($130,000) for a four-year bachelor's degree course at an American university.

The support from the business community itself marks a turning point in South African corporate behaviour. Business in this country does not have a history of generosity or public-spiritedness. Perhaps because of its origins in the buccaneer mining-camp days of the 1880s and 1890s, it has tended to be rough and exclusive, monopolistic in structure and, during the apartheid years particularly, deliberately blind to the social injustices inflicted all around it. The favoured dictum was to keep out of politics and concentrate solely on business.

Perhaps the new spirit may be a guilt reaction to that long consent by silence. Or simply business's age-old instinct to curry favour with the incumbent government. Or possibly a case of enlightened self-interest, for the gross imbalance between the supply and demand of skilled black labour is inflating wages and retarding productivity. But Blecher has a more generous and encouraging explanation. "I think there is a general trend towards social upliftment," he says. "A new economic theory, or way of thinking. The old way was a zero-sum game: you win, somebody else loses. I think that is changing. Now I realize that you can't buy from me if you are poor. So if you are poor, in a sense I am poor too. If I am to be wealthy I need a bigger mass market. So if I can educate this mass market, then I will make a lot of money."

If that is true, if that is really the new culture taking hold in South Africa's business community, it could indeed mean a paradigm shift for the country. Business's efforts to help with training and education and to combat the crime problem through an organization called Business Against Crime, which contributes money, helps equip the police and funds training courses, do constitute new rays of light. South Africa is collectively responsible for these wretched legacies of the past; only a collective response can overcome them.

CHAPTER TWELVE

DEATHS AND BIRTHS

The old order changeth, yielding place to new.
— ALFRED LORD TENNYSON

As you drive into the city of Welkom today you pass by a long yellow slimes dam, its rain-rutted walls stepped up in platforms like an ancient Babylonian ziggurat, giving the entrance to the city a faintly tomb-like aspect. Nearby are the tall ungainly headgears of the mine shafts, their skip-wheels still, dead. It is not yet a ghost city, but the decline is palpable. For Welkom was a city born of gold and now it is dying of gold's decline.

Fifty years ago, in the heyday of apartheid, this was a dazzling boom town that had sprung up like an instant El Dorado on the flat feature-less plains of the Free State province after a gold strike that had set the stock markets of the world alight. No honky-tonk Ferreira's camp this time, with shacks and brothels and gambling joints, for by now the mining industry was a massive organism with immense wealth that was able to move in and establish what it envisioned as a model city. People were flocking to the place for the highest wages in the land. The times were good, the atmosphere heady.

Today everything is changed. The city is an elaborate infrastructural shell with little to support it. Houses and shops and whole mine compounds are empty. The economically active population has halved. And it has all happened so quickly. In 1992, AngloGold, then the world's biggest gold mining company whose progenitors built the city in the 1950s,[1] had 22 deep-level shafts operating here. Today, nine years later, it has five. It had 122 000 employees then; it has 17 000 now.

The effect of this precipitous decline in gold has rippled through the city's entire economy. "The impact on the community has been enor-mous," says Aubrey Neychens, chairman of the Welkom Chamber of Commerce. "We have lost 80 000 jobs in 10 to 15 years." Property prices have plummeted: homes worth R3 million are on the market for R500 000. Few are sold. AngloGold alone has 1 500 staff houses vacant. Even some churches have closed.

And all this has happened at the very moment of political transition when the African National Congress, after 82 years of struggle against segregation and apartheid and economic exploitation, finally came to power and inherited a country they thought was rich and would endow them with the means to undertake the transformation into an equalitarian society that they had dreamed of during their long years in prison and exile. Instead they inherited a financial crisis, epitomized in its most vivid form here in this struggling city whose name mockingly bade them welcome. The political transformation of Welkom itself turned out to be remarkably smooth, given its location in the heart of the National Party's *platteland* power-base where the notion of black majority rule had always been beyond imagination. Serake Leeuw, the ANC mayor, can recall no serious conflicts, not even when the schools were integrated. But the city's economic crisis has been an altogether tougher issue to confront. "When I came here last year," Leeuw said when I met him in mid-2001, "I realized immediately that Welkom needed to find an alternative industry, that we could not rely on a recovery of gold." Accompanied by local business leaders he has travelled widely overseas and at home trying to attract industrialists with details of the city's extensive infrastructure, but so far without success. He is still trying as the one-time El Dorado's decline continues.

The gold rush here was surprisingly slow in coming. There was extensive prospecting all over the highveld following the discovery of gold on the Witwatersrand in 1890. One prospector found outcrops of quartzites and conglomerates which contained small quantities of gold on a farm called Aandenk, 30 kilometres north of where Welkom now stands, but the yields were too low to mine economically. Thirty years later, in 1932, a dental mechanic and amateur prospector named Alan Roberts (after whom the nearby mining town of Alanridge is named), together with a lawyer, Emmanuel Jacobson, decided to explore this site more thoroughly. They formed a company and drilled to a level of 1 350 metres before they ran out of funds and had to stop – just 40 metres short of the narrow but incredibly rich basal reef which later became the Free State goldfields.[2]

Seven years later another exploratory borehole struck the basal reef on a nearby farm called St Helena, but then World War II broke out and all prospecting was suspended. Not until after the war was it resumed – and then on 16 April 1946 a prospecting syndicate announced a major strike on the border of the farms Geduld and Friedenheim, 8 km southeast of the hamlet of Odendaalsrus. It was a stunning find. The samples assayed 6 $^1/_2$ ounces of gold to a ton of ore, a hundred times richer than the best Witwatersrand results. It set the whole financial world abuzz.

It also caused a surge of excitement in sleepy little Odendaalsrus, where the locals sensed they were about to make a killing in property values. But they overplayed their hand. By now the giant Anglo American Corporation, progenitor of AngloGold, had acquired a controlling interest in most of the companies prospecting in the area, and its founder and chairman, Sir Ernest Oppenheimer, decided the prices being asked for real estate in the town were outrageous. He drove 20 km south, climbed a nearby hillock called Koppie Alleen – hill alone – from where he looked down at where his company was preparing to sink the shafts of five new gold mines, and announced that he would build his own town, a "garden city", within the circle of those shafts.

Property speculators who had already rushed in to Odendaalsrus were dismayed, and lodged objections to Oppenheimer's plan. So the matter went to the provincial Townships Board for arbitration where, ironically, a brilliant lawyer named Abram Fischer, later to become leader of the outlawed South African Communist Party and be imprisoned for life for underground activities in the struggle against apartheid, represented Oppenheimer at the hearing. It was a toughly contested case, in which – more irony – it was Fischer's argument that the establishment of a new town that could be planned from scratch would enable the corporation to build good houses for the miners in the town that won the decision for Oppenheimer. Welkom's birth certificate came in the form of a letter, dated 15 April 1947, stating that the Provincial Council had approved the establishment of the new town.[3]

In the event, by the time the town was built the National Party had come to power to implement apartheid, and while housing was indeed built for white mineworkers in Welkom the new Group Areas Act decreed that black miners could not live in a "white" town. They were accommodated instead in large, men-only hostels and family villages around the mine shafts out on the broad flat Free State *veld*.

It was a massive enterprise. Five new, very large gold mines were developed simultaneously; five more were developed soon afterwards and three others followed them. Said Oppenheimer at the time: "The establishment of 13 large mines at virtually the same time is the most extensive mining development the world has ever seen." The building of Welkom was an equally big task. In his 1950 Christmas message – the year the mines came into production – Oppenheimer described the joint operation as "probably the biggest single enterprise in the history of our country".[4]

Anglo American lavished money on the project. Oppenheimer engaged a leading town planner, William Backhouse, to design a model town, and a landscape gardener, Joane Pim, to lay out a series of sweeping parks and gardens. "To plan a new town has always been every town planner's dream," Backhouse enthused.[5] His vision was to build an open city that would avoid congestion. The problem with most cities, he felt, was that they had too many buildings on too little land. So he decided to use the abundance of space available on these Free State plains. No high-rise buildings, broad one-way streets, and no traffic lights, only circles at every intersection to keep the traffic moving. Backhouse also conceived of a Roman Forum in the city centre, a central place where the townsfolk would gather and have all their communal facilities.

It didn't quite work out that way. His forum was too big to serve the purpose he had in mind: a 75-metre wide four-lane roadway forming a horseshoe around a low-rise shopping complex, with an 11-acre park in the centre. To the plebeian miners who came to settle in the town it became known as the *hoefie,* a vulgarized reference to its horseshoe shape, and it spawned more of a hotrod culture than anything resembling ancient Rome. The overall effect is of an extravagance of spaciousness, an urban creation that perhaps looked better on the town-planner's drawing board than it turned out in practice for it lacks the cohesion and bustle and central business core that one associates with a vibrant city.

Extravagance is its essential feature. Here is a city that was built of and for gold, by the world's greatest gold-producer, out of the immense wealth that lay beneath its soil. Money was thrown at it. No expense was spared. Lavish sports and entertainment facilities were provided to lure people to come and work. There were golf clubs, sports clubs, stadiums, recreation complexes with Olympic-size swimming pools and pools for babies and toddlers, parks with landscaped lawns, rockeries and waterfalls, hospitals, cinemas and theatres.

People came in their thousands. "Guys would arrive with a couple of tools in a shopping bag and get jobs as tradesmen," recalls Dennis Emmenis, who arrived in 1951 to run the Oppenheimer Theatre. "Jobs were there for the asking." And they were well paid. The average wage for white miners was between R8 000 and R9 000 a month at a time when the rand was worth 40% more than the US dollar, according to

Daan Mostert, who was Human Resources Manager for the mining company at the time. And if they lived in a company house the rent was a paltry R9,50 a month, with a subsidy for water and electricity that effectively made the house rent-free. There was cash aplenty to blow.

Things were startlingly different for the black miners who also arrived by the thousand. The average wage was R35 a month, and they lived in the huge single-sex hostels at the mine compounds. The miners' contracts were onerous, too. The terms were laid down by law, which meant breaking the contract was a criminal offence. There were instant trials by government commissioners, and miners were fined on the spot. They then had a criminal record. There were no defence lawyers nor any other form of representation. The commissioner would simply question the accused miner and if he was not satisfied with the answers the miner was fined and his contract was withdrawn. The employers had no say in the proceedings.

But if life was tough in the black hostels, the white miners of Welkom were whooping it up. "The place exuded an aura of wealth," Emmenis recalls. "People had plenty of money and they liked to flash it. Young guys would walk around with a roll of banknotes in their pockets, thousands of rands at a time, and flash them in a cafe or Wimpy. They paid cash for everything."

And they bought cars. A new car every year was de rigueur, although Emmenis knew one young blade who bought ten in one year. "People would say if the ash tray was full it was time to get a new car," he chuckles. "And every third house had a new caravan, or speedboat, anything that money could buy." Kobus de Jager, who lived in Welkom for 27 years, adds another twist to the jests about its lifestyle. "It was a litre-town," he says. "The culture was one litre of brandy, two litres of Coke, and a three-litre Ford Cortina."

Then there was the *hoefie* culture. The young lads would turn out on Saturday nights to cruise around the *hoefie* showing off their latest status symbols. "They would cruise around slowly in their swanky new cars," Emmenis recalls. "It was like a fashion parade. Some of the cars had big eagles painted on the bonnets, fur on the dashboards, and plastic oranges stuck on the radio antennae." Some would take the baffles out of the exhaust to make a racy noise. Occasionally, too, they would dice around the *hoefie,* turning it into a race track in the middle of the city. Life was a carnival.

It lasted for half a century. At its peak in the 1970s the Free State goldfields produced 35% of South Africa's gold, which in turn was three-quarters of the free world's gold. Everyone knew the gold could not last forever, but when the decline came it was still a shock. The residents had always believed there would be something to replace the gold. The official history of the town was sanguine about the long-term future. "Nature was very kind to this area," it gushed. "Apart from gold, Welkom is situated in the centre of a coalfield that spreads out from west of Odendaalsrus to the Henneman-Virginia railroad. These coal deposits and the abundance of water from the Sand-Vet rivers, which can be augmented from the Caledon River and the Oxbow in Lesotho, will without doubt form the basis of a large chemical industry that will in due course replace the gold-mining industry."[6]

Wishful thinking. No coal-mining or chemical company has shown any interest in these manifestations of nature's kindliness. The coal is low grade. And so the decline set in, draining the lifeblood from the city but leaving its skeleton intact like a starving dinosaur whose time has passed. "The mine volume was driving everything," says De Jager. "As soon as the volume started declining you sat with this substantial infrastructure but without the volume to sustain it. So the council, the business community, everyone is facing the same squeeze."

AngloGold is doing what it can to sell, lease or otherwise put to use what it euphemistically calls its "under-utilized assets", in other words whole gold mines 3 000 metres deep and the elaborate infrastructure surrounding them. It has sold one mine to another company, Harmony, which is running a leaner operation that keeps it profitable. The others are being unbundled. The mines were self-sustaining in all their technological needs, so that each became a self-contained industrial town with workshops, blacksmith shops, repair shops, machine shops, locomotive stations, housing suburbs, fine homes for the mine managers and the huge hostels for the black mineworkers together with large stores where they could shop. Each of these facilities must now be put to new use or closed down.

It is an enormous task, but then that is the nature of mining. It is a finite operation. Resources become depleted and the mining company moves on. AngloGold has no cause for complaint. Its investment in Welkom has been amortized a thousand times over. Its profits have been stupendous. What it is doing now is largely out of parental concern for a community to which it gave birth. The real problem rests with that community – and with Mayor Leeuw and his ANC council.

The Mayor is confronting his problem with stoic resolve. He is not well equipped for the task. He used to work as a counter clerk in the

Welkom post office, selling stamps and handling small savings bank deposits, then moved for a time to the human resources department of the postal services in Pretoria. His only experience of dealing with policy issues came from his five years as an ANC parliamentarian. Then he was "relocated" here to take charge of a domain that had expanded with the redrawing of the geo-political map of South Africa. Welkom had been included with five other neighbouring towns – Odendaalsrus, Alanridge, Virginia, Henneman and Ventersburg – to form the metro-council of Matjhabeng, with a total population of just under half a million people. All are now suffering the effects of the goldfields' decline.

Leeuw says he has a programme of action to tackle the crisis. Top of his list is to try to persuade the government to build a major cargo airport at Welkom. "We are almost in the geographic centre of the country," he says. "Johannesburg airport is too congested. The air cargo companies also find it too expensive to refuel and park there while they wait for their next load. So they fly to Botswana and wait there until the cargo is ready and then fly back to Johannesburg. It would make more sense to have a cargo airport here and then they wouldn't have to fly back and forth." The airport itself and the many support services it would require would create a substantial number of jobs.

Astonishingly for a city that has no beach, no river and no mountains, just the flat Free State plains, Leeuw believes Welkom has potential as a tourist attraction. The mines for a start. "All we have to sell are holes in the ground," he quips. There is the prospect of taking tourists down one of the deep mines. St Helena, the oldest and deepest, could accommodate a mine museum. It also has a wine cellar and could offer tourists the novelty of cocktails 1 500 metres underground.

Perhaps as an inheritance of its *hoefie* culture, Welkom already has a world-class race track which AngloGold helped build as a parental bequest to help establish a new economic base. It is an elaborate multi-circuit affair, part of it banked, that can accommodate go-kart racing, motor-cycle grands prix, as well as Formula One, Indianapolis 500, and stock car racing. It has already drawn big crowds and obviously has potential.

Leeuw also sees his troubled city as a potential processing centre for the beneficiation of the gold it still produces and of the agricultural produce from its earlier economy. He talks of jewellery. South Africa produces all this gold, all these diamonds, it is the world's largest producer of platinum and there is an abundance of semi-precious stones, yet none of this has spawned a significant jewellery industry. South Africa's economy, and its colonial mentality, has been that of a primary producer that sends its products elsewhere for processing. It has sold its gold not only to Fort Knox but to jewellery makers in Italy and India and Taiwan, its diamonds to Amsterdam and Israel for cutting, and no-one has ever considered making jewellery right here at home. Only now with the decline of gold is this particular penny beginning to drop. A substantial project is in the making at the Rand Gold Refineries near Johannesburg, and there is a small pilot project under way at Welkom's Harmony mine. Leeuw thinks there is potential in this for his troubled city. He also thinks there could be processing plants for the agricultural produce of the surrounding countryside. Welkom is in the country's richest maize-producing region and he thinks this as well as wheat, sunflower seed, ground nuts and sorghum could be processed here. His eyes lit up when I suggested making bourbon whiskey.

Finally, there is the possibility of using the city's redundant mining facilities, its empty hostels and its human skills, its retired mining engineers and other specialists, to create a training centre here.

This is good imaginative thinking by a good committed man. Yet the results can only be limited. Welkom's golden age, like South Africa's, is over and it is entering a new and much tougher economic phase which brave souls like Serake Leeuw must try to handle though the old South Africa did nothing, absolutely nothing, in the way of education or job experience to prepare them for such a task.

* * *

The cycle of death followed by new life may be less immutable in national economies than in nature, but the effort to transform South Africa from a primary producing economy into a manufacturing exporter has not been without its success stories. There have been significant increases in a range of manufactured exports, from wine to mining machinery and weapons of war, but the most striking success has been in the motor industry. In the eight years since the ANC came to power the industry has expanded exponentially. Vehicle exports have more than quadrupled from 15 764 in 1995 to 68 031 in 2000, while the value of vehicle components exported has gone up from R3,3 billion to R11,5 billion.[7] By the end of 2001 the total motor manufacturing industry had become the third-largest contributor to the South African economy, after mining and agriculture.[8]

Yet astonishingly the number of workers employed in the motor industry has declined in that time, in the motor assembly plants from 38 600 to 32 300, and in the components industry from 47 000 to 38 500.[9] It is a striking illustration of the demands of rationalization and increased efficiency to become competitive in the international marketplace after years of operating in a protected domestic market. It is also a vivid illustration of the single most difficult and demoralizing problem facing the new government as the decline of the old economy swells the ranks of the unemployed and the growth of the new one fails to take up the slack.

The South African motor industry is old. Ford and General Motors established assembly plants in Port Elizabeth in the 1920s, and over the years a substantial components industry arose to supply them. The industry grew rapidly in the early years but soon reached a ceiling in its small domestic market. As new manufacturers came the number of models multiplied, which together with the small market meant low-volume output. With no economies of scale, unit costs were higher than on the world market and so high import tariffs were imposed to protect the domestic industry.

This typified the South African economy throughout the apartheid years. As the country's pariah status deepened and particularly after sanctions were imposed, it became increasingly a siege economy. The objective was to achieve self-sufficiency: industrial development was aimed at import substitution and domestic growth took place behind high protective tariffs. "We made everything from ice cream to atom bombs, and that shaped the business mindset in this country," says Christoph Kopke, chief executive of Daimler-Chrysler South Africa.[10]

In line with this inward-looking strategy and culture, the apartheid government began imposing local content requirements on the motor industry. The amount of local materials that every domestically manu-factured vehicle had to contain was stepped up in phases to a peak of 66% in 1971. This, too, increased the cost of locally-made vehicles. Bizarrely, too, the amount of local content was calculated by weight, not value. Customs officials would arrive once a month, put a car on a scale, weigh the local components, and check whether the regulatory requirements had been met. "The result is that you would make the local content as heavy as possible," says Kopke, who is also president of the National Association of Automotive Manufacturers of South Africa (NAAMSA). "South African cars had the heaviest chassis in the world. You would also skimp on imported things like paint and under-body protection."

With the political transition came a complete change of outlook and of strategy as the new regime realized South Africa would have to break out of its isolation and plunge into the global economy. That meant turning the old inward-looking economy on its head. To become a successful exporter has meant a massive restructuring of the whole economy, of the tariff structures, of the way industries structured themselves, of the whole outlook of the business community and the labour force. "South Africa still doesn't properly understand what it means to be an exporter," says Kopke. "Our mindset is still one of import substitution. To become an exporter requires a whole change of culture and strategy."

The motor industry has done best in making this change of mindset and strategy, largely because of its relationships with parent companies in Germany, Japan and the United States. The motor manufacturers put their heads together with the government, and a Motor Industry Task Group was established to devise a strategy for the industry to break out of its protected isolationism into the harsh world of international competition. What emerged was an innovative programme that has proved remarkably successful.

The Motor Industry Development Programme (MIDP), which came into effect in 1995, struck a delicate balance between the phased reduction of protective import tariffs and increased incentives to export. It did this by allowing manufacturers to offset their exports against the local content requirements. In other words the more they exported, the less local content they had to use. They could also use these export credits to reduce import duties on models made abroad, or even sell export credits to other manufacturers to import their vehicles into South Africa. It worked wonderfully. "We never realized at the time how smart it was," says Kopke.

The balance of incentives built into the MIDP has encouraged manufacturers to rationalize their operations. The German manufacturer, BMW, for example, used to manufacture its small three-series model at a plant in Rosslyn, near Pretoria, for the domestic market only. Its other, bigger models were imported from Germany with heavy import duties on them. But after the MIDP came into effect the parent company in Germany decided in 1997 to upgrade the Rosslyn plant at a cost of R1,3 billion and use it to manufacture the three-series BMW for the world market. Now it is able to use the credits from those exports to import its other models from Germany duty free. It also sells export credits to Porsche, Ford and Peugeot.

Thus at a stroke BMW South Africa became a player in the world automobile market, forcing it to trim costs and upgrade quality to become competitive in that tough environment. The higher volume coming off the Rosslyn production line reduced unit costs, and the company boasts that the quality of its Rosslyn cars now exceeds those produced in Bavaria. Its production figures have increased exponentially, from 8 000 before 1997 to 20 000 in 1999, 40 000 in 2000, 50 000 in 2001 and 55 500 in 2002. The cars are exported to the United States, Japan, Australia, New Zealand, Singapore and Taiwan, to a total value of about R15 billion a year. Exports to the US alone doubled between 2001 and 2002, from 11 000 vehicles to 22 000.

Now BMW Germany has decided to invest another R1,5 billion in the Rosslyn plant to expand its capacity to 60 000 units in preparation for the launch of BMW's new three-series model in 2004. "The MIDP is this government's crowning achievement as a way of encouraging foreign direct investment," says BMW South Africa's spokesman, Richard Carter. "We certainly wouldn't be doing all this without it."[11]

Daimler-Chrysler is doing much the same. It used to make a wide range of models for the South African market at its plant in the port city of East London. Now it makes only the right-hand-drive version of its C-Class model there – and exports about 12 000 of them a year to other right-hand-drive countries such as Japan, Australia, New Zealand, Britain, Singapore and Hong Kong. Like BMW, it uses the credits from these exports to import its other German made models duty free.

Now other manufacturers are following the trend. Toyota is planning to double production at its Durban plant, with almost all of its new cars destined for the export market. The prediction overall is that the South African automobile industry will generate R75 billion a year in exports by 2005.

The value of these exports aside, Kopke believes the exporting of prestige vehicles from here boosts South Africa's image as a quality manufacturing country. "When a Mercedes-Benz arrives in Japan and they see 'Made in South Africa' imprinted on it, that makes it a very important ambassador for this country," he says.

Both Daimler-Chrysler and BMW have invested billions of rands in the components industry as well, boosting its export capacity almost as much as the vehicles themselves. Leather upholstery is the big thing. "Sixty-five percent of all leather seating for BMW cars manufactured in Germany is made in South Africa," says Carter. "It's a R1 billion-a-year business, and constitutes the largest exporter by volume on the

Johannesburg-Frankfurt airfreight route." Catalytic converters to prevent exhaust pollution are another major export, along with alloy wheels, jacks, electric wiring harnesses, rubber mats, seat covers and other trim components.

It is a success story, and the manufacturers are generous in their praise of the role the government has played in it. "I don't know of another regime in the world that has done better," says Kopke. "It has done ninety-nine percent of what we hoped it would do." But the sad thing is that it has failed to create more employment. As Welkom disgorges its miners by the thousand, this successful export industry is not absorbing any of them. Not yet anyway.

CHAPTER THIRTEEN

WHEN SAINTS GO MARCHING OUT

"The long walk is not yet over.
The prize of a better life has yet to be won."
— NELSON MANDELA

South African diplomats abroad called it the WHAM question – What Happens After Mandela? The question itself and the frequency with which it was asked echoed the old doomsday expectations, a feeling that somehow the new South Africa was too good to be true, that it had happened only because of one magic man and that with his retirement after only one five-year term the country would surely return to its pre-destined road to disaster.

This view was not shared to nearly the same extent at home. Sure Mandela would be a hard act to follow, but Thabo Mbeki had shown himself to be a highly competent deputy and, as Mandela himself acknowledged, had pretty well been running the country these past few years as the old man withdrew more and more into a symbolic role above the cut-and-thrust of everyday politics. It was, moreover, going to be a most predictable and orderly succession in a continent given to violent transitions. Here surely was compelling evidence that South Africa was different. And so there was no sense of apprehension as the first Parliament of the new country met for the last time and to bid farewell to its Founding Father.

It was a mild, grey day in Cape Town, the streets damp with over-night rain and dark clouds hanging over the great mountain. The National Assembly was decked out for a special sitting: MPs in their yellowwood benches with tan upholstery; cross-benches set in rows like church pews down the centre aisle for members of the National Council of Provinces, facing the Speaker's chair flanked on each side by the colourful new South African flag. It is an ugly chamber, not graceful like the old House of Assembly which was built for the newly formed Union of South Africa in 1910, for this one was built to accommodate joint sittings of P W Botha's crazy tricameral parliament and

251

with its gaudy carpeting smacks of the architectural grandiosity of apartheid's triumphalist days.

There was a festive atmosphere with heavy overtones of nostalgia, rather like a graduation day, as members of this historic Parliament bade farewell to one another and were suddenly overwhelmed, after five years of verbal combat, with an awareness of what they had accomplished. Of the history they had made together. Of their role in avoiding what Mandela called a racial Armageddon. Of the democratic foundations they had laid.

There were handshakes and hugs. Members took snapshots of one another in little groups. Later Parliament presented Mandela with a giant framed photograph of a joint sitting in session. The legislators themselves formed a colourful sartorial picture. The Minister of Sport, Steve Tshwete, arrived looking like some sectarian priest in a flowing purple gown with elaborate gold trimmings; there were Xhosa women in traditional dresses dyed with red ochre; and a few white MPs observed an ancient British parliamentary tradition allowing them to wear a hat in the House on the last day of a session – incongruously the most conspicuous being burly Koos van der Merwe, the most Afrikaner of Afrikaners, with a white straw Panama.

It was a time for graciousness as Mandela, the most universally beloved man in the history of his country and probably the most admired in the world right then, took his bows. He had paid generous tribute to his political opponents the day before, now it was their turn. The normally acerbic Tony Leon was the most generous, saying Mandela was one of only two or three leaders of the century, including Mahatma Gandhi and the Dalai Lama, who had "a special grace", adding that "we shall not see the likes of him again". And Marthinus van Schalkwyk, the Afrikaner Nationalist whose party had jailed Mandela for so long: "It is one of the great ironies that people who have suffered greatly have the capacity to forgive greatly."

It was more than just the end of the first democratic Parliament and the departure of the great Mandela, it was also a generational change with power passing from the heroic Robben Islanders who had waged their struggle for half a century and were now handing over to a new and very different generation. Paying tribute to the comrades of his time, many of whom had died in the struggle, Mandela said: "I hope that decades from now, when history is written, the role of that generation will be appreciated and that I will not be found wanting against the measure of their fortitude and vision." Few in his audience doubted it was a hope assured.

And so the baton was passed. Thabo Mbeki took over in the smoothest of transitions and with hopes running high. Mandela's role had been reconciliation, it was said, now Mbeki's would be delivery – and he was the right man for the job.

Yet it has not been plain sailing. Mbeki has not fulfilled the high expectations many had of him. He is bright – "one of the brightest guys I've come across, and easily the brightest politician", says Frederik van Zyl Slabbert, the former liberal opposition leader.[1] He is urbane, he is elegant, he is highly literate with a use of language that can reach poetic heights, he has charm and he is deeply experienced, a consummate politician having been nurtured in the business since infancy and virtually brought up by the ANC. Yet curiously he keeps stumbling and then struggles to steady himself, often seeming stubborn and recalcitrant in the process. The result is that he has drawn a constant stream of harsh criticism, both at home and abroad, to the point where two years after he assumed office the influential *Business Day* newspaper posed the question: "Is Thabo Mbeki fit to govern?"[2]

Of course it is always difficult to follow in the footsteps of a towering figure like Mandela. A few have managed, such as Truman after Roosevelt, but not many. And it was made more difficult in Mbeki's case by the fact that, while Mandela did not have to fight his way to the top, he did. Mandela was that unprecedented and unassailable phenomenon, a living martyr who descended from above as it were, canonized even before he arrived on the scene. Even his lifelong friend Oliver Tambo, who had led the ANC during its three decades in exile, was incapacitated by a stroke shortly before Mandela's release and died soon afterwards. So unlike any other politician I can think of, Mandela never made any enemies on his way to the leadership of his party and to the presidency of his country. No enemies, only disciples.

Mbeki, by contrast, did indeed have to fight his way to the top, in the tough and often treacherous milieu of exile politics that was laden with intrigue. In the course of doing so he not only made enemies but acquired a manipulative style of operating. "Thabo sends you obscure messages," a prominent ANC member once remarked to me metaphorically, "and if you don't read them right you can find yourself dead in the morning – and there'll be no fingerprints."

Mbeki has also been unlucky. Things beyond South Africa's control have gone wrong on his watch. As Deputy President he was responsible behind the scenes for much of the acclaim that Mandela was accorded, but by the time his turn came the honeymoon was over and a crisis of expectations was beginning to set in. He was the one who was expected to deliver, who laid himself on the line with the about-turn to the market-based GEAR policy, but the anticipated foreign direct investment stubbornly failed to materialize despite all the applause from the World Bank and the IMF for doing "the right thing". Mbeki was the one who had to face the cold winds of globalization, and the wrath of his trade union and communist allies as unemployment continued to mount. On the political front there were power games and intrigues as comrades vied for position. Fate also intervened unkindly: the global recession, Robert Mugabe's sudden mania in neighbouring Zimbabwe, and worst of all the terrible, unmanageable HIV/AIDS pandemic.

The two men are in any event almost opposites in style and personality. Mandela, tall and regal, is a man of action who dislikes paperwork and theoretical discussion but who revels in the spotlight, moving easily and graciously through crowds, smiling and greeting people with that special grace Leon spoke of, or as his biographer Anthony Sampson says, looking more like a monarch or an archbishop than a politician. Mbeki, small and scholarly, is a strategic thinker to the core; a backroom operator who is uncomfortable in crowds, and a workaholic who sets himself impossible standards of trying to become an expert on every subject his government has to deal with and ends up delegating little and keeping his aides and ministers on edge lest he second-guess them. Where Mandela's leadership style was transparent and collegiate, Mbeki's is less visible, more centralized and controlling.

They are different away from politics, too. Mandela loves children and is never happier than when immersed in his own large extended family, while Mbeki is uncomfortable with children and has none of his own. He did have a son, Kwanda, when he became involved in a teenage affair with a rural girl in the Transkei, but he hardly knew the boy. Kwanda was only two when Thabo went into exile, and when he was 17 he disappeared after leaving to try to meet up with his father in exile. He was never seen again. Mbeki married Zanele Dlamini, who was then studying for a social sciences doctorate in the United States, in London in 1974 – after having to get permission to do so from the ANC leadership in terms of disciplinary rules that applied to the exiles. He was 32 years old. The couple have not had children. Zanele later worked for the United Nations High Commission for Refugees. Today she heads the Women's Development Bank in South Africa, an organization that finances micro-enterprises for poor women.

* * *

In large measure the differences between the two stem from the different life experiences that moulded them in the course of the long, searing struggle against apartheid. There were three different sets of experience that produced three markedly different cultures within the ANC, which do not always mesh comfortably. There were the Robben Island prisoners, the exiles, and the township activists who formed the United Democratic Front (UDF) and mounted the great black uprising of the 1980s.

Mandela was the quintessential product of the long-term prison experience. I did not know him before he went to Robben Island in 1962, but those who did say he was austere and dedicated, militant and uncompromising. It was prison that moulded him into the personality the world so admires today. It not only gave him his remarkable resilience but it humanized him, taught him patience and gave him a much deeper insight into human nature. It also gave him time, to read and to reflect, and to study Afrikaans literature and poetry the better to understand his adversary and how best to deal with him.

But it was a harsh experience. One has only to visit the island, 7 km offshore from Cape Town, to get a sense of what it must have been like to be incarcerated there. Despite its breathtaking view of the Cape Peninsula "the fairest Cape in all the circumference of the earth", as Sir Francis Drake called it – one is struck by the isolation of the place, and its starkness, its flat and featureless surface exposed to the wild weather of what Bartholomeu Dias called the Cape of Tempests, lashed by blistering winds and driving winter rains.[3] And by the prison itself, grey and forbidding, a place of rock and concrete and harsh lines. Yet out of this pitiless place with its sadistic punishments came these wonderful men, steeled but also imbued with a humility and a depth of human understanding. They learned how to negotiate with the racist warders and how in the end to humanize them. The island has been called a university, for the educated ran clandestine lecture courses for the untutored as they crushed rock and laboured in the blinding heat of a lime quarry, but it was more than that. It was a place of meditation and introspection, where this generation of older leaders learned about human courage and frailty, about themselves and each other. Above all, it bred in them a strong sense of equality and comradeship despite ideological differences which were sometimes quite sharp.

The exile experience was quite different. Whereas the prisoners were thrown together in close proximity for years on end, the exiles lived a peripatetic and often precarious existence scattered around the globe. It meant that being in the good books of an individual leader could decide whether you were located in relatively comfortable circumstances, such as a posting in Stockholm or London, or given an uncomfortable and even dangerous assignment somewhere in the African bush. The dominant role of the military wing, *Umkhonto we Sizwe* (Spear of the Nation), and the fact that most ANC leaders were expected to undergo military training, also gave the exile community more of a commandist culture than either the prisoners or the activists back home.

More important still, the exiles were vulnerable to infiltration by agents of the apartheid regime and over time the devastating success of these spies engendered a paranoia within the exiled leadership that discouraged openness and led to a more centralized command structure. Indeed for the exiles paranoia was common sense. Pretoria *was* out to get them and its agents were everywhere. When I first met Thabo Mbeki in London, he was accompanied by another senior ANC member, Solly Smith, who sat in on our discussion saying nothing. I assumed he was there for security reasons, that it was a safety precaution to have at least two members present at meetings with outsiders. Later it turned out that Smith was an apartheid mole who had been in the ANC's London office for years. A number of prominent exiles were assassinated. Mbeki himself was the target of an assassination attempt: Pretoria sent an agent to blow up his Lusaka home with him inside, but the Zambian police arrested the man before he could make his attack.

But if paranoia was understandable, it was also damaging. It resulted in some leading figures forming intelligence networks of their own, which fostered mutual suspicions and rivalries and tended to produce a manipulative political culture. And as the level of paranoia escalated in the late 1970s with the arrival of large numbers of new exiles after the Soweto riots – and with them new infiltrators – it also resulted in some members being arrested, summarily tried by makeshift courts in the military camps, imprisoned, tortured and even executed. These human rights violations were later censured by the Truth and Reconciliation Commission.

This is not to say there was no spirit of comradeship among the exiles. There was. And it is a tribute to Oliver Tambo's leadership that the ANC, alone among the southern African liberation movements, never split in its 30 years in exile. But the rivalries and suspicions left their stamp on the exile culture.

Then there were the "internals", the activists of the black townships and the trade unionists who took to the streets and confronted the apartheid regime's security forces during the climactic years of the 1980s. They formed the UDF as a loose alliance of more than a thousand community organizations, with the trade unions providing the organizational spine. Because of the looseness of their alliance, in which each affiliated body retained its own identity and autonomy, the activists formed an elaborate system of collective decision-making and developed a strong aversion to any cult of personality or any individual having overriding authority. As a reporter, I found dealing with them a nightmare because you could never get a statement from anyone: there had always to be a meeting to produce a collective "mandate". Nor was it easy to interview individual leaders, since it was considered unacceptable for any individual to presume to speak on behalf of the alliance. You would have to meet with a representative group all of whom would have a say.

It was called "people's democracy" and it rapidly became not just a political culture but an ideology, with the young comrades inspired by the vision of a liberated South Africa being governed in this way, with everyone having a say in the affairs of state. It was a romantic notion of democracy taken to impractical extremes.

Under the Mandela administration the prison culture was dominant, with its collegiate style and its emphasis on reconciliation. Mandela left his ministers to get on with their jobs, and except on a few issues in which he took a special interest he did not immerse himself in detail the way Mbeki does. He did not even chair Cabinet meetings, although he always attended them, preferring to let his deputies, at first De Klerk and Mbeki and later Mbeki alone, do so while he sat back and listened. As for political strategizing and the day-to-day management of the administration, he left that to Mbeki too. Mandela was a hands-off President, an inspirational figurehead like a charismatic chairman of the board rather than a company CEO.

But with the generational change that came with the change of presidency, power passed from the prison to the exile culture. The collegiate style gave way to centralized control. Mbeki is totally hands-on, totally engaged, totally committed. He seeks to be in personal command of every issue his administration has to deal with, always a step ahead of every Minister, always the best informed and brightest person in the room whatever the subject.

The paranoia of exile is there, too. Unlike Jack Kennedy, who handpicked his advisers for their intelligence and willingness to challenge and sharpen his thinking, Mbeki has chosen his closest aides and ministers for their proven loyalty. Some, like Essop Pahad, who is Minister in the Presidency and the single person closest to the President, have been with him since student days at Sussex University. What is more disturbing has been Mbeki's habit of moving against anyone he senses may be a potential rival. He is a master of the silent strategic thrust, with the result that some of the ANC's most talented people have either been marginalized or have quietly slipped out of his way into the private sector.

Nor is it only the prison generation that has faded from power, in their case because of advancing years, but under Mbeki the UDF culture has been eclipsed. To a degree this was inevitable, since the UDF's style of "people's democracy" was never a practical proposition for governing anything larger than a Greek city-state, but the extent of the difference has rankled. The new commandist style, with decisions taken by a small leadership group and handed down to the members who are expected to show disciplined obedience, is as far removed as one can imagine from the bottom-up collectivism of the UDF with all its meetings and mandates.

This has become a major source of tension within the ANC-led alliance. While there are indeed serious ideological differences between the Mbeki government and its alliance partners, who are unhappy about the U-Turn from socialism to GEAR and about the growing unemployment they believe that has caused, the government's commandist style has also become a major source of grievance. Cosatu in particular is rooted in the old UDF, and it finds the new culture objectionable. Whereas it expects to be a participant in policy formulation, it complains that it is consulted but ignored; that the government hands down decisions and demands obedience. Public criticism has been declared unacceptable. Members of the ANC and its partner organizations may criticize within party structures, but not outside. This, say the critics, is destroying the ANC's long-established tradition of vigorous debate within its ranks and turning it into a commandist organization whose members and partner organizations must be submissive flunkeys.

Yet it must be said that there are sound practical reasons for Mbeki's tightening of control. The ANC has always been a movement rather than a party with a coherent ideological identity, an alliance of disparate political elements, with trade unionists and capitalists, liberals and communists, all rubbing up against one another and held together only by a common commitment to overthrowing apartheid. The rumbustious debates of this "African parliament", as Mandela liked to call it, were all very well in a liberation movement, but a government needs to have a greater measure of policy coherence. Moreover, as the ANC gained power, and especially after Mbeki took over, power games and intrigues broke out in the provinces as comrades vied for positions and jobs. Tighter discipline from the centre became necessary, and Mbeki himself took over the appointment of provincial premiers and directors-general from the provincial branches.

There is an inescapable contradiction within this kind of necessity. As Van Zyl Slabbert points out, there are many conflicting choices in the tough situation Mbeki faces. There are tensions, for example, between liberty and equality, justice and mercy, tolerance and order, or between free speech and ending racism. All are good values, but they are not always compatible.

"The ANC want to consolidate the liberal democracy and they want to go for growth, and pursuing the one creates problems for the other," says Slabbert. "If you are going for growth you have to get rid of exchange controls, keep the deficit before borrowing low, privatize and get a flexible labour policy, all of which have direct political consequences which can cause problems of instability. The flexible labour market sticks a finger in the eye of the unions, and privatization must lead to unemployment in the short term. So you have to manage those political consequences, which is what Mbeki is trying to do. He's doing it by co-option – using the communists in his government to deal with the unions and carry out the privatization – and he's doing it by taking control of the ANC. He is determining the public representatives right through from the national to the local level, which is authoritarian and undemocratic. So he makes the ANC undemocratic in order to preserve a democratic system."

Similarly, to stop the conflicts of policy between different ministries that arose under Mandela's collegiate style, Mbeki has asserted more authority over the Cabinet to ensure a greater degree of policy co-ordination. Again authoritarian action to preserve democracy

Slabbert is not critical of these paradoxical choices. He regards them as shrewd, essential political management of a tough transition. "If I were in his (Mbeki's) position I think I would make the same choices," he says.[4]

* * *

It has become a cliche to describe Mbeki as an enigma. Yet I must confess to being puzzled by the contradictory features of the man that swing one in a dizzy pattern between admiration and exasperation. I first met him in London 20 years ago and liked him immediately. We talked for two hours in the lounge of a hotel, he in a tweed jacket puffing on a curved pipe, looking every inch an English gentleman and speaking in tones of understanding and moderation that dispelled all the alarming images of radical revolutionaries that I had listened to back home. He was, quite simply, wonderful.

Later, through the eighties, I met him frequently in Lusaka, either at his modest suburban home or at a room in the Pamodzi Hotel where he was prone to arrive late at night and chew the fat with a small group of us journalists over a bottle of whisky until sunrise. I can testify to the fact that he has a formidable capacity to hold his drink. He saw many of us under the table many a night.

I was also present at a celebrated meeting in Dakar, Senegal, in May 1989 when Mbeki led an ANC team in four days of intense talks with a group of about sixty white South Africans, mostly Afrikaners, headed by Van Zyl Slabbert. It was the first encounter between the ANC and a sizeable group of Afrikaners, and Mbeki was the star. He disarmed his white adversaries with his charm, and fascinated them with his highly articulate analysis of the South African situation from an ANC perspective, which made them aware not only that there could be no soft options of modifying the apartheid system, that the whole thing had to go, but also, to their surprise and relief, that these black revolutionaries had a keen awareness of the Afrikaners' own fears of identity and cultural survival and would be sensitive to them. It was a command performance which, as John Battersby, another journalist who was there with me and later became editor of Johannesburg's *Sunday Independent*, has said completely transformed the political landscape and laid the foundation for crucial secret talks with Afrikaner Nationalists in Britain over the next two years which – in parallel with Mandela's secret talks in prison with members of the government and its security establishment – paved the way for the unbanning of the ANC in 1990 and the negotiated settlement that followed.[5]

Watching all this I came to like and admire Mbeki enormously. I thought he was brilliant. In 1989 I participated in organizing a big South African conference at Duke University in North Carolina, where I introduced him for his keynote address as the person I believed would be the first black President of a post-apartheid South Africa. Mandela at the time was still locked away in prison with no hint of his release.

Others were equally captivated. In a profile article written when Mbeki became President, Anthony Sampson described him as "a brilliant diplomat, able to charm and disarm the most hostile Western businessmen – as I often witnessed in London in the Eighties."[6] Patti Waldmeir of the *Financial Times*, who knew him in both Lusaka and South Africa, wrote with great insight of Mbeki's elegance and charm in her book on South Africa's political transition, *Anatomy of a Miracle*. "His greatest weapon was always his charm," she wrote. "Not the easy openness of character that is sometimes denoted by that term, but a personality tool wielded sharply to advantage. For Mbeki, charm is a form of self-discipline; it masks his feelings, and ensures that he never gives anything away. It was the perfect weapon for the battle to hand. Mbeki wielded it skilfully to win liberation for his people, and a formidable position of power for himself in the new South Africa."[7]

Back in South Africa after the unbanning, Mbeki was again the key player in some of the most important strategic moves that led to the negotiated settlement. It was he who was instrumental in persuading the ANC, first, to abandon its armed struggle, then to agree to the dropping of international sanctions against South Africa. Both were highly emotional issues that encountered fierce resistance within the liberation movement, but Mbeki won his colleagues over with his cool, reasoned arguments that they were weapons of the past that would have to go and that it was therefore better for the ANC to manage their removal and win the moral high ground in doing so. Together with Mandela, Mbeki also played a key role in engaging with Afrikaner right-wingers who were bent on sabotaging the democratic election and persuading them instead to fight for their ideal of a separate Afrikaner *volkstaat*, or homeland, by constitutional means. And when Chief Mangosuthu Buthelezi, too, seemed to pose a real secessionist threat in the Zulu-dominated province of KwaZulu-Natal, it was again Mbeki who intervened to placate the Inkatha Freedom Party leader and crucially to draw him and his party in at the last minute to participate in the election and become a partner in the Government of National Unity.

That is a formidable record of achievements. Mbeki must go down in history as one of the key players in bringing about South Africa's miracle of transition.

As Deputy President, too, he played a crucial role as Mandela's key strategic adviser, his fixer, administrative manager and, not least, as a highly articulate expositor of the new government's principles and policies. He wrote and delivered speeches of sublime eloquence to express its highest ideals, as when he explained the inclusiveness of his concept of Africanness in a speech on behalf of the ANC at the adoption of the new South African Constitution on 8 May 1996. Beginning with the declaration that "I am an African," he went on:

"I owe my being to the Khoi and the San whose desolate souls haunt the great expanses of the beautiful Cape – they who fell victim to the most merciless genocide our native land has ever seen, they who were the first to lose their lives in the struggle to defend our freedom and independence and they who, as a people, perished in the result.

Today, as a country, we keep an audible silence about these ancestors of the generations that live, fearful to admit the horror of a former deed, seeking to obliterate from our memories a cruel occurrence which, in its remembering, should teach us not and never to be inhuman again.

I am formed of the migrant who left Europe to find a new home on our native land. Whatever their own actions, they remain still, part of me.

In my veins courses the blood of the Malay slaves who came from the East. Their proud dignity informs my bearing, their culture a part of my essence. The stripes they bore on their bodies from the lash of the slave master are a reminder embossed on my consciousness of what should not be done.

I am the grandchild of the warrior men and women that Hintsa and Sekhukhune led, the patriots that Cetshwayo and Mphephu took to battle, the soldiers Moshoeshoe and Ngungunyane taught never to dishonour the cause of freedom.

My mind and my knowledge of myself is formed by the victories that are the jewels in our African crown, the victories we earned from Isandhlwana to Khartoum, as Ethiopians and as the Ashanti of Ghana, as the Berbers of the desert.

I am the grandchild who lays fresh flowers on the Boer graves at St Helena and the Bahamas, who sees in the mind's eye and suffers the suffering of a simple peasant folk – death, concentration camps, destroying homesteads, a dream in ruins.

I am the child of Nongqause. I am he who made it possible to trade in the world markets in diamonds, in gold, in the same food for which my stomach yearns.

I come of those who were transported from India and China, whose being resided in the fact, solely, that they were able to provide physical labour, who taught me that we could both be at home and be foreign, who taught me that human existence itself demanded that freedom was a necessary condition for that human existence.

Being part of all these people, and in the knowledge that none dare contest that assertion, I shall claim that – I am an African!"

That is as profound and poetic an exposition of the principle of non-racialism, of Nelson Mandela's Covenant and his vision of a rainbow nation, as one could ever hear. Small wonder, therefore, that there was little anxiety within South Africa when Mbeki took over from Mandela.

* * *

He made an impressive start, winning a larger majority in the 1999 election than even Mandela mustered five years before. Only one seat short of a two-thirds majority, Mbeki was soon offered the support of a maverick Indian politician, Amichand Rajbansi, the sole representative of his Minority Front party, which gave the new President the power even to amend the Constitution if he chose to do so. Mbeki's inaugural speech on 16 June, the anniversary of the Soweto student uprising 23 years before, was low-key, but in it he gave an indication that there would be a change of emphasis. After paying tribute to the older generation, who he said had pulled the country out of the abyss and placed it on a pedestal of hope, he spoke of the millions still living in misery. Quoting a proverb of the Tswana people, he said the country was at a stage of "the dawning of the dawn", when only the tips of the cattle's horns could be seen etched against the morning sky. Now the sun would continue to rise to banish the darkness of the long years of colonialism and apartheid. "The full meaning of liberation will not be realized," he said, "until our people are freed both from oppression and from the dehumanizing legacy of deprivation we inherited from our past." Clearly the emphasis was going to shift from reconciliation to transformation – a delicate balancing act once again between two conflicting needs, where too much emphasis on one can cause problems with the other.

The remainder of that first year went well, and the *Mail & Guardian*, which publishes an end-of-year school report-card in which it grades the performance of individual ministers, gave Mbeki an A.

Then the wheels came off. The millennium year turned out to be Mbeki's *annus horribilis*, at the end of which the *Mail & Guardian* gave him a D.

His first stumble came in April with the leaking of an extraordinary letter to Bill Clinton, Tony Blair and other foreign leaders, justifying his inclusion of a number of maverick scientists on a special panel of experts he formed to advise him on AIDS, which had swelled into a massive epidemic in South Africa on a scale that threatened the whole future of the country. These scientists were challenging the orthodox medical conclusion that the HIV retrovirus causes AIDS, claiming the virus did not exist, or that if it did it was harmless, that AIDS was not contagious but was caused by poverty and the very drugs used to treat it, and that the orthodox view was part of a conspiracy by the big pharmaceutical companies to rip off Africa's poor. Mbeki's inclusion of the dissidents in his panel raised a flurry of criticism, because their theories had long since been discredited in the scientific community. Mbeki explained in the letter that he had included them because he was searching for answers and wanted to canvass all views on the subject, which sounded fair enough, but then his letter launched into an extraordinarily intemperate defence of the dissidents.

"Not long ago in our country people were killed, tortured and imprisoned because the authorities believed that their views were dangerous," Mbeki wrote. "We are now being asked to do the same thing that the racist apartheid tyranny did, because there is a scientific view against which dissent is prohibited."

The White House was so astonished at this equating of criticism of the dissidents with apartheid tyranny that it ran a check to see whether the letter was a hoax. It then tried to keep it under wraps to avoid embarrassing Mbeki, but the letter was leaked and there was an avalanche of adverse publicity in the US and elsewhere. I happened to be in Washington at the time, on a scholarship at the Woodrow Wilson Center for International Studies, and everywhere I went people would question me about Mbeki. "What gives with your new President?" they would ask. "Is he crazy? Does he really believe HIV doesn't cause AIDS?" The doubts about WHAM were back.

It was a situation that cried out for damage control, and over lunch with the South African ambassador, Sheila Sisulu, I suggested that since Mbeki was about to visit the US he should clarify his position with an address to the National Press Club in Washington. It was an ideal platform, I felt, since the representatives of all the world's major media, as well as the American media, were housed in the National Press Building and all belonged to the Press Club on the 13th floor. They would all attend if it were known that Mbeki was going to talk about AIDS. He would be able to reach the whole world at once and put the issue to rest with a simple statement that could go something like: "Of course I believe HIV causes AIDS, but in South Africa we have some special circumstances which I will now tell you about ..."

But as we talked I came to realize that it would not be as easy as I had imagined. It was my first glimpse into the degree of confusion that Mbeki's complex statements on AIDS were creating in his administration. In the end Mbeki had a private meeting over lunch with the editors of *The Washington Post,* but when I spoke to them afterwards they were as baffled and critical as before. They said he had been convoluted and obscure on the subject. Mbeki was also interviewed on *The NewsHour with Jim Lehrer,* but again he came across as evasive when questioned about his views on AIDS.

And so it remained throughout the millennium year. A close scrutiny of all Mbeki's speeches on the subject shows he has never denied that HIV causes AIDS, but his statements frequently reflect the attitudes and assumptions of the dissidents so that he has become identified with them. And if he never openly declared himself to be a dissident, he did not deny it either, and the dissidents themselves certainly claimed him as their champion. Their websites carry pictures of him and one runs a petition of support for him.

The result was confusion and paralysis in the administration, where nobody seemed to know what government policy was or what the President was thinking. Civil servants seemed afraid of doing the wrong thing and so did nothing, with the result that in 2000 the Health Department failed to spend 40% of its AIDS budget. There were more intemperate statements from Mbeki and from his Minister of Health, Manto Tshabalala-Msimang. When 5 000 doctors signed a declaration before an international AIDS conference in Durban in July 2000 that HIV was the direct cause of AIDS, Tshabalala-Msimang dismissed it as "an elitist document". Soon after that Mbeki's office issued a statement accusing AIDS activists who were demanding that the government provide anti-retroviral drugs in the public hospitals of trying to poison black people. "Our people are being used as guinea pigs and conned into using dangerous and toxic drugs," the statement declared, likening this to "the biological warfare of the apartheid era."

The whole administration seemed to be in a state of denial, including people who were literally dying of the disease themselves. In March 2000 the President's spokesman, Parks Mankahlana, wrote an article saying the anti-retroviral drug AZT was not only expensive and toxic, but pressure for its use was part of a corporate conspiracy to profit from the misery of Africa's poor.

"Like the marauders of the military industrial complex who propagated fear to increase their profits," Mankahlana wrote, "the profit-takers who are benefiting from the scourge of HIV/AIDS will disappear to the affluent beaches of the world to enjoy wealth accumulated from a humankind ravaged by a dreadful disease ...

"Sure, the shareholders of Glaxo Wellcome (the manufacturers of AZT) will rejoice to hear that the SA government has decided to supply AZT to pregnant women who are HIV-positive. The source of their joy will not be concern for those people's health, but about profits and shareholder value."

Seven months later, Mankahlana died of AIDS.

Another fiery AIDS dissident, Peter Mokaba, a former ANC youth leader who later became an aide in the President's office, wrote an equally pungent article in March 2002. "The story that HIV causes AIDS is being promoted through lies, pseudo-science, violence, terrorism and deception," Mokaba wrote. "We are urged to abandon science and adopt the religion and superstition that HIV exists and that it causes AIDS. We refuse to be agents for using our people as guinea pigs and have a responsibility to defeat the intended genocide and dehumanization of the African child, mother, family and society."

Three months later, Mokaba died of AIDS.

At the end of 2000 Mbeki announced he was "withdrawing from the debate" on AIDS, but the issue bubbled on through 2001. Eventually the pressure on the government found a sharper focus on the issue of providing the anti-retroviral drug neviropine to prevent the transmission of HIV from pregnant women to their babies. At first the government refused to provide the drug on cost grounds, then when a German pharmaceutical company offered to provide it free the government insisted the drug had first to be cleared through clinical trials in a handful of research sites that would only be completed in December 2002. With a survey finding that 25% of pregnant women were HIV-positive and that an estimated 70 000 to 100 000 babies were being infected every year, public outrage escalated. Cosatu joined the chorus of criticism, then in September 2001 Mandela added his enormous moral weight to the pressure when he urged the government to save the babies. Finally AIDS activists in an organization called the Treatment Action Campaign took the matter to court, and in December 2001 a High Court judge ruled that the government was violating the constitution by denying children the right to life. The government lodged an appeal with the Constitutional Court, but with public feeling running high and provincial health departments threatening to defy Pretoria, it backed down before the appeal was heard and agreed to reassess its policy.

It was a triumph of sorts and an encouraging demonstration of the strength of South Africa's civil society, but it remains troubling that the President should have been obdurate for so long. In the next chapter I shall explore in more detail how Mbeki became involved with the dissidents and the strange mixture of political and psychological pressures that appear to have influenced him. That it has done him great political damage is beyond question. Mbeki's approval ratings have declined steeply since the AIDS saga began. In May 2000, 71% of South Africans thought he was doing a good job, by June that had dropped to 66% and by August it was down to 50,2%. A poll of urban adults of all races in early 2002 indicated that nearly 60% disagreed with his viewpoint on AIDS, and only one in 10 agreed fully with it.

* * *

Mbeki's second stumble also came in the millennium year, and again his efforts at recovery were hesitant and only partially effective. In February 2000, President Robert Mugabe of Zimbabwe suffered a blow to his oversized ego when the citizens of his country voted at a referendum to reject a new constitution Mugabe had drafted to increase his already formidable executive powers. It was an event that was to transform the man and the fortunes of his country and confront Mbeki with yet another debilitating problem.

When he first came to power in 1980, winning independence for his country after a long and bitter guerrilla war, Mugabe pronounced a policy of racial reconciliation that won worldwide acclaim, just as Mandela's did a decade later. He struck a deal with the country's white commercial farmers who, though comprising only 1% of the population, owned the bulk of the commercial farmland and generated 38% of the gross domestic product. Mugabe promised the farmers security of tenure if they would go on laying the country's golden eggs for him, and as a gesture of goodwill appointed the president of the Commercial Farmers Union, Dennis Norman, as his Minister of Agriculture. Zimbabwe prospered for a decade and a half, then began running into economic difficulties which critics blamed on cronyism and rampant corruption.

I shall deal in a later chapter with the events that culminated in the Zimbabwean crisis, for they make a cautionary tale, but at this stage it is enough to note that the humiliation of the referendum defeat triggered the transformation of Mugabe from a benign reconciler into a raging tyrant. Smelling defeat in a presidential election due the following year, and with the aid of a private militia of self-styled liberation war veterans, he launched a wildly destructive populist campaign of seizing the white-owned commercial farms for free distribution to black Zimbabweans, while at the same time setting out to smash the newly-formed opposition Movement for Democratic Change (MDC) which had spearheaded the referendum campaign against him.

Mugabe blatantly ignored Supreme Court rulings declaring his actions unconstitutional, allowed the war veterans to intimidate the judges until even the Chief Justice resigned, then restructured the judiciary with his own appointees. His police arrested and harassed the few independent journalists left in the country and expelled foreign correspondents, and military agents blew up the presses of the main opposition newspaper, the *Daily News*, and an independent radio station called *Voice of the People*. He issued a decree ordering the remaining white farmers to cease working their land on pain of imprisonment – surely the only time farming has ever been made a crime – and as the agricultural economy collapsed and the Zimbabwe dollar with it, the country faced the prospect of mass starvation.

As international outrage mounted at this wilful destruction of a once-promising country, Mbeki and some other leaders of the 14-nation regional alliance called the Southern African Development Community (SADC) flew to the Victoria Falls in April to meet with Mugabe. The following night I cringed as I sat in my Washington apartment watching a CNN newscast that showed Mbeki standing beside Mugabe holding his hand and smiling, while Mozambique's President Joaquim Chissano, who was the chairman of SADC at the time, extolled the Zimbabwe leader's democratic virtues, telling viewers: "No one can teach President Mugabe anything about the rule of law. He is the expert."

The sickening scene appeared on screen again and again over the following days and weeks as CNN rolled over its news items the way 24-hour news channels do. I know African men hold hands, it is a cultural thing the way Frenchmen kiss cheeks, but here was Mbeki with his British education and sophisticated understanding of the Western world, the super-diplomat and skilled persuader, allowing this impression of smiling support for Mugabe's outrageous actions to be broadcast globally.

The imagery has stuck. And again Mbeki has been slow to redress the impression of support that it projected to the world. The next day he appeared together with Mugabe at the Zimbabwe Trade Fair, and as guest speaker paid fulsome tribute to Mugabe as a southern African liberator. When it came to the issue that was making headlines around the world, he could hardly have been more tentative. Land dispossession, he said, had been one of the most iniquitous results of the colonization of Zimbabwe. It had to be redressed, but redistribution should ensure that the land was used productively. It should also be done in a co-operative and non-confrontational manner. "Accordingly, we trust that ways and means will be found to end the conflict that has erupted in some areas of Zimbabwe," he said.

That was all. Not a word of censure for the violence, the seizures, the violations of the rule of law, and the wholesale disregard for legal property rights.

"To you, the people of Zimbabwe, I would like to convey the message that the overwhelming majority of your brothers and sisters south of the Limpopo share with you the hope that the land question in Zimbabwe will be addressed successfully," Mbeki said. "At the same time, as a people, we are convinced that it would be best that this important matter is dealt with in a co-operative manner among all the people of this sister country, both black and white."

The administration called it "quiet diplomacy", and perhaps there was a case for trying initially to moderate Mugabe in this low-key way, but it soon became clear that the Zimbabwean had the bit between his teeth and was treating the younger Mbeki with contempt. He resented the new South Africa anyway, and Mandela particularly, feeling they had stolen his thunder as the most important leader of the most important country in the southern African region.

"Mugabe's problem," Mandela once muttered to me in a moment of exasperation after one of their many spats, "is that he was the star – and then the sun came up."

Now Mugabe felt he could twist Mbeki around his little finger. He seemed to enjoy publicly humiliating him. He did so right after the Victoria Falls summit. At that meeting Mbeki thought he had negotiated a deal in which Mugabe agreed to withdraw the war veterans from the white farms they had started invading and occupying, in return for South Africa interceding with Britain to reinstate a 1998 donors' agreement to provide money to compensate white farmers whose land was to be expropriated. But a few days later Mugabe reneged on the deal by publicly encouraging the war veterans to continue occupying white farms. Later, when Mbeki met with the British government, he discovered that, contrary to what Mugabe had told him, it was in fact Zimbabwe, not Britain, that had abandoned the donors' agreement. Britain said that as far as it was concerned the agreement, worth £36 million, was still on the table. The British attitude was that the money would be made available as soon as Mugabe returned to the rule of law, stopped the land invasions and agreed to implement a legal resettlement programme, but until then it refused to subsidize lawlessness. To which Mugabe replied that he would not be dictated to by Britain. "Keep your money," he thundered at a political rally.

It happened again four months later. After another meeting with Mbeki on 2 August, Mugabe pledged in a televised news conference, with Mbeki sitting beside him, that the war veterans would be removed from all the commercial farms they had occupied and be resettled on "designated" properties by the end of August. But the very next day Mugabe reversed himself, saying he had been misquoted – even though the public had seen and heard him make the statement on TV. In a ranting speech to the black Zimbabwe Farmers Union in the northern town of Bindura, he declared that 3 041 white commercial farms would now be seized, though he had gazetted 804 as "designated" only a month before, and that the war veterans need not leave the farms they were occupying. They would be settled on either those farms or others, he said, adding that he was mobilizing the army to speed up the resettlement.

What is more, Mugabe indicated that this would not be the end of the land grabs. "That will just be the start," he said. "We will be going on from there."

Clearly Mbeki's "quiet diplomacy" was not working, and it was not hard to see why. Reapportioning farmland was not the real issue; Mugabe was on a crusade to establish his credentials as a revolutionary hero bent on expunging the last vestiges of white neo-colonialism from his country and he was damned if he was going to let any compromise deal stop him. As one observer remarked, it was Pol Pot in slow motion.

Despite that, and despite the public humiliations, Mbeki and his ministers stuck to their timid approach. A chorus of voices, both inside the country and abroad, urged Mbeki to take a tougher line, noting that as the most powerful country on the continent only South Africa could bring meaningful pressure to bear on Mugabe. But Mbeki would not. He agreed in several statements that what Mugabe was doing was wrong, but insisted that only Zimbabweans could bring about change in their own country – an assertion that sounded strange coming from the leader of a liberation movement whose whole history had been devoted to lobbying for international pressure to end apartheid in South Africa.

Mbeki's impotence in the face of the increasingly outrageous behaviour of his northern neighbour has done great harm to South Africa. Zimbabwe was by far South Africa's biggest trading partner on the continent, so that the collapse of its economy had a serious knock-on effect. Moreover, the two countries are so closely interwoven historically and economically that foreign investors tended to assume it would be only a matter of time before the contagion spread to South Africa. In fact some read Mbeki's reticence as an indication that he was secretly supportive of Mugabe and would like to go the same way if he thought he could get away with it. While this was certainly not true, the fact is that Mugabe's propagandists in Zimbabwe emulated the AIDS dissidents and claimed Mbeki as their champion. There can be nothing more off-putting to a would-be investor than the suspicion that property rights may not be respected in the country he is assessing. And although Mbeki kept saying that land grabs could not happen in South Africa, he failed to put sufficient distance between himself and Mugabe to convince the sceptics.

The suspicions about where the Mbeki administration's real sentiments lay were deepened during the Zimbabwean presidential election in March 2002, when despite months of violent intimidation of opposition supporters and blatant vote-rigging at the polling stations, two South African observer missions, one from the ANC and the other from the government, declared the election legitimate, while other outside observer missions declared it stolen. This put Mbeki in a tight spot. While accepting the reports of his own observers, he found himself on a three-member Commonwealth sub-committee, with Australia's John Howard and Nigeria's Olusegun Obasanjo, having to deal with a Commonwealth mission report roundly rejecting the election result. Eventually Mbeki concurred with the sub-committee's decision to recommend that Zimbabwe be suspended for a year from the 54-nation club, but it left him in a position that looked both ambiguous and painfully weak. This impression was reinforced six months later when the sub-committee met in the Nigerian capital of Abudja to reassess the Zimbabwean situation in the light of its rapid deterioration and Mugabe's continued recalcitrance. This time Howard pressed hard for Zimbabwe's immediate expulsion from the Commonwealth, but again Mbeki demurred, this time with Obasanjo's support, and so the Zimbabwean leader was left to continue on his destructive course.

Worst of all, perhaps, is that Mbeki's failure to act clearly and force-fully in the face of a moral crisis that threatened to polarize racial attitudes in South Africa, much as the O J Simpson trial did in the United States, amounted to a betrayal of the ANC's vision of a non-racial society and of Mandela's Covenant.

The third major stumble was the most bizarre of all. In April 2001, the then Minister of Safety and Security, Steve Tshwete, informed Parliament that the police were investigating a conspiracy against President Mbeki, and named three prominent ANC members as being implicated – former Secretary-General Cyril Ramaphosa, who was Mbeki's chief rival for the deputy presidency in 1994, Tokyo Sexwale, former Premier of Gauteng province, and Mathews Phosa, former Premier of Mpumalanga province. All three were now successful businessmen.

The conspiracy allegation, it turned out, was based on an affidavit by one James Nkambule, a former ANC Youth League leader who at the time was facing more than 70 charges of fraud. In it Nkambule, who had once been close to Phosa but had then fallen out with him, spelled out a convoluted plot in which he claimed that Phosa, in col-laboration with Ramaphosa and Sexwale, planned to run a smear cam-paign against Mbeki so that he, Phosa, could replace him as ANC president. The plot involved trying to implicate Mbeki in the killing of the popular leader of the Communist Party, Chris Hani, who was gunned down in his own driveway by a white right-wing extremist, Janusz Walus, in 1993. According to Nkambule, Phosa arranged for Walus, who was serving a life sentence for the murder, to draw up an affidavit saying that Mbeki prompted him to kill Hani, and through an unnamed aide gave him the murder weapon. Walus was to say that Mbeki told him Hani wanted to sideline him so that he, not Mbeki, would succeed Mandela, which would be bad for the country.

That anyone should have taken seriously this farcical tale from a discredited source seemed astonishing, and the reaction both at home and abroad was a mixture of ridicule and concern, for it seemed clear that the naming of three such senior and respected ANC figures could not have been done without Mbeki's approval. With no serious evidence of anything remotely like a coup, *The Economist* asked: "Does this mean that Mr Mbeki is going off the rails?" No, it then responded to its own rhetorical incredulity. "Mr Mbeki is not barmy, merely paranoid."[8]

In an interview with Britain's Channel 4, Mbeki conceded it may have been wrong to disclose names, but he continued to insist that there had been a conspiracy against himself. This prompted several publications to comment that, while they dismissed Nkambule's allegations as nonsensical, given the number of able ANC members who had been locked out of Mbeki's inner circle it would not be surprising if there were a plan to challenge his leadership at the organization's next national conference. Soon afterwards the affair took a further bizarre twist when Deputy President Jacob Zuma issued a statement saying he had no intention of challenging Mkeki for the presidency at the ANC's next national conference – remarkable in that it was a denial of something no one had suggested. It came as further evidence of a pervasive atmosphere of paranoia and suspicion in the inner circle.

⚜ ⚜ ⚜

So what ails Thabo Mbeki? Why should this highly intelligent and able politician, so secure in his seat of power with a two-thirds majority in Parliament and no prospect of anyone challenging him when he runs for a second term in 2004, be prone to these spasms of eccentricity that do himself and his country so much harm? What explains the failure of Mbeki the President to be Mbeki the genial genius we all knew in the past; the paradox of the great communicator's failure to communicate, the great charmer's failure to charm?

There are no shorthand answers to the nuanced complexity of the man. I suspect it is all wrapped up in his past, in his experiences as a child of the struggle who was brought up more by the movement than by his parents, who was educated for a role that he himself was never allowed to choose or define, whose whole life was controlled and directed and dedicated for him with little thought for his own wishes. He became in every respect an instrument of the movement, and the person who made him that was his own father.

Govan Mbeki was an icon in Thabo's life rather than a parent to his son. There was mutual admiration but there appeared to be little warmth in the relationship. I caught a glimpse of this when Govan Mbeki and other newly released prisoners flew to Lusaka in 1990 to meet with the exiled leaders from whom they had been cut off for more than a quarter of a century. It was an emotional moment. The exiles, with Oliver Tambo at the head, waited in a formal reception line to greet their old comrades as they filed down the gangway from the Zambian Airways jet, but as the 78-year-old Walter Sisulu stepped on to the tarmac his son Max broke from the reception line and ran forward to throw his arms around his father and the two men stood there hugging each other and weeping with joy. But when Govan Mbeki

273

appeared, Thabo, who had not seen his father since leaving for Britain 28 years before, did not break ranks. He waited his turn in the reception line and formally shook his father's hand.

I asked Govan Mbeki about this when I interviewed him at his home in Port Elizabeth much later. The conversation which followed was illuminating:

SPARKS: You greeted each other but you didn't embrace with the enthusiasm and warmth one would have expected.
GOVAN MBEKI: That's right. I didn't do it in the way I was expected to.
SPARKS: How did you feel at that moment? Didn't you feel a great rush of warmth towards your son? You hadn't seen him for so long?
GOVAN MBEKI: I don't think I had a special feeling for seeing him after so long a time. I was meeting a group of young men who we understood were following in our footsteps.
SPARKS: And your son was just one of them?
GOVAN MBEKI: He was one of them. That's the important thing.
SPARKS: He wasn't special to you?
GOVAN MBEKI: No.
SPARKS: Isn't that unusual for a father? Had you grown distant because of the lapse of time, or was it a matter of discipline?
GOVAN MBEKI: It might have been both. We were brought up over a long period of time to fight for a certain cause in a certain way. We are not going to be moved easily, and I think that is important. We are not going to show our emotions. I think we have strong feelings about what we are at, about the cause of liberation that we have been fighting for.
SPARKS: Are those feelings stronger than the ties of blood?
GOVAN MBEKI: In a way I think they are.

Later, when I asked Thabo Mbeki about his relationship with his father, he agreed that it had been distant. This was by design, he said. In the early fifties there was a general expectation that the ANC leadership was going to be arrested and imprisoned for a long time, so both his parents decided the children should become accustomed to growing up without them. They farmed them out to relatives and friends.

"They deliberately wanted to break any close attachment," Mbeki explained, "because in their absence we would miss them and do wrong things. So we had to learn to live with other people, on our own without our parents. I mean, that's how we grew up. So it would have been very fake of me to pretend (at Lusaka airport) that we had a relationship other than that. These are parents, but they are also comrades, because that's what they sought to communicate to us children – that they would disappear into jail and we must continue the struggle and not wait around and mope. That's how it was."[9]

Dedication and discipline were obviously the watchwords of Thabo Mbeki's upbringing. It must have been a loveless childhood. There seemed to be little affection, either, between Govan Mbeki and his wife, Epainette. Both were members of the Communist Party and deeply involved in politics. For most of their long marriage they led separate lives. In 1953, after a fire destroyed the family's general dealer store in the small Transkei village of Mbewuleni, Govan took a teaching job in Ladysmith, in Natal province, then later moved to Port Elizabeth to edit a left-wing newspaper called *New Age*, while Epainette remained in Mbewuleni 500 km away running the rebuilt family store. Even after his release from prison in 1987 Govan did not rejoin his wife. He returned to Port Elizabeth and lived alone there with his nurse until his death in 2001 at the age of 91.

The relationship between father and son was further strained by a history of political conflict between Govan Mbeki and Nelson Mandela, who clashed frequently while they were together on Robben Island. Govan Mbeki had a reputation as a didactic and difficult man and by his own admission he and Mandela were "both men of strong views which we express openly and unashamedly to each other". Fellow prisoners described the relationship as "very bad". This meant that when Thabo Mbeki returned to South Africa realizing that his political future lay in Mandela's hands, he distanced himself from his father and saw little of him. Nor did Thabo see his mother or sister Lindiwe for two years after he became Deputy President. Then he paid a flying half-hour visit to Mbewuleni in a military helicopter.

It was in Mbewuleni that Thabo Mbeki was born on 18 June 1942. He had two brothers, Jama, a lawyer, who went missing believed killed by the South African security forces in 1980, and Moeletsi, who is now a media consultant and deputy chairman of the South African Institute of International Affairs, and his sister Lindiwe. Both his parents were teachers, and Govan had a university degree and had written several books and political articles for left-wing journals, which meant Thabo was part of an intellectual and economic elite who lived a considerable social distance apart from the poor and almost wholly uneducated peasants of the village who traded their meagre produce and bought

275

goods at the family store. He grew up surrounded by books, which he read avidly and omnivorously, from novels to the *Communist Manifesto*, and from when he was very small he was exposed to intense political debates with his parents and the many activist colleagues who visited the home.

Yet for all the distance between himself and the *amaqaba* of the village – the tribal folk who painted their faces with red, white and yellow ochre – he became aware at an early age of the painful hardships that afflicted their lives. The Mbeki store also served as the local post office, and as young Thabo became literate he had to help with reading letters that came to the illiterate families from fathers and sons who had left as migrant workers for the mines of the Witwatersrand and Welkom, and with writing the dictated replies. It was a searing exposure at an impressionable age to the bitter realities of their lives that left him with a depth of anger at the degradation inflicted on his people by colonialism and apartheid that lies just beneath the surface of his controlled charm and occasionally reveals itself in brief flashes of intemperate rancour.

There was a history of personal injustice and bitterness in the family, too. Govan Mbeki's father had been part of a small landed elite, but a Land and Trust Act in 1936 declared the area "white" and the family was dispossessed. It was this which drew Govan Mbeki into protest politics when he was at high school, and it still rankled more than sixty years later when he told me with bitter sarcasm that the prime minister responsible for this and other legislation stripping blacks of their limited voting rights and restricting their movements, James Barry Hertzog, founder of the National Party, was "the real founder of the ANC".

But it was the control over Thabo Mbeki's life that I think shaped the young man most profoundly. Almost from the beginning his future was mapped out for him. There was the decision that he should learn to live without his parents and grow up to be a strong comrade. When he was only nine his parents sent him to live with an uncle in the Eastern Cape town of Queenstown, where he attended primary school. Later he transferred to another primary school in the Transkei town of Butterworth. From there he went to Lovedale Institute, the most prestigious black high school in the country founded by Scottish Presbyterian missionaries. There he was placed in an "academic" stream and required to immerse himself in Shakespeare and the Latin texts of Julius Caesar, Livy and Catullus. When he was 15 he joined the ANC Youth League, was elected to the executive, and in his final year at

Lovedale was expelled from the school for his part in organizing a protest strike.

Govan Mbeki, by then a leading figure in the South African Communist Party, next dispatched his son to Johannesburg to live with the then general-secretary of the ANC, Duma Nokwe. Govan Mbeki also asked a leading white communist, Michael Harmel, to take the young man under his wing. This was the beginning of Thabo Mbeki's managed political education and preparation to become a future ANC leader. Between Harmel and Nokwe, the young Thabo met all the leading ANC and communist figures of note in the city. "Thabo and my father were very close," recalls Harmel's daughter, Barbara. "He used to just pitch up at our home any time." Other communists of that time say Harmel was a hard-line ideologue, but he was charming, witty and popular and led something of a bohemian lifestyle. The young Mbeki warmed to him and clearly the older man had a considerable influence on him, and the influence spread beyond politics. "Govan was a very harsh and distant father," says Barbara Harmel, "and I think Mick became something of a father substitute for him. Mick was a fun person who enjoyed being with young people, especially young black people, and I think he gave Thabo some warmth that he had not had at home." Harmel, an Irishman, was also a highly literate man with a master's degree in English literature. He worked periodically as a journalist, first on *The Star*, then for a time on the *Daily Worker*, the Communist Party mouthpiece in London, and finally on various left-wing publications in South Africa. It was through him that Mbeki acquired an abiding love of the literary giants, particularly William Butler Yeats whom he frequently quotes. "Mick had this long-playing record of Irish revolutionary poems and speeches that he would play for me," Mbeki recalls. "It had Yeats's poems about the Irish uprising against the English, very fine poems recited by Michael MacLeammour, who was the lead actor from the Abbey Theatre in Dublin. Mick took me to meet MacLeammour when he came to South Africa and gave a performance at Wits University. It was wonderful. His record was banned here but Mick managed to get a copy somehow. I later bought one when I was in exile and I still have it. I'll play it for you one day. That was my introduction to Yeats. And as I listened to his poems I felt I needed to understand more about Yeats, so I began to read Yeats and about Yeats in my spare time."[10]

While in Johannesburg Mbeki studied through the South African Committee for Higher Education (SACHED), where he obtained both the British A-levels, qualifying him for entry into British universities, and the University of London's junior degree in economics.

By now the ANC had been banned, its members were being arrested in droves, and Nelson Mandela had gone underground to form *Umkhonto we Sizwe*, its military wing, and begin an armed struggle. Mbeki's teacher at SACHED, Anne Welsh, realizing that he was exceptionally talented and fearing that these talents were going to be wasted in a dark prison cell, wrote a letter to his parents. "Your boy has a gift," she wrote. "I have written to the University of Sussex in Britain recommending him for a scholarship to study for a Masters in economics. If you can see to him getting there, I will see to his fees."[11]

Young Thabo, meanwhile, had other ideas. He wanted to be part of the struggle. Like many of his age he wanted to join *Umkhonto we Sizwe* and go abroad for military training, but at his father's instigation the ANC leadership intervened to stop him. His future had been decided for him. He was to study at Sussex in order to become a future leader of the movement. And it was Govan Mbeki who delivered the instruction from the ANC to his son. What followed was an illustration of how his life was being managed.

"When they told me I had to go to Sussex, I said no," Mbeki told me. "I told my father and Duma Nokwe that I wanted to stay here and be part of the struggle. They said OK, but if you refuse to go and you get arrested you will have to care for yourself. We will not bother about you. So after more discussion they said, Let's reach a deal. You go, and if after one year you want to come back you can do military training and then come back to fight in the struggle. So I agreed that we would raise the matter again after one year. At the end of that year Oliver Tambo (the ANC leader in exile) called me. I told him I wanted to go for military training. He said, OK, that's fine we'll organize it. So I cancelled my scholarship and told the university I was leaving. They pleaded with me to stay, but I was insistent. Then a week before the end of the summer holidays Oliver Tambo called me again and said, We've changed our minds. You must go back to university. I said, You can't say that to me. I've cancelled my scholarship, my place in the university, everything. But he just said, You go back, talk to them, they'll take you back."

So he returned, and was indeed welcomed back by Sussex. But not before he had negotiated another deal with Tambo to review his situation after his second year of studies. But when that time came the ANC again insisted he stay at Sussex and complete his junior degree. And when that was duly done he was instructed yet again to stay and complete a master's degree in economics. "It was the same thing over and over again," he recalled in the interview. Years after leaving Sussex, when he was already Deputy President, Thabo Mbeki expressed his bitterness about this management of his life and denial of his own wishes in an unpublicized speech to a group of ANC women parliamentarians. But the point is, he obeyed. Discipline and self-control had already been instilled in him at that early age.

The trip to Britain without travel documents was a hazardous affair. Mbeki, then just turned 20, was arrested first in the north-western town of Zeerust and charged with failing to produce a reference book, required then under the apartheid pass laws. After managing to persuade the magistrate to postpone the case, he slipped across the border into Botswana, from where he was escorted on foot into Zimbabwe (then Southern Rhodesia) by fighters of the ZANU guerrilla movement. There Mbeki was arrested again for travelling without a passport and held in prison for six weeks before being sent back to Botswana. Eventually he and a group of other ANC students were able to fly to Dar es Salaam where Tanzanian President Julius Nyerere gave them asylum. Finally, he was put on a plane to London in the care of Kenneth Kaunda, who was on the same flight to Britain to negotiate Zambia's independence. And so he arrived in Britain and entered Sussex.

After completing his studies, Mbeki worked for another two years in the ANC's London office. So he was in Britain throughout the "Swinging Sixties", the stimulating decade of the Beatles, the mini-skirt, Carnaby Street and the flower children. Mbeki absorbed it all, the culture, the literature, the arts and the mannerisms of modern Britain, becoming the smooth, polished, urbane sophisticate who later dazzled the white businessmen and Afrikaner intellectuals who came to meet him in exile.

Mbeki had other experiences, too, which perhaps left other imprints. In 1969 he went to Moscow for three years where he studied at the Lenin Institute of Social Sciences and finally underwent his long-delayed military training, in the course of which he was exposed to lectures by Soviet intelligence agents. This plunged him into a world of conspiracy theories, of perceived threats to the nation-state, and a belief in the supreme importance of information as the key to power. Some exiles who were close to Mbeki believe this experience infused itself deeply into him. They note that when he became Deputy President he ensured that all arms of the intelligence services reached

Mandela through him, that he was the filter. As one put it: "The insecurity of his early life, and of life in exile, was on top of this underlying milieu."

Wrap all that up in a man of high intelligence and a wonderful strategic thinker, and perhaps you come close to the complexity of his personality.

Some who have known him a long time think perhaps he is too intelligent to be a good leader, that he can become so absorbed in an issue and so sure that he is right that he fails to see the obvious that is clear to others. Nearly all observers, both inside and outside the movement, agree that he was a superb number two, both to Oliver Tambo whose special adviser he was for many years in exile, and to Nelson Mandela. But he is less impressive in the top job.

As one insider puts it: "Where Oliver Tambo had Thabo Mbeki to advise him, and Nelson Mandela had Thabo Mbeki to advise him, Thabo Mbeki's problem is that he has no Thabo Mbeki to advise him."

* * *

So what of Nelson Mandela in the post-Mandela era? He remains a towering moral figure, the ultimate custodian of his Covenant, but he is careful to remain in the background on most issues. He likes to use his enormous international prestige to speak out on global issues that he feels strongly about, such as his criticism of Israel's military invasions of the West Bank and Gaza to try to crush the Palestinian *Intifada*, and his telephone calls to President George W Bush to urge him not to destroy the United Nations by bypassing it with a unilateral attack on Iraq. He has also involved himself deeply in trying to negotiate peace in the war-ravaged Great Lakes region. But the home front is different. Mandela has always prided himself on being a loyal and disciplined member of the ANC, and it would clearly be improper for him to interfere in his successor's running of the country.

That said, it is also clear there have been issues that have disturbed him and where he has felt impelled to speak discreetly to Mbeki. Mandela's intercession to plead for the government to make neviropine freely available to prevent pregnant women transmitting HIV infection to their babies is a case in point, and he has campaigned vigorously and publicly in AIDS awareness campaigns, showing that he at least has no doubts that HIV causes the disease.

Although Mandela was thoroughly supportive of his deputy and skilfully smoothed his way to the succession, he dropped a few oblique hints along the way which indicated that he had some niggling worries. He let it be known that he had personally favoured Cyril Ramaphosa to be his deputy and thus almost certainly his successor, but said this was because of his concern that Mbeki was from the same Xhosa tribe as himself which might arouse fears of ethnic domination, while Ramaphosa was from the small Venda tribe. More pointedly, at the ANC congress in December 1997 he made a speech that included a thinly veiled reference to some of the more widely held concerns about Mbeki in the ANC. The congress had just made Mbeki president of the ANC in preparation for his succession to the national presidency 18 months hence, and Mandela warned in the speech that there could be problems with a leader being elected unopposed, as Mbeki had been.

"He may use that powerful position," Mandela said, "to settle scores with his detractors, to marginalize or get rid of them and surround himself with yes-men and women." Mandela hastened to add that he was sure Mbeki understood these problems. "He is not the man who is going to sideline anybody," he said. But it was significant that the huge audience of more than 2 000 delegates punctuated Mandela's statement with applause at precisely the points that showed they understood what he was getting at.

Later Mandela had a more frontal clash with Mbeki when the new president of the ANC tried to prevent the Truth and Reconciliation Commission including in its final report a condemnation of the ANC's own abuses of human rights during its struggle against apartheid. These passages of the report referred to the killing of civilians in landmine attacks inside South Africa, and more specifically to the drumhead trials, torturing, imprisonment and execution of suspected spies in the ANC's Quatro prison camp in Angola. Mbeki objected strenuously to what he saw as the TRC's equating the ANC's struggle for liberation with the atrocities committed by the oppressors of the apartheid regime, but Mandela pulled rank as President of the country who had appointed the commission and insisted that the TRC report be published in full. "I set up the TRC," he said. "They have done not a perfect but a remarkable job and I approve of everything they did."

Mandela will be careful, he will be proper, but he will not be silent if he feels his country really needs him. As he told his biographer, Anthony Sampson, as he stepped down: "As an ordinary ANC member I will have the privilege to be as critical as I can be."[12] So far he has been prudent, but he has served notice that if things should go wrong he will intervene.

281

So will others. As the AIDS issue has already shown, South Africa has a strong civil society, backed by a strong Constitution and a strongly independent judiciary which together form a strong counterweight against the kind of egocentric tyranny so many other African countries have suffered. Thabo Mbeki has his faults and has made his stumbles, but he is an intelligent and pragmatic politician with the right ideals who I do not believe will try to defy Mandela's legacy. It may well be that when he is safely into his second term, as he surely will be, his inner insecurities will subside and the great potential that is undoubtedly within him will blossom.

CHAPTER FOURTEEN

AN AFRICAN HOLOCAUST

"In the midst of the heroic efforts to build a new,
pluralistic South Africa, the HIV epidemic simply
became one challenge too many."
— PROFESSOR MALEGAPURU MAKGOBA,
PRESIDENT OF THE SA MEDICAL RESEARCH COUNCIL[1]

Not since the Black Death which decimated the population of Europe in the fourteenth century has a pandemic posed such a terrible threat to an entire continent as HIV/AIDS does to Africa today. As it is, this is the world's most marginalized continent, ravaged by floods, droughts, famines, civil wars and chronic misrule, and with 250 million of its people living on less than $1 a day.

Now, like the plagues of ancient Egypt, comes one more to afflict this birthplace of the human race and source of its earliest civilization. There are 34 million people worldwide with the HIV virus, and 25 million of them are in Africa, the continent least able to cope with the pandemic. AIDS has been brought to the level of a containable disease in the United States and Western Europe, thanks to sustained education programmes on how it is spread and cocktails of anti-retroviral drugs that cost $12 000 per patient each year – something the poor countries of Africa cannot begin to afford.

So rampant is the disease that it is undermining even Africa's brighter success stories. Botswana has one of the world's fastest economic growth rates and has increased its per capita income 219% since 1975, yet now it has the continent's steepest fall in the United Nations Human Development Index which weighs per capita incomes along with educational standards and life expectancy. Botswana is a model democracy and its government has won praise for the prudent management of its diamond wealth. It is the darling of the World Bank and the International Monetary Fund. But its HIV infection rate of 36% is among the world's highest, as a result of which life expectancy has fallen from 53 years in 1975 to 47 in 2000.

South Africa, too, with the continent's most highly developed economy and the country many look to as the engine for an African Renaissance, is also among the worst hit with 4 200 000 of its 41 million people HIV positive, and about 1 700 more are infected every day. Projections are that by 2010 6 million South Africans will have died of AIDS – the same as the number of Jews who perished in the Holocaust.

AIDS is a surreptitious disease. It creeps up on you. It incubates in your body for six to eight years after you become infected with the HIV virus before it kills you, and even then it does not kill you directly. It destroys your immune system to the point where you die from something else, malaria perhaps, or tuberculosis, or measles, or pneumonia, or influenza, or even a common cold when your immunity has been reduced to the point of no resistance. All of which makes it difficult to categorize the cause of death specifically, especially in unsophisticated communities where there is also a stigma attached to the disease.

And so the disease caught South Africa off guard. It made its silent inroads mainly between 1990 and 1995, as guerrilla and anti-guerrilla fighters, lonely men with pay, made their way home from infected areas to the north and while the apartheid regime and the liberation movements were locked in intense negotiations that absorbed all their attention. The ANC's seminal 1992 document, *Ready to Govern*, devoted only four lines to AIDS.

These returning fighters, together with truck drivers coming down the long transport routes from the north, were probably the principal vectors of the disease. But the main problem lay here at home, where the virus these carriers brought with them struck a set of social conditions that caused it to spread with explosive ferocity. This once again is a legacy of apartheid. That appalling system, with its aim of segregating the races into separate and highly unequal compartments, forced a system of migrant labour on the black population. Men who went to work in the mines and factories of "white" South Africa were prohibited by law from bringing their families with them, so they lived in single-sex hostels for months and years at a time. This created a culture of urban and rural wives and resulted in high levels of prostitution. At its height in 1985, there were 1 833 636 South Africans registered as migrant workers, and another 288 705 from neighbouring countries, with thousands more who came illegally – a vast army of men severed from their families and forced into an unnatural lifestyle where they had multiple sexual relationships.[2] The system also drove millions of people into crowded, impoverished bantustans, and into crowded, impoverished squatter camps around the cities – again conditions conducive to multiple sexual relationships and high levels of prostitution.

According to Professor Malegapuru Makgoba, a renowned microbiologist who is now president of the Medical Research Council of South Africa, the pandemic could have been curbed during the early period of its incursion. But it was not: between 1990 and 1995 both the old regime and the ANC were too preoccupied with their negotiations, and with the drama and excitement of writing a new constitution and transferring power. And when the new ANC-led government found itself facing an array of problems across the full spectrum of governance, the HIV epidemic, Makgoba suggests, "simply became one challenge too many". The ANC, in his judgement, went into denial. First, with the personal backing of Mbeki, who was then Deputy President, it endorsed a cheap quack remedy called virodene that had been developed by a group of Pretoria University researchers and which the new government hoped would reduce the crippling costs of dealing with the disease. When that hope collapsed ignominiously, with the Medicines Control Council's discovery that virodene's active ingredient was a solvent used in freezing animal organs that had no impact on HIV, the government, according to Makgoba, "retreated behind revisionist theories".[3]

Mbeki did not hold these revisionist theories at the outset. His eager backing of virodene in 1997 and his anger when the Medicines Control Council stopped its tests on humans is proof of that. Mbeki accused the council of sacrificing lives by holding up a "miracle cure" amid "the pressing crisis of an escalating pandemic of HIV/AIDS". There was no talk then of poisoning people with dangerous drugs. That first came during a parliamentary speech in October 1999, six months into Mbeki's presidency, when he questioned the value of the anti-retroviral drug AZT, suggesting it was so toxic it might do patients more harm than good. "It would be irresponsible for us not to heed the dire warnings which medical researchers have been making," he said.

What had happened in the interim is that the President had found the websites run by the AIDS dissidents, an eclectic bunch of medical scientists and lay persons who call themselves simply "The Group". Among them are Peter Duesberg, Professor of Molecular and Cell Biology at the University of California at Berkeley, David Rasnick, a California biochemist and former president of "The Group", Kary Mullis, who won the 1993 Nobel Prize for Chemistry, Harvey Bialy, a molecular biologist from Mexico, Sam Mhlongo, head of the department of family medicine and primary health care at the Medical University of South Africa (Medunsa), Celia Farber, a New York journalist, John Lauriston, a market research executive, and Nicholas Regush, a television journalist. There is also a "Perth Group" in Australia headed by Eleni Papadopulos-Eliopolus, a professor at the Royal Perth Hospital. Others crop up in Britain, France, Germany, Scandinavia and India.

Mkebi himself confirmed that the first person to draw his attention to these dissident websites was a lawyer and part-time jazz musician named Anthony Brink, then practising in the provincial city of Pietermaritzburg. He was closely followed by a febrile Johannesburg journalist, Anita Allen. Both are passionate crusaders in the cause that the HI virus and AIDS do not exist and that the whole thing is a monumental scam by the big international pharmaceutical companies. Brink came upon the writings of the AIDS dissidents in 1996, and after much surfing and reading became convinced they were right and that the drug AZT in particular was dangerously toxic. "A medicine from hell", he called it in an article in a Johannesburg newspaper in March 1999.[4] This prompted a response defending the drug from Desmond Martin, president of the Southern African HIV/AIDS Clinicians Society. After more exchanges, Brink contacted President Mbeki and sent him copies of the debate between himself and Martin. "That was the first time I became aware of this alternative viewpoint," Mbeki told me. Allen was in touch with him soon afterwards. In July 1999 she sent him a 100-page dossier, the essence of which was an assertion that the orthodox scientific view on AIDS violated fundamental principles of science in contending that the HI virus caused the disease.

It must be said in Mbeki's defence that Brink in particular is an able lawyer who makes his case with persuasive force. He was able to persuade the country's most experienced investigative journalist, Martin Welz, of the validity of his case, so that Welz not only published a series of Brink's articles on AIDS in his investigative magazine, *Noseweek*, but also wrote a rapturous foreword to Brink's book on AZT. Friends describe Brink's commitment to his crusade as obsessive, to the point where he once challenged a group of them who were arguing with him to inject him with HIV-infected blood there and then. Allen is no less obsessive. When I visited her at her home in Johannesburg, she followed me out to my car afterwards urging me not to fall for the "propaganda" of the orthodox scientists. "They are wrong, and more and more people are realizing this," she said.

Both are improbable Galileos to be challenging the general body of world science in this way, although they clearly see themselves in that light. Galileo was a scientist challenging laypersons trapped in religious dogma; these are laypersons challenging the very body of modern science that Galileo fathered. Neither Brink nor Allen has any formal training in any branch of medicine or science. Brink presents his credentials for taking on the global scientific establishment in the preface to his book on AZT. "At heart I'm a science geek," he writes, adding that he was "keenly interested in chemistry and microscopy as a boy".[5] Brink goes on to say he is also "one of those annoying inquisitive types with little respect for authority", which is admirable, except that one wonders how he might react to a geek of a sea lawyer who might challenge his fundamental understanding of the law in a life-and-death case affecting millions of his fellow countrymen.

Allen likewise has had no scientific training of any sort, nor indeed any formal education beyond high school. Her only scientific involvement has been a stint as science correspondent of *The Star* newspaper in Johannesburg. Her interest in AIDS, she told me, was sparked when her husband, David Allen, a former editor of the *Saturday Star*, gave her a book by Kary Mullis called *Dancing in the Mind Field*. As the book itself reveals, Mullis, whom Brink also credits with having ignited his early interest in the subject, is a brilliant but eccentric scientist. He won the Nobel Prize for Chemistry for inventing a procedure called the polymerase chain reaction (PCR), which enables scientists to multiply a segment of DNA millions of times in a few hours so that they can in effect "see" the genetic structure.[6] It was a breakthrough in biochemical and genetic research. But in his book, which is a kind of breezy autobiography that encompasses a rollicking sex life as a surf hunk on the beaches of California, Mullis also reveals a frankly nutty side to his personality. He has experimented with hallucinogenic drugs, is enthusiastic about astrology, and condemns orthodox scientists for not taking the configuration of the stars and planets at the time of one's birth more seriously, and who even suggests he may have had an encounter with aliens. He thinks the idea of a hole in the ozone layer is nonsense, as is global warming. He says you can turn a light bulb on with your mind, and believes the United States should spend money defending itself against an asteroid hit.

It was Mullis's two chapters on HIV/AIDS that captured Allen's imagination. Mullis does not dispute the existence of HIV – which ironically his PCR process helped to identify – but says he does not believe it causes AIDS. He says he has seen no papers or proof that link HIV and AIDS.

After reading the book, Allen told me, she "got into the subject" of HIV and AIDS in March 1999. Five months later she wrote her 100-page dossier to Mbeki – a remarkably short time for a lay person to become a specialist confident enough to challenge the great body of scientific knowledge on so complex a subject. Allen then visited Mbeki at ANC headquarters in Johannesburg in November 1999. By then, she had been working on the subject for eight months. The meeting lasted about 45 minutes, she told me, during which she handed the President four computer discs that "gave him the pick of the science on the subject". This, she told me, was material that had been sent to her and which she gleaned off the Internet. "A selection from my electronic database," she said.

* * *

Trawling through the dissidents' websites is a surreal experience. There are upwards of a dozen of these sites, and the same names appear repeatedly as the dissidents quote one another in a repetitive cycle of self-reinforcement. A number are academics, often of emeritus vintage, while others, like Anita Allen, are lay persons, but all engage in a discourse laden with scientific jargon intended to give their arguments an aura of learned authority.

Some, like Kary Mullis, hold views that are distinctly odd. Here, for example, we find one Fintan Dunne, an Irishman who is joint editor of a website called Aidsmyth. A little surfing reveals he is also involved with an organization called the UFO Resource Centre, on whose behalf he reports that contact has been established with what he believes to be an extra-terrestrial humanoid intelligence. In 1974, Dunne reports, he and his associates at the UFO Resource Centre sent a digitally-encoded message describing earth and mankind into deep space from a radio telescope in Puerto Rico. The target was 21 000 light years away, so they didn't expect a response for 42 000 years, but lo and behold a reply came to another radio-telescope in Hampshire, England, in August 2001. Dunne says he has decoded the message from this wandering outer-space humanoid intelligence, who inform earthlings that "we are also a hydrocarbon lifeform with a similar mathematics and logic. However we have a slightly different DNA structure and we are smaller than you, with very large heads ..."

Other groups have jumped on the dissidents' bandwagon. A women's group in Canada rails against the notion that HIV causes AIDS as an attempt to stifle breast-feeding. Gay groups claim it is part of an ongoing war against homosexuals. One gay website, demanding the reopening of bathhouses in San Francisco, claims "the media-fed virus of fear called AIDS" is aimed at "the repression of sex through the demonization of the anus".

Conspiracy theories lie at the heart of the dissident cause. Here Dunne ranks supreme. In one astonishing article on his website he contends that state institutions of medicine and public health are waging a genocidal campaign to eliminate gay men, who, he suggests, constitute the Men's Liberation Movement whose aim is to make this a kinder, gentler world. The AIDS wards of hospitals, Dunne thunders, are "death camps posing as treatment centres, where hundreds of thousands are dead. They did not die of AIDS. They were exterminated ... These sexual aliens have been medicated to death by lethal overdoses of toxic drugs supposed to save them from AIDS."

Dunne claims, too, that the notion of an AIDS pandemic in Africa is another genocidal conspiracy, this time intended to cull the continent's population for the benefit of the developed nations. "African AIDS is the Trojan horse of the West," he writes. "Inside the horse are millions of condoms for you so-fertile Africans, you who would otherwise so-selfishly use up African natural resources we covet for Western benefit."

Not all the dissidents are as cranky as that, but conspiracy theories are the common denominator among them. One reads of "the AIDS rethinkers" waging their campaign against "the AIDS establishment" who are supported by "the AIDS stooges" of the mainstream media and the "AIDS police" of the pharmaceutical industry. The argument goes around in a self-validating cycle: the HI virus has never been isolated, and if it exists at all it is harmless; the HIV tests are worthless; AIDS is caused by the lethal toxicity of drugs such as AZT which are used to treat this otherwise non-existent disease. It is an unchallengeable cycle because, while the dissidents deny that AIDS really exists as a sexually transmitted disease, they account for its rising death toll by pointing to the very drugs used to treat it.

The pharmaceutical companies are presented as the real villains of the piece. Duesberg and his colleagues contend that the big drug companies form a cartel that manipulates research funding to shut out dissident scientists and maximize profits by getting "orthodox" researchers they have funded to present the drugs they have developed as the only acceptable remedies.

Again, of course, it is a self-fulfilling condition. Get yourself categorized as a scientific crackpot and you are unlikely to get much research funding from the pharmaceutical industry. Announce that you believe the moon is made of green cheese and you will be lucky if the Royal Astrological Society comes rushing with money for you to test your thesis.

The dissidents' take on AIDS in Africa follows a similar line, again portraying the pharmaceutical companies as guilty not only of exploiting the poor but of inflicting lethal medicines on them. AIDS has manifested itself differently in Africa from the way it has in Europe and the United States, in both numbers and form. While South Africa has 4 200 000 HIV-positive people in its population of 41 million, North America and Western Europe, with their much larger populations, have only 920 000 and 520 000 respectively. And while the disease in the developed countries is confined largely to homosexuals, in Africa it is overwhelmingly a heterosexual disease.

Indeed in South Africa, according to Tim Tucker, director of the South African Medical Research Council's AIDS Vaccine Initiative, the disease actually arrived in the two forms at different times. The first was when two South African Airways stewards, both male homosexuals, contracted AIDS in 1983, which suggests they were infected in North America or Europe six to eight years before. The much larger heterosexual epidemic started in 1990, as truck drivers, soldiers and other immigrants arrived from infected African countries to the north.[7]

The orthodox scientists ascribe the different forms of the disease to different mutations of the HI retrovirus – Sub-Type B in North America and Western Europe, and Sub-Type C in Africa – and with that to the critical mass of a particular mutation that goes down a particular pathway but has no significant biological differences from the core type.

The dissidents, on the other hand, cling to their belief that there is no viral cause at all. AIDS in Africa, they say, is a collapse of the immuno-suppressive system caused by malnutrition and other poverty-related ailments as well as other endemic Third World diseases such as tuberculosis and malaria. These afflicted patients, the dissidents claim, are being killed by the new toxic anti-retroviral drugs being given them to treat these "old diseases" that have been around Africa for centuries. The patients involved are being "poisoned". Stop the medicines, stop the HIV tests, and everything will return to normal.

Again the dissidents' arguments are difficult to refute. Point to the ballooning death toll in South Africa and its neighbouring countries, tell them there is obviously something causing this, and they will agree. Yes, they say, but it's the combination of deepening poverty and the killer drugs being given to these depleted people. The dissidents do not believe that AIDS is a sexually transmitted disease. All medical authorities agree that deficiency diseases weaken the immune system, which is what AIDS does, but the difference is that AIDS is infectious, transmitted by the HI retrovirus through sexual contact, through blood transfusions and needle-stick accidents, and that it needs to be treated and the onset of the disease restrained with anti-retroviral drugs that will attack the HIV infection and allow the immune system to recover if only temporarily.

It is a life-and-death difference. If you don't believe AIDS is infectious but merely a deficiency disease, you will not practise safe sex. And then the disease will spread exponentially.

This is where Mbeki's culpability looms large. It is true, as his office likes to point out, that he has never said he does not believe HIV causes AIDS, but neither has he warned his people from his bully pulpit that it does.

* * *

How has this highly intelligent man been drawn into this situation that is so damaging to himself and his country? Some have wondered whether Mbeki may be a desperate man in denial, but he is too much in control for that to be true. Others have suggested that he is trying to assert an African intellectual independence, to show that he is not simply a captive of Western thought systems, but that hardly squares with the fact that nearly all the dissidents are white Westerners, while his most potent critics are Professor Malegapuru Makgoba, who has impeccable Africanist credentials, and the black workers of Cosatu.

Mbeki himself insists he has merely been asking questions. "You can't respond to a catastrophe merely by saying I will do what is routine," he wrote in his letter to Clinton and Blair. He defends his decision to invite dissidents onto his presidential advisory panel on AIDS on the intellectually respectable grounds that he should explore all views on the subject, however deviant or unpopular.

This is all very well, but the trouble is Mbeki is not only an intellectual. He is a political leader in a world spotlight, and whatever he does sends out political signals. He should be aware of the impressions he is giving and of the conclusions that might be drawn from his actions and associations. Mbeki is correct when he says the majority is not always right, but if a political leader goes out of his way to seek counsel from a deviant figure in any field he must know that he is bound to be associated with that person's views – unless he makes his purpose and the distinction abundantly clear.

This is where Mbeki erred. By becoming involved with the dissident scientists he gave the group credibility – and they certainly embraced him as their champion – after their views had been roundly dismissed by the overwhelming majority of the world's top scientists working in this field, who were dismayed at having what they regard as a damaging distraction revived in this way. And by defending in such vehement language his right to consult the dissidents, he then gave the impression that he shared their basic beliefs. He was judged a dissident himself by association.

In fact I believe it was the dissidents' charges against the pharmaceutical companies that first attracted Mbeki's attention. When Brink and Allen drew his attention to their websites, Mbeki was himself in the throes of a bitter conflict with these companies. They had responded aggressively to an amendment which the government had passed to its Medicines and Related Substances Act in 1997, just when the HIV infection rate was beginning to balloon in South Africa. The amendment, introduced by the then Health Minister, Nkosazana Zuma, and strongly supported by Mbeki, who was then Deputy President, enabled the Department of Health to acquire generic versions of badly-needed drugs at much lower prices than the big drug companies that had developed them were charging. Although the Trade-Related Intellectual Property Rights agreement, supervised by the World Health Organization, allows countries facing a national emergency to do this, the big American drug companies – among them Glaxo Wellcome, the manufacturers of AZT – objected strongly. More than forty of them filed suit in the South African Constitutional Court to bar the amendment, claiming it violated their intellectual property rights.

The Clinton Administration backed the drug companies, which had made heavy donations to the Clinton-Gore re-election campaign, and there followed two years of heavy US diplomatic pressure which included placing South Africa on a "watch list" for possible punitive action. All this infuriated the South African government, and Mbeki particularly. Then, in the face of mounting international criticism, the drug companies backed down in September 2001 and withdrew their case at the last minute – finally, with a belated generosity that smacked of hypocrisy, offering to slash the prices of their anti-retroviral drugs, AZT included.

It was while he was in this angry state of mind, I believe, that the dissidents' accusations that the drug companies were manipulating the research funding and ripping off the poor resonated with Mbeki. It also goes some way to explaining the intemperate language of his letter to Clinton, written while the drug companies' case was still pending.

The dissidents' views on AIDS in Africa also resonated with Mbeki. I recall listening to him speak to the Foreign Correspondents Association in Pretoria in early 2001 about how the different manifestations of the disease in Africa and the developed countries was the core question in his mind. If African AIDS was different and much more virulent, he said, then surely one could not simply assume that the American and European drugs were effective in treating it, particularly given their high toxicity.

This is when he began speaking about the need to develop an African remedy for the disease here. In his letter to Clinton he questioned the relevance of Western medical models to the "uniquely African catastrophe" of AIDS, adding that it "would constitute a criminal betrayal of our responsibility to our own people" simply to mimic Western methods of treating the disease.[8] This assertion was widely, and I believe wrongly, interpreted as stemming from an Africanist ideology on the part of the President, who was thus seen as placing ideological considerations ahead of the welfare of his people. In this at least he was innocent, although he was almost certainly wrong in assuming that Western medicines would be ineffective in treating African AIDS.

But there is more to Mbeki's attitude towards AIDS than all of this. Somehow in this complex man there seems to be a deep-seated anger that the disease and those who point to its catastrophic scale in Africa are maligning black people, that the whole thing amounts to a calumny against African culture and sexual behaviour; that the disease is being used as a means to smear black people the way homosexuals were demonized when AIDS first appeared in the US. He gave a glimpse of this in an extraordinary outburst during a lecture at Fort Hare University in October 2001. He did not mention AIDS or HIV in the lecture, but his meaning was clear enough. Implying that the AIDS scientists were denigrating black people as vice-ridden germ carriers, he went on: "And thus does it happen that others who consider themselves to be our leaders … demand that because we are germ carriers, and human beings of a lower order that cannot subject its passions to reason, we must perforce adopt strange options, to save a depraved and diseased people from perishing from self-inflicted disease."

There was an earlier hint of the same mindset during an acrimonious exchange of letters about AIDS between Mbeki and opposition leader Tony Leon in July 2000. Referring to the declaration signed by 5 000 doctors at the international AIDS conference in Durban, Mbeki wrote somewhat cryptically: "You may ... be unaware of the desperate attempt made by some scientists in the past to blame HIV/AIDS on Africans, even at a time when the United States was the epicentre of reported deaths from AIDS. To me as an African, it is both interesting and disturbing that the signatories of the so-called 'Durban Declaration' return to the thesis about the alleged original transmission of HIV from (African) animals to humans, given what science has said about AIDS during the past two decades. I accept that it may be that you do not understand the significance of this and the message it communicates to Africans ..."[9]

The same touchiness showed up again following an article in *The Washington Post* by a South African journalist, Charlene Smith, who had suffered a terrifying rape at the hands of a black man who invaded her home. Smith had managed to beat down the barriers of bureaucratic obstruction to obtain a dosage of AZT to safeguard herself from HIV infection. Her article contended that the AIDS epidemic in South Africa was being spurred by men's attitudes towards women. "We won't end this epidemic," she wrote, "until we understand the role of tradition and religion – and of a culture in which rape is endemic and has become a prime means of transmitting the disease to young women as well as children. There is no doubt in my mind: attitude is the father of rape, and the incubator of AIDS."[10] In a country with an appalling rate of 50 000 rape cases a year, Smith's point seemed pertinent enough, but her allusion to black culture touched that raw nerve in Mbeki. He exploded with wrath, publicly accusing Smith of "a naked racist statement".

Whatever the reasons for Mbeki's involvement with the AIDS dissidents and his strange reactions to those warning of the awful realities of the disease, it would be difficult to exaggerate the damage he has done to his own image and that of his government, both at home and abroad. The only bright side to the saga is that despite the centralizing of power and control upon himself and his office, the President has been forced to back down. Mbeki has been roundly criticized in the media for his statements on AIDS. The influential Professor Makgoba has spoken out frequently and forcefully, coming close to warning the President that he would be guilty of genocide if he continued to hide behind "revisionist theories" about the disease. AIDS activists have campaigned vigorously and taken the government to court. Cosatu and the SACP have criticized Mbeki publicly. Nelson Mandela added his immense moral authority to calls for a more positive government policy and the use of anti-retroviral drugs. And for all the ANC's public appearance of solidarity behind its leader, there has been persistent internal pressure for a change of stance. As early as September 2000, while Mbeki was still in the midst of his *annus horribilis*, leaders of the ANC's health committee wrote a confidential memorandum urging the President and Health Minister Manto Tshabalala-Msimang to acknowledge that HIV caused AIDS. While neither did so personally, the government published a series of advertizements saying the President had been misunderstood and that he had never denied a link between HIV and AIDS. Soon afterwards Mbeki announced that he was withdrawing from the AIDS debate. Finally, in April 2002, in what was clearly a response to irresistible pressure from many quarters, the Cabinet announced a major policy reversal. It issued a statement accepting the usefulness of anti-retroviral drugs and announcing that rape survivors should be able to demand them from state hospitals to protect themselves from HIV infection. Towards year's end, Mbeki paid his first visit to an AIDS ward where the anti-retrovirals were being distributed.

In other words civil society has shown its effectiveness as a safeguard against misrule. That more than anything else is what distinguishes South Africa from the rest of the African continent.

* * *

Russel Kaufman sits comfortably at his desk in the Dean's Suite of the big Duke University Medical Center in Durham, North Carolina. This is in the heart of North Carolina's Research Triangle, which is to the pharmaceutical industry what Silicon Valley is to the IT industry. So the Duke Centre, with an annual $300 million research budget, is at the cutting edge of medical research, with HIV/AIDS as one of its major projects, and Dean Kaufman himself is at its control panel. Without sounding boastful, he says matter-of-factly that the Duke researchers are among the best in the world. More important, he also knows what other researchers are doing worldwide, because all are working together closely in the race to find a cure for this terrible disease. And he believes the race is being won. Already, he says, there are a few people who may have been cured by anti-retroviral treatments: they have been on the drugs for a long time and tests are showing them consistently

HIV negative. But it is the search for a preventative vaccine that holds out the hope of wiping out the disease altogether, as smallpox and polio have been eliminated – and here, too, Kaufman is "very confident" that it will be achieved.

Promising vaccines are already being tested in the United States, Thailand, Britain, Kenya, India, Haiti, Brazil, Peru and South Africa. Unfortunately this testing phase is the most time-consuming part of the production of a new vaccine, because the researchers have to make sure it is absolutely safe. After that the vaccine has to be commercialized, then produced in large quantities and distributed globally.

All this normally takes twenty to twenty-five years, but in mid-2001 I interviewed Tim Tucker, head of the newly formed South African Vaccine Initiative, which falls under Makgoba's Medical Research Council, who told me the project's researchers were trying to halve that time and produce a vaccine in ten to twelve years. A year later they were well on track, and in September 2002 three vaccines developed at the University of Cape Town, which Tucker said had shown "very promising" test results on laboratory mice, were approved to go into a manufacturing phase in preparation for clinical trials. The trials move through three phases: the first, involving twenty or thirty patients, will last a year to eighteen months, and if the results are positive the tests will advance to phase two with a larger sampling that will last two years. If one or more of the vaccines still look good they will go to the third and final phase which could last two to three years. An eight or nine-year process altogether.

The failure rate along the trial course is heavy. About eighty have entered the test phase so far, but only two – one in Thailand and the other in the US – have reached phase three.

When I put Tucker's target of having a vaccine ready for use in ten to twelve years to Kaufman and asked whether he thought that was a realistic possibility, he was emphatic in his reply. "Absolutely," he said. Pressed for his own estimate of how long it might take, Kaufman replied: "I think 15 years would probably be safe. The wonderful thing about science is that knowledge builds on knowledge, so it is an expanding inverted cone. As you understand one part of the puzzle it helps you understand other parts, and then understanding three parts helps you to understand nine parts."

Kaufman is a genial man, surprisingly laid back for one in such a high-tension job. He is politely but comprehensively dismissive of the AIDS dissidents and their theories. "I know of no reputable scientist in the field," he says, "who still believes the HI virus does not exist or that it does not cause AIDS. It has been isolated, it has been characterized, the genes have all been cloned and sequenced. We now understand the life cycle of the virus, we understand how it infects cells, we understand the molecules it uses to gain access to the cells, we understand a lot of the genetic variation, and we are continuing to learn about the relationship between the virus and the host which is important for developing vaccines."

Other research specialists are equally emphatic. Robert Gallo, an American specialist who headed the National Institutes of Health team that contributed to the discovery of HIV in 1984, says that now, 18 years later, "we know more about HIV than we know about any other microbe ever studied."[11]

Why then do the dissidents persist? "In any scientific research," says Kaufman, "there is always the leading edge who will draw conclusions before all the story is in, and a trailing edge that will continue to dispute almost any area of science."

In any event, he explains, scientific research proceeds by the development of an hypothesis which is then countered by a no-hypothesis. Both are tested. "We never say the hypothesis is truth," says Kaufman. "If the evidence is overwhelming, we say that the no-hypothesis is not true. So we use this negative assertion, saying that if there is no evidence that the hypothesis is not true then we accept it until we have a better theory. That is the nature of science and the best scientists understand it, but it always leaves you susceptible to people saying you've never really proved it.

"However, after one has accumulated a massive amount of data and evidence, which is what we have done with the AIDS virus, then the hypothesis becomes synonymous with the truth."

To understand how retroviruses work, Kaufman explains, you have to understand how genes and genetic information work. Every human being has his or her own set of genetic information, which is encoded in the DNA of the individual cells of the body. Normal cells make copies of the DNA, which is then called RNA, and this RNA then directs the cellular machinery to make proteins.

Most viruses are DNA viruses, so that their genetic material looks like the genetic material inside our cells. But there is an exotic family of viruses, called retroviruses, which are made of RNA – in other words they are made of the copy of the DNA. These RNA retroviruses then go into the human cell, and a copy of them is made and so reverse-transcribed into DNA – hence the name retrovirus. This DNA then inserts itself into the human genome and becomes part of the genetic material of the individual.

"So it's a different way of getting this genetic material into the body," says Kaufman. "There's nothing particularly complex about that, except for one tiny thing. The process isn't as precise as the usual copying of the DNA, so that in making copies that aren't exact it gives the virus a chance to mutate. And they mutate quickly, so instead of having a single target for our immune systems to attack, it's a constantly changing target which makes it difficult for our immune systems to recognize them."

The irony is that the HIV retrovirus then attacks the very immune cells in our bodies, called T-cells, that are meant to fight it.

It is like a stealthy attack on your body. The HIV sneaks in, lies waiting unrecognized in your cells while it duplicates itself, then when it has made lots of copies of itself they attack your defenders, the T-cells, and overwhelm them. Then when next you contract a disease that a healthy immune system would deal with quite easily, your body cannot fight it and the disease kills you.

Two lines of research are being pursued to counter the HIV assault – anti-retroviral cocktails to treat people already infected, and the search for a vaccine to prevent infection.

The anti-retrovirals come in several forms. Some block the virus and prevent it attaching itself to and infecting the cells. Others, called protease inhibitors, stop an enzyme called protease from clipping a protein on the retrovirus into several smaller pieces which then enable the retrovirus to duplicate itself. By targeting the enzyme, or the protein directly, the medicine can stop, or at least slow down, the HIV's ability to multiply itself to the point where its army of copies can attack and destroy the T-cell defenders of your immune system.

The proteins themselves vary, which is why the anti-retroviruses come in cocktail form – to enable them to attack all the proteins on the virus. As Kaufman says, it's like having multiple defences. If you attack all the proteins at once, you stand a better chance of killing the virus and not getting resistance to the drug.

But there are problems. The anti-retroviral cocktails are toxic, just as the chemo-therapy drugs used to treat cancer patients are, and they can produce nasty side effects. It is also much more difficult to attack the virus once it is inside the cell and has taken up a home there. This is why anti-retroviral treatment is regarded as a palliative and not a cure – although Kaufman believes a few patients may have been cured. It is also why the main hope lies in developing a vaccine that can prevent the virus from entering the cell in the first place.

Vaccines in general involve using a part of a virus, or a similar one such as the harmless cowpox virus used in smallpox vaccine, to produce a serum which enables the immune system to recognize viruses as invaders and stop them before they have a chance to get inside the cells. The researchers are following several different approaches. One is to kill an HIV virus and try to use that as a vaccine, although this raises the obvious concern that not all of the virus may have been killed. Another is to take parts of the proteins that are attached to the virus and make a vaccine from them. Two of the South African candidate vaccines are made from different HIV proteins, while the third is an interesting variation that uses a form of the old smallpox vaccine which has been genetically engineered to produce HIV proteins in addition to its normal set of proteins.

What of the different sub-groups of the HIV virus that appear in different parts of the world, and Mbeki's apparent belief that this means Western medications will be ineffective in Africa and that this continent must produce its own? Kaufman doubts this. He thinks the sub-groups are "subtleties" rather than basic differences in the biology of the virus, but that in any event all scientists the world over are interacting closely with a view to producing what he calls a "multiple target" vaccine. This in any case is necessary, he says, to deal with the way the HIV virus mutates. "If you are making a vaccine with five targets, it's unlikely all five of them will mutate, so you give the body multiple chances to make an immune response against the virus. That's why vaccine makers try to give a broad range of targets."

* * *

What does all this mean for the future of South Africa and the predictions of an African holocaust? If Kaufman and Tucker are right and there is going to be a preventative vaccine in ten to fifteen years, then at least the apocalyptic predictions of the state of the nation in 2020 and beyond will be alleviated. The United Nations, for example, has predicted that AIDS will kill a further 65 million people worldwide by 2020, equalling the number of people killed in all wars in the twentieth century.

Nevertheless an appalling number of people are still going to die, most of them young, in the prime of their lives. It is a terrible human tragedy.

Just how many is difficult to estimate, especially now that a preventative vaccine may be on the way and anti-retroviral treatments are becoming more effective. The demographics are further complicated by the time lag of six to eight years between infection and the onset of the disease, which means the level of infection is already high before anyone gets sick, and AIDS deaths will continue rising long after the HIV infection rate has started to fall. The HIV infection rate, the AIDS prevalence rate and the AIDS death rate are therefore three different things, but they are often conflated confusingly in the media.

The AIDS death rate in South Africa is just beginning to climb as I write this. The HIV infection rate is expected to peak in 2010. Love-Life, an American-funded non-governmental organization, has projected a sharply rising graph starting at 120 000 deaths in 2000 and rising to between 354 000 and 383 000 in 2005 and between 545 000 in 635 000 in 2010.[12] Other sources predict 800 000 deaths in 2010. By that time, says the 2002 annual report of NGM-Levy, a labour relations and actuarial consultancy, 1 million South Africans will have AIDS and a total of 6 million will have died of it.

The tragedy is not measurable in deaths alone. Millions of families will be broken up, adding to the massive social dislocation and destruction of traditional institutions already caused by apartheid. Breadwinners will die, plunging their dependants into destitution. But most tragic of all will be the impact on children.

Appalling numbers of babies are dying already from mother-to-child transmissions. A public hospital serving Mdantsane, a large black township in the Eastern Cape, recently recorded 200 infant deaths from AIDS in a month, while a cemetery established in Pietermaritzburg in mid-2002 that was expected to last at least a year was almost full with 300 tiny mounds of earth after only four months.[13]

The child mortality graph plunges to zero after the age of four and remains there for the next ten years, after which it begins to rise again with the onset of puberty, peaking between the ages of 20 and 40. But many of the surviving children will also suffer the consequences of AIDS as one or both of their parents die. The number of orphans is projected to increase to nearly two million by 2010. As it is South Africa has a disproportionately large number of children brought up by people other than their parents, because of the migrant labour system and the long history of apartheid's disruption of families. Now this fragile system of foster and community care will become overloaded: grannies and aunts will have their meagre resources stretched to the point where they can no longer cope. Some children will be orphaned more than once, as grandparents and other older relatives also die. Already the phenomenon of child-headed households is beginning to appear, and institutions intended for pre-school education are turning into residential hostels. Meanwhile the elderly, too, will suffer as they are left with no one to take care of them.

The effects will ripple throughout society, pushing poor households deeper into poverty, impacting on education as teachers die, on social development and not least on the crime rate as AIDS orphans become street children, turn to petty crime and then get sucked into crime gangs.

Of course some of the rich and healthy will die too, but in every respect it is the poor who will suffer the most. The AIDS Foundation of South Africa offers the concept of a "deprivation trap" to explain why this is so.

"The starting point is the poor household. Families are generally large, consisting of many children, as well as the aged and disabled. The family has too little money to provide adequately for basic needs. Malnutrition is rife, leading to poor performance in school and lower labour output. As most of the households live in rural areas or peripheral urban squatter settlements, they are isolated from social infrastructure such as transport routes, schools and medical facilities, and often employment opportunities. As a result they are isolated and illiteracy is high. The household is also vulnerable due to dependence on landlords and traditional authorities. They live from hand to mouth. If the father dies, survival becomes even tougher. The mother must find work and the children are left in the care of the elderly or without care at all. Finally, the household is powerless, intimidated by those on whom they rely for a livelihood. Their ability to influence policy decisions that would improve their well-being is virtually nonexistent. Thus they occupy a very low status in society."[14]

* * *

What of the impact on the economy? Again there have been apocalyptic predictions. When AIDS first appeared in the mid-1980s, one South African author offered the dire prediction that the disease would cause economic collapse and change the balance of global power.[15] Subsequent predictions have been less alarmist but still grim. LoveLife, noting that the pandemic would hit working-age adults hardest, predicted in 2000 that some companies could lose up to half their workforce, and that by 2010 15% of the country's highly skilled employees would have contracted AIDS.

The International Monetary Fund, in its World Economic Outlook report in September 2000, said that in the worst-affected countries, which includes South Africa, per capita gross domestic product could fall by 5% within a year. "The epidemic creates a vicious cycle," the report said, "by reducing economic growth which leads to increased poverty which, in turn, facilitates the rapid spread of HIV/AIDS as household food and health spending declines, thereby reducing resistance to opportunistic infections." In fact that predicted drop in per capita GDP did not come about, at least not in South Africa.

A study by two World Bank researchers, Channing Arndt and Jeffrey Lewis, concluded that AIDS would cut South Africa's GDP growth rate to a miserable 1% in 2008 from the 3,5% they reckoned it would be without AIDS. However they added, rightly I believe, that there would be no decrease in per capita GDP because the population size would decrease in proportion to the decrease in productivity.[16]

Ing Barings Bank, meanwhile, produced a research document suggesting that while the largest number of deaths would be among unskilled and semi-skilled workers, the skilled and highly skilled sectors would also be affected which would hurt an economy already struggling with a skills shortage. The result, Barings forecast, would be a GDP growth rate between 0,3% and 0,4% lower than if there were no AIDS epidemic.[17]

Most recently Stellenbosch University's Bureau for Economic Research contended that while South Africa "is likely to retain an economic growth rate of around 3% per annum, the overall effect of the disease will be to shave roughly 0,5% off gross domestic product every year until 2015."[18]

These varying forecasts underline my own inherent scepticism about all doomsday predictions, especially those pronounced by economists: it is not for nothing they are known as practitioners of the gloomy science. I believe societies, and businesses in particular, have ways of adapting to crises that lessen their impact and sharpen creative thinking and initiative. This is all the more likely in the case of AIDS because its impact is gradual, giving everyone time to plan and adjust in the light of unfolding experience.

Nor have the economic and other forecasters taken sufficient account of the possible impact of this pandemic on that other doomsday scenario we were hearing so much about only a few years ago – the population explosion. Ever since Thomas Malthus, perhaps the original gloomy economist, first raised the issue at the turn of the eighteenth century, demographers have been frightening us with predictions of how the snowballing growth of populations is going to outstrip the global resources necessary to sustain them. In South Africa it was suggested that the present population of 41 million would reach 51,3 million by 2010 and then soar to Everest proportions after that. Well, AIDS is not going to *reduce* South Africa's overall population, but it is going to slow its growth rate so that we are now looking at a population of 47 million in 2010.[19] The lower growth rate will not be due only to increased mortality but also to lower fertility and to changes in sexual behaviour, including the increased use of condoms, which probably indicates a flatter growth trajectory in the longer term. Moreover, a smaller population can be better educated, and better education, especially of women who are then in a stronger position to determine their own choices, is by far the most effective method of birth control.

If one is to try to extrapolate some kind of economic equation from the interaction of these two demographic doomsday scenarios, it may be helpful to start with a couple of historical examples. The Black Death of the fourteenth century, which killed a third of Europe's population, was not only one of the greatest human disasters the world has known but also marked a turning point in Europe's economic development.

The plague began incongruously in early 1347 when a Genoese trading post in the Crimea was being besieged by an army of Hungarian Kipchaks and Mongols from lands further east. The Mongols brought a new form of plague with them and began falling ill and dying during the siege. The Kipchak commander, thinking he could take advantage of this misfortune, catapulted several corpses into the Genoese town, and the defenders promptly began to die in droves. At that point one of the Genoese ships managed to escape from the blockade and make its way to Messina, in Sicily. It brought the plague with it. The disease spread with terrifying speed, wiping out half the population of Messina in two months, then it spread to mainland Italy and from there throughout Europe. The plague killed more than 14 million people before it ended in 1350.

Half the farm labourers died, which resulted in a huge increase in agricultural wages. At the same time the survivors inherited everything that the dead had owned, money, lands, buildings, clothing, furniture, and with this sudden surge in wealth went one of history's great spending sprees that gave a major boost to the cultural and economic expansion of the Renaissance.

By contrast, another major European catastrophe, World War I, had an opposite effect. It was a disastrous war in every respect: it was not fought over any great and specific issue, but followed the assassination of Archduke Francis Ferdinand of the Austro-Hungarian Empire and his wife by a young Serb, Gavrilo Prinzip, in the streets of Sarajevo on 28 June 1914. Ferdinand's name meant little to the ordinary people of France, Britain and Russia, yet as Austria and Serbia went to war with each other over the incident country after country was sucked in through a complex network of mutual defence alliances until a huge percentage of the world's population was involved.

The trench warfare that followed on the Western Front was the first in history where defence weaponry proved more deadly than arms of attack. Rapid-firing machine guns cut down whole waves of young men as both sides sought in vain to overrun the other in a deadly stalemate that dragged on for four years. At the battle of the Somme six hundred thousand British soldiers died capturing six miles ($9^1/_2$ km) of territory. In all ten million men perished in the war and millions more were wounded in a struggle that ended with an armistice as inconclusive as the war's beginnings were obscure. The war eliminated a huge section of an entire generation of men in the flower of their productive youth, and this, combined with a general feeling of the futility of it all, plunged the world into the Great Depression and a mood of profound pessimism from which it took 30 years – and another more decisive world war – to recover.

The lesson to be drawn from these two conflicting historical examples brings us to a touchy subject. Describing a great human tragedy is one thing, assessing its economic consequences quite another. As Alan Whiteside and Clem Sunter note in their excellent little book, *AIDS: The Challenge for South Africa*: "It is a harsh *economic* reality that not all lives have equal value. If the majority of those infected are unemployed, subsistence farmers or unskilled workers, then the impact on the national economy will not be as great as if they are skilled and highly productive members of society." It is even true, the authors add, that "if the majority of people (who die) were unskilled and resources were not taken from savings to fund provision of care, then in *pure economic terms* the survivors could be better off and per capita income could rise!"[20]

Nasty but true. It depends on who does the dying.

The Black Death, or bubonic plague, was spread by fleas on rats and it spread fast and indiscriminately, killing rich and poor, skilled and unskilled, men and women, young and old alike. Perhaps it killed marginally more of the poor, because there would have been more rats in their crowded and less salubrious settlements, but the difference would have been slight. World War I, by contrast, took out one specific segment of the population – young, able-bodied men at their productive peak.

It requires someone with more knowledge than I possess to assess the light, if any, that these two historical examples cast on the long-term economic impact of the AIDS pandemic in South Africa. My sense of it is that AIDS falls somewhere between. It will kill people of all sectors of the community, but all studies suggest it will kill more of the poor and unskilled than of the skilled and more affluent. But many of the skilled will die too, and as Baring Bank says their loss will hurt an economy that is short of skills. So we are unlikely to have a post-tragedy boost to a new Renaissance. But we are not going to have a Great Depression either.

CHAPTER FIFTEEN

A BAD NEIGHBOURHOOD

"When something goes wrong in Somalia, the residents
of Dead Man's Creek, Mississippi, don't say something
has gone wrong in Somalia. They say something has gone
wrong in Africa. And when somebody steals a presidency in Togo,
they don't say somebody has stolen a presidency in Togo.
They say the Africans have done it yet again."
— THABO MBEKI

In the words of actress Whoopie Goldberg describing her lot as a black woman in America, South Africa's geographic location is a double whammy. In the first place, as Harvard economist Jeremy Sachs has noted, proximity to a developed country, as Poland is to Germany and Mexico to the US, is a huge advantage for an emerging economy; but here is South Africa at the bottom of the world's most marginalized continent far from the economic hubs of North America, Europe and Japan. Its chances, says Sachs, would be immeasurably better if it were located where Morocco is.¹ The second and even bigger whammy is that Africa has this terrible reputation of being "the hopeless continent" in a world where few are disposed to differentiate between its 54 countries. South Africa gets lumped in with the rest, tarred with the brush of Afro-pessimism.

There is, of course, a compelling logic about not investing in a bad neighbourhood. Who would want to set up a new business in a declining district with a rampant crime wave? Investors fear contagion, so that when things go wrong in one country they red-line those around it. That has pretty well happened to the entire African continent.

This is perhaps South Africa's most burdensome albatross. If this new democracy has inherited more than its fair share of domestic problems from the apartheid era, it has inherited almost as many from its desperate neighbourhood. But unlike the apartheid legacy, it cannot renounce these. The temptation may be there to say we are not like the rest, we are different, please don't equate us with the hopeless continent. But the new South Africa cannot do that. By geographic location, by racial identity, by emotional commitment, and above all by the logic of our circumstances, we are inextricably part of the African continent. More than that, we are its regional superpower and therefore in an abandoning world, its last best hope. We carry the responsibility for resurrecting a continent *in extremis*, and if we fail the world will live to regret it for the global village cannot live with the decline and terminal decay of such a major sector of its own community. The domestic imperative is even stronger. If ever the need to be your neighbour's keeper was evident it is here, for already the economic refugees are pouring in and provoking a xenophobic reaction that often turns to violence from South Africa's own hard-pressed unemployed. As Federal Reserve Chairman Alan Greenspan once said of the United States in a global context, South Africa, too, cannot survive as an oasis of prosperity if the rest of its continent is in chaos.

Not all of Africa is in chaos, of course. There are some bright spots, Botswana, Mozambique, Senegal, Mauritius, Cameroon, Ghana and a newly democratized Nigeria among them; and as President Mbeki likes to point out there have been some 50 multi-party elections in the continent since 1990, although as Zimbabwe has shown elections do not always signify democracy. But for the most part Africa presents a dismal picture to the world. Four decades after the bulk of its 54 countries attained independence, much of the continent is mired in poverty, despotism, corruption and violence. Throughout the nineties a broad band of warfare involving a dozen countries and as many warlords and rebel militia stretched diagonally right across Africa, from Angola in the south-west through the Democratic Republic of Congo, Congo-Brazzaville, the Great Lakes countries of Rwanda, Burundi and Uganda, through the Sudan to Ethiopia, Eritrea and Somalia at the Horn of Africa in the far north-east; while over on the west coast little Sierra Leone became a charnel house at the hands of Foday Sankoh's Revolutionary United Front whose drugged militiamen set a new standard of gratuitous cruelty by kidnapping children and chopping off people's hands and feet, and in neighbouring Liberia the egregious warlord-president, Charles Taylor, enriched himself as a conduit for the blood diamonds that funded much of the carnage.

From a personal perspective, the events in Sierra Leone have been the most poignant, for they illustrate more vividly than anything else I have witnessed the tragic gap between political greed and a people's hopes that is such a widespread feature of the African experience.

Sierra Leone is not an important country. With its 4 275 000 population, harsh malarial climate and meagre resources, it is one of the world's poorest. But it has a great history which fills its people with a sense of pride. Its capital, Freetown, was established in 1787 by the British government as a haven for freed slaves, and the emancipatory zeal which accompanied that event also saw sub-Saharan Africa's first university, Fourah Bay College, and its first newspaper established there. So it has a self-image as a place of freedom and a place of learning. The "Athens of Africa", its citizens like to call it. But its modern experience, pock-marked with coups, military dictatorships and Africa's most terrible civil war, has been a cruel denial of that historical imagery.

In February 1996 I flew to Sierra Leone as part of a Commonwealth observer team to witness an election that was as remarkable as its aftermath was heartbreaking. After 18 years of single-party rule and successive military dictatorships, a new palace coup had brought to power a certain Brigadier Maada Bio who unexpectedly committed himself to returning the country to civilian government. Elections were scheduled with 15 parties registered to take part. There was a palpable air of excitement as we landed in Freetown. People were talking optimistically of a new beginning, of their determination to build a country based on liberty, democratic values, peace and development. There was only one problem. The country was at war. Foday Sankoh's rebels, operating out of neighbouring Liberia and funded by diamonds looted from Sierra Leone's alluvial diggings, had been ranging across the countryside for the past five years, terrorizing the population with their amputations, kidnapping thousands of children, forcing them to watch their own parents being murdered and then indoctrinating and drugging them to become cruel, almost dehumanized child-soldiers themselves. Compounding the problem was the fact that the poorly trained and undisciplined Sierra Leone army was itself more of a threat than a stabilizing force, with many conscripts being labelled "sobels" – soldiers by day, rebels by night – as they, too, harassed and looted the local population.

I was assigned with eight other observers to the south-eastern town of Kenema, just 50 km from the Liberian border. It was in the heart of the war zone. The town itself was filled with refugees from the surrounding countryside, and more were streaming in as we arrived – some hobbling on makeshift crutches or with arms that ended in stumps, evidence of encounters with Sankoh's psychopaths.

We were billeted in a pastoral centre on the outskirts of the town, and as we settled in news reached us of encroaching rebel attacks on nearby villages. Sankoh had vowed to stop the elections. The polling stations were due to open at 7 am on 26 February, but at exactly 6.15 am the rattle of small-arms fire broke out around the centre. It was still dark and for a while we watched the battle from the grounds of the centre, which was on a rise overlooking the town. We could see tracer bullets flare through the darkness, while intensive small-arms fire came closer down the valleys on either side of us. The distinctive slow, heavy bark of AK-47 automatic rifles was everywhere, and we could also hear the sharp rip of a 12,7 mm anti-aircraft machine-gun which the army had mounted on a truck to use as an anti-personnel weapon. But then the heavy crunch of mortar bombs and RPG rockets sent us scurrying indoors. We ran into a dormitory and huddled on the floor of a passageway in the centre of the building, which gave us a measure of protection at least from the small-arms fire.

For two-and-a-half hours the firefight raged. At times the rebels ran close past our building and we could hear them shouting: "No election! No election!" between their bursts of AK-47 fire. Then, indistinctly at first but gradually increasing in volume, we heard a counter-chant coming from the direction of the town: "We want vote! We want vote!"

Thousands of people were pouring into the streets, and as the chanting crowd swelled they ran through the town waving palm leaves. An electoral commission van drove ahead of the crowd with an election song blaring over its loudspeaker system and the voice of the local electoral commissioner calling on the people to come out of their houses and join the throng. Part of the crowd made their way up to the pastoral centre. There, with gunfire still rat-tat-tatting all around, the Electoral Commissioner leaped from the van to address the observers. "We are going to have an election," he cried. "Come and observe."

Whether it was this display of public courage or a successful counter-attack by the local military was unclear, but the rebels began to withdraw and the shooting subsided. As the observers made their way gingerly into the town, crowds lining the streets yelled impatiently at us: "Bring the boxes. We want vote!" The polling stations opened late, some not until the afternoon, but electoral officials worked frantically to open extra stations, and by the time the polls closed at 6 pm nearly every registered adult in Kenema had voted.

There were similar rebel attacks all over the country, including in Freetown itself, but these, too, failed to scare away the voters. The turnout nationwide was enormous, and all the observer missions declared the election "free and fair". Seldom can there have been a more dramatic demonstration of a people's yearning for democracy. But to no avail.

A generous allocation of aid to reward the people of Sierra Leone for their remarkable courage and commitment to the democratic ideal would have done much to enable the new President, Ahmad Tejan Kabbah, to improve the lives of his people, and the British and American ambassadors pleaded passionately for that. They pointed out that a modest amount of aid could make a big difference in such a small community. But the big powers did not respond. Boredom with Africa and its endless woes had set in, and not a single foreign press team had been there to report on the remarkable election. So democracy was not able to deliver any of the hoped-for improvements, and over the next three years Sankoh's brutes were able to take advantage of this failure to continue plundering the country's diamond wealth and extending their military control over the countryside until eventually they entered the capital itself where their special brand of violence rose to a climactic orgy of killings, rapes and the hacking off of limbs.

* * *

It would be a mistake to regard the tragic mess in Sierra Leone and the rapacious power-hunger that has caused it as typifying all of Africa, just as it is wrong to blame all the continent's woes on the developed world's treatment of Africa, from the slave trade to colonialism and now on unfair trading relations and the IMF and World Bank's tough demands for economic reforms. But the truth is there are elements of all these factors present in the condition of the continent. The slave trade certainly wrought havoc, but the African slave-raiders who captured and sold their brethren into bondage must share at least some of the blame with those of both the Arab and Western worlds who bought, used and abused them; and while colonialism certainly robbed Africans of their land and resources it also brought the modern world and its technology to them.

With the wisdom of hindsight, one can see that the cycle of problems that has brought Africa to its present condition begins with the fact that the colonial era was long enough to be disruptive but too short to impart enough modernizing benefits. In 1873, when David Livingstone died at Ulala in the heart of present-day Zambia, most of Africa was still ruled by Africans. By 1902 five European powers – Britain,

France, Germany, Italy and Portugal – together with King Leopold II of Belgium had grabbed control of nearly the entire continent and carved it up arbitrarily into 30 new colonies. A mere 60 years later, roughly two generations, most of those colonies were independent countries.

Never before had an entire continent been colonized so rapidly – and then decolonized even more swiftly. It was a process that first destabilized Africa's traditional social systems and institutions, then ended before it could replace them with new social and governmental systems or even establish a common sense of nationhood among the disparate tribes that had been lumped together. The hasty carve-up paid no heed to economic viability or ethnic coherence: the prestige of the rival imperial powers was all that counted. Thus the boundary between Kenya and Tanganyika was drawn so as to give Otto von Bismarck Africa's highest peak, Mount Kilimanjaro, and Britain its second highest, Mount Kenya, in the course of which the Masai tribe were heedlessly cut in half. The hasty decolonization paid equally little heed to administrative capacity and political viability. Thus the Democratic Republic of Congo, geographically the largest country in Africa with a population of 40 million, had no university until five years before independence in 1960 when it was left to run itself with only 13 graduates. There were few qualified administrators, no Congolese had been able to advance beyond the level of medical assistant to become a doctor, and none had been able to rise above the rank of non-commissioned officer in the army.

It was Africa's misfortune, too, that independence coincided with the deepest phase of the Cold War so that both the Soviet bloc and the West sought to strengthen their positions on the geo-political chessboard by propping up corrupt regimes with aid and personal handouts and providing them with weapons with which to suppress their subjects. In the Congo again, a connivance of US and Belgian conspiracies saw a regional leader, Moise Tshombe, lead a secessionist rebellion by the copper-rich province of Katanga, followed soon afterwards by the assassination of the democratically elected prime minister of the Congo itself, Patrice Lumumba, and his replacement by the military dictator, Mobutu Sese Seko. Mobutu ruled the country for the next 32 years, winning American support by proclaiming his opposition to communism and turning the Congo, which he renamed Zaire, into a prototype kleptocracy. His was a regime of thieves who plundered the Congo's considerable mineral wealth to the point where Mobutu himself became one of the richest men in the world while his country became one of the poorest. His self-indulgence was such that he reportedly flew a hairdresser out first class from New York every six weeks to cut his hair. He built 11 palaces for himself in the Congo and owned luxury villas in Europe. Under his venal rule the Congo degenerated into a suppurating sore at the very heart of the continent which over time infected others around it.

Next door in Angola, meanwhile, a long war of liberation against the Portuguese colonizers mutated into an even longer civil war as rival liberation movements, funded and armed by the two Cold War super-powers, became locked in a struggle for supremacy that stretched the total span of bloodshed and destruction to four full decades. It became in effect a proxy war between the Soviet Union and Cuba on one side and the United States in an uncomfortable alliance with apartheid South Africa on the other.

The Soviets backed the overtly Marxist *Movimento Popular de Libertãcao de Angola* (MPLA), which had its main power base in the north of the country and was therefore able to gain control of the capital, Luanda, and establish itself as the internationally recognized government. Initially the Americans backed the rival *Frente Nacionãl Libertacao de Angola* (FNLA), led by Holden Roberto, a brother-in-law of Mobutu Sese Seko, but when it was quickly defeated by the MPLA they turned to the more charismatic and effective Jonas Savimbi, whose *União Nacional para a Independência Total de Angola* (UNITA) had its main support in southern and central Angola. South Africa, meanwhile, was using Savimbi as its own proxy to protect its western flank against incursions from the ANC and Namibia's liberation fighters, the South West African People's Organization (SWAPO), who were also operating out of southern Angola. In response to this South African involvement, which at one point saw South African troops penetrate to within 100 km of Luanda, Fidel Castro sent Cuban troops and pilots to help the MPLA, while the Soviets supplied the MPLA with T-54 tanks, Mi-24 helicopter gunships, Mig-23 jet fighters and 122 mm BM-21 multiple rocket launchers, the so-called Stalin Organ, to counter South Africa's light armoured cars and French-built Mirage fighters. American funding and supplies reached Savimbi across Angola's porous border from Mobutu's Zaire.

The end of the Cold War and the start of South Africa's negotiated revolution in 1990 removed these proxy elements from the Angolan conflict. But that did not end the war. It merely changed it. With money and weapons no longer pouring in from the superpowers, a new form of insurgency took over, in Angola and in other parts of Africa, as rival warlords turned to easily exploitable natural resources within their own countries to finance their war efforts – and to enrich themselves in the process. Greed became a primary motive for prolonging these wars, for the generals and other senior officers share in the loot along with the politicians. Even the foot soldiers get their cut, and their weapons give them the ability to rob and rape. It is the ordinary people who do the suffering as they struggle to survive in collapsing economies and at the mercy of rapacious predators.

These resource wars present global peace-makers with a daunting problem, for how do you stop a war when all the people engaged in fighting it, the politicians and the generals on both sides, are profiting mightily from its continuation? What is more they have a vested interest in perpetuating disorder, for it is easier to plunder a country in a state of chaos than one where there is peace and an orderly legal system.

There is a simple if crude method of political control embodied in this process which operates outside of wartime as well. Richard Cornwell, Africa specialist at the Institute for Strategic Studies in Pretoria, once described it to me as "the privatization of sovereignty". The instruments of the state, such as the army, the police and the civil bureaucracy, are appropriated for personal use. Soldiers involved in the Congo war, for example, are engaged in resource exploitation as part of their official duties – partly to offset the costs of the military operation and partly to reward the governing elites, who in turn use the proceeds as patronage to secure themselves in power. It means that political leaders cease to be dependent on the support of the broad population to remain in power and become dependent instead on keeping the critical power brokers of the inner circle – the generals, the police chiefs and the key regional warlords – adequately rewarded and happy.

But again it would be wrong to suggest that the plundering of resources and the enrichment of politicians began only with the end of the Cold War, or that it is only Africans who are involved in the corruption. Profiteering from Africa's plentiful natural resources has accompanied all its conflicts from the start, and it is the developed world that has provided the procuring agents and ultimately been the receivers of these stolen goods, whose banks have accepted vast sums from the thieving presidents and whose estate agents have sold them luxury villas in Europe.

It would also be wrong to suggest that greed is the only factor driving these wars. There are ethnic, sociological and cultural divisions that were the initial cause of many African conflicts and which are still salient today. But as an excellent study of Angola's war economy by the Institute for Strategic Studies makes clear, "resource wars" are an additional phenomenon that have kept old wars going in the post-Cold-War era and ratcheted up the motive of greed to produce new armed conflicts.[2]

The Angolan struggle became the prototype resource war. With the Soviets, Cubans, Americans and South Africans out of the picture, the MPLA government turned to its oil revenues to fund its ongoing war against UNITA. These revenues are vast. Angola is one of the world's fastest-growing oil-producing regions: production has soared from 140 000 barrels a day in 1973 to a projected 1,4 million barrels a day by the end of 2003, and Angola is now the US's sixth-largest oil supplier. Oil revenues and oil-backed loans funded arms purchases of up to $1 billion a year through the 1990s as the MPLA built up its strength and acquired more and more sophisticated weapons, including T-72 tanks with laser-guided target-sighting systems, liquid air fuel bombs, and radar systems to monitor planes flying supplies to UNITA. The oil revenues also enabled the governing elite to enrich themselves and secure their positions through patronage. President Jose Eduardo dos Santos is himself reportedly a dollar billionaire. But none of this vast wealth has been spent on building or maintaining infrastructure or providing services to the population. After 41 years of war the country is in ruins and its 10 million people are destitute. There are some estimates that Angola has more landmines than people, and they have left it with the world's highest amputee rate.

For its part, UNITA turned to Angola's other major natural resource, diamonds, to fund its war effort. Angola is the world's fourth-largest diamond producer, and since UNITA controlled most of the countryside it was able to seize 70% of the diamond fields, force the diggers to work for it, and then sell the diamonds through middle-men to dealers in Belgium, Israel, India, the US and even to De Beers, the big South African company which controls the international diamond market through its London-based Central Selling Organization. In seven years, beginning in 1992, Savimbi extracted an estimated $4 billion from the Angolan diggings. Like Fodah Sankoh's diamonds from Sierra Leone, many of these UNITA stones found their way to the world markets through Liberia, which serves as a kind of flag of convenience for the illicit diamond trade. In 1999 Liberia was listed as having exported

31 million carats of rough diamonds, while its actual domestic production was only 500 000 carats.

Although Savimbi's diamond loot was not as abundant as the government's from oil, it enabled him to sustain his war for another 12 years
after the end of the Cold War, until eventually he was killed in battle in
February 2002 and the remnants of his army surrendered within weeks
of his death. Now for the first time since the war of liberation from
Portuguese colonial rule began in 1961, Angola faces a real prospect
of peace. There have been only two lulls in all those years of fighting,
in 1992 and again in 1994 when the United Nations tried to broker
peace agreements and on the first occasion managed to hold an election in which the MPLA won 54% of the vote to UNITA's 34%. But
each time the deals collapsed and Savimbi went back to war.

The Angolan pattern of resource war has been repeated elsewhere
in Africa, most notably in the Democratic Republic of Congo, where
Uganda, Rwanda, Burundi, Angola, Namibia, Zimbabwe, Sudan and
Chad all became involved, together with a number of Congolese rebel
armies and Hutu rebels from Rwanda and Burundi. It has become a
maelstrom of plunder. With Mobutu gone, his corrupt successor Laurent
Kabila assassinated and Kabila's youthful son Joseph now trying to run
things, the central government's writ barely extends beyond the city
limits of the capital, Kinshasa, in the west of the country. The eastern
provinces, where most of the resource wealth is located, has no effective government at all. While the Congolese government emulated
Angola by funding its military operation with oil revenues, the other
combatants looted the eastern provinces of diamonds, gold, copper,
cobalt, ivory, timber and, most rewarding of all, a new wonder mineral
called col-tan. The name is short for columbite-tantalite and it is used
in the manufacture of cellphones, jet engines and the components that
maintain an electric charge in computer chips. When col-tan was first
discovered in 1998 the price was $29 for 500 grams; three years later
it was $200. The eastern Congo has some of the richest deposits of this
substance in the world.

Nor did the looting stop when peace agreements saw the foreign
armies leave the Congo in mid-2002. A special United Nations investigative team reported a few months later that as the armies withdrew
their governments set up criminal cartels to continue plundering the
resources. The report named 54 individuals involved, including top
Congolese officials, Ugandan and Rwandan army chiefs, a Zimbabwean
businessman named Johan Bredenkamp who has close ties to the

Mugabe government, and the Speaker of the Zimbabwe Parliament, Emmerson Mnangagwa, who is said to be President Mugabe's chosen successor and whom the UN report described as the "key strategist for the Zimbabwean branch of the elite network" operating the cartels. A South African company called Tandan, run by an Israeli businessman, Niko Shafer, was also named.[3]

* * *

But of all the misrule that is afflicting so much of Africa, none is so sad and so damaging to South Africa as the strange case of Robert Mugabe's madness in Zimbabwe. Sad because it is such a wonderfully endowed country which began its passage into independence with such high promise and now is being wilfully wrecked by the very leader who seemed so enlightened. Damaging because, as South Africa's most important neighbour with whom we have a shared history, its sudden plunge into irrational behaviour fills foreign investors and many South Africans with fears that the same could happen here. Fears which, as I have said, President Mbeki has not done enough to dispel.

But as a study in itself, Zimbabwe's catastrophic nosedive is a cautionary tale of how one man's egomania and obsession with power can destroy a country if its civil and state institutions are not strong enough to stop him.

I first caught a glimpse of Mugabe's egotism and hyper-sensitivity during an interview with him in December 1981, just 20 months after he had become prime minister of independent Zimbabwe and while he was still basking in international acclaim for his gestures of reconciliation towards the white Rhodesians his guerrillas had fought in that country's long and bitter liberation war. Mugabe interrupted the interview when I asked him about a young Dutch-born student named Kees de Jongh who had been summarily deported the week before. He dispatched his private secretary to fetch what he said was the incriminating evidence. The man returned a few moments later bearing two posters that had been found at a gas station, one of the prime minister and the other of the non-executive president, Canaan Banana. The posters had been mildly defaced with a felt pen: two devil's horns on the president's head and a small moustache and beard for Mugabe. They seemed innocent enough, but Mugabe was clearly agitated as he showed them to me. With short, mirthless chuckles he asked: "What do you make of someone who can do a thing like that?" I recall thinking at the time that Margaret Thatcher or even South Africa's P W Botha would count themselves lucky to get away with such light lampooning. But Kees de Jongh had been given 24 hours to leave the country.

If that revealed an intolerance of criticism, Mugabe soon afterwards revealed his ruthlessness in dealing with opposition. He had come to power with remarkable gestures of reconciliation, even inviting his bitter enemy, the hardline old white leader, Ian Smith, to State House and charming him with his reasonableness, and inviting his main black rival, Joshua Nkomo, leader of the Zimbabwe African People's Union (ZAPU) which had its power base among the Ndebele and Kalanga people of Matabeleland province, to join his cabinet as Home Affairs Minister. But from early 1982 Mugabe began to show an increasing resentment of Smith's white followers, accusing them, with some justification it must be said, of retaining racist attitudes and failing to respond to his gestures of reconciliation. More seriously, he turned on ZAPU and set about crushing it.

The trigger for this came when a renegade group of Nkomo's former guerrillas staged an uprising in Etumbane township on the outskirts of Zimbabwe's second city, Bulawayo, which turned into a two-day battle with government troops before it was put down. The incident occurred against a background of friction between members of the two former guerrilla armies and complaints that ZAPU was being short-changed in the coalition government. It was in itself not a truly serious threat to national security, but Mugabe seized on it to precipitate a showdown with Nkomo. As the leaders of his Zimbabwe African National Union-Patriotic Front (ZANU-PF) stepped up the rhetoric against ZAPU, Mugabe announced that a major arms cache had been discovered in Matabeleland. It was well known that both armies had cached arms around the country during the liberation war, but Mugabe used this as a pretext for launching a massive campaign to stamp out what he called an attempted ZAPU coup.

It was clearly a premeditated campaign, for a year earlier Mugabe had concluded an agreement with North Korea to train a special military unit that fell outside the command structures of the national army and answered directly to Mugabe's generals. In early 1983 Mugabe unleashed this new Fifth Brigade on the people of Matabeleland, accusing them of supporting dissidents from Nkomo's guerrillas. Likening Nkomo's role in the cabinet to "having a cobra in the house", Mugabe added that "the only way to deal effectively with a snake is to strike and destroy its head." He first demoted Nkomo, then fired him from the cabinet.

In a comprehensive book analyzing Mugabe's disastrous rule,

Martin Meredith, a veteran journalist and Africa specialist, estimates there were never more than 400 dissidents in Matabeleland, but the Fifth Brigade's operation turned into a full-scale war against the Ndebele and Kalanga people.[4] Mugabe first gave his men immunity from prosecution, then launched them into a campaign of unrestrained ruthlessness. Villagers were rounded up, marched to some central spot, then systematically beaten for hours. The names of alleged dissenters, often randomly chosen, were read from lists and they were publicly executed. The villagers would then be forced to sing songs praising ZANU-PF and to dance on the graves of their families and friends who had been killed and buried only moments before.[5]

At one point Mugabe even resorted to starving the people of southern Matabeleland. He closed shops, stopped food supplies and imposed harsh curfews. Nor did he make any bones about his indiscriminate harshness. "We have to deal with this problem quite ruthlessly," Meredith quotes him as telling an audience in Matabeleland at the height of the repression. "Don't cry if your relatives get killed in the process … Where men and women provide food for the dissidents, when we get there we eradicate them. We do not differentiate who we fight because we can't tell who is a dissident and who is not."[6]

As the terror raged Nkomo fled the country, while two of his former army commanders were arrested and charged with treason. When a court acquitted them, Mugabe rearrested them and held them in prison for the next four years. In December 1987 Nkomo capitulated and signed a unity accord with Mugabe which absorbed his party into ZANU-PF, effectively turning Zimbabwe into a one-party state – at least for the next 12 years.

There is no official figure of the number of casualties inflicted during this reign of terror in Matabeleland, but two investigations conducted concurrently by the Catholic Conference for Peace and Justice and the Zimbabwe Legal Resources Foundation compiled a report based on 2 000 sworn affidavits which estimated the number of people killed at 20 000.

What has driven this intelligent and articulate man to such levels of brutal power-hunger remains unclear. He was born and brought up in a Catholic mission run by Jesuit Fathers near Harare, which was then called Salisbury. Meredith believes this instilled in him a self-discipline that was "almost puritanical in its intensity". Mugabe graduated from a teacher-training school there, then went on to acquire six university degrees, in law and economics. One was from that South African political hothouse,

Fort Hare, where Mandela, Tambo and many other prominent ANC figures had their baptism; the other five were by correspondence while he was in Rhodesian prisons for his political activities. Later he went to Ghana where he became a devotee of its first liberation leader, Kwame Nkrumah, with his messianic vision of building a mighty United States of Africa. This instilled in Mugabe strong Africanist ideas, linking him ideologically to South Africa's Pan-Africanist Congress rather than to the non-racialism of the ANC. Above all he saw himself as a revolutionary, committed to the radical transformation of his country into an egalitarian people's state. He was bitterly opposed to a negotiated settlement of the conflict in white-ruled Rhodesia because of the compromises it would inevitably entail, and resented the pressure his independent black neighbours, Kenneth Kaunda in Zambia and Samora Machel in Mozambique, put on him to reach such a settlement at the Lancaster House conference in 1979. Yet once in power Mugabe embarked on his remarkable policy of compromise and racial reconciliation.

Some observers think that honeymoon was simply a facade Mugabe put on until he felt strong enough to embark on the Africanist revolution of his dreams. If so it was a good act. I think the answer is more psychological than ideological. I believe he enjoyed the international acclaim he was accorded at the beginning, but then weaknesses in his character – his huge ego and his obsession with power – caught up with him and as his star waned, particularly after Mandela's release outshone him, he resorted to a populist agrarian revolution to try to secure his place in history as an Africanist revolutionary hero.

For the first decade and a half of his presidency Mugabe made no effort to establish an egalitarian people's state. He may have mouthed the rhetoric in his early years, but once in power he neglected the rural poor notoriously – to a degree that shocked some of his old Jesuit mentors. He headed a corrupt regime whose members scrambled for farms, businesses and other perks while Mugabe secured his own position through a network of patronage that embraced old cronies, sycophants and family members. He had fought the liberation war on the land issue, expressing outrage that nearly half the farmland and two-thirds of the best commercial land was owned by 6 000 white farmers and vowing to redistribute it when victory was won. But when the time came he struck a deal with the white Commercial Farmers Union, and although Britain as the departing colonial power made substantial funds available for land resettlement few black peasants were in fact resettled. Eighteen months after independence the Mugabe government had bought up 435 000 acres of white farmland, but resettled fewer than 3 000 black peasants. In a pattern that was to become even more apparent in the years that followed, scores of government-owned farms were being handed out on leases to cabinet ministers, MPs, top civil servants and other senior members of the ruling party – few of which were put to productive use. Writing from Salisbury at the time Howard Barrell, who much later was to become editor of the *Mail & Guardian* in Johannesburg, warned presciently that "Robert Mugabe is sitting on a time bomb primed by his victory at the pre-independence poll: land hunger ... It constitutes a potential political threat both to his government and continued peace and stability in the country."[7]

The time bomb exploded in the mid-1990s when a newspaper exposed the full extent of the land corruption scandal. Farms had gone to a former minister of agriculture, to the head of Mugabe's office, to the commissioner of police and the former commander of the Fifth Brigade: in all 8% of commercial farmland had ended up in the hands of Mugabe's acolytes. Outraged, the British government, which at that point had spent £44 million to aid the land resettlement programme, stopped all further support. The government's unpopularity began to soar, but instead of responding to this Mugabe increased the size of his cabinet from 29 to 42 despite World Bank and IMF warnings to cut government spending.

In July 1997 another corruption scandal erupted. As disgruntled former guerrillas demanded that the government release money from a special compensation fund for their wartime injuries, it emerged that large sums had disappeared from the fund and there was nothing left to pay them. Again senior politicians and officials were said to be involved, including Mugabe's wife Grace. Hundreds of angry war veterans demonstrated in the streets of Harare, and to mollify them Mugabe appointed a commission of inquiry into the scandal – but it never reported.

Four months later the situation worsened when the War Veterans Association, now headed by an unsavoury character named Chenjerai "Hitler" Hunzvi, who boasted of his admiration for the Nazi leader, confronted Mugabe at State House and demanded compensation payments. The meeting is said to have turned ugly with Hunzvi's men threatening the President, who then made a series of extravagant promises. He committed the government to making a bonus payment of Z$50 000 and a monthly pension of Z$5 000 to each of some 60 000 veterans. He also offered them free education and health care. There was no budget for these payments, which knocked a Z$4,5 billion hole in the fiscus at a time when the Zimbabwe dollar was about 10 to the US dollar. This triggered a run on the Zimbabwe dollar which has continued ever since. By November 2002, it had collapsed to 1 500 to the US dollar on the parallel market and was still in free fall.

Later that month, after Hunzvi's men demanded land in addition to the cash payouts, Mugabe announced that 804 white-owned commercial farms would be expropriated without compensation – later increased to 3 900 or 95% of the white commercial farms. At this point the IMF and the World Bank suspended collaboration with the Zimbabwe government.

As the economy began to sputter and go into a tailspin, Mugabe perversely plunged his country into a major foreign war, sending 12 000 troops to the Democratic Republic of Congo to support Laurent Kabila in his fight against rebels supported by Uganda and Rwanda. Again it was a decision that stemmed from his enormous ego. Mugabe had clashed with Nelson Mandela over the definition of his own role as chairman of the 14-nation Southern African Development Community's Organ of Politics, Defence and Security. Mugabe argued that as the senior statesman of SADC – a status he was damned if he was going to yield to Mandela – he should be permanent chairman of the Organ, which should be an independent body headquartered in Harare. Mandela, who was chairman of SADC at the time, disagreed, insisting that the Organ should be a division of the regional organization with its chairman rotating among the national leaders as the SADC chairmanship itself did. With the issue still unresolved, Mugabe decided to assert his independence as acting chairman of the security body by joining with the presidents of Namibia and Angola in sending troops to the Congo. It was a decision that committed his financially strapped country to expenditure of US$1 million a day for the next four years.

With inflation and unemployment soaring, Zimbabweans grew increasingly resentful of the President's autocratic and wasteful behaviour. When Mugabe presented a new draft constitution with clauses that increased his already wide executive powers and allowed the government to expropriate land without compensation, a new opposition group calling itself the Movement for Democratic Change (MDC) formed around the trade union movement to oppose it at a national referendum. Led by former trade unionist Morgan Tsvangirai, the MDC managed to mobilize the popular discontent and stunned Mugabe by defeating him.

This was the turning point. Outraged at the injury to his pride Mugabe began lashing out at those he perceived to have humiliated him – the MDC, the white farmers and the international community, especially Britain. Turning to Hunzvi's veterans association, who by now had been joined by hundreds of opportunistic thugs too young ever to have been involved in the liberation war, Mugabe offered them the opportunity of looting farms and grabbing land in return for their services as a private militia. And so the land grabs began. The so-called "war veterans" invaded scores of commercial farms, staking out claims on them, appropriating vehicles and equipment and generally terrorizing, beating up and sometimes murdering the white farmers, their families and their black workers. It became an officially sanctioned campaign of intimidation and theft. Initially the Zimbabwe High Court declared the farm invasions illegal and on several occasions ordered that the trespassers be evicted, but on Mugabe's orders the police declined to evict them and ultimately, after Mugabe was able to pack the Supreme Court Bench, the invasions were legally condoned.

This also marked the start of Mugabe's campaign for the 2002 presidential election campaign. As the world now knows, it was a campaign of systematic violence and intimidation against the MDC and its supporters, and on election day itself of vote-rigging and stuffed ballot boxes that ensured Mugabe's re-election. All international observer teams rejected it as a stolen election except those from the ANC and the South African government, which, while acknowledging irregularities, pronounced the outcome "legitimate".

As I write this the situation in Zimbabwe is deteriorating rapidly. The agricultural economy, which used to account for 38% of the country's gross national product and provide sorely needed foreign exchange, has collapsed and the economy as a whole is in steep decline. Only 600 of the original 4 500 commercial farms are still functional, and some of them only partially. Tobacco exports, which used to account for 60% of the agricultural economy, are down to one-third what they were three years ago, while the cattle population is one quarter of what it was three years ago. Hundreds of thousands of farm workers are out of work : total unemployment is more than 70%, while inflation is 220% and rising fast. The Zimbabwe dollar, at parity with the British pound at independence in 1980, is now 2 200 to the pound on the black market. Basic commodities such as bread, milk and salt are almost unobtainable, while queues at filling stations stretch up to 2 km on the rare days when fuel is available.

Politically, Zimbabwe has been suspended from the Common-wealth, and the European Union, the United States and Australia have slapped a visa ban on Mugabe and 71 of his associates and frozen their assets, and are also refusing to deal with SADC if Zimbabwe is included in the deliberations.

Worst of all, the official assault on the farming community com-bined with a severe drought has turned this one-time food exporter into a starving nation. The country has run out of maize and wheat and there is no foreign exchange to import any. The World Food Pro-gramme estimates that six million people face starvation, while the World Health Organization estimates that at least a quarter of the pop-ulation are HIV positive. Put those two facts together and they spell a terrible prospect. Malnutrition hastens the onset of AIDS for those who are already HIV positive, which means hundred of thousands of Zim-babweans are facing an early death. To make matters worse Mugabe is manipulating food aid to starve MDC supporters, much as he did dur-ing the 1980s campaign against Nkomo's supporters.

Meanwhile a small privileged elite are living high on the hog. The Congo war may have helped impoverish the country, but it has enriched a few. By a deal struck with the Congolese government, diamonds extracted from a jointly owned concession at Mbuji-Mayi in eastern Congo are flown to Harare, then smuggled to Antwerp where they are sold. The proceeds, running into many millions of US dollars, are divid-ed among Zimbabwe's ruling elite. As Lord Robin Renwick, who was one of the chief architects of the Lancaster House agreement that gave Zimbabwe its independence, remarked to journalist John Carlin who investigated the racket: "The Zimbabwean army has been rented out in the Congo for the benefit of Mugabe and the mafia around him. Mugabe was always power-hungry," Renwick added, "but not, I thought, corrupt. I never imagined he would end up presiding over the most corrupt regime in Africa."[8]

* * *

What can be done about the malaise that afflicts so much of the African continent and has given it such a dismal reputation? The problem is that Africa's hopelessness is now so widely perceived that it has become a self-fulfilling prophecy, deterring investors from creating the new enter-prises that might arrest its downslide and causing a continuous brain-drain with thousands of African professionals and other enterprising spirits abandoning the continent annually. Somehow this vicious cycle must be turned around so that Africa's people can begin to regain their self-confidence through role models of achievement and success.

In his BBC Reith lectures more than a decade ago, Professor Ali Mazrui, the distinguished Kenyan intellectual, recommended what he called "the internal recolonization of Africa", by which he meant that the strongest country in each of the continent's four regions – Egypt in the north, South Africa in the south, Nigeria in the west and Kenya or Ethiopia in the east – should assume responsibility for establishing order, democratic rule and economic upliftment in its region. It was an unfortunate choice of words which the professor came to regret, and later at a seminar in Johannesburg he also noted wryly that some of the "doctors" who featured in his proposal were themselves "patients", a reference to Sani Abacha's military dictatorship in Nigeria at the time as well as corruption and misrule in Kenya and war in Ethiopia.

Yet his core idea, which was that Africa should cease looking outside for help but would have to uplift itself, had merit which was later to find a new expression in Thabo Mbeki's concept of "an African Renaissance". Mbeki first articulated this idea in April 1997 when he mistakenly saw the overthrow of Mobutu in the Congo and a short-lived ceasefire in Angola as signs of an African rebirth beginning. Although both countries were soon to slump back into conflict and corruption, Mbeki clung to the idea of putting together a programme to uplift the continent. "It is very directly in the interests of South Africa that there should be direct development in the rest of the continent," he told an interviewer. "I don't think you can have sustainable, successful development in this country if the rest of the continent is in flames."[9]

In 2000 Mbeki came up with a Marshall Plan for Africa, asking the developed world to invest urgently in the continent to remove the image of emaciated African children with begging bowls from the television screens of the world. A year later this evolved into a more detailed aid plan which Mbeki called the Millennium Africa Recovery Plan (MAP), which in turn formed the basis for discussions with other key African leaders, Presidents Olusegun Obasanjo of Nigeria, Abdoulaye Wade of Senegal and Abdelaziz Bouteflika of Algeria. What emerged was a more practical and hopefully more palatable proposal to put to the aid-weary major powers which the four leaders called the New Partnership for Africa's Development (Nepad) plan. In an effort to shake off the begging-bowl image, they presented the plan as a trade-off: Africa would commit itself to democracy, good governance, financial discipline and market-oriented policies in return for more help from the developed countries, especially by giving better access to Africa's exports.

The plan has obvious merit. It was drafted by Africans for Africans and so is free of any imperialist taint. Its aim is to end Africa's conflicts, encourage accountable government and achieve growth rates of between 7% and 8%. Its emphasis is on trade rather than aid, and to that end it seeks $64 billion annually in global assistance for investment and trade.

But the nub of it is a commitment to good governance and financial discipline. In its founding document, the 15 nations that have signed on to Nepad pledge themselves to work, both individually and collectively, to promote the principles of peace, security, democracy, good governance, human rights and sound economic management in their own countries and in the sub-regions of Africa. They undertake "to respect the global standards of democracy, the core components of which include political pluralism, allowing for the existence of several political parties and workers' unions, and fair, open and democratic elections."

Mbeki and his co-sponsors of Nepad know the developed countries are tired of pouring aid into Africa only to see it end up in the pockets and offshore accounts of corrupt leaders while the ordinary people sink ever deeper into poverty. They have pledged to set up a peer review mechanism.[10] They are also trying to widen the application of these commitments beyond Nepad's 15 signatories. To this end they have managed to convert the 39-year-old Organization of African Unity (OAU), which includes all the continent's 54 counties, into a new African Union (AU). The key difference between the old organization and the new one is that whereas a cardinal principle of the OAU was that no African country could interfere in another's affairs, a Constitutive Act setting up the AU – which has to be ratified by the various African legislatures to bring it into being – says the new organization should be able to intervene actively in wayward African countries to prevent genocide and crimes against humanity. It provides for sanctions against member countries which violate principles contained in the Constitutive Act, including "respect for democratic principles, human rights, the rule of law and good governance" – and in particular for unconstitutional changes of government. In other words, the AU will refuse to recognize military regimes that gain power through coups.

The Constitutive Act envisages the establishment of an African Court of Justice which can hear cases emanating from any of the member states on the basis of the Constitutive Act, a Human Rights Commission, an African Parliament and, in effect, Africa's own version of the UN Security Council, consisting of elected members with the power to advise, mediate and even intervene in a member country held to be a threat to the peace or violating human rights.

But here's the rub! How do these fine principles and all the mechanisms for guaranteeing good governance square with Mbeki's reluctance to take a stronger line against Mugabe's blatant misrule? What price peer review if the man whose brainchild this is cannot exercise it on his delinquent neighbour?

Mbeki and his colleagues were able to get the G-8 nations – the world's richest seven, the US, Japan, Germany, Britain, France, Italy and Canada, plus Russia – to sign on to Nepad at their summit in Kananaskis, Canada, in June 2002, but their pledges of help were lukewarm. The G-8 leaders were plainly sceptical of Africa's ability to deliver its side of the bargain. Zimbabwe is Nepad's credibility test, and so far Mbeki has failed to pass it. The G-8 were also sceptical of the AU's prospects for success after Mbeki and his colleagues were unable to prevent the election of Libya's Muammar Gadaffi, widely regarded as a rogue leader, onto its management committee.

What inhibits Mbeki in his dealings with Mugabe? In his defence it must be said that South Africa suffers from a number of restraining factors in the role it must play on the continent. Regional superpower though it may be, it has limited resources in the face of massive domestic demands. As I have noted earlier, it also suffers in the regional context from the same mixture of envy and resentment that the United States encounters globally. This is aggravated by the fact that South Africa is the new boy on the block, the last African country to be liberated from white minority rule and one which holds many IOUs from poorer states in its region who suffered greatly in its liberation struggle, so it would be resented if it were to start throwing its weight around.

South Africa must move delicately, and no one is more sensitive – indeed over-sensitive – to this than Mbeki. His entire political life was spent as a supplicant, pleading the ANC's cause, begging support, accepting refuge from whoever was willing to offer it and often at great cost to his hosts, and never, ever, jeopardizing any of this by meddling in their domestic affairs and certainly not by criticizing them publicly. It became a way of life, a political culture. And it is deeply embedded today in the psyche of the ANC exiles – if not in the minds of the internals and ex-prisoners such as Nelson Mandela who can and often do speak out much more sharply about the behaviour of Africa's delinquent leaders.

It must be said, too, that there are no easy options for bringing Mugabe to heel. Theoretically South Africa could close its borders with landlocked Zimbabwe, but that would precipitate a national catastrophe among a population already under stress. It could cut off the electricity that it supplies from its Eskom power grid, or simply slow down all cross-border traffic as the apartheid-era prime minister John Vorster did to Ian Smith in the 1970s to force him to the Lancaster House negotiating table. But again that would inflict hardship on the ordinary Zimbabweans while having little effect on the well-heeled ruling elite who care little for the plight of their people.

But in a lengthy interview with Mbeki it became clear that the main thing influencing him on Zimbabwe is a conviction that the intense concern with the issue reflects a racist perspective on the part of white South Africans particularly and the white developed world generally. As he sees it, the white world is indifferent to the suffering and death of millions of black people all over Africa, but becomes agitated when a handful of whites are harassed and have their farms confiscated in Zimbabwe. "The reason Zimbabwe is such a preoccupation here, in the United Kingdom and the United States and Sweden and everywhere," he said, "is because white people died, and white people were deprived of their property."

When I suggested that Zimbabwe was likely to be seen by the developed world as a test for the credibility of Nepad's commitment to good governance, the president showed a rare flash of anger. "Why is the question not asked, What about the Ivory Coast and Nepad?" he demanded. "You've had negotiations in Sudan, which broke down and have now resumed after 2 million people have died. Why doesn't anybody say, What about Sudan and Nepad? No, all they say is Zimbabwe, Zimbabwe, Zimbabwe.

"I'm not saying the things that are going on in Zimbabwe are right," he went on. "But I am saying the extraordinary preoccupation with what is going on in Zimbabwe in reality has got to do with white fears in South Africa. What they are afraid of is, Here are these black people across the border doing these terrible things to white people. What assurance do we have that they won't do the same thing to white people here? That's the issue. And that's all. A million people die in Rwanda and do the white South Africans care? Not a bit. You talk to them about the disaster in Angola, to which the apartheid regime contributed, and

327

they're not interested. Let's talk about Zimbabwe. Does anyone want to talk about the big disaster in Mozambique, from which it is now recovering? No. Let's talk about Zimbabwe. You say to them, Look at what is happening in the Congo. No, no, no, let's talk about Zimbabwe. Why? It's because 12 white people died!"

No doubt there is much truth in Mbeki's charge that many whites are shamefully indifferent to the plight of black people in Africa's many trouble spots, and that they are worried that what is happening to the white Zimbabweans might one day happen to them here. But it is not the whole truth. The fact is, what is happening in Zimbabwe is a major African tragedy in the making. Hundreds of thousands of black people are going to die there over the next few years, perhaps more than died in the Rwanda genocide, because of Mugabe's wilful destruction of the agricultural economy and the combination of starvation and AIDS this is going to cause. "I'm saying that Zimbabwe is a big obsession in this country," Mbeki said at one point in the interview. "It isn't anywhere else on the African continent."

I know this is wrong, that there is widespread dismay among black South Africans at the human tragedy unfolding in Zimbabwe, among many members of the ANC and of Cosatu and the SACP, including Mbeki's own brother, Moeletsi, who has been outspoken on the subject in his capacity as deputy chairman of the South African Institute of International Affairs.

But if what Mbeki says is true at a political level, if Africa, Nepad and the AU notwithstanding, really does not see the Zimbabwean crisis as a major issue and get active about it, then the bad neighbourhood will remain just that.

CHAPTER SIXTEEN

THE FOOT OF THE RAINBOW

*"We South Africans like to look on the dark
side of the moon. We sometimes can't believe that
we're actually doing OK."*
— MARIA RAMOS, D-G OF THE TREASURY.

As we approach the end of the first decade of the new South Africa, what is the status of Mandela's Covenant? Are we making progress towards building a rainbow nation at peace with itself and the world? The answer almost certainly is yes, although many South Africans will tell you and themselves otherwise. We have, as Maria Ramos says, this tendency to look on the dark side of things. Perhaps it is a psychology born of the insecurity of our past, of life in a land of struggle and wars, of oppression and abuse, of having been isolated and labelled a pariah among nations and always living with the dark unspoken expectation that a doomsday lay ahead, that sometime there surely had to be a day of reckoning. So we are slightly manic-depressive, given to extremes of over-reaction. It shows in our responses to our sports teams. When they win we are ecstatic, convinced we are on the way to becoming world champions. When they lose we flagellate the useless team and fire the coach.

"I think South Africans are very hard on themselves," Archbishop Desmond Tutu replied when I asked him, the single most truly non-racial person I know, whether he thought we were making progress towards becoming a rainbow nation. He had just returned from a church conference in Germany where he was shocked by the attitudes that still separate the western and eastern sectors of that country. "Here are people who are of the same ethnic group, who speak the same language, and yet they are still very far from being reconciled," the little archbishop said." And here we are with our many races and ethnic groups and our 11 official languages. I think it's amazing that we have the level of stability that we have. Look at Northern Ireland, look at Yugoslavia. We could so easily have gone that way." But we should not have unrealistic expectations, Tutu warns. It will take time to build a sense of national unity across such a wide spectrum of diversity with such a history of conflict. But he is encouraged by his experiences as head of the Truth and Reconciliation Commission, where he witnessed many remarkable acts of personal forgiveness. "I think we are going to make it," he said. "The world needs a South Africa that has succeeded."

What is the measure of success? When people can relate to each other naturally but without trying to wipe out their differences, Tutu says. "I don't want to be a white person. I just want to be me, and I want you to be you, gloriously you, and for us to celebrate this diversity. It's enriching. Of course there will be moments when we say, They are doing this to me because I am black, or because I am white. It happens even among people of the same ethnic group. People will say, Oh he does that because he comes from a particular area, or because he didn't go to such and such a university."

It is a matter of inculcating a culture of mutual respect and tolerance. The differences of race, colour, culture, of the religious and the secular, of different perspectives and world views, will all remain, but as a society we must learn to contain them within a broad entente and hopefully infuse all with a transcendent sense of common nationhood. To mix the metaphors, the rainbow nation must be a mosaic society, not a melting pot, and for it to hold together and prosper we must be constantly aware of Isaiah Berlin's warning about Schiller's bent twig: groups can live together peacefully and can even be bent a little, but bend one too far with a sense of collective grievance or humiliation and it will lash back painfully. Like Desmond Tutu, I believe South Africans are learning that. We have made considerable progress along the rocky road from institutionalized racism to mutual tolerance.

We have made progress in other ways, too. A decade ago we were not only racially divided and locked in social conflict, we were also in a fiscal mess. We were politically and economically, even psychologically, isolated in a globalizing world, inflation and interest rates were sky-high, our businesses were inefficient and uncompetitive, hiding behind high protective tariffs, and economic growth had been in decline for years.

Today all that has changed. Our apartheid society has become integrated across the board, from schools to workplaces to boardrooms and even bedrooms. We have a functioning multi-party democracy with regular free, fair and peaceful elections underpinned by the world's most progressive Constitution and protected by perhaps the world's finest panel of judges in the Constitutional Court. Economically, too, South Africa is transformed. The economy has averaged 3% growth a year over that decade, it is projected to average 3,6% from 2003 to 2006, it has stayed above the international average through the post-September 11 global recession, and it has shown the least degree of volatility of all emerging economies since 1994. It is in far better shape than the Latin American giants of Brazil and Argentina.

But daunting problems remain. Despite the improvements the economy is still too sluggish to get the country on the high road to real development, unemployment is high, the skills level is low, there is a huge wealth gap, crime persists, foreign investment is only a meagre 1% of gross domestic product, the AIDS pandemic is inflicting great tragedy on the population, and although the wars in Angola and the Democratic Republic of Congo are ending, Zimbabwe continues to blight the region so that the neighbourhood remains bad. How to tackle these problems is the challenge that faces us in the decade ahead.

* * *

South Africa's problems are dialectical: they interact with each other and feed off one another. Each of the critical issues has powerful implications for the others. Poor education leads to a low skills level, which deters investment, which slows growth, which aggravates unemployment, which increases the crime rate, which deters investment, and so on.

Somehow there must be a dynamic intervention in that process to reverse its cycle. An improved educational system would do it, and much attention is being given to that. But that is a slow road. As I noted earlier, it takes 21 years and nine months to produce a new skilled worker, and first you must produce a new corps of skilled teachers in the face of competition for their skills from much better paying occupations. Something faster is needed.

That brings me to the conclusion that if the rainbow nation is ultimately to be attained, it will have to be via the pot of gold supposedly at its foot. As Bill Clinton famously told his campaign office: "It's the economy, stupid!" Get the growth rate up above 5% for five to ten years in a row and the cycle will turn into a virtuous one: reduced unemployment will bring down the crime rate, it will begin to close the wealth gap, which will reduce racial and class tensions, which will increase political stability – all of which will make the country more attractive to foreign investors.

South Africa's macro-economic policy has been acclaimed in all the right circles, but is it has not produced the growth rates needed to start that virtuous cycle. Why? Because I do not believe investors rush to invest in a country simply because it has an orthodox economic policy. They invest where they see growth. Because that is where they believe they can make money. So simply liberalizing the economy and then waiting for the foreign investors to come does not work. One must produce growth first to attract them. How?

I am indebted to Derek Keys for a lesson in what is perhaps the simplest and most fundamental law of economics. It is that there are only two ways to make an economy grow – by increasing investment, or by improving productivity. Keys reckons improved productivity would deliver not much more than 1% growth. So getting more investment is vital. Again the question is how? If you cannot get foreign investment until you get growth and you cannot get growth until you get foreign investment, are you not trapped in a Catch 22 situation?

The point is that growth, like charity, begins at home. The foreign investors will not come if they see the locals holding back. They will come only when they hear a buzz of excitement coming from the local investors and when they see the growth figures start to rise. So an effective strategy must start with boosting local investment.

Here, I think, is where South Africa needs to modify its neo-liberal approach. It is not working for us, and it has not worked for a number of Latin American and East European countries which have had slow and volatile growth. The lesson is that one-size-fits-all formulae are no good, whether they emanate from Washington or pre-perestroika Moscow. Economic jackets, strait or otherwise, must be tailored to fit individual circumstances, as the more successful examples of India, China and Vietnam have shown. This does not mean South Africa should abandon its GEAR policy or undertake a radical change of course. But some modifications are needed to meet our special circumstances.

The crux of the problem is that South Africa has a double-decker economy – its First World sector and its Third World sector – and what is working for those on the upper deck of this economic bus is not working for those on the lower deck. So unemployment is increasing and the wealth gap is widening.

It is a question of skills. The new globalized economy places a premium on skills. Those at the top of the bus have skills, while those on the lower deck do not. Which means that while those on the upper deck are prospering, growing numbers of those down below are unemployed and rapidly becoming unemployable – and if nothing is done about it South Africa faces the socially dangerous prospect of this unemployment becoming generationally repetitive. The children of the unemployed will themselves be unemployable.

There is a further troubling feature to this double-decker bus. Those on the top deck are a multiracial group. It used to be a whites-only deck, but now it is integrated. They are all getting on pretty well, working together, making money together, their kids going to the same schools and universities. It is a rainbow deck. But those down below are nearly all black, just the odd pinched face of a poor white here and there. And another thing, there is no stairway from the lower deck to the upper one. If you are unskilled you cannot climb up to the top of the bus.

A single neo-liberal macro-economic policy, which is what South Africa has, is insufficient to deal with this dual economy. It may be good for the skilled sector, but not for the unskilled. What is needed is a two-pronged strategy to cater for the different needs of both. The developed sector must be encouraged and energised to build on the good start it has made. It is this sector that will attract the foreign investors. But the unskilled sector, which is far larger, needs a different set of strategies, not only for humanitarian reasons, though those are important enough, but to draw them into the economy from which they are now excluded so that they can begin to contribute their huge numbers to its growth and also build a stairway to the top.

* * *

The developed sector is actually doing fine, although as President Mbeki's International Investment Council, a panel of friendly global tycoons, keeps telling him, the country needs to sell itself better. Considering how effectively the ANC sold its case to the world when it was a struggling exile movement, its failure to do so now is puzzling. It has to overcome the bad neighbourhood image, and it has to overcome the widely held perception that the South African economy is all about mining and agriculture. It must make investors aware that the new South Africa is shifting to become a high-technology, high-value manufacturing economy. The rapid growth of the motor industry is evidence of this. So, too, is its Information Technology sector. South Africa is the 23rd largest country in terms of IT investment; it is the fourth largest in networked PCs; it is 23rd in world-wide telecommunications spending, and 18th in terms of internet hosts.[1]

333

Learning what a country is good at producing is important, says Dani Rodrik, an economist at Harvard's Kennedy School of Government, because that can guide investments of other entrepreneurs.[2] The motor industry has already demonstrated the truth of this, with the success of BMW and Daimler-Benz's operations in South Africa encouraging Toyota Japan to make a large direct investment in Toyota SA. Harvard's Jeremy Sachs believes South Africa is also potentially good at a range of other middle-technology industries, such as textiles and clothing, generic drug production, consumer appliances, food processing and some simple forms of assembly operations.[3] The government could replicate its hugely successful Motor Industry Development Programme, which gives manufacturers export credits to reduce import duties, to attract foreign manufacturers into some of these sectors. It would enable them to use South Africa as a comparatively cheap but efficient base for manufacturing export goods, while at the same time entering the South African domestic market cheaply with their foreign-made goods.

But what is needed above all is to build a closer partnership, a social contract if you will, between government and business. They need to forge a greater unity of purpose, both to act more effectively and to avoid costly misunderstandings. In July 2002 a draft government proposal for a mining charter that envisaged blacks owning more than 51% of new mining operations by 2015 was leaked to the media, causing a panic in the investor community that resulted in a staggering R84-billion being whipped out of mining shares on the Johannesburg Stock Exchange. Eventually government and business were able to negotiate a compromise charter, but it was a brutal illustration of how costly a blunder stemming from the lack of a common vision between the two can be.

Too often South African business leaders whinge to their foreign associates, painting a bleak picture of a government they feel does not understand business and keeps committing acts of folly that are hurting the economy. "Things are going down the tubes," is a common phrase. This is hardly calculated to encourage foreigners to invest here, so that ultimately the bad-mouthing by the local business community is doing as much damage as, if not more than, the supposedly foolish acts of the government.

While it is certainly true that government's understanding of business and market forces is sometimes defective – apartheid allowed few black people to acquire any meaningful business experience – it is equally true that few in business have an understanding of politics. The South African economy has always been dominated by the English-speaking white community, who have been on the political sidelines for a hundred years. They have not had a political leader since Cecil John Rhodes at the end of the nineteenth century; even in opposition politics they have mostly followed Afrikaner leaders. Of government they know nothing. Unlike other democracies where individuals shuttle between top jobs in government and the private sector, South Africa has no Robert McNamaras or Dick Cheneys or Michael Bloombergs, with experience of both.

The result is a failure on the part of business to understand the political imperatives with which Mbeki has to deal. They berate the President because he does not do exactly what they want, failing to appreciate the mounting pressures he has to deal with in his own constituency where huge numbers have not reaped any benefits at all from his market-friendly reforms and some are worse off than before. There is no appreciation of the tensions the government has to manage between securing investment and bringing about greater equity in the economy. Nor even, for that matter, of the imperative necessity of greater economic equity. Having forsaken nationalization, the government is trying to redress the gross imbalance between white and black shares in the economy through policies of affirmative action and black empowerment. While business pays lip service to the principle underlying these policies, it shudders when they are applied. Mbeki says he has to push them – and when he does there is a panic, with fears that South Africa is starting to go down the road to Zimbabwe-style confiscations.

Yet redressing the imbalance is not only a political necessity, it is in the long-term interests of business itself and the security of the white population as a whole. Amy Chua, a Chinese Filipino now teaching law at Yale, offers a stark warning of how globalization is adding explosively to the tensions between economically dominant minorities and indigenous majority populations around the world. Globalization's free-market policies are making the rich richer and the poor poorer, she points out, and where the rich are minorities, as the Chinese are in the Philippines and much of Southeast Asia, and the poor are the indigenous majority, the resentment becomes dangerous. Chua's favourite aunt, she tells us, had her throat slit by her Filipino chauffeur out of bitter resentment of her conspicuous wealth and racially arrogant attitudes. The combination of free-market policies and democracy in such

335

situations, Chua suggests, is particularly dangerous, because then the poor hold political power while the increasingly resented ethnic minority commands the economy – opening the way for political demagogues to exploit ethnic hatreds for political advantage.[4]

Mbeki knows this very well, which I sense is one of the reasons he is so tense about Zimbabwe. He resents white South Africa's opposition to what he calls the deracialization of the economy and sees it as a replication of the same mindset that failed to bring about a voluntary reapportionment of land ownership in Zimbabwe. It's all about property, he says. Whites don't mind losing political power, but don't touch their property. In other words, don't touch their wealth.

While I disagree with Mbeki's interpretation of the Zimbabwe crisis, which I believe is more about Mugabe's power hunger than it is a mass popular uprising and clamour for white farms, I think his concern about business's defensive reaction to his strategies to achieve greater economic equity is justified. I am reminded of a wisecrack by Archbishop Desmond Tutu during the struggle days. Referring to the attitudes of white South Africans as the old regime played games with various power-sharing formulae, Tutu remarked: "Everyone is in favour of change, so long as things remain the same."

Mbeki is emphatic. "When you talk about the creation of a non-racial South Africa," he says, "it's not only about political institutions and the vote. It's got to be across the board. There has got to be deracialization of the economy as well." He would prefer the business community to come forward with its own proposals about how this should be done rather than wait for the government to push it into making the changes. That would mean less acrimony and less risk of accidents like the leaked draft mining charter.

"What I think needs to happen is that the business people should say, I am a banker and I think these are the things we need to do in our sector to contribute to the overall process of the deracialization of the economy. If they want to express that by way of a banking charter, that's fine. Or they can do it in any other way. The critically important issue is that the initiative should come from the property owners," Mbeki says.[5]

* * *

But that still leaves the bottom deck of the bus. Business is right when it says putting capital in the hands of a black entrepreneurial class is not going to trickle down to the mass of the black population any more than if it had stayed in white hands. Blacks may argue otherwise, that whites have no long-term confidence in the new South Africa and will not invest here unless the costs are low and the profits quick. But the evidence so far is that black empowerment has not increased black employment. The economic imperatives of globalization are colour-blind. All it has done is ensure that the top of the bus is not a whites-only deck, which in itself is vitally important because it means it is no longer just a rich ethnic minority sitting up there. But we still have the problem of the overcrowded bottom deck.

President Mbeki says skills training is the key. The government has set up a skills development fund and he feels business should be making better use of it than it is. In the course of an interview he recounted a visit to a German-owned automobile components factory near Pretoria, where he said half the trainees were apprentices employed by the company, and half were unemployed youths from the Pretoria area. "They are doing this because the sector is developing fast," Mbeki said. "When new activity is generated they will be looking for people with skills, and then these young people who were unemployed because they had no skills will get jobs."

But while skills training is obviously vital, it is not enough. What South Africa needs, I believe, is a state-driven public works programme on the scale of Franklin D Roosevelt's New Deal which put millions of Americans to work during the Great Depression. There are already a number of state-sponsored public works programmes run at community level. One of these, the *Zivusemi* (lift yourselves up) programme in Gauteng province, pays people in local communities a small allowance to tackle projects in their communities, such as renovating schools or improving access roads to townships. But what I think is needed is a national programme to build vital infrastructure that is big enough to capture the public imagination and energize the nation.

Choosing the right projects will require some lateral thinking, and I certainly do not know enough about the country's infrastructural needs to make concrete suggestions. But simply to illustrate the concept let me offer a thought. The economic geography of South Africa is unique in that its industrial heartland, the Pretoria-Johannesburg-Witwatersrand complex where 65% of the GDP is generated, is in the centre of the country 600 km to 1 500 km from the seaports. To get to the ports goods have to be transported along a narrow-gauge railway system built in the nineteenth century, which means the trains are short and slow by international standards. At the same time, as our volume of exports swells, the ports are becoming congested and ships are beginning to bypass them. Together these two factors are becoming a serious bottleneck in our important export drive. So why not take 1% of our R250-billion budget and engage large numbers of unemployed people for a massive labour-intensive project to widen the railway track and enlarge the port facilities. Negotiate an agreement with the trade unions to pay these people the equivalent, say, of the old-age pension which in February 2003 was R700 a month. Such a project could no doubt be undertaken more efficiently and economically by contracted companies, and the conventional argument against such public works projects is that they are not a long-term solution to unemployment: when the project is completed the workers are unemployed again. But a New Deal project of the kind I have suggested could be combined with on-the-job skills training to help the workers find other jobs afterwards and uplift the general skills level of the country. Above all it would re-establish the dignity and satisfaction of work for a large sector of the population now afflicted by the demoralization and other harmful psychological effects of unemployment, a factor that is important not only for the workers themselves but also for their families, particularly their children. It would help build a national work ethic to counter the culture of entitlement now afflicting so many in our society. All of which would be a human investment of great importance, as much as the improved infrastructrure itself.

But there is more to be done than this to mobilize the people on the lower deck of our economic bus.

Thirty-five percent of South Africa's economically active population work in the informal sector, according to Frances Lund of Natal University's Informal Sector Research Unit, and their numbers are growing fast.[6] It is an amorphous category of people who work for themselves in unregistered activities and pay no tax, and ranges in a continuum from what is called the survivalist segment, like street vendors, to bigger and more dynamic operations which sometimes employ a small staff. These are the people at the bottom of our bus, and the fascinating thing about this lower deck is that it is packed with energy, creativity and resilience. It's just that the people have great difficulty growing their enterprises. They need help to do that.

The informal sector is ballooning everywhere in the developing world as globalization, with its downsizing and outsourcing, drives more people out of the formal economy. It accounts for between 40%

and 60% of the total workforce in most of the developing countries. In some of these, informal workers are craftsmen and -women who work from home and contribute to key export industries such as garments, textiles and footwear. In Mexico the informal economy contributes about 12% of the country's gross national product, in Asia it ranges from 17% to 48%, and in India it is a whopping 62%. In South Africa it is 7%.[7] There is obviously room for growth there. What is needed are strategies to help it grow. When it does grow the migration will turn around, and successful informal-sector operators will begin to move into the formal sector.

The first thing needed is to recognize the informal sector is an important job creator and contributor to the national economy. It must be accepted that the city-centre traders are not a nuisance but a permanent and important part of the city. The different sectors should be organized into viable trading areas, provided with proper storage facilities and linked to the tourist industry. There should also be training programmes for them in simple skills such as basic accounting. But they need more than that, too. They need financial help to improve themselves.

Three-quarters of the adult population of South Africa are not bankable, in that they have no legal title to property or possessions that they can use as collateral to get a loan from a bank. That means they are locked in a poverty trap. If you have nothing and you cannot raise a loan to start a small enterprise of your own, you cannot begin to improve your circumstances. Millions of our people are in that situation. Helping to lever them out by enabling them to raise loans would transform many of their lives and transform the economic face of the country. For years their only recourse has been to private loan sharks, known in the vernacular as the *mashonisa* (the sinkers) who charge extortionate rates of interest.

The Peruvian economist, Hernando de Soto, makes a compelling case in his seminal work, *The Mystery of Capitalism*, for giving the poor in the developing world formal, legally recognized property rights to the land they occupy but to which, because of bureaucratic tangles and outdated legal systems, they do not have title. Do that, says De Soto, and they will be able to turn their assets into liquid capital to generate new wealth. That, he contends, is the key to the mystery of capitalism, of why the Western countries have been able to develop and the rest have not. You cannot, as he puts it, build capitalism without capital.

De Soto talks of economic apartheid, with a relatively small elite who have access to formal property living inside a "bell jar" of economic access to the privileges that formal property provides. The remainder live outside. The bell-jar makes capitalism a private club, De Soto says.[8]

He and his research team have done extensive work in developing countries, and report findings that the poor of the world have accumulated an astonishing number of assets. Their tally for Egypt alone was US$ 240-billion, or thirty times more than the value of all the shares on the Cairo Stock Exchange. "By our calculations," writes De Soto, "the total value of the real estate held but not legally owned by the poor of the Third World and former communist nations is at least $9,3-trillion. This is about twice as much as the total circulating US money supply . . . (and) more than twenty times the total direct foreign investment into all Third World countries in the ten years after 1989."[9]

But all this is "dead capital." It cannot be used as collateral to raise loans to generate additional wealth. You need to have legally enforceable transactions on property rights, with mortgages and accountable addresses, to do that. De Soto's solution, therefore, is to cut out the red tape and revamp the legal system so that the poor can be given legal title to the assets they own. Then their dead capital will come to life.

This is a great and valuable insight. It highlights the double value of the new South Africa's massive provision of housing for the black community and the need for a major programme to assess and grant legal title for the land and shacks occupied by the millions living in informal settlements.

But De Soto's idea does have snags. As any banker will tell you, one of the most difficult tasks in the business is assessing the granting of loans. One has to judge whether the proposed enterprise is a viable one, then whether the person applying for the loan has the ability to make it work. If you get it wrong on either count and the enterprise fails, you will dispossess the humble defaulter of the only asset he has. It could sow large-scale catastrophe, and even cause unrest as there would almost certainly be community resistance when the lending institutions arrived in townships to attach the property of poor families.

More appropriate, perhaps, is the example of the Grameen Bank in Bangladesh which grants tiny loans without collateral to the poorest of the poor in rural villages. Founded in 1976 by a Bangladeshi economics professor, Muhammad Yunus, the bank grants loans of as little as 50 taka, or just a few dollars, to help poor people start or upgrade small informal-sector enterprises. It charges interest rates of between 5% and

20%, calculated on a declining basis and astonishingly claims a repayment rate of more than 95% as borrowers try to maintain a good credit rating so that they can come back for more. In September 2002, the bank reported that it had 2,4-million borrowers and that it was operating in 60% of all the villages of Bangladesh. It has clearly had a significant impact on the lives of the poor in one of the world's poorest countries.

Significantly, too, 95% of Grameen's borrowers are women. The bank now lends only to women, saying it finds them a much better credit risk than men and more responsible managers of meagre resources.

There are some micro-lending operations in South Africa, but they are small and isolated. In every way, much more attention needs to be focussed on the informal sector and the very poor. The government's macro-economic policies are indeed praiseworthy and the top of the bus is doing well. But there is no trickle-down effect. We need strategies for the lower deck and if those masses can be better mobilized I believe there will in fact be a trickle-up effect that will boost the entire economy.

Uplifting the poor in the globalized world is a global challenge, and in this, too, South Africa must become a pathfinder. It is the key to our domestic success, to ending the legacy of economic apartheid as we have done in the political and social spheres. To achieve it we must not feel hidebound by the "Washington consensus" and its orthodox neo-liberal economic formula. That is not a credo. We must make our own modifications and march to our own drummer. As De Soto says in his concluding chapter: "I am convinced that capitalism has lost its way in developing and former communist nations ... With its victory over communism, capitalism's old agenda for economic progress is exhausted and requires a new set of commitments. It makes no sense continuing to call for open economies without facing the fact that the economic reforms under way open the doors only for small and globalized elites and leave out most of humanity."[10] We should not be afraid that innovation will scare away the foreign investors. When they see growth, they will come no matter what policies produced it.

I believe this country has the political courage and innovative intelligence to do this. We have demonstrated that in the political and social spheres South Africa has achieved remarkable things in this first decade of its new incarnation. It is a difficult country to govern and it is beset with many problems. It has a wildly diverse population of disputatious people who are both crazy and creative and, as I have said, somewhat manic-depressive. It is an exciting place to live in because it is at the cutting edge of so many of the world's most challenging problems. Whenever I spend time in one of the world's more mature democracies, as I do from time to time, I am reminded of that old pop song of the Sixties: "Heaven is a place where nothing ever happens."

So in the final analysis I am confident that we shall fulfill Nelson Mandela's pledged Covenant and attain the rainbow nation. It will not come easily and it will not come soon. But that we shall get there I am as certain as anyone can be in this uncertain world. When you have just escaped Armageddon, that is no time to become a pessimist.

CHRONOLOGY

1486 Portuguese explorer Bartholomeu Dias rounds the Cape.

1492 Christopher Columbus reaches America.

1497 Vasco da Gama pioneers the Cape sea route to the Far East.

1652 Dutch settlement under Jan van Riebeeck at the Cape.

1688 Arrival of French Huguenot settlers at the Cape.

1702 Xhosa people and Boers first meet in the Eastern Cape.

1795 First British occupation of the Cape.

1803 Dutch Batavian Republic at the Cape.

1805 Second British occupation of the Cape.

1834 Emancipation of slaves at the Cape.

1836 Beginning of the Great Trek by Afrikaners into the interior.

1843 British annex Natal.

1852 Transvaal gains independence as a Boer Republic.

1854 Orange Free State gains independence as a Boer Republic.

1867 Discovery of diamonds.

1886 Discovery of gold on the Witwatersrand.

1899 Anglo-Boer War begins.

1902 Anglo-Boer War ends with Peace of Vereeniging.

1910 Union of South Africa founded with merging of the conquered Boer Republics of Transvaal and Orange Free State and the British Colonies of the Cape of Good Hope and Natal.

1911 South African Party under leadership of Prime Minister Louis Botha established in Bloemfontein.

1912 African National Congress founded to resist Native Land Act.

1913 Native Land Act makes provision for reserves for black occupation, prohibiting black land ownership elsewhere.

1913 Afrikaner National Party founded.

1915 Capture of South West Africa (later Namibia) from Germany.

1918 Nelson Mandela born.

1919 South Africa given League of Nations mandate to administer South West Africa.

1920 Louis Botha dies and General Jan Smuts becomes leader of the SAP and Prime Minister.

1924 Nationalist-Labour pact defeats Smuts's SAP, General Barry Hertzog becomes first Nationalist Prime Minister.

1934 Fusion of National Party and SAP to form United Party with Hertzog as Prime Minister, Smuts as Deputy. Daniel Malan breaks away, forms "Purified" National Party.

1936 Second Native Trust and Land Act further restricts black land ownership, setting aside 13% of South Africa as reserves for black people.

1939 Hertzog defeated as United Party splits over going to war against Germany. Smuts becomes wartime Prime Minister.

1942 Thabo Mbeki born.

1948 Nationalist-Afrikaner Party coalition wins election on apartheid platform. Malan becomes Prime Minister.

1950 Suppression of Communism Act and Group Areas Act passed.

1952 ANC's Defiance Campaign begins.

1953 Nationalists win election with increased majority.

1954 Malan retires, Hans Strijdom becomes Prime Minister and intensifies apartheid.

1955 Congress of the People adopts the Freedom Charter.

1956 Treason Trial begins. Thabo Mbeki joins ANC Youth League.

1958 Nationalists win increased electoral majority. Strijdom dies and Hendrik Verwoerd becomes Prime Minister.

1959 Promotion of Bantu Self-Government (Bantustan) Act passed. Pan-Africanist Congress (PAC) breaks away from the ANC with Robert Sobukwe as president. Progressive Party breaks away from the United Party.

1960 Sharpeville massacre. State of Emergency declared. Attempt on Verwoerd's life. ANC and PAC banned. End of African parliamentary representation by three white MPs.

1961 Treason trial ends with the acquittal of all accused. South Africa becomes a republic outside the Commonwealth. Nationalists win an increased electoral majority. First acts of sabotage take place.

1962 Sabotage made a capital crime. House arrest introduced. Nelson Mandela arrested. Thabo Mbeki leaves for exile.

1963 Ninety-day detention without trial introduced. Mass trials begin.

1963 Looksmart Ngudle becomes the first political detainee to die in Security Police custody.

1964 Rivonia Trial begins. Mandela and other ANC leaders sentenced to life imprisonment.

1965 180-day detention without trial introduced.

1966 Nationalists again win election with increased majority. Verwoerd assassinated. John Vorster becomes Prime Minister and introduces intensified security laws. Thabo Mbeki graduates from Sussex University with a master's degree in economics.

1969 Steve Biko forms the South African Students Organisation (Saso), a precursor of the black consciousness movement. Thabo Mbeki goes to Moscow to enter the Lenin Institute of Social Studies and, a year later, undergo military training.

1974 Thabo Mbeki marries Zanele Dlamini in London.

1975 Thabo Mbeki becomes acting chief ANC representative in Swaziland. Elected to the ANC's National Executive Committee.

16 June 1976 Soweto student uprising begins.

December 1976 Thabo Mbeki becomes ANC representative in Nigeria.

1977 Steve Biko banned. Black Consciousness organisations outlawed.

17 August 1977 Steve Biko detained.

6 September 1977 Security Police "Day Squad" interrogates Biko.

12 September 1977 Steve Biko dies.

February 1978 Thabo Mbeki appointed political secretary to ANC president Oliver Tambo, as well as director of information, based in Lusaka.

1978 Information Department scandal leads to downfall of John Vorster. P W Botha becomes Prime Minister.

1980 Zimbabwe becomes independent.

1982 Mandela and three other ANC leaders transferred from Robben Island to Pollsmoor Prison in suburban Cape Town.

1983 P W Botha introduces a new constitution providing for separate White, Coloured and Indian Chambers of Parliament, but still leaving black Africans unrepresented. Botha becomes Executive President.

1983 Heavily boycotted black township elections take place.

1983 President Mugabe uses North Korean-trained Fifth Brigade to crush Joshua Nkomo's opposition ZAPU party in Matabeleland. Nkomo flees to London.

September 1984 Mass black township uprisings begin. P W Botha declares State of Emergency.

27 June 1985 Murder of the "Cradock Four".

1986 Broederbond chairman Pieter de Lange meets Thabo Mbeki at Ford Foundation conference in New York. Attempt on Thabo Mbeki's life by a South African military officer in Lusaka.

February 1986 Olusegun Obasanjo, co-chairman of the Common wealth Eminent Persons Group, meets Mandela in Pollsmoor Prison.

May 1986 Defence Minister Magnus Malan orders attacks on refugee camps in Zambia, Botswana and Zimbabwe, aborting Commonwealth EPG mission to SA.

August 1987 Frederik van Zyl Slabbert leads a group of Afrikaners to meet the ANC in Dakar, Senegal.

November 1987 Professor Willie Esterhuyse leads a group of Afrikaners to meet the ANC in Britain. Eleven similar meetings followed over the next four years. Govan Mbeki released from Robben Island prison under restrictions.

December 1987 Joshua Nkomo capitulates, signs unity accord with Robert Mugabe.

345

May 1988 Special committee of government officials headed by Niel Barnard, head of the National Intelligence Service, begins a series of secret meetings with Mandela in prison.

December 1988 Mandela moved to head warder's house in the grounds of Victor Verster prison near Paarl to facilitate secret meetings.

2 February 1989 President Botha suffers a stroke, resigns as leader of the National Party. F W de Klerk takes over party leadership.

5 July 1989 President Botha meets Prisoner Mandela at Tuynhuys.

8-13 July 1989 Lausanne colloquium between ANC economists and government officials.

14 August 1989 P W Botha resigns as President, F W de Klerk takes over.

6 September 1989 National Party wins general election. President de Klerk vows during the campaign "never to speak with terrorists".

12 September 1989 Thabo Mbeki and Jacob Zuma meet secretly with intelligence chiefs in Lucerne, Switzerland.

15 October 1989 Walter Sisulu and five other black political leaders released from prison.

19 October 1989 Almond Butana Nofomela makes statement to Lawyers for Human Rights, leading to exposure of police hit-squad activities.

2 February 1990 President de Klerk announces unbanning of ANC, PAC, SACP and other black political organisations.

11 February 1990 Nelson Mandela released.

April 1990 ANC, Cosatu and SACP economists meet in Harare to draft an economic policy. Thabo Mbeki returns to South Africa.

21 March 1990 Namibia becomes independent.

2 May 1990 ANC and government leaders meet and sign historic Groote Schuur Accord charting the way to negotiations.

July 1991 ANC national conference at Durban-Westville University. Canadian aid agency visits SA and recommends formation of a policy body to construct a macro-economic policy for the ANC. Macro Economic Research Group (MERG) established.

21-22 December 1991 Congress for a Democratic South Africa (Codesa) at World Trade Centre, near Johannesburg Airport.

February 1992 Nelson Mandela makes his first visit to economic summit in Davos, Switzerland.

March 1992 President de Klerk wins whites-only referendum to approve negotiations with ANC. ANC economists hold Mont Fleur scenarios. Trade unionists, meeting separately, draft "Economic Policy in Cosatu" document.

May 1992 Codesa-2 convenes, then breaks down. ANC policy conference drafts "Ready to Govern" document.

16 June 1992 ANC-led alliance begins "rolling mass action" camapign.

17 June 1992 Zulu hostel dwellers murder 38 in Boipatong massacre.

7 September 1992 ANC demonstrators march on Bisho, capital of Ciskei bantustan. Police open fire, killing 28 marchers and wounding more than 200.

March 1993 A new Negotiating Council convenes at the World Trade Centre.

10 April 1993 Chris Hani, general-secretary of the South African Communist Party, assassinated.

25 June 1993 *Afrikaner Weerstandbeweging* (Afrikaner Resistance Movement) mob led by Eugene Terre'Blanche break into the World Trade Centre and disrupt proceedings.

14 October 1993 Right-wingers Janusz Walus and Clive Derby-Lewis found guilty of Hani murder. Death sentence later commuted to life imprisonment.

November 1993 MERG report presented to ANC.

18 November 1993 National Council adopts Interim Constitution.

11 March 1994 Armed right-wing invasion of BophuthaTswana bantustan collapses ignominiously, with three whites killed. Disillusioned, General Constand Viljoen quits the rebels and flies to Cape Town to register the Freedom Front party to participate in the democratic election as a party for Afrikaners.

27-29 April 1994 South Africa's first democratic election.

10 May 1994 Nelson Mandela inaugurated as the first President of a democratic South Africa. Thabo Mbeki and F W de Klerk become Executive Deputy Presidents.

February 1995 Eugene de Kock trial for Vlakplaas murders begins.

5 December 1995 Truth and Reconciliation Commission formed.

26 February 1996 Thabo Mbeki unveils the free-market based Growth, Employment and Redistribution (GEAR) policy.

16 April 1996 First TRC hearing, in East London.

8 May 1996 Constitutional Assembly adopts new SA Constitution.

14 June 1996 GEAR policy presented to Parliament.

1997 Thabo Mbeki backs Virodene as an AIDS remedy.

December 1997 Asian economic crisis begins in Thailand.

August 1998 Mugabe sends Zimbabwean troops to support regime of Laurent Kabila in Congo civil war.

April 1999 Pietermaritzburg lawyer Anthony Brink attacks AZT as a dangerous AIDS medicine, draws Mbeki's attention to the AIDS dissidents.

2 June 1999 ANC wins massive parliamentary majority in general election.

14 June 1999 Thabo Mbeki inaugurated as President.

August 1999 Freelance journalist Anita Allen sends Mbeki dossier on the views of AIDS dissidents.

October 1999 President Mbeki warns against the dangers of AZT in a parliamentary speech.

February 2000 Mugabe loses referendum to change Zimbabwe constitution.

April 2000 SADC leaders, including Mbeki, meet with Mugabe at Victoria Falls. Mbeki causes stir by writing to Bill Clinton, Tony Blair and other Western leaders justifying his inclusion of a number of AIDS dissidents on a panel of experts to advise him on the disease.

August 2000 Mbeki meets Mugabe again, secures promise to withdraw war veterans from farms – but Mugabe reneges on the pledge the next day.

April 2001 Minister of Safety and Security, Steve Tshwete, announces police are investigating a conspiracy against Mbeki by top ANC members Cyril Ramaphosa, Tokyo Sexwale and Mathews Phosa.

2001 Mbeki takes initiative in forming a new aid plan for Africa called the Millennium Africa Development Plan (MAP).

2002 Mbeki develops the MAP concept into the New Partnership for Africa's Development (Nepad) plan, proposing that the G-8 developed nations give aid to Africa in return for guarantees of democracy, good governance and financial discipline.

February 2002 Jonas Savimbi killed in battle, ending Angola's four decades of civil war.

March 2002 Mugabe re-elected in controversial presidential election. Commonwealth suspends Zimbabwe.

April 2002 Cabinet announces acceptance of the usefulness of anti-retroviral drugs in treating HIV/AIDS. Mbeki withdraws from the debate.

June/July 2002: The African Union is launched in Durban.

March 2003 Mbeki and Nigerian President Olusegun Obasanjo oppose majority decision to suspend Zimbabwe from the Commonwealth for another year.

NOTES

PROLOGUE

1 The Knight-Ridder news service, published in the Raleigh *News and Observer*, 16 September 2001.
2 *The New York Times*, 20 September 2001.
3 The vivid metaphor of the "electronic herd" is used in Thomas L Friedman's seminal book on globalization, *The Lexus and the Olive Tree: Understanding Globalization* (New York, 1999), to denote the speed at which international investors move money around in the electronic age.

CHAPTER ONE

1 While all schools are open to all races throughout the country, many in black urban and rural areas still have only black pupils and staff. All former whites-only schools, public and private, and all universities and tertiary training institutions, are racially integrated.
2 *The Great Debate: Unity, Diversity and Race in South Africa.* Supplement in weekly newspapers, 7-10 June 2001.
3 Ibid.
4 *Sunday Times*, Johannesburg, 27 June 1999.
5 *The Great Debate,* Op Cit.
6 A Land Act passed by the Union Parliament in 1913 supplemented by a further Act in 1936, prohibited Africans from owning land outside demarcated tribal reserves which together comprised 13% of the land area of South Africa. Within the reserves land was vested communally in tribal chiefs. There was therefore no freehold title for Africans anywhere in South Africa.
7 *Business Day*, 30 December 1999. For a full account of this saga see Helena Dolny, *Banking on Change* (Sandton 2001), pp 218-296.
8 *The Star*, 29 October 2002.
9 *Sunday Times*, Johannesburg, 8 April 2001.
10 F W de Klerk, *The Last Trek: A New Beginning* (London 1998), p 344.
11 Quoted by Frederik van Zyl Slabbert in *Tough Choices* (Johannesburg, 2000), p 155. The word "kaffir" is a crude racist term, derived from the Arabic word for a disbeliever, used by white South Africans to demean blacks.
12 *Sunday Times*, Op Cit.

CHAPTER TWO

1   *The Economist*, 13-17 December 1997.
2   Interview with the author.
3   In 2001 South African Breweries acquired Millers, the US brewing company, making it the world's second-largest brewer.
4   Dolny, Op Cit, p 42.
5   Standard Bank, Agricultural Division.
6   For a lively account of the Thai crisis see Friedman, Op Cit, pp ix to xix.
7   Frederick Johnstone, *Class, Race and Gold* (London, 1976), p 182.
8   Interview with the author.
9   Ibid.
10 Roger Baxter, Chief Economist, SA Chamber of Mines.
11 Ibid.
12 Haroon Bhorat, "Impact of Trade and Structural Changes in Sectoral Employment in South Africa", in *Development Southern Africa*, Vol 17, No 3, September 2000.
13 Ibid, p 6.
14 Labour Force Survey Round 5, Statistics South Africa, released September 2002.

CHAPTER THREE

1   Anthony Sampson, *Mandela: The Authorised Biography* (Johannesburg 1999), p 496.
2   *Business Day*, 4 June 2002.
3   Helena Dolny, *Banking on Change* (Sandton 2001), p 301.

CHAPTER FOUR

1   "In new S. Africa, a new apartheid". Report in *The Washington Post,* 31 May 2000.
2   Quoted by President Thabo Mbeki in his State of the Nation speech to Parliament, 9 February 2001.
3   Statement at the opening of the debate on reconciliation and nation-building in the National Assembly, Cape Town, on 29 May 1998.
4   *The Washington Post*, Op Cit.
5   Robert D Kaplan, "The Coming Anarchy", *The Atlantic Monthly*, February 1994.

CHAPTER FIVE

1   I published this extract in a front-page editorial on the day I took over as editor of the *Rand Daily Mail*, 16 April 1977, to highlight how the paper had entered a "new and dynamic" phase in its history which I pledged to carry forward – "one which wrenched it out of the conventional and set it on a vigorously reformist course that has brought it both fame and pain."
2   This tally of the number of laws affecting the press was made by the late Kelsey Stuart, legal adviser to the *Rand Daily Mail* and its sister newspapers, and conveyed to me verbally.
3   Afrikaans newspapers published the official statement, English papers did not.

4 Several other white journalists were detained, banned and exiled for political activism and membership of outlawed political organizations rather than for their journalistic activities.

5 John P Phelan, *Apartheid Media,* Laurence Hill & Co., 1987, p 65.

6 Initially the new licensing body was called the Independent Broadcasting Authority (IBA). Later it was merged with the telecommunications licensing authority to form ICASA.

7 Anthony Lewis, *Make no Law: The Sullivan Case and the First Amendment* (Vintage Books, New York 1992), p 153.

8 Ibid, p 72.

9 Ibid, p 78.

10 Ibid, p 83.

11 Ibid, p 100.

12 Ibid, p 96.

13 Ibid, pp 140-152.

14 *General Lothar Paul Neethling v Max du Preez*, 4 December 1993.

15 *National Media v Bogoshi*, 29 September 1998.

16 *South African National Defence Force Union v Minister of Defence and Chief of the South African National Defence Force*, 26 May 1999.

17 *Khumalo and others v Holomisa*, 14 June 2002.

18 Wim Trengove, SC, in a keynote address at the Legal Journalist of the Year Award, 6 November 2002.

19 *Mail & Guardian*, "Pityana Prejudged the Media", 25 February 2000.

20 Claudia Braude, "Cultural Bloodstains: Towards Understanding the Legacy of Apartheid and the Perpetuation of Racial Stereotypes in the Contemporary South African Media", p 136.

21 Ibid, p 135.

22 Edward S Herman and Noam Chomsky, *Manufacturing Consent* (Pantheon Books, New York, 1988), p 300.

23 Ibid, p 302.

24 Keynote address at the presentation of the Legal Journalist of the Year Award, Johannesburg, 9 November 2001.

25 "Sympathy for the Media out of Place", *Mail & Guardian*, 15-22 March 2001.

CHAPTER SIX

1 Quoted by W A de Klerk, *The Puritans of Africa: A Story of Afrikanerdom* (Penguin, London, 1976), p 214. It was pure National Socialism.

2 Although the party had no English version of its name it means "Reconstituted National Party". Hertzog broke away from the NP in 1969 in protest at an attempt by Prime Minister John Vorster to stave off sports isolation by permitting a French rugby touring side to include a black wing three-quarter.

3 Hultman, T J, *Culture Clash*, a PhD thesis submitted to the University of North Carolina (Chapel Hill, 1997), p 71. Hultman and her husband, Reed Kramer, published a specialist news periodical, *Africa News*, in the US for more than 30 years before launching an on-line publication, AllAfrica.com. Because of her reputation Hultman was given extraordinary access to key executives at the SABC, including

permission to attend board and management meetings, as she conducted five months of research on the corporation for her thesis on its transformation.

4   Ibid, pp 47-48.
5   *Weekly Mail*, 14 May 1993.
6   Professor Ndebele is now Vice-Chancellor of the University of Cape Town.
7   *Tough Choices*, Op Cit, p 110. Slabbert says in his book that he heard about these "secret meetings" while in Dakar, Senegal. A strange place indeed to pick up a rumour of events in Johannesburg, thousands of kilometres away. Stranger still that Slabbert, a politician who has had extensive dealings with the media over the years and knows the importance of checking facts, never checked with either Raymond Louw or myself whether there was any substance to the rumour. He also states in his book that Meer, Louw and I were members of the ANC, implying that this meant he was the victim of a "struggle clique". This is also untrue. Neither Louw nor I has ever belonged to any political organization.
8   *Culture Clash*. Op Cit, pp 5-6.
9   Ibid, p 71.
10 Quoted by Hultman, Ibid, pp 194-5.
11 In May 2000 the IBA was merged with the South African Telecommunications Authority to form the Independent Communications Authority of South Africa, or ICASA, which handles all licensing for broadcasting and telecommunications.
12 *Delivering Value: Submission by the SABC to the IBA*, June 1994, pp 6-7.
13 Presentation by Group Chief Executive Zwelakhe Sisulu to the IBA Triple Inquiry, 8 November 1994.
14 With some poetic justice, Matsepe-Casaburri later became Minister of Communications in the Mbeki Cabinet, which includes responsibility for broadcasting.
15 This was at the 1998 exchange rate of R6 to the US dollar. At today's exchange rate, which would apply had the SABC retained the transponders, the deal would be worth more than R2 billion.
16 *Culture Clash*, Op Cit, p 248.

CHAPTER SEVEN

1   Schalk Pienaar, "Safeguarding the Nations of South Africa", in a volume co-authored with Anthony Sampson, *South Africa: Two Views of Separate Development* (London, 1960), pp 3-4.
2   Anthony Sampson, *Mandela: The Authorized Biography* (New York, 1999), p 293.
3   Allister Sparks, *Tomorrow is Another Country: The Inside Story of South Africa's Negotiated Revolution* (London 1999), p 204.
4   Ibid, p 214.
5   Wilhelm Verwoerd, *My Winds of Change* (Randburg, 1997).
6   *The Washington Post*, 20 April 2000.
7   *Beeld*, 18 May 2001.
8   Isaiah Berlin: *The Crooked Timber of Humanity*, ed Henry Hardy (New York, 1991), pp 243-245.
9   Op Cit, pp 147-182.
10 Antjie Krog, *Country of My Skull* (Johannesburg, 1998), p 238.
11 Willem de Klerk, *Afrikaners: Kroes, Kras, Kordaat* (Cape Town 2000), pp 9, 52.

12 Ibid, p 9.
13 Ibid, p 14-21.
14 Ibid, p 29-39.
15 Ibid, p 57.
16 *Beeld*, 1 May 2000.
17 Ibid. Chris Louw uses the Afrikaans word "Outa", which I have translated here as "The old black uncle." Afrikaner children, especially in conservative rural areas, commonly refer to their elders as "oom", or uncle, but in the case of elderly black men they use the term "outa", an ambiguous word which has mixed connotations of paternalistic condescension and respect for age.
18 The terms, literally translated, mean "the enlightened ones" and "the cramped ones".
19 Guy Willoughby, *Mail & Guardian*, 22-28 June 2001.
20 Carl Niehaus, *Om te Veg vir Hoop* (Cape Town, 1993), pp 65-66.
21 *The Crooked Timber of Humanity*, Op Cit, pp 236-261.

CHAPTER EIGHT

1 George Bizos, the most tenacious of all South Africa's courageous civil rights lawyers, has published an anthology of these cases which I found an invaluable source in refreshing and adding to my own memory of them as a journalist. See *No One to Blame: In Pursuit of Justice in South Africa* (Cape Town, 1998).
2 Eugene de Kock, *A Long Night's Damage: Working for the Apartheid State* (Johannesburg, 1998), p 91.
3 Guillermo O'Donnell and Philippe C Schmitter, *Transitions from Authoritarian Rule: Tentative Conclusions about Uncertain Democracies* (Baltimore, 1986), p 30.
4 Alex Boraine, *A County Unmasked: Inside South Africa's Truth and Reconciliation Commission* (Cape Town, 2000), p 99.
5 Ibid, p 102.
6 Op Cit, p 42.
7 Op Cit, p 145.
8 Op Cit, p 32.
9 Op Cit, p 44.
10 Op Cit, p 352.
11 Op Cit, p 96.

CHAPTER NINE

1 The ANC's adoption of the Freedom Charter led eventually to a breakaway by radical members who formed the Pan-Africanist Congress (PAC). The Africanists objected to the charter's guarantee of equal status to all racial groups, contending that other groups had a right to remain in South Africa only if they recognised their position as "guests" of the African nation and accepted rule by an African majority. The Africanists also claimed white communists had manipulated the Congress of the People behind the scenes.
2 Thomas Karis and Gail M Gerhart, *From Challenge to Protest, Vol 3: Challenge*

and Violence 1953-1964 (Stanford, 1977, pp 63-64). The Treason Trial ended in 1961 with the acquittal of all the accused.

3 Quoted by William Kentridge, *Turning the Tanker: The Economic Debate in South Africa*, a study undertaken for the Centre for Policy Studies (Johannesburg, 1993), p 4.

4 *Daily Mail*, 15 August 1990. This newspaper was a brief attempt by the founders of the *Weekly Mail* (later renamed the *Mail & Guardian*) to launch a daily version of their paper to replace the crusading *Rand Daily Mail* which had been controversially closed by its proprietors five years before. But the venture was badly under-funded and failed.

5 *Mandela: The Authorised Biography*, Op Cit, p 434.

6 Interview with Ambassador Lyman.

7 Op Cit, p 435.

8 Mandela's speeches, ANC web site http://.anc.za.org, 2 February 1992.

9 Op Cit, p 435.

10 Details of this secret negotiating process are contained in my book, *Tomorrow is Another Country: The Inside Story of South Africa's Negotiated Revolution* (London and Johannesburg, 1994).

11 Interview with the author.

12 Interview with Pieter le Roux.

13 Terence Moll, *Growth Through Redistribution: A Dangerous Fantasy?* The South African Journal of Economics, Vol 59, No 3, 1991, pp 319-320.

14 *Ready to Govern,* p 15.

15 Ibid, p 16.

16 *Turning the Tanker,* Op Cit, p 10.

17 Ibid, p 56.

18 *Making Democracy Work: A Framework for Macroeconomic Policy in South Africa* (Bellville, 1993), p 255.

19 Ibid, pp 5-7.

20 Ibid, p 163.

21 *Weekly Mail, Review/Economy*, 11-12 August 1990.

22 Nicoli Nattrass, *South Africa: The economic restructuring agenda – a critique of the MERG report*, in the "Third World Quarterly", Vol 15, No 2, 1994, pp 219-225. Soon after publishing this Nattrass was appointed Professor of Economics at the University of Cape Town.

23 Op Cit, pp 255-256.

24 Ibid, p 156.

25 Iraj Abedian is now Chief Economist at the Standard Bank of South Africa.

26 *Mail & Guardian*, 13 November 1998.

27 Interview with the author.

28 I am indebted to Jeremy Cronin, Deputy General-Secretary of the SACP, for being the first to draw my attention to the "two parliaments" feature of South African politics.

29 Speech by President Thabo Mbeki to the ANC policy conference at Kempton Park, 27 September 2002.

30 Interview with the author.

CHAPTER TEN

1 Thomas L Friedman, *The Lexus and the Olive Tree: Understanding Globalization* (New York, 1999), p 26. Friedman is an international affairs columnist for *The New York Times*.
2 Anthony Giddens, *Runaway World: How Globalization is Reshaping Our Lives* (London, 1999), pp 15-16.
3 Jay Mazur, "Globalization's Dark Side: Labour's New Internationalization", in *Foreign Affairs* magazine, January/February 2000, pp 80-82. Mazur is chairman of the AFL-CIO's International Affairs Committee.
4 *UN Millennium Report* (New York, 2000), p 10.
5 Ibid, pp 14-15.
6 Giddens, Op Cit, p 10.
7 Ibid, p 5.
8 Op Cit, p 32.
9 Friedman, Op Cit, pp 86-7.
10 Ibid, p 199.
11 Joseph Stiglitz, *The New Republic*, 17 April 2000.
12 *The New York Times*, 21 March 2002. Soros's criticisms of the global financial system are set out in his book, *The Crisis of Global Capitalism: Open Society Endangered* (New York, 2000).
13 Ibid.
14 Robert H Frank and Philip J Cook, *The Winner-Take-All Society: Why the Few at the Top Get So Much More Than the Rest of Us* (New York, 1996), p 5.
15 Ibid, p 24.
16 Ibid, p 29.
17 Ibid, p 28.
18 *Business Day*, 29 January 2001.
19 Interview with the author.

CHAPTER ELEVEN

1 House of Assembly Debates, 1953, col 3576.
2 *Business Day*, 25 July 2002.
3 Peter Gastrow, *Organized Crime in South Africa: An Assessment of its Nature and Origins*, Institute of Strategic Studies Monograph No 28, August 1998.
4 Quoted by Gastrow, Ibid.
5 Ibid.
6 Ted Leggett, *Everyone's an Inspector: The Crisis of Rank Inflation and the Decline of Visible Policing*, Institute of Security Studies document, July 2002.
7 Makubetse Sekhonyane and Antoinette Louw, *Violent Justice, Vigilantism and the State's Response,* Institute of Strategic Studies Monograph No 72, April 2002.
8 Media briefing, 17 February 2003.
9 Interview with the author.
10 The national drop-out average is made worse by the dismal results at the former bantustan universities. The major universities do significantly better.

CHAPTER TWELVE

1 The Anglo American Corporation, South Africa's biggest mining, industrial and financial services conglomerate, restructured itself in 1998 to create core, focussed companies in its various fields of operation. In the course of this it merged all its gold mining companies into AngloGold.

2 This account of early prospecting that led to the discovery of the Free State goldfields and the founding of Welkom which followed is based largely on the official history of the town, *Welkom*, Felstar Publishers, Johannesburg, 1968.

3 After the town had been built by the Anglo American Corporation, Welkom's assets were transferred to a Village Management Board in 1953 and the town became a municipality with its own council in 1961.

4 *Welkom*, Op Cit, p 12.

5 Ibid, p 11.

6 *Welkom,* Op Cit, p 98.

7 National Association of Automotive Manufacturers of South Africa's (NAAMSA's) annual report for 2000/2001. It must be noted, however, that the increased value of component exports cited in the report was partly due to the decline of the rand.

8 National Association of Automotive Component and Allied Manufacturers (NAACAM) statement, 10 August 2002. The figure given is 5,5% of gross national product.

9 NAAMSA's annual report, Op Cit.

10 Interview with the author.

11 Interview with the author.

CHAPTER THIRTEEN

1 Interview with the author.

2 *Business Day*, 8 May 2001.

3 The Portuguese navigator, Bartholomeu Dias, was the first to round the Cape in 1488, encountering fierce storms as he did so. However, on his return to Lisbon King John II changed the name to the Cape of Good Hope, since its discovery opened Europe's sea route to the rich spicelands of the East.

4 Interview with the author.

5 *Sunday Independent*, 7 April 2002.

6 *Mail & Guardian*, 16 June 1999.

7 Patti Waldmeir, *Anatomy of a Miracle* (London, 1997), p 68.

8 *The Economist*, 5 May 2001.

9 Interview with the author.

10 Interview with the author.

11 Adrian Hadland and Jovial Rantao, *The Life and Times of Thabo Mbeki* (Rivonia, 1999), p 26.

12 *Mail & Guardian*, 16 June 1999.

CHAPTER FOURTEEN

1 From an article in *Science* magazine, Vol 288, 19 May 2000.

2   Alan Whiteside and Clem Sunter: *AIDS: The Challenge for South Africa* (Cape Town, 2000), p 63.
3   Makgoba, Op Cit.
4   *The Citizen*, 17 March 1999.
5   Anthony Brink, *Debating AZT: Mbeki and the AIDS drug controversy* (Pietermaritzburg, 2000), p xvi.
6   Kary Mullis shared the 1993 Nobel Prize for Chemistry with Canadian Professor Michael Smith, of the University of British Columbia, Vancouver, who developed another method for studying the DNA molecules of genetic material.
7   Interview with the author.
8   *The Washington Post*, 19 April 2000.
9   Exchange of letters published in the *Mail & Guardian*, 6-12 October 2000.
10 *The Washington Post*, 4 June 2000.
11 *National Geographic*, February 2002.
12 LoveLife: *The Impending Catastrophe* (Johannesburg, 2000), p 9.
13 *Natal Witness*, 25 September 2002.
14 Information retrieved 29 April 2002 from http://www.aids.info.org.za.
15 Keith Edelston, *AIDS: Countdown to Doomsday* (Johannesburg, 1988).
16 Channing Arndt and Jeffrey Lewis, *The Macro Implications of HIV/AIDS in South Africa: A Preliminary Assessment,* in the South African Journal of Economics, Vol 68, No 5, December 2000.
17 Ing Barings, *Economic Impact of AIDS in South Africa: A dark cloud on the horizon*, April 2000.
18 Quoted by Michael Dynes in *The Times*, London, 18 April 2002.
19 Whiteside and Sunter, Op Cit, p 78.
20 Ibid, pp 85-86.

CHAPTER FIFTEEN

1   Interview with the author.
2   Jakkie Cilliers and Christiaan Dieterich, eds, *Angola's War Economy: The Role of Oil and Diamonds* (Pretoria, 2000).
3   *Business Day*, 22 October 2002.
4   Martin Meredith, *Robert Mugabe: Power, Plunder and Tyranny in Zimbabwe* (Cape Town, 2002), p 66.
5   Ibid, p 67.
6   Ibid, p 68.
7   *Sunday Tribune*, 18 October 1981.
8   John Carlin, an old Africa hand, conducted a wide-ranging investigation into Zimbabwe's "blood diamonds" racket for the Spanish Newspaper, *El Pais*. His reports were reprinted in the courageous Zimbabwean newspaper, *The Daily News*, on 13-14 October 2002.
9   *The New York Times*, 22 February 2002.
10 There has been some confusion about how the peer review system will operate. Initially the 15 Nepad signatories presented it to the G-8 nations as part of their partnership proposal, but in an interview on 25 October 2002 President Mbeki told me the Nepad review system would be for economic issues only, while political peer reviewing would be done by the African Union. This caused dismay in diplo-

mätic circles, where it was seen as serious backtracking by the Nepad group. However, the group announced in Nigeria a week later that Nepad would indeed establish a "voluntary" political peer review mechanism to operate until the new African Union structures are established – probably not for several years.

CHAPTER SIXTEEN

1 Global Information Technology Study by the World Information Technology Alliance, 1999.
2 *Business Day*, 17 October 2002.
3 Interview with the author.
4 Amy Chua, "A World on the Edge", in *The Wilson Quarterly*, Autumn 2002.
5 Interview with the author.
6 Interview with the author
7 Martha Alter Chen, Renana Jhabvala and Frances Lund, *Supporting Workers in the Informal Sector: A Policy Framework*. A paper prepared for the International Labour Organisation's task force on the informal economy, November 2001.
8 Hernando de Soto, *The Mystery of Capitalism: Why Capitalism Triumphs in the West and Fails Everywhere Else* (New York 2000), p 69.
9 Ibid, pp 35-35.
10 Ibid, pp 226-227.

INDEX